Apple Training Series

Mac OS X
Support Essentials
v10.6

Kevin M. White

Apple Training Series: Mac OS X Support Essentials v10.6
Kevin M. White
Copyright © 2010 by Apple Inc.

Published by Peachpit Press. For information on Peachpit Press books, contact:
Peachpit Press
1249 Eighth Street
Berkeley, CA 94710
510/524-2178
510/524-2221 (fax)
www.peachpit.com

To report errors, please send a note to errata@peachpit.com.
Peachpit Press is a division of Pearson Education.

Apple Training Series Editor: Rebecca Freed
Production Editors: Danielle Foster, Becky Winter
Copyeditor: Peggy Nauts
Tech Editor: Gordon Davisson
Apple Editor: Shane Ross
Proofreader: Suzie Nasol
Compositor: Danielle Foster
Indexer: Valerie Perry
Cover design: Mimi Heft
Cover illustrator: Kent Oberheu

ISBN 13: 978-0-321-63534-1
ISBN 10:   0-321-63534-5

9 8 7 6 5 4 3 2

Acknowledgments

In addition to the amazing Peachpit staff members who were instrumental in completing this work, I would like to thank the development team for their hard work: Shane Ross, Patrick Gallagher, and Gordon Davisson. Additional thanks go to John Signa, Tilla Torrens, Jason Deraleau, Tommy Hann, Schoun Regan, Arek Dreyer, Simon Wheatley, Brian Gupton, and the Blue Man Guild. Finally, I could not have made this journey without the support of my family and loving wife, Michelle.

This book is dedicated to my new best friend and son, Logan Michael White.

Contents

Getting Started

This book is based on the same criteria used for Apple's official training course, Mac OS X Support Essentials 10.6, an in-depth exploration of troubleshooting on Mac OS X. It serves as a self-paced tour of the breadth of functionality of Mac OS X and the best methods for effectively supporting users of Mac OS X systems.

The primary goal is to prepare help desk specialists, technical coordinators, service technicians, system administrators, and others who support Macintosh users to knowledgeably address customer concerns and questions. This includes the ability to return a Mac OS X computer to normal operation using the proper utilities, resources, and troubleshooting techniques.

Whether you are an experienced system administrator or just want to dig deeper into Mac OS X v10.6, you'll learn in-depth technical information and procedures used by Apple-certified technicians to install, configure, maintain, and diagnose Macintosh computers running Mac OS X.

This book assumes a basic level of familiarity with Mac OS X. Unless otherwise specified, all references to Mac OS X refer to Mac OS X version 10.6.0, which was the most current version available at the time of writing. Due to subsequent upgrades, some screen shots, features, and procedures may be slightly different from those presented on these pages.

Learning Methodology

This book is based on lectures and exercises provided to students attending Mac OS X Support Essentials 10.6, a three-day, hands-on course that provides an intense and in-depth exploration of how to troubleshoot on Mac OS X. For consistency, we follow the basic structure of the course material, but you may complete it at your own pace.

Each chapter is designed to help experienced users become experts who are able to support other Mac OS X users by:

▶ Providing *knowledge* of how Mac OS X works

▶ Showing how to use diagnostic and repair *tools*

▶ Explaining troubleshooting and repair *procedures*

For example, in Chapter 7, "Network Configuration," you'll learn basic networking concepts (knowledge). You'll acquire network configuration and troubleshooting techniques using the Network preferences and Network Utility (tools). And you'll explore methods for trouble-shooting networking issues (procedures). In addition, each chapter includes troubleshooting techniques for dealing with common issues related to the topic of the chapter.

Each chapter focuses on a different aspect of Mac OS X:

▶ Chapter 1, "Installation and Initial Setup"—Preparing and partitioning the drive; installing Mac OS X; using the installer log files to verify a successful installation; config-uring Mac OS X with the Setup Assistant; updating software with Software Update and Installer; learning tips and techniques for troubleshooting an installation problem.

▶ Chapter 2, "User Accounts"—Creating and managing user and administrator accounts; locating directory attributes; implementing security; selecting passwords; managing the keychain; FileVault.

▶ Chapter 3, "Command Line and Automation"—Introduction to command-line fun-damentals, navigation, and administration tools; using Automator; using AppleScript; and basic command-line scripting.

▶ Chapter 4, "File Systems"—Identifying the file systems supported by Mac OS X; managing file and directory ownership and permissions; using Disk Utility; repairing files; using the command line for file management.

▶ Chapter 5, "Data Management and Backup"—Exploring the root volume, file system layout, preferences, frameworks, and file types unique to Mac OS X (i.e., file system metadata and packages); using Spotlight, file archives, and disk images; archiving and restoring data with Time Machine; managing backup data; accessing data outside of Time Machine.

▶ Chapter 6, "Applications and Boot Camp"—Understanding applications supported in Mac OS X, applications created with different developer APIs, the UNIX concept of a process, and the relationship of processes to applications; using tools to monitor and manage processes; setting application preferences; troubleshooting; using Boot Camp.

▶ Chapter 7, "Network Configuration"—Configuring basic networks; setting up TCP/IP networking, Ethernet, and AirPort; connecting multiple networks; using network locations; isolating and troubleshooting network elements.

▶ Chapter 8, "Network Services"—Connecting to common network resources; enabling network services on a Mac OS X client; accessing AFP, SMB, SSH, FTP, and WebDAV connections; using Bonjour, NetBIOS, and the network browser; sharing files between Macs and Windows; sharing web documents; taking advantage of screen sharing and remote login; using firewalls; isolating sharing issues from network issues; configuring and troubleshooting network directory services.

▶ Chapter 9, "Peripherals and Printing"—Connecting peripherals to a Macintosh; identifying cabling, connections, and device drivers for common peripherals; managing printers and print jobs; understanding printer PPDs and PDF workflow; learning techniques for isolating cabling, driver, or application issues.

▶ Chapter 10, "System Startup"—Troubleshooting boot issues with a Mac at startup; understanding the phases of the startup process; identifying the active part of the system during each phase; exploring issues that can arise; launching processes automatically with the `launchd` and `loginwindow` startup items.

An appendix of general Apple troubleshooting information is available online, at www.peachpit.com/snowleopard-support. It may be valuable to you, but it's not essential for the coursework or certification.

Chapter Structure

Each chapter begins with an opening page that lists the learning goals for the chapter and an estimate of time needed to complete the chapter. The explanatory material is augmented with hands-on exercises essential to developing your skills. For the most part, all you need to complete the exercises is a Macintosh computer running Mac OS X v10.6 or later. If you lack the equipment necessary to complete a given exercise, you are still encouraged to read the step-by-step instructions and examine the screen shots to understand the procedures demonstrated.

> **NOTE ▶** Some of these exercises can be disruptive—for example, they may turn off network services temporarily—and some exercises, if performed incorrectly, could result in data loss or damage to system files. As such, it's recommended that you perform these exercises on a Macintosh that is not critical to your daily productivity. Apple, Inc. and Peachpit Press are not responsible for any data loss or any damage to any equipment that occurs as a direct or indirect result of following the procedures described in this book.

We refer to Apple Knowledge Base documents throughout the chapters, and close each chapter with a list of recommended documents related to the topic of the chapter. The Knowledge Base is a free online resource (www.apple.com/support) containing the very latest technical information on all of Apple's hardware and software products. We strongly encourage you to read the suggested documents and search the Knowledge Base for answers to any problems you encounter.

You'll also find "More Info" resources throughout the chapters, and summarized at the end of each chapter, that provide ancillary information. These resources are merely for your edification, and are not considered essential for the coursework or certification.

At the end of each chapter is a short chapter review that recaps the material you've learned. You can refer to various Apple resources, such as the Knowledge Base, as well as the chapters themselves, to help you answer these questions.

Apple Certification

After reading this book, you may wish to take the Mac OS X Support Essentials 10.6 Exam to earn the Apple Certified Support Professional 10.6 certification. This is the first level of Apple's certification programs for Mac OS X professionals:

▶   Apple Certified Support Professional 10.6 (ACSP)—Ideal for help desk personnel, service technicians, technical coordinators, and others who support Mac OS X customers over the phone or who perform Mac OS X troubleshooting and support in schools and businesses. This certification verifies an understanding of Mac OS X core functionality and an ability to configure key services, perform basic troubleshooting, and assist end users with essential Mac OS X capabilities. To receive this certification, you must pass the Mac OS X Support Essentials 10.6 Exam. This book is designed to provide you with the knowledge and skills to pass that exam.

> **NOTE** ▶ Although all of the questions in the Mac OS X Support Essentials 10.6 exam are based on material in this book, simply reading it will not adequately prepare you for the exam. Apple recommends that before taking the exam you spend time actually setting up, configuring, and troubleshooting Mac OS X. You should also download and review the Skills Assessment Guide, which lists the exam objectives, the total number of items, the number of items per section, the required score to pass, and how to register. A 10-item sample test is also available for download. Items on the sample test are similar in style to items on the certification exam, though they may vary in difficulty level. To download the Skills Assessment Guide and sample test, visit http://training.apple.com/itpro/snow101

▶   Apple Certified Technical Coordinator 10.6 (ACTC)—This certification is intended for Mac OS X technical coordinators and entry-level system administrators tasked with maintaining a modest network of computers using Mac OS X Server. Since the ACTC certification addresses both the support of Mac OS X clients and the core functionality and use of Mac OS X Server, the learning curve is correspondingly longer and more intensive than that for the ACSP certification, which addresses solely Mac OS X client support. This certification is not intended for high-end system administrators or engineers, but may be an excellent step to take on an intended career path to system administration. This certification requires passing both the Mac OS X Support Essentials 10.6 Exam and Mac OS X Server Essentials 10.6 Exam.

▶ Apple Certified System Administrator 10.6 (ACSA)—This certification verifies an in-depth knowledge of Apple technical architecture and an ability to install and configure machines; architect and maintain networks; enable, customize, tune, and troubleshoot a wide range of services; and integrate Mac OS X, Mac OS X Server, and other Apple technologies within a multiplatform networked environment. The ACSA certification is intended for full-time professional system administrators and engineers who manage medium-to-large networks of systems in complex multiplatform deployments. ACSA 10.6 certification requires passing the Mac OS X Server Essentials 10.6 Exam, Mac OS X Directory Services 10.6 Exam, Mac OS X Deployment 10.6 Exam, and Mac OS X Security and Mobility 10.6 Exam.

▶ Mac OS X 10.6 certification offerings now include new Specialist certifications for the ACSA-level Directory Services, Deployment, and Security and Mobility exams.

Apple hardware service technician certifications are ideal for people interested in becoming Macintosh repair technicians, but also worthwhile for help desk personnel at schools and businesses, and for Macintosh consultants and others needing an in-depth understanding of how Apple systems operate:

▶ Apple Certified Macintosh Technician (ACMT)—This certification verifies the ability to perform basic troubleshooting and repair of both desktop and portable Macintosh systems, such as iMac and MacBook Pro. ACMT certification requires passing the Apple Macintosh Service exam and the Mac OS X Troubleshooting Exam.

About the Apple Training Series

Apple Training Series: Mac OS X Support Essentials v10.6 is part of the official training series for Apple products developed by experts in the field and certified by Apple. The chapters are designed to let you learn at your own pace. You can progress through the book from beginning to end, or dive right into the chapters that interest you most.

For those who prefer to learn in an instructor-led setting, Apple also offers training courses at Apple Authorized Training Centers worldwide. These courses are taught by Apple Certified Trainers, and they balance concepts and lectures with hands-on labs and exercises. Apple Authorized Training Centers have been carefully selected and have met

Apple's highest standards in all areas, including facilities, instructors, course delivery, and infrastructure. The goal of the program is to offer Apple customers, from beginners to the most seasoned professionals, the highest-quality training experience.

To find an Authorized Training Center near you, please visit http://training.apple.com.

1

Time   This chapter takes approximately 3 hours to complete.

Goals   Prepare a computer for installation of Mac OS X v10.6

Successfully install Mac OS X v10.6 software

Troubleshoot potential installation problems

Complete initial configuration of Mac OS X v10.6

Install software and updates

Chapter 1

Installation and Initial Setup

Without software, a computer is nothing more than an expensive collection of sand, metals, and plastic. That's not to say that hardware doesn't matter. It would be foolish to ignore the exceptional quality and panache with which Apple creates its hardware. However, due to the homogenization of PC hardware, today's Macs use many of the same parts found in standard computers. So neither the processor, nor storage, nor even the trend-setting design set Apple's computers apart from the competition. The same thing that makes the Mac special is also responsible for elevating simple hardware to a functional computer. This, the true "soul" of a computer, is its operating system.

Every Mac computer had some version of Mac OS preinstalled when it was built. The particular version of Mac OS X that ships with a computer is usually the latest available at the time. Thus, the operating system on every Mac will at some time need a newer version to have the latest features and bug fixes. This chapter starts with a brief introduction of Mac OS X v10.6 and then guides you through the installation, initial configuration, and updating of the system. This will also include troubleshooting issues that may arise during these processes.

NOTE ▶ Several of the operations that you will learn about in this chapter involve significant changes, and many of them are difficult to reverse, if not irreversible. Therefore, if you plan to experiment with the topics discussed in this chapter, you should do so on a spare computer or external hard drive that does not contain critical data.

About Mac OS X v10.6

Mac OS X v10.6, also known by its development code name "Snow Leopard," is the latest revision of Apple's primary operating system. Since its introduction in 2001, Mac OS X has become an increasingly attractive alternative to more common operating systems due to its unique combination of innovative technologies. Mac OS X is the only operating system that combines a powerful, open-source UNIX foundation with a state-of-the-art user interface, including all the easy-to-use features for which Apple is known. Further, the Mac provides an exceptional development platform, as evidenced by the large selection of high-quality, third-party software titles available for the Mac.

In addition to all the features found in older versions of Mac OS X, the latest version includes significant refinements across the board. It also adds several new core technologies that will improve the Mac experience for everyone from casual users to seasoned administrators. Almost everywhere you look in Mac OS X v10.6 there are small enhancements and improvements, but one new feature is especially significant: built-in support for Microsoft Exchange.

> **MORE INFO** ▶ A full list of Mac OS X v10.6 enhancements can be found at www. apple.com/macosx/refinements/enhancements-refinements.html.

> **MORE INFO** ▶ Apple's online Macintosh Products Guide is the definitive resource for finding hardware and software designed to work with the Macintosh: http://guide. apple.com.

Integration Through Standards

Much of the success of Mac OS X can be attributed to Apple's wholehearted embrace of industry-standard formats and open-source software. The historic perception of the Macintosh platform being closed or proprietary is far from today's reality. Nearly every technology in Mac OS X is based on well-known standards. Adoption of common standards saves engineering time and allows for much smoother integration with other platforms. Even when Apple developers must engineer a technology for a new feature, Apple often releases the specs to the developer community, fostering a new standard. An example of this is the Bonjour network discovery protocol, which Apple pioneered and has maintained as an open standard for others to develop and use.

Some examples of common standards supported by Mac OS X are:

▶ Connectivity standards—Universal Serial Bus (USB), IEEE 1394 (FireWire), Bluetooth wireless, and the IEEE 802 family of Ethernet standards

▶ File system standards—UNIX File System (UFS), File Allocation Table (FAT), New Technology File System (NTFS), ISO-9660 optical disc standard, Universal Disc Format (UDF)

▶ Network standards—Dynamic Host Configuration Protocol (DHCP), Domain Name Service (DNS), Hypertext Transfer Protocol (HTTP), Internet Message Access Protocol (IMAP), Simple Mail Transfer Protocol (SMTP), File Transfer Protocol (FTP), Network File System (NFS), and Server Message Block/Common Internet File System (SMB/CIFS)

▶ Application and development standards—Single UNIX Specification v3 (SUSv3), Portable Operating System Interface 1003.1 (POSIX), C and C++, Java, Ruby, Python, and Perl

▶ Document standards—ZIP file archives, Rich Text Format (RTF), Portable Document Format (PDF), Tagged Image File Format (TIFF), Portable Network Graphics (PNG), Advanced Audio Codec (AAC), and the Moving Picture Experts Group (MPEG) family of media standards

Layers of Mac OS X

In contrast to the apparent simplicity presented to the user on its surface, Mac OS X is a highly complicated operating system made up of hundreds of different processes and several hundred thousand files and folders. However, a bird's-eye view reveals that this operating system is made up of four primary components. Though covered briefly here, many of these concepts will be further discussed in Chapter 6, "Applications and Boot Camp."

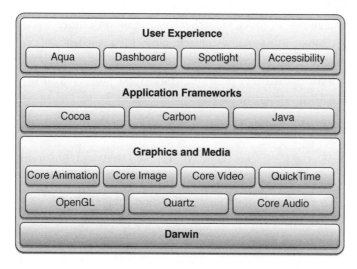

Starting from the lowest levels of the system to the user interface, the four primary layers of Mac OS X are:

▶ Darwin—This is the open-source UNIX core of Mac OS X. This lowest level of the system provides advanced functionality such as protected memory, preemptive multitasking, symmetric multiprocessing, a secure multiple user environment, and advanced multiple-link multihoming networking. Though based on the Mach micro-kernel and Berkeley Software Distribution (BSD) UNIX, Darwin has evolved into its own distinct version of UNIX. Since Mac OS X v10.5, Darwin is no longer simply "based on UNIX," but is now an Open Brand UNIX 03 Registered Product—meaning it boasts full compatibility with the Single UNIX Specification, Version 3 (SUSv3) and POSIX UNIX applications and utilities.

▶ Graphics and Media—Though close to the bottom, these technologies provide fundamental services that add tremendous value to the Apple user experience. Residing here are technologies such as OpenGL, OpenAL, Core Audio, Core Image, Core Video, Core Animation, Core Data, and QuickTime. These services allow developers to rapidly create advanced applications that require much less knowledge of complicated low-level code. Apple has done all the hard work commonly associated with creating an application with a graphical user interface, allowing developers to create higher-quality applications in less time.

▶ Application Frameworks—Here you find the primary development platforms that engineers use to create Macintosh applications. Cocoa is based on Objective-C and is the primary development platform for Mac OS X. Carbon, largely based on C and C++ code, is a development platform with roots in Mac OS 9 that allows developers to easily move their legacy code forward. Finally, Java is a highly portable development platform originally created by Sun Microsystems.

▶ User Experience—This is as deep as most users ever get with Mac OS X, and for good reason. This is where most users interact with the system and its applications. Technologies that really make the Macintosh platform stand out are on display at this level. The Aqua user interface, Spotlight search engine, and Dashboard widgets are present here. UNIX applications accessed via the command line and the X11 windowing environment can also be considered part of this level.

MORE INFO ▶ For more on Mac OS X system architecture, see Apple's development resources: http://developer.apple.com/macosx/architecture.

Using Installer Disc Utilities

Apple is well known for designing every operation to be as easy as possible, and the installation process is an example of this. The installation process for Mac OS X is so well engineered that most users could easily complete it with no training. However, anyone tasked with supporting Mac OS X computers should be more familiar with all the necessary procedures to ensure a smooth installation. This starts with understanding the processes and utilities associated with the Mac OS X Install DVD.

> **NOTE ▶** New Macs usually come with a computer-specific release of Mac OS X that was engineered specifically for that model and may include additional software bundled with that model. This book assumes that you will be using a standard retail package of Mac OS X v10.6, so you may find that some details vary if you are using a computer-specific install disc. For more information, see Knowledge Base document HT2681, "What's a 'computer-specific Mac OS X release'?"

While the installation process can be started while running from an existing system, this is not always an option. For this reason, the Mac OS X Install DVD can be used as the startup volume for any Mac that meets the Mac OS X v10.6 installation requirements. This DVD not only provides a stable operating system to perform installations, but it also provides other important utilities for administering and troubleshooting the Mac.

Start Up from the Installation DVD

The following methods can be used to start your Mac from the Mac OS X Install DVD:

▶ Insert the DVD in a currently running Mac, and then select it as the startup destination using the Startup Disk preferences.

▶ Turn on the Mac while holding down the C key, and as soon as possible, insert the installation DVD and the computer will start up from it.

▶ Turn on the Mac while holding down the Option key, and as soon as possible, insert the disc. The computer will enter Startup Manager mode, where you'll use the cursor to select the installation DVD as the startup drive. If you have a tray-loading optical drive, you can open it with the keyboard Eject button after the Startup Manager appears.

Once the Mac has started up from the installation DVD, you will be presented with a language-selection dialog. Select your preferred main language and click the blue right arrow. You will then be presented with the system installer interface. At this point you could begin the installation, as outlined in the "Installing Mac OS X" section later in this chapter, but for now this guide will cover using the installation DVD utilities.

Installation DVD Utilities

The Mac OS X Install DVD is very useful as an administrative and troubleshooting resource. When you start up from this DVD, you will have access to several system administration and maintenance tools that are available from the Utilities menu. There are even a few indispensable utilities on this disc that you cannot find anywhere else in Mac OS X.

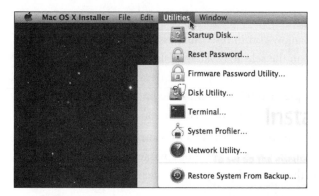

TIP It's also worth noting that, when booted from this DVD, Ethernet and AirPort networking is available if the network provides DHCP services. While Ethernet is automatically enabled if physically connected, you can connect to a wireless network from the AirPort menu item.

The utilities available on the Mac OS X Install DVD include:

▶ Startup Disk—This utility will allow you to select the default system startup disk. The default startup disk can be overridden using any of the alternate startup modes discussed in Chapter 10, "System Startup."

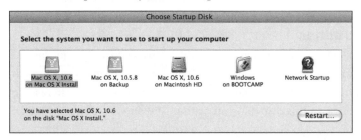

▶ Reset Password—This utility will allow you to reset the password of any local user account, including the root user, on the selected system disk. Obviously, this is a dangerous utility that can lead to a serious security threat. Because of this, the Reset Password utility will not run if copied from the original media. You can find out more about the Reset Password utility in Chapter 2, "User Accounts."

▶ Firmware Password Utility—This utility will allow you to secure the Mac's startup process by disabling all alternate startup modes without a password. You can disable or enable this feature and define the required password. You can find out more about the Firmware Password utility in Chapter 2, "User Accounts."

▶ Disk Utility—This application is responsible for storage-related administration and maintenance. This is especially useful when the Mac has started up from the Mac OS X Install DVD, because Disk Utility can be used to manage a system disk that otherwise can't be managed when in use as the startup disk. Specifically, Disk Utility can be used to prepare a drive for a new installation of Mac OS X or to attempt repairs on a drive that fails installation. Disk Utility usage is covered later in this chapter and also further discussed in Chapter 4, "File Systems."

▶ Terminal—This is your primary interface to the UNIX command-line environment of Mac OS X. Terminal will be further discussed in Chapter 3, "Command Line and Automation."

▶ System Profiler—This application allows you to inspect the status of both the hardware and software on your Mac. You will be using this application throughout this guide, including the very next section of this chapter.

▶ Network Utility—This is the primary network and Internet troubleshooting utility in Mac OS X. Network Utility will be further discussed in Chapter 7, "Network Configuration."

▶ Restore System From Backup—You can use this utility to restore a full-system Time Machine backup from either a network or locally connected volume. Time Machine will be further discussed in Chapter 5, "Data Management and Backup."

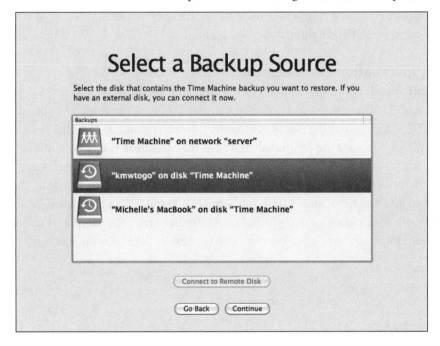

NOTE ▶ The utilities available from the Mac OS X Install DVD can certainly be used to compromise system security. Then again, any system where the default startup disk can be overridden during startup is wide open to compromise. Therefore, it is very important that you use the Firmware Password Utility to protect your secure systems from this attack vector.

Before You Install Mac OS X

Because every Mac ships with Mac OS X preinstalled, the majority of installations of Mac OS X are actually upgrades. An upgrade installation implies that there is a preexisting system that the installer will be replacing. There will probably also be preexisting user data on this system that is important to the user. The Mac OS X installation process is designed to retain non-system data during an upgrade installation.

Upgrading an operating system is a complicated process that isn't entirely free from issues. Apple has worked hard to improve the Mac OS X v10.6 upgrade experience, but there are other variables involved that could still lead to issues. For instance, a hardware failure issue could prevent a successful upgrade installation. For these reasons, you should take some preparatory steps to prevent installer issues and data loss.

Verifying Installation Requirements

It's important to understand the installation requirements for the copy of Mac OS X you plan to use and also the requirements of the particular Macintosh you intend to install it on. If you're not sure what the intended computer's specifications are, use the System Profiler application to view the computer's status. If the Macintosh is already running Mac OS X, you can simply open System Profiler (in the /Applications/Utilities folder). Also, you can get to System Profiler by clicking About This Mac in the Apple menu, then clicking More Info. If you've booted from the Mac OS X Install DVD, the System Profiler is available from the Utilities menu. Within System Profiler, verify the computers' specifications by selecting and viewing the various content areas in the Hardware section.

Mac OS X v10.6 requires:

▶   A Mac computer with an Intel processor

▶   1 GB of memory

▶   5 GB of available disk space

▶   DVD drive for installation (Installation on a MacBook Air requires either an external DVD drive or another computer with a DVD drive.)

▶   A built-in display or a display connected to an Apple-supplied video card supported by your computer

▶   Some features require a compatible Internet service provider; fees may apply

▶   Some features require Apple's MobileMe service; fees and terms apply

MORE INFO ▶ Some Mac OS X v10.6 features have additional requirements beyond these minimum system requirements. You can learn more about feature-specific requirements at the Mac OS X v10.6 technical specifications website: www.apple.com/macosx/specs.html.

As you can see from these requirements, Mac OS X generally supports hardware a few years older than the latest version of the operating system. However, older versions of Mac OS X do not support hardware that is newer than the operating system release. In other words, you may come across a Mac that's newer than the Mac OS X installation disc you're trying to use. If this is the case, the installation disc will fail to boot or refuse to install the older operating system. In this case, you should use the installation disc that came with the Mac.

MORE INFO ▶ For more, see Knowledge Base document HT2186, "Don't install a version of Mac OS X earlier than what came with your Mac."

Preparing for Installation

While you could jump right into Mac OS X installation without any preparation, completing some preliminary steps will reduce your chances of experiencing installation problems or losing important data. There are four crucial steps you should take before any system installation: check for firmware updates, verify application compatibility, back up important files and folders, and document critical settings.

Check for Firmware Updates

Firmware is low-level software that facilitates the startup and management of system hardware. Though it's quite rare, Apple may release firmware updates that older Macintosh computers need to operate properly with new system software.

You can identify the firmware version on a currently running Mac by opening /Applications/Utilities/System Profiler, or on a Mac booted from the Mac OS X Install DVD by choosing System Profiler from the Utilities menu. The default view for System Profiler will identify the two types of firmware on Intel-based Macs. The first type, listed as "Boot ROM Version," is in reference to the Extensible Firmware Interface (EFI), which is responsible for general hardware management and system startup. The second type, listed as "SMC Version," is the System Management Controller (SMC) firmware responsible for managing hardware power and cooling. Once you have located your computer's firmware versions, you can determine if you have the latest updates by accessing Knowledge Base document HT1237, "EFI and SMC firmware updates for Intel-based Macs."

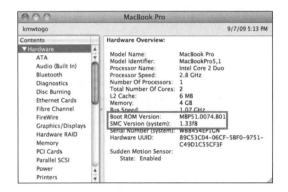

If you determine that your Mac requires a firmware update, you will need to find the appropriate update at the Apple Support Download website, http://support.apple.com/downloads. Installing a firmware update is very similar to a normal system software update in that it requires administrative user authorization and a reboot. However, most firmware updates have an extra requirement: After the initial installation process, you must shut down and restart the computer, holding down the power button until you hear a long tone. This will initiate the remainder of the firmware update process. Be sure to carefully read any instructions that come with a firmware updater! Failure to properly update a Mac's firmware could lead to hardware failure.

> **NOTE ▶** If you experience an unsuccessful update you can restore your Mac's firmware with a Firmware Restoration CD. You can find out more about acquiring and using this CD from Knowledge Base document HT2213, "About the Firmware Restoration CD (Intel-based Macs)."

Verify Application Compatibility

When moving to a new operating system, many third-party applications may require updates to function properly. You can easily collect a list of installed applications on a currently running Mac by opening /Applications/Utilities/System Profiler. In System Profiler, you will need to verify that View > Full Profile is selected, to reveal the Applications section in the Contents list. Selecting Applications from the Contents list causes System Profiler to scan the current startup volume for all available applications.

NOTE ► Using System Profiler while booted from the Mac OS X Install DVD will only show applications located on the DVD.

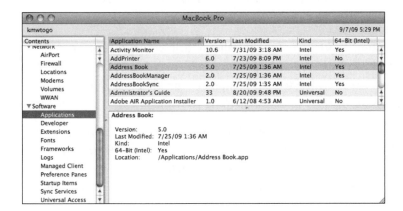

You don't have to worry about the applications installed as part of the operating system, as those will obviously be replaced when you run the new system installer. However, you may have to do your own research to determine if the installed third-party applications require updates. A good starting point is Apple's own Macintosh Products Guide, http://guide.apple.com.

Also, Mac OS X v10.6 has a useful new list of known incompatible software. If the Mac OS X installer detects certain incompatible software during an update installation, it will move it to a folder named "Incompatible Software." In some cases the incompatible software isn't moved, but the system prevents you from opening the software, instead displaying a warning dialog stating that the software is known to be incompatible. You can find out more about this new feature of Mac OS X from Knowledge Base document HT3258, "Mac OS X v10.6: About Incompatible Software."

Back Up Important Files and Folders

Experienced computer users should already know to keep current backups of their important files and folders. Having a current backup is even more important before making significant changes to the computer. Installing a new operating system is a significant change that, if done improperly, could result in catastrophic data loss.

If the system is already running Mac OS X v10.5, you can use the built-in Time Machine software to easily create a backup before you start your installation. Using Time Machine and other archival tools is covered in Chapter 5, "Data Management and Backup."

Document Critical Settings

Apple has designed Migration Assistant and the Installer to help ensure that previous settings are not lost when you are upgrading from an older version of Mac OS X. Nonetheless, some settings are so critical to your computer's function that you would be well served to document those settings should something go wrong.

Specifically, network settings are very critical and should be documented before a system upgrade is attempted. Network settings for all previous versions of Mac OS X can be located in the Network pane of System Preferences. System Preferences are easily accessed from the Apple menu. Avoid missing crucial settings by navigating through all the available network interfaces and configuration tabs.

> **TIP** ▶ You can quickly document your settings by using the screen capture keyboard shortcut, Command-Shift-3, to create picture files of the dialogs onscreen.

Keeping Up to Date

The latest information regarding known issues at the time your installation disc was created can be found in the "Instructions" folder. This folder is easy to find—it's one of the two visible folders when you're viewing the contents of the Mac OS X Install DVD in the Finder. When presented with any new software, it's always a good idea to read the "getting started" documentation, especially if you are replacing something as fundamental as the computer's operating system.

For the most recent information regarding the installation process, your best source is the Apple Support page and Knowledge Base. A good place to start is the Snow Leopard Support page at www.apple.com/support/snowleopard. Any time you intend to install Mac OS X you should visit these resources to catch any recently discovered issues. The Apple Knowledge Base documents are sprinkled throughout this guide for a reason: They are simply the best source for up-to-date support information.

Preparing the System Drive

Again, because most Mac OS X installations are of the upgrade variety, further system drive preparation isn't necessary. Any drive containing a version of Mac OS X for Intel-based Macs is already properly formatted for Mac OS X v10.6. In other words, if an upgrade installation describes your situation, then you should move right to installing Mac OS X.

However, if you need to perform an erase and install for a "clean" system or you are planning on repartitioning the drive, you will have to prepare the system drive prior to installing Mac OS X. Specifically, Mac OS X is only supported for installation on drives partitioned with GUID Partition Table (GPT) and volumes formatted for either Mac OS X Extended (Journaled), or Mac OS X Extended (Case Sensitive, Journaled).

Erasing the system drive before a Mac OS X installation may be necessary for various reasons. Obviously, erasing the system drive will effectively erase any existing data, but sometimes this may be necessary. For example, if you are upgrading the Mac's internal drive to more spacious or faster hardware, it must be properly formatted for Mac OS X. Another instance is when an operating system has serious issues; in this case erasing and installing a "clean" copy of Mac OS X may resolve the situation.

The reasons to repartition your system drive are a bit more complex, so they are covered in the next section. Nevertheless, the process of repartitioning your system drive can also effectively erase previous data, and thus is generally done prior to installing Mac OS X. You will use Disk Utility both for erasing and repartitioning the disk. Disk Utility can be found on any Mac in the /Applications/Utilities folder or, as covered previously, from the Utilities menu when started up from the Mac OS X Install DVD. Obviously, if you're going to make changes to the system drive before you install Mac OS X, doing it while started up from the installation disc is very convenient.

> **MORE INFO** ▶ This chapter does not include details about erasing or repartitioning disk drives; these procedures are covered extensively in Chapter 4, "File Systems."

Understanding Partition Options

Before selecting a destination volume, you may want to pause and consider the various partition methodologies that are available as installable Mac OS X destinations. Most Macs have a single hard drive formatted as a single volume that defines the entire space on that hard drive. However, by repartitioning the hard drive you can choose to break up that single large volume into separate smaller volumes. This allows you to treat a single physical storage device as multiple separate storage destinations.

Just as installing a new operating system will have long-lasting ramifications on how you use your computer, so does your choice of partition options. Thus, before you install a new operating system you should reconsider your partition methodology. The following lists present the pros and cons of various partition options. Again, many of these concepts will be further discussed in Chapter 4, "File Systems."

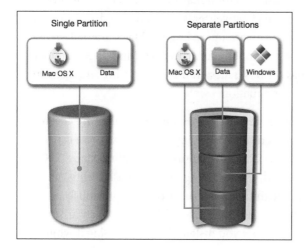

Single Partition

▶ Pros—Most drives are formatted with a single partition by default, so no changes are necessary and no data will be lost. Also, a single partition is the most efficient use of space on your drive, as you won't have wasted space due to having separate volumes.

▶ Cons—Having only a single partition severely limits administrative flexibility. Many maintenance and administrative tasks require multiple volumes, so you will have to use an additional physical storage device to accommodate those needs. Further, because system and user data are combined on a single drive, administration can be more difficult.

Multiple Partitions

▶ Pros—Multiple partitions allow you to have multiple operating systems and multiple storage locations on a single device. Having multiple operating systems allows you to run different versions of Mac OS X from one drive or create utility systems that can be used to repair the primary system. With multiple storage locations, it's much easier to replace a damaged operating system because all the user's data resides on another volume.

▶ Cons—Most drives need to be repartitioned to use multiple partitions. While Mac OS X supports dynamic partitioning without losing data, it can only do so when working within the free space of a drive. Therefore certain partition configurations may require you to completely erase the drive. Any future partition changes may also require you to sacrifice data on the drive as well. Additionally, Boot Camp Assistant, used to configure a Windows partition, does not support multiple partition drives. Finally, multiple partitions can be very space inefficient if you don't plan carefully, as you may end up with underused volumes or volumes that run out of space too soon.

Installing Mac OS X

One of the many improvements to Mac OS X v10.6 is a new system installer. The new installer is easier to use because there are fewer choices for the user to make, but the big improvements are in the underlying reliability of the installation process. The single most significant change is that there are now only two primary types of installations; upgrade installs that replace an existing Mac OS X system, and new installs that place a copy of Mac OS X on a drive without a system. The installer will automatically choose the appropriate installation type based on your selected destination.

> **NOTE** ▶ If you want to perform an erase and install, you must manually erase the system drive using Disk Utility before selecting the installation destination.

The installation process itself involves just a few simple choices up front, followed by the actual execution of the installation. This allows the user to spend just a few minutes choosing the installation options, and then leave the computer unattended while the time-consuming installation process completes.

TIP▶   The Mac OS X v10.6 installation process has a new feature that can safely restart the installation process after a power loss or drive disconnection. If this occurs, simply restart the installation process.

TIP▶   MacBook Air supports system installation via Remote Disk sharing. Several Apple Knowledge Base articles contain more information about Remote Disk, including articles HT1131, HT1777, and HT2129.

Starting the Installation Process

There are two methods for starting an installation. The first method, for installations on top of an existing system, allows you to start the installation while still running the old system. The second method can be used for any type of installation, but it requires that you start up from the installation disc before you can begin. This second method also allows you to use the tools in the Utilities menu.

Start Installation from Existing System

To start the installation while still in the previous system:

1   Insert the Mac OS X Installation DVD.

    A view of the disc contents automatically opens in the Finder.

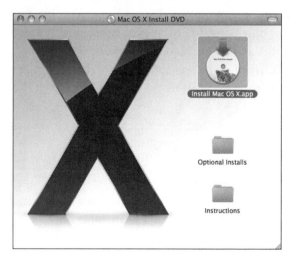

2   Open the Install Mac OS X application from the disc.

This starts an application that allows you to select installation options.

3   Continue through the Welcome screen.

TIP   Clicking the Utilities button from this screen prompts you to restart the computer from the installation disc.

4   Agree to the Apple Software License Agreement.

5   Select the installation destination. Details regarding this step are covered in the next section of this chapter.

TIP   The default selection is the current startup disk; to select other drives, click the Show All Disks button.

6   Optionally customize the installed items to suit your needs. Details regarding this step are covered in the "Selecting Installation Options" section later in this chapter.

7   Click the Install button to start the installation.

The installation will execute automatically without further interaction. Eventually the computer will restart from the installation disc to complete the installation and then restart into Mac OS X v10.6 when complete.

Start Installation from Disc

To startup from the installation disc and then install:

1   Start up from Mac OS X Install DVD. The most common method is to restart the Mac with the installation disc inserted in the drive and hold down the C key to force the Mac to start up from the optical drive.

Further details regarding this step are covered in the "Startup from the Installation DVD" section earlier in this chapter.

2   Select your main language.

3   Continue through the Welcome screen.

4   Agree to the Apple Software License Agreement.

5   Select the installation destination. Details regarding this step are covered in the next section of this chapter.

6   Optionally customize the installed items to suit your needs. Details regarding this step are covered in the "Selecting Installation Options" section later in this chapter.

7   Click the Install button to start the installation process.

The installation will execute automatically without further interaction. Eventually the computer will restart into Mac OS X v10.6 when the installation is complete.

Selecting the Destination

After you have passed the initial installation screens, you will be prompted to select the installation destination. You are simply selecting the disk volume where Mac OS X will be installed. This can be an internal or an external drive as long as it's formatted properly.

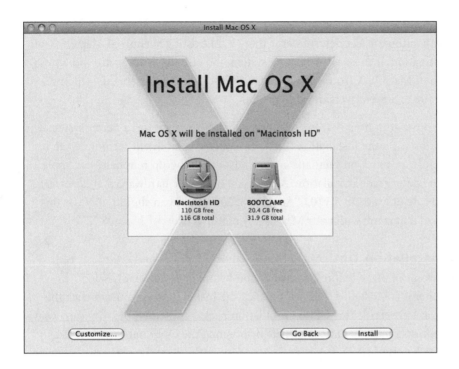

TIP ▸ The default selection is the current startup disk; you may have to click the Show All Disks button to choose an alternate destination.

You may notice that the installer will not let you select certain volumes. This is because the installer has determined that your Mac cannot boot from that volume. Possible reasons are:

▸ The disk does not use the proper partition scheme for your Macintosh. Intel Macs use GUID Partition Table (GPT). You can resolve this issue by repartitioning the drive using Disk Utility.

▸ The volume is not formatted properly. Mac OS X v10.6 requires either Mac OS Extended (Journaled) or Mac OS Extended (Case Sensitive, Journaled). You can resolve this issue by reformatting the volume using Disk Utility.

   NOTE ▸ The installer will also prevent you from selecting a Time Machine backup drive as the installation destination. For more information see Knowledge Base article TS2986, "Mac OS X v10.6: Cannot install Mac OS X v10.6 on a volume used by Time Machine for backups."

Again, the system automatically determines if there is an existing version of Mac OS X on the selected destination. If there is an existing system, the installer will replace the system with the version of Mac OS X from your installation disc. For most users this will probably be an upgrade to a newer version of Mac OS X.

However, it's important to note that the installer will also "downgrade" a newer system to whatever version is on the installation disc. This system replacement technique can be used as a last resort to "fix" a problematic system. Just remember to reupdate any Apple software after the downgrade installation. Also, if you have Mac hardware that is newer than the release date of Mac OS X v10.6, August 28, 2009, then you should only use the system install disc that came with your Mac or any newer version of Mac OS X.

Selecting Installation Options

The last choice you can make before the installation begins is to optionally select which software items are installed. Before you click the Install button, you can click the Customize button to override the default installation packages. Remember, you can always reinstall these optional packages at a later date by opening the Optional Installs package from the Mac OS X Install DVD.

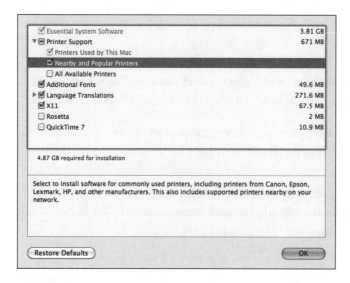

TIP ▸ Click the disclosure triangle to reveal any subinstallations, and select any item to reveal a brief description of the item's contents.

The default, or "Easy Install" as it was known in earlier versions of Mac OS X, is to install almost all the items that make up the complete system installation. Only the base Essential System Software items are required, so you can save a great deal of space by electing to not install various languages and printer drivers that you don't intend to use. The following is a brief description of each optional installation package to help you decide if they are required in your situation:

▶ Printer Support—This item defaults to installing new printer drivers for printers currently being used by the existing system, printers advertising via Bonjour on the local network, and any popular printers from a variety of printer manufacturers. If you have access to the Internet, you can choose to not install these items, as Mac OS X v10.6 can automatically download and install many printer drivers automatically.

▶ Additional Fonts—This item will install high-quality non-Roman fonts to support writing in foreign languages. Non-Roman fonts use many special characters in their alphabets and can take up quite a bit of space.

▶ Language Translations—This item will install non-English versions of all the system resources. Mac OS X supports a variety of languages, so this can take up quite a bit of storage space.

▶ X11—This item will install Apple's X11 windowing environment. X11 is a common graphical user interface platform for UNIX workstations. X11 is covered in Chapter 6, "Applications and Boot Camp."

▶ Rosetta—This item, not installed by default, is the software that allows your Intel-based Mac to open applications created for PowerPC-based Macs. If you have access to the Internet you can choose to not install Rosetta, as Mac OS X v10.6 can automatically download and install it later. Rosetta is also covered in Chapter 6, "Applications and Boot Camp."

▶ QuickTime 7—This item is a bit of a misnomer, as most of the legacy QuickTime 7 technology is installed by default on Mac OS X v10.6. This item installs only the QuickTime 7 player application. If your existing system had a QuickTime 7 Pro key configured, this item will automatically be selected and installed. This is because the new QuickTime X player application is missing several of the previous "pro" features.

MORE INFO ▶ You can find out more about QuickTime support in Mac OS X from Knowledge Base articles HT3678, "Installing QuickTime Player 7 on Mac OS X v10.6 Snow Leopard," and HT3775, "Media formats supported by QuickTime Player in Mac OS X v10.6."

Installer Troubleshooting

Apple has worked hard to make the Mac OS X installation process as painless and reliable as possible. Yet, as with any complicated technology, problems may arise. The good news is that the new Mac OS X v10.6 installer has the ability to "back out" of an installation and restart to the previous system. If this is the result, then obviously the installation did not complete, but at least you still have a functioning Mac. This particular issue is documented by Knowledge Base TS2951, "Mac OS X v10.6: After installing, Mac still starts up into Mac OS X v10.4 or v10.5."

Thoroughly verifying that your computer meets the requirements for Mac OS X v10.6 and completing the installation preparation steps outlined earlier in this chapter will go a long way toward preventing or resolving any serious problems. Beyond appropriate preparation, the most common installation failures arise from bad installation disc media or a problematic destination disk. You can use Disk Utility to verify both the Mac OS X Install DVD and the system drive, as covered in Chapter 4, "File Systems."

> **MORE INFO** ▸ Two other Knowledge Base documents that will help you troubleshoot general installation issues are document TS1394, "Mac OS X: Troubleshooting Installation and Software Updates," and document HT2632, "Mac OS X: Troubleshooting the Mac OS X Installer."

Using the Installer Log

The granddaddy of all troubleshooting resources for Mac OS X is the log file. Nearly every process writes entries in a log file, and the Installer is no different. The Installer Log contains progress and error entries for nearly every step of the installation process, including steps not shown by the standard interface. Information in the Installer Log will allow you to more precisely pinpoint problems or verify installation.

> **TIP** ▸ You can also use this technique to check on the progress of any general software installation via the Installer application.

> **TIP** ▸ After installation you can access the Installer Log on a normally running Mac from the /Applications/Utilities/Console application. Once Console is open, select the /private/var/log/install.log.

Any time during the installation process you can bring up the Installer Log by following these steps:

1 Choose Window > Installer Log from the menu bar or hold down the Command-L keyboard shortcut.

2 Choose Show All Logs from the Detail Level pop-up menu to view the entire contents of the Installer Log.

3 Use the Spotlight search field in the toolbar to isolate specific entries in the Installer Log.

4 To save the Installer Log, choose File > Save or click the Save button in the toolbar.

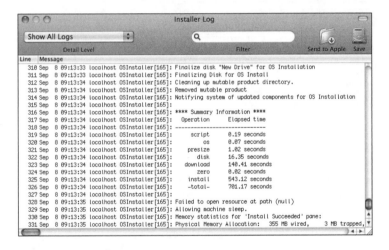

TIP If you start the system installation while running from the Mac OS X Install DVD, the Mac will not automatically restart during the system installation process as long as the Installer Log window is the foremost window.

You can leave the Installer Log window open during the entire installation process to monitor progress. You may find that, even during a successful installation, the Installer reports many warnings and errors. Many of these reported issues are benign, and you should only concern yourself with these issues if you are trying to isolate a showstopping problem. When the installation successfully completes, you should see summary entries in the Installer Log that look similar to the screen shot above.

Mac OS X Setup Assistant

If you are using a brand-new Mac for the first time or you have just installed Mac OS X on a volume with no previous system, you will be presented with the Setup Assistant. The Setup Assistant will guide you through the preliminary configuration required to use a new system. Any of the configurations made while using the Setup Assistant can be easily changed later by accessing the appropriate System Preferences.

Welcome

In just a few steps, you can register and set up your Mac. You can also sign up for a MobileMe subscription, Apple's premium Internet service which lets you easily share photos and files online, create a website, sync important information, and more.

To begin, select the country or region you're in, then click Continue.

> United States
> Canada
> United Kingdom
> Australia
> New Zealand
> Ireland

☐ Show All

Do you need to hear instructions for setting up your Mac?
To learn how to use VoiceOver to set up your computer, press the Escape key now.

(Go Back)   (Continue)

NOTE ▶ If you pause for a few moments at the Startup Assistant Welcome screen, the VoiceOver Tutorial will begin. This is an optional tutorial that explains how to use the VoiceOver assistance technology designed for people who are visually impaired. VoiceOver will be further discussed in Chapter 6, "Applications and Boot Camp."

First you will choose the primary language. This ensures that the appropriate language and dialect are used by the applications on your system. At the Setup Assistant Welcome screen, you'll need to choose a country or region to continue. This information is used to complete the registration process. At this point you will also select the primary keyboard layout.

TIP ▶ Both language and keyboard layout settings can be changed later from the Language & Text preferences.

Migration Assistant

After you select the appropriate language, country or region, and keyboard layout, the Setup Assistant switches to the Migration Assistant. If you are migrating from a previous Mac or version of Mac OS X, the Migration Assistant is a huge time-saver. It enables you to easily transfer all the settings, user accounts, and data from another system to your new system.

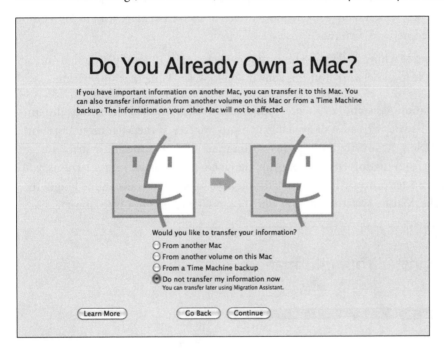

TIP ▶ You can use the Migration Assistant at any time after the initial setup by opening /Applications/Utilities/Migration Assistant.

If you choose to transfer your previous settings with the Migration Assistant you will skip much of the remaining Setup Assistant configuration process. If you do not have a previous system to migrate from, then simply leave the default choice of "Do not transfer my information now" and click Continue to proceed through the rest of the Setup Assistant.

However, if you choose to use Migration Assistant, you can migrate:

▶   From another Mac—This option will instruct you on how to set up a FireWire or network connection between your new system and your previous Mac. Choosing FireWire involves connecting the two computers with a FireWire cable and then boot-ing your previous Mac while holding down the T key. Choosing Ethernet involves running the Migration Assistant application from another Mac to establish a network connection.

▶   From another volume on this Mac—This option will scan all locally mounted vol-umes for a previous system. This includes drives connected via FireWire or USB but not mounted network volumes.

▶   From a Time Machine backup—This option will also scan all locally mounted vol-umes and the local network, but this time it will look for Time Machine backups.

When the Migration Assistant finds a previous system volume or backup, it scans the con-tents and presents you with a list of available items to migrate. If the Migration Assistant discovers multiple system volumes or archives, you must select the specific system you wish to migrate from the Information pop-up menu. Once you make your selections, you can begin the transfer process. The more data you have selected to transfer, the longer the process will take. Mature systems with lots of data can take several hours to migrate.

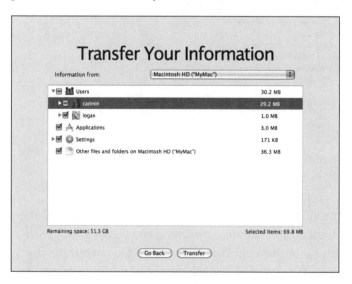

NOTE ▶ If multiple volumes are available on a system, you can choose to migrate that data as well. However, the migration process does not create new volumes on the new system; instead, it creates folders on the new system with the contents of the old volumes.

Setup: Network Settings

If you elect to skip the Migration assistant, the Setup Assistant will attempt to establish a connection to the Internet by automatically configuring the Mac's network settings. It will first attempt to automatically detect the network settings via DHCP on a wired Ethernet network. If it finds an Internet connection via wired Ethernet, you won't be prompted to set up networking, and the Setup Assistant will move on to the registration process.

If you are not connected via wired Ethernet, you will see a configuration screen. The assistant will try to figure out which type of network connection you need to set up first and present you with the appropriate configuration screen. On most Macs this will be the wireless network setup screen. From here you can select an open wireless network or choose "Other Network" from the list to specify a closed wireless network.

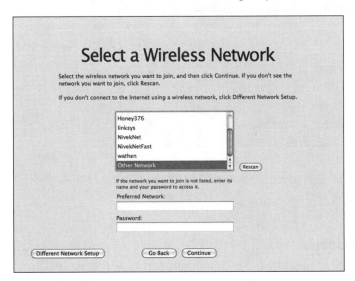

For other network types, you can click the Different Network Setup button and choose a different connection type to configure. Only one active network connection needs configuration to enable the Setup Assistant to move on with the setup. If you decide to manually configure one of the network settings, your choices will vary depending on your Mac's hardware capabilities. Alternatively, you can select the "My computer does not connect to the internet" radio button, which also enables the Setup Assistant to move on. Remember, you don't have to set up networking at this point, and you can do so at any time from the Network preferences.

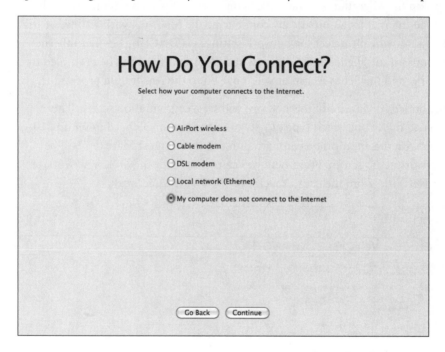

MORE INFO ► Network configuration concepts will be further discussed in Chapter 7, "Network Configuration."

Setup: Registration Process

The registration process, though not required, is an important part of system setup. If you're connected to the Internet at this point, the registration process will send the registration information to Apple. You will also be able to create an Apple ID and MobileMe subscription at this time if you do not already have either. An Apple ID is the login you will use for all Apple online services, including access to the Apple Support pages and the iTunes Store. An Apple ID is completely free to set up. A MobileMe user account will also serve as a valid Apple ID, but MobileMe is a paid subscription service.

Enter Your Apple ID

Your Apple ID is the email address you used if you made a purchase on the iTunes Store, iPhoto, or the online Apple Store. If you have an email address ending in @mac.com or @me.com, you can use that as your Apple ID.

If you don't have an Apple ID, just click Continue. You will set up one later. For more information about the benefits of an Apple ID, click Learn More.

Apple ID: [　　　　　　　　　　　]
Example: annejohnson1@me.com

Password: [　　　　　　　　　　　]

(Learn More)　　(Go Back) (Continue)

MORE INFO ▶ For more information about the Apple ID, the MobileMe service, or the registration process, click the Learn More button. You can also visit the Apple ID FAQ page at http://myinfo.apple.com/html/en_US/faq.html, and the .Mac website, www.apple.com/mobileme.

If you do not want to complete the registration process during the initial setup, you can skip it now by leaving the fields blank and clicking the Continue button through the next few screens. You can also cancel the registration process at any point by using the keyboard shortcut Command-Q and then click the Skip button when the Cancel Registration dialog appears. Remember, you can always complete it later by visiting www.apple.com/register.

NOTE ▶ Attempting to use the Command-Q keyboard shortcut while viewing non-registration screens in the Setup Assistant will not allow you to skip those screens. Instead, you will be forced to shut down or continue.

Setup: Initial Account Creation

The most important part of the setup process is the creation of the initial administrative user account. The account you create here will be the only administrative user account initially allowed to modify all system settings, including the creation of additional user accounts. Therefore, until you create additional administrative user accounts, it is important that you remember the authentication information for this first account.

MORE INFO ▸ User accounts will be further discussed in Chapter 2, "User Accounts."

If Setup Assistant has established a network connection and detected a properly configured Mac OS X Server, then you will see the Connect to Mac OS X Server screen. From this screen simply select your server from the pop-up menu and enter the server account name and password. This will simultaneously create a local administrative user, automatically configure directory service settings, and tie that user to a Mac OS X Server account. Alternatively, you can skip this process by simply leaving all selections blank and clicking the Continue button.

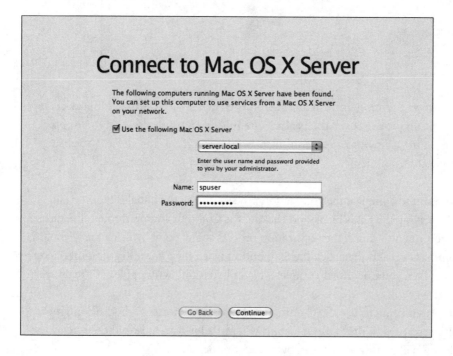

MORE INFO ▶ The behind the scenes details of the Connect to Mac OS X Server screen are covered in Chapter 8, "Network Services."

If the Connect to Mac OS X Server screen never appears, or if you elect to skip that step, then you will be presented with the Create Your Account screen. From this screen you must create the initial administrative user account to continue the Setup Assistant process.

Create Your Account

Enter a name and password to create your user account. You need this password to administer your computer, change settings, and install software.

Full Name: `Client Administrator`

Account Name: `cadmin`

This will be used as the name for your home folder and can't be changed.

Password: ●●●●●●●●●●

Verify: ●●●●●●●●●●

Password Hint:

Enter a hint to help you remember your password. Anyone can see the hint, so choose a hint that won't make it easy to guess your password.

(Go Back)   (Continue)

To create the initial administrative user account:

1   Enter a long user name. This name can contain nearly any alphanumeric character.

2   Enter an account name. This name cannot contain any spaces, capitals, or special characters.

3   Enter the password twice (not three times) to verify it was typed correctly.

4 Only enter a password hint if you think you may forget this password.

The password hint should not match your password.

5 Once you have double-checked your work, click the Continue button to create the new account.

If you didn't set a password hint, the system will advise you to set one. You can set one now or simply leave it blank and click the Continue button.

6 If your Mac is attached, or includes, an iSight camera, then you will be prompted to take a snapshot as a picture for the account.

You can also choose a picture from the library if you're camera shy.

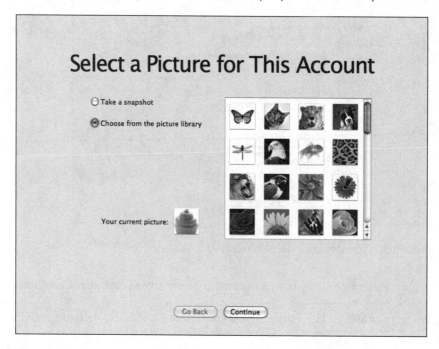

Setup: MobileMe Subscription

At this point in the Setup Assistant process, if you have successfully connected to the Internet and completed the registration process but you don't already have a MobileMe subscription, the assistant will help you acquire one. Apple's MobileMe service is an annual subscription–based Internet service that provides a variety of useful and fun features. If you're not convinced you need a MobileMe account, you can still try it out for 60 days free of charge by completing the MobileMe registration.

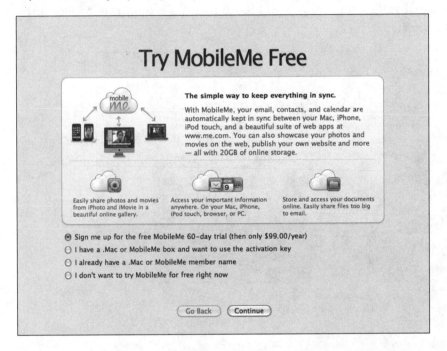

If you are a MobileMe member, select the third option and enter your information. This automatically configures your MobileMe settings for your local account. You can also configure and adjust any MobileMe settings from the MobileMe preferences in System Preferences.

If you do not want to sign up for MobileMe during the initial setup, you can skip it now by selecting the last option and clicking Continue. You can also complete MobileMe registration later by visiting an Apple retail store and purchasing a .Mac box, or by registering online at www.apple.com/mobileme.

Setup: Time Zone, Date, and Time

Finally, the last step in the Setup Assistant process is to configure your Mac's time zone, date, and time settings. Mac OS X v10.6 now features automatic time zone selection if your Mac includes a wireless Ethernet card and has a connection to the Internet. Select the checkbox at the top of the Select Time Zone screen and the Mac will automatically locate your closest time zone by connecting to an Internet database that tracks networks and their Earthly location. If the system is able to locate your closest city and time zone, click Continue to complete the setup. The Mac will also automatically connect to Apple's time servers to set the date and time.

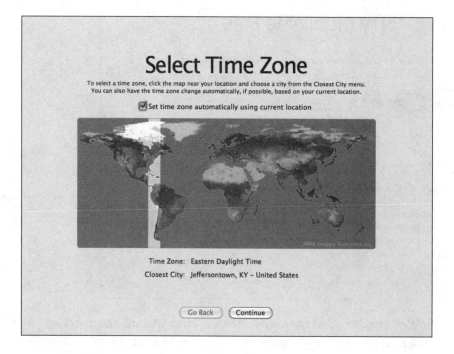

TIP Time zone, date, and time settings can all be reconfigured via the Date & Time preferences.

If your Mac has yet to establish an Internet connection, you will have to manually set the time zone. Start by clicking on the map near your current location. Then, from the pop-up menu at the bottom of the screen, you can select the current best choice and click Continue. If your Mac isn't connected to the Internet you will also be prompted to set the date and time. Set them and click Continue to complete the setup.

Configure Mac OS X

Once your Mac has completed its initial configuration via Setup Assistant you will rely on an array of system tools for administration and troubleshooting. In this section you will learn about the fundamental Mac OS X configuration application System Preferences, and how to gather essential system information with the About This Mac dialog and the System Profiler application.

Using System Preferences

The System Preferences application is the primary interface for adjusting user and system settings. (In other operating systems these settings would be accessed using Control Panels.) You will use System Preferences quite frequently throughout this book and any time you are setting up a new Mac. The quickest access to System Preferences is via the Apple menu because it's almost always available from any application.

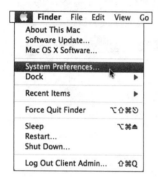

TIP The System Preferences application can also be found in the /Applications folder. You can use any shortcut method you like to access the System Preferences application, including using its icon in the Dock and placing it in the Finder sidebar.

The first time you access System Preferences, you'll notice it is divided into four separate rows representing the four main categories of System Preferences: Personal, Hardware, Internet & Wireless, and System. Further, any third-party preference panes you install will appear automatically in a fifth row categorized as simply "Others."

The categorization of the individual System Preferences is deliberate:

▶ Personal—These preferences panes will generally only affect settings for the active user account. In other words, for most of the System Preferences in this category, each user has his own discrete settings.

▶ Hardware—These preferences panes are specific to hardware settings. For example, the Energy Saver and Print & Fax preferences in this category can affect every user on the Mac, and thus they require administrative access to make changes.

▶ Internet & Wireless—These preferences panes are used to configure various network-related services. The Network preferences pane is the primary graphical interface for managing your Mac's network and Internet configuration. Also, the Network and Sharing preferences in this category can affect every user on the Mac, and thus they require administrative access to make changes.

▶ System—These preferences panes have a systemwide effect when changed. Consequently, most of the System Preferences in this category, save for the Software Update and Universal Access preferences, require administrative access.

▶ Others (optional)—There is no rhyme or reason to the classification of these preferences panes except that they are not part of the standard Mac OS X installation. The
developers of third-party System Preferences decide whether their preferences require
administrative access.

Accessing a set of preferences is as simple as clicking once on the icon. Most System
Preferences changes are instantaneous and don't require you to click an Apply or OK but-
ton. Clicking the Show All button in the upper-left corner returns you to the view of all
System Preferences.

If you're not sure where a specific feature setting is located in the various System
Preferences, you can use the Spotlight search field in the upper-right corner to quickly
locate the hidden setting.

You'll notice that some System Preferences have a lock in the bottom-left corner. These
preferences can be accessed only by an administrative user account. If a set of preferences
you need to access is locked from editing, simply click the lock icon, and then authenticate
as an administrative user to unlock it.

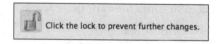

NOTE ▶ The lock icon is a general indication that access to the item requires administrative authentication. The lock icon shows up in a variety of places, not just in
System Preferences.

Information About Your Mac

Knowledge of your Mac's specifications is always important when installing new software, updating installed software, performing maintenance, or troubleshooting a problem. Your first stop to discovering a Mac's specifications is the About This Mac dialog. You can open this dialog at any point by choosing About This Mac from the Apple menu.

Initially, the About This Mac dialog will show you the Mac's system software version, processor type and speed, total system memory, and currently booted startup disk. You can also find the system build identifier and hardware serial number by repeatedly clicking the system version number directly below the bold "Mac OS X" text:

▶ System version number—This number represents the specific system software version currently installed on the Mac. The first digit, 10, obviously represents the tenth generation of the Mac operating system. The second digit, 6, represents the sixth major release of Mac OS X. The final digit represents an incremental update to the operating system. Incremental updates generally offer very few feature changes but often include a number of bug fixes.

▶ System build number—This is an even more granular representation of the specific system software version currently installed on the Mac. Apple engineers create hundreds of different versions of each system software release as they refine the product. The build number is used to track this process. Also, you may find that the computer-specific builds of Mac OS X, which come preinstalled on new Mac hardware, will differ from the standard installation builds. This is an important detail to note if you are creating system images for mass distribution, as computer-specific builds of Mac OS X may not work on other types of Mac hardware.

▶ Hardware serial number—The hardware serial number is also located somewhere on the Mac's case. However, Apple has a tendency to choose form over function, so the serial number may be quite difficult to find. Like many other complicated products, the Mac's serial number is a unique number used to identify that particular Mac for maintenance and service issues.

TIP This information, along with other useful information, is also available at the login screen by clicking just below the words "Mac OS X." This allows you to check a Mac's vital statistics quickly, without even having to log in first.

TIP Macs that have had their logic boards replaced may not properly display the serial number in the About This Mac dialog.

System Profiler

The system information in the About This Mac dialog is only the tip of the iceberg compared with what can be found via the System Profiler application. From the About This Mac dialog, click the More Info button to open System Profiler.

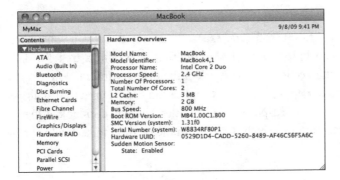

TIP ▶ The System Profiler application can also be found in the /Applications/ Utilities folder. You can use any shortcut method you like to access the System Profiler application, including placing it in the Dock and the Finder sidebar.

You will use System Profiler to locate critical system information in nearly every chapter of this book. Additionally, one of the most important uses of System Profiler is as a documentation tool. Any time you need to document the current state of a Mac, you can use System Profiler to create a detailed system report. To create this report while in System Profiler, simply choose Save from the File menu. Enter a name and destination for this report and be sure to choose an appropriate File Format option from the pop-up menu; then click the Save button.

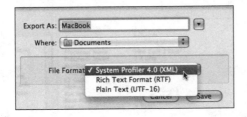

NOTE ▶ The XML code used by the default System Profiler file format is not easily legible when opened by standard text-viewing applications. Applications that can understand Rich Text Format are common, and nearly every text reader understands plain text format.

Install Software and Updates

Adding new capabilities is the very reason "software" exists. It's expected that you will add new applications to increase the capabilities of your Mac and that, as products are refined, new software updates as well. In this section you will look at the primary installation technology in Mac OS X, the Installer application. This application can be used to install Apple software and updates and many third-party software titles. You will also look at the built-in Apple software update technology, which is an automatic method to keep all your Apple software up-to-date.

Using the Installer Application

A great feature of Mac OS X is the relative ease with which most new software is installed. In fact, many applications require only that the user copy a single application file to the local system drive. At the same time, more complicated software may require multiple resources placed at a variety of specific locations on your Mac. A prime example of a complicated software installation is any Mac OS X system software update.

The Installer application makes complicated application installations simple. Often, software developers will create an "installer package" with all the instructions necessary for the Installer application to set up the new software on your system.

> **MORE INFO ▶** Though covered briefly here, packages will be further discussed in Chapter 5, "Data Management and Backup."

**Optional
Installs.mpkg**

Double-clicking one of these software installer packages will open the Installer application and begin the installation process. Much like the Mac OS X installation process, the Installer application will guide you through the steps necessary to install or update software. This may include agreeing to software licenses, selecting a destination, selecting package options, and authenticating as an administrative user.

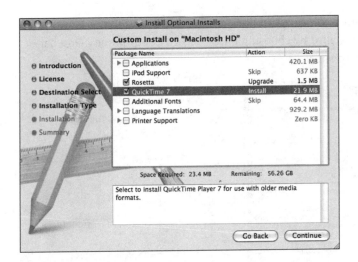

NOTE ▶ Third-party software developers may choose to use a proprietary non-Apple installer for their product. These installers will behave differently than the Apple Installer.

NOTE ▶ Proceed with caution if an installer requires you to authenticate as an administrative user. These installers need administrative access so they can make changes to the system software.

Advanced Installer Features

If you're curious about what an installation package is actually doing to your Mac, you have two ways to find out. First, you can view the Installer Log at any time while using the Installer application by choosing Window > Installer Log or using the Command-L keyboard shortcut. The Installer Log is a live view of any progress or errors reported during the installation process.

MORE INFO ▶ Accessing the installer log is covered in the "Using the Installer Log" section previously in this chapter.

If you want to inspect an installer package before installing the application you can do so, but not using the Installer Log. After passing the initial installation welcome screens and agreeing to any software license agreements while using the Installer application, you can preview the list of files to be installed by choosing File > Show Files from the menu bar or using the Command-I keyboard shortcut.

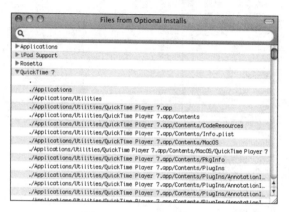

TIP Save time looking for what you need by using the Spotlight search field in the toolbar when examining the Installer Log or file list.

With Mac OS X v10.5, Apple introduced a few new significant Installer application features. For starters, users may specify their home folder as the installation destination for applications that allow it. Apple also introduced a dynamic installation package that remains up to date as long as the Mac has Internet access. Network-based installation packages automatically download the latest software from a vendor's servers during the installation process.

Finally, Apple increased the security and reliability of software installation packages by supporting signed packages. These packages contain special code used to validate the authenticity and completeness of the software during installation. This makes it nearly impossible for nefarious hackers to insert illegitimate files in trusted installation packages. You can identify a signed installer package by a small certificate icon in the far right of the installer window title bar. Clicking this icon reveals details about the signed package, including its certificate status.

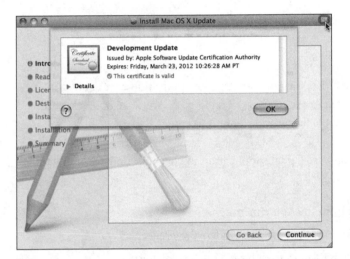

Using Apple Software Update

Keeping current with software updates is an important part of maintaining a healthy Mac. Fortunately, Mac OS X includes an easy-to-use Software Update application that automatically checks Apple's servers via the Internet to make sure you're running the latest Apple software. Automatic Software Update checking is enabled by default the first moment you start using your Mac. If an update is detected it will be downloaded in the background, and you will be presented with a Software Update dialog.

You have three choices when presented with this dialog:

▶ Click the Show Details button to open the full Software Update, so you can further inspect all the available updates, as covered in the next section of this chapter.

▶ Click the Not Now button to dismiss the automatic update until the next scheduled update check.

▶ Click the Install button, and then authenticate as an administrative user to have the updates install immediately.

NOTE ▶ An Internet connection is required to use Software Update for both automatic and manual updates. Also, the Software Update application checks only for updates of currently installed Apple software. Finally, some software updates require that you also agree to the Apple Software License Agreement.

You can manually open the Software Update application to check for updates at any time via any of the following methods:

▶ Choose Software Update from the Apple menu.

▶ Click the Check Now button in the Software Update preferences.

▶ Click the Software Update button in the About This Mac dialog.

TIP ▶ The Software Update application can also be found in the /System/Library/ CoreServices folder. You can use any shortcut method you like to access the Software Update application, including placing it in the Dock and the Finder sidebar.

When you choose to have Software Update install new software for you, it will do so in one of two ways. First, if the new software does not require a restart for installation, the software will automatically install without any further user interaction.

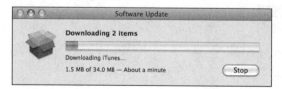

But if the new software requires a restart after the install process, you will be presented with a dialog featuring a Log Out and Install button. You can, of course, choose to install these updates later, but you will eventually have to restart to take advantage of the new software.

Software Update Details

When Software Update opens to the discovery of new updates, selecting the Show Details button reveals its full interface. This allows you to individually inspect all the available Apple software updates. The information provided includes the update name, version, file size, and a detailed description. You will also be able to deselect and ignore updates that you do not wish to install.

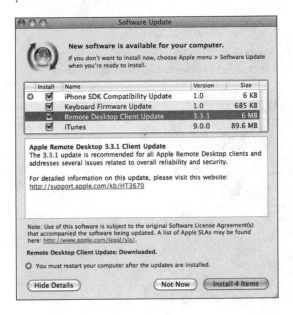

TIP Updates in the list that require a restart will have a small grey icon of a triangle inside a circle next to their name.

If you don't want to be reminded of a particular update again, you can choose to ignore the update by selecting it from the list of available updates and then choosing Update > Ignore Update from the menu bar. You can bring back all ignored updates by choosing Software Update > Reset Ignored Updates.

Also from this menu you can open a web browser to Apple's downloads website. With Mac OS X v10.6 this is the only official method for saving an Apple update installer. This is unlike previous versions of Mac OS X, which allowed you to download updates from within Software Update. Updates downloaded from Apple can be installed by the Installer application or any other application that can process Apple installation packages, such as Apple Remote Desktop.

Software Update Preferences

The Software Update preferences, accessed via System Preferences, enable you to adjust the schedule of automatic software updates and review previously installed updates.

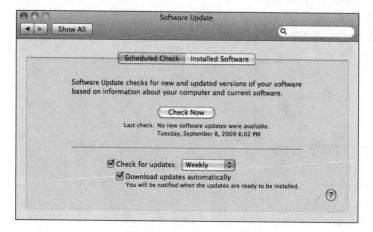

The default view is the Scheduled Check pane; from here you can:

► Click the Check Now button to manually open Software Update.

► Enable or disable automatic software updates by toggling the "Check for updates" checkbox.

► Adjust the frequency of automatic updates using the "Check for updates" pop-up menu.

► Enable or disable the automatic download of updates by toggling the "Download updates automatically" checkbox.

NOTE ▶ The Software Update schedule is saved separately for each user of a Mac. Thus another user's account may automatically download updates even when your account has them disabled.

NOTE ▶ You will need to authenticate as an administrative user to complete the installation of any automatically downloaded updates.

When you select the Installed Software tab, you can investigate previously installed Apple software updates. You will be able to view the name, version, and date installed for any software update. It's important to know that this interface shows only Apple software that was installed after the system installation, although it shows both manually and automatically installed Apple software. You can view the full installer log from the Console application as covered in the "Using the Installer Log" section of this chapter.

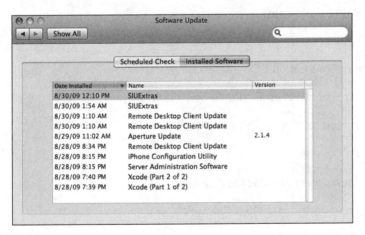

What You've Learned

▶ Mac OS X v10.6 requires a Mac computer with an Intel processor, 1 GB of memory, 5 GB of available disk space, and a DVD drive for installation.

▶ The Mac OS X Install DVD includes a variety of administration and troubleshooting utilities.

▶ The Mac OS X Install DVD guides you through system installation.

▶ The Mac OS X Setup Assistant guides you through the initial configuration of your Mac system.

▶ The Migration Assistant can be used to easily transfer user accounts, settings, and data from a previous system.

▶ Apple provides updates to Mac OS X through the Software Update service. To ensure that your system is up-to-date, run Software Update on a regular basis.

References

You can check for new and updated Knowledge Base documents at www.apple.com/support.

Firmware and Startup

HT2568, "Determining BootROM or firmware version"

HT1237, "EFI and SMC firmware updates for Intel-based Macs"

HT2213, "About the Firmware Restoration CD (Intel-based Macs)"

HT1352, "Setting up firmware password protection in Mac OS X"

HT1310, "Startup Manager: How to select a startup volume"

System Installation

HT2632, "Mac OS X: Troubleshooting the Mac OS X Installer"

HT2681, "What's a 'Computer-Specific Mac OS X Release'?"

HT2186, "Don't install a version of Mac OS X earlier than what came with your Mac"

HT3258, "Mac OS X v10.6: About incompatible software"

TS2986, "Mac OS X v10.6: Cannot install Mac OS X v10.6 on a volume used by Time Machine for backups"

HT3678, "Installing QuickTime Player 7 on Mac OS X v10.6 Snow Leopard"

HT3775, "Media formats supported by QuickTime Player in Mac OS X v10.6"

TS2951, "Mac OS X v10.6: After installing, Mac still starts up into Mac OS X v10.4 or v10.5"

Installers and Updates

TS1394, "Mac OS X: Troubleshooting Installation and Software Updates"

HT1569, "Troubleshooting Automatic Software Update in Mac OS X"

HT1222, "Apple security updates"

URLs

Mac OS X v10.6 enhancements and refinements: www.apple.com/macosx/refinements/enhancements-refinements.html

Apple's product guide: http://guide.apple.com

Mac OS X system architecture overview: http://developer.apple.com/macosx/architecture

Mac OS X v10.6 detailed technical specifications: www.apple.com/macosx/specs.html

Apple's software downloads: http://support.apple.com/downloads

Main Mac OS X v10.6 support website: www.apple.com/support/snowleopard

Apple ID FAQ: http://myinfo.apple.com/html/en_US/faq.html

MobileMe subscription service: www.apple.com/mobileme

Apple product registration: www.apple.com/register

Review Quiz

1. What utilities are available when booted from the Mac OS X Install DVD?

2. What are the minimum hardware requirements for installing Mac OS X v10.6?

3. What four preparation steps must you take before installing Mac OS X?

4. What are the advantages and disadvantages of using a single-partition drive with Mac OS X? How about a multiple-partition drive?

5. Which packages are installed by default when installing Mac OS X?

6. Where can you locate the system version number, build number, and serial number? What is the significance of these numbers?

7. How do the four default System Preferences categories differ?

8. How do you ensure that you have the latest Apple software?

Answers

1. The Utilities menu when booted from the Mac OS X Install DVD includes Startup Disk, Reset Password, Firmware Password Utility, Disk Utility, Terminal, System Profiler, Network Utility, and Restore System From Backup.

2. The minimum requirements are:

   A Mac with an Intel processor

   1 GB of memory

   5 GB of available disk space

   DVD drive for installation (Installation on a MacBook Air requires either an external DVD drive or another computer with a DVD drive.)

   A built-in display or a display connected to an Apple-supplied video card supported by your computer

   Some features require a compatible Internet service provider; fees may apply.

   Some features require Apple's MobileMe service; fees apply.

3. Check for firmware updates, verify application compatibility, back up vital files and folders, and document critical settings.

4. Single-partition drives are easier to set up initially, but they aren't as flexible for administration and maintenance. Multiple-partition drives require repartitioning during setup but provide several separate volumes, which can be used to segregate user data and host multiple operating systems.

5. Items installed by default include the essential system software, printer drivers for currently used printers, additional fonts, language translations, and X11. Optional items include more printer drivers, Rosetta, and QuickTime 7.

6. The system version, build number, and hardware serial number are located in the About This Mac dialog or the login screen. The system version number defines the specific version of Mac OS X currently installed. The system build number is an even more specific identifier used primarily by developers. Finally, the hardware serial number is a unique number used to identify your specific Mac.

7. Generally, Personal preferences affect only a single user, Hardware preferences adjust hardware and peripheral settings, Internet & Wireless preferences affect personal and system network settings, and System preferences affect all users and often require administrative access.

8. The Software Update application checks for Apple software updates via the Internet. You can adjust automatic update settings or manually open the Software Update application from the Software Update preferences.

2

Time   This chapter takes approximately 2 hours to complete.

Goals   Recognize various user account types and user attributes
Create and manage user accounts and home folders
Understand and implement user security techniques
Resolve issues that prevent users from accessing their account

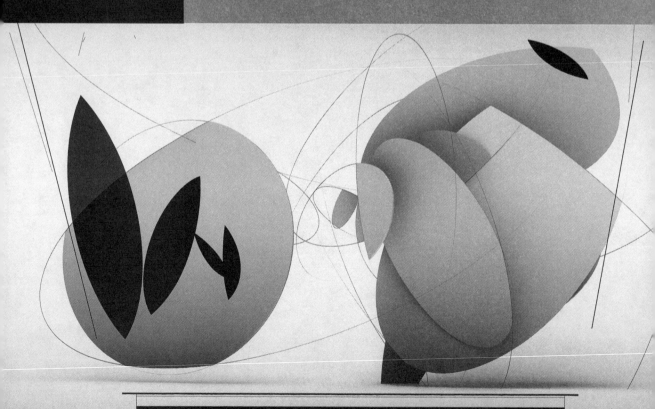

Chapter **2**

User Accounts

One of the hallmarks of a modern operating system is support for multiple user accounts. Mac OS X v10.6 delivers in spades with a robust, secure, and highly polished multiple-user environment. Mac OS X's UNIX foundation is primarily responsible for providing such a sophisticated multiple-user environment. UNIX operating systems have a long history of providing such services, but Apple has made many improvements by providing advanced user management features and streamlined administration tools, all with Apple's traditional ease of use.

In this chapter, you will explore the fundamental technologies that allow individuals to log in and use the Mac. Further, you will learn how to create and manage multiple user accounts on Mac OS X. Finally, you will learn account security and troubleshooting techniques.

Understanding User Accounts

Mac users have been known to identify their beloved computer with a pet name; nevertheless, your Mac absolutely identifies you via a user account. With the exception of the rarely used single-user mode, you are required to log in with a user account to perform any task on the Mac. Even if the Mac is sitting at the login window and you haven't yet authenticated, the system is still using a handful of system user accounts to maintain background services. Every single file and folder on your Mac's hard drive belongs to a user account—in short, every single item and process on your Mac belongs to some user account. Consequently, a thorough understanding of user accounts is necessary to effectively administer and troubleshoot Mac OS X.

NOTE ▶ This chapter focuses on user accounts that are available only to a single local Mac. Network user accounts, on the other hand, are available to multiple Macs and are hosted from shared servers. Network user accounts are briefly covered in Chapter 8, "Network Services."

User Account Types

The vast majority of home Mac users are only aware of, and therefore only use, the account created when the Mac was initially set up with the Setup Assistant. Apple has engineered Mac OS X to appear as a single-user operating system by default. However, Mac OS X supports multiple simultaneous user accounts. Mac OS X also supports several types of user accounts to facilitate different levels of access. Essentially, you choose a specific account type to grant a defined level of access that best meets the user's requirements. User accounts are categorized into one of five types: standard users, administrative users, the guest user, sharing only users, and the root user.

Standard Users

Ideally, standard is the account type most should use on a daily basis. Standard accounts are also commonly used when multiple people share a computer, as is the case with computer labs. This is because the standard account strikes the best balance between usability and security. Standard users are members of the "staff" group and have read access to most items, preferences, applications, and other users' Public and Sites folders. Yet they are only allowed to make changes to personal preferences and items inside their own home folders. Essentially, standard users are not allowed to make changes to systemwide preferences, system files, or anything that might affect another user's account.

> **TIP** ▶ Standard users can be further restricted using parental controls. The account type known as Managed with Parental Controls is a standard account with parental controls enabled.

Administrative Users

Administrative users aren't much different from regular users, save for one important distinction: Administrative users are part of the "admin" group and are essentially allowed full access to all applications, system preferences, and most system files. By default, administrative users do not have access to protected system files or other users' files outside the Public and Sites folders. Despite this, administrative users can bypass these restrictions in both the graphical environment and at the command line if needed. For example, administrative users are allowed to update system software as long as they successfully authenticate when the installer application asks for authorization.

Because administrative access is required to make changes to the system, this is the default account type for the initial account created when Mac OS X is set up for the very first time with the Setup Assistant. Additional standard user accounts can be created for daily use, but the Mac should have access to at least one administrative account.

Guest User

Older versions of Mac OS X use only the guest account to facilitate file sharing by allowing nonauthenticated access to users' Public folders. Starting with Mac OS X v10.5, support was added for a full guest user account. Once enabled, the guest user is similar to a nonadministrative user but without a password. Anyone with access to the Mac can use it to log in. However, when the guest user logs out, the guest user's home folder is deleted. This includes preference files, web browser history, or any other trace that the user might have left on the system. The next time someone logs in as a guest, a brand-new home folder is created for that user.

NOTE ▶ The guest user is enabled by default for file-sharing access only.

Sharing Only Users

Again, starting with Mac OS X v10.5, support was added for special user accounts that have access only to shared files and folders. Sharing only users have no home folder and cannot log in to the Mac's user interface or command line. Administrative users can create multiple shared users with unique names and passwords. Sharing users start out with access similar to that of the guest user, with access only to other users' Public folders. Administrative users can, however, define specific shared user access to any folder via the Sharing preferences. File sharing will be further discussed in Chapter 8, "Network Services."

Root User

The root user account, also known as System Administrator, has unlimited access to everything on the Mac. In other words, the root user can read, write, and delete any file; can modify any setting; and can install any software. To help prevent abuse of this account, by default no one is allowed to log in as root, as a password hasn't been set for the root user. Since many system processes run as the root user, it needs to exist on the system; otherwise, Mac OS X wouldn't be able to boot. The root user is covered in greater detail in "Fundamental Account Security," later in this chapter.

User Account Attributes

Although the loginwindow process enables you to log in to the Mac environment, the DirectoryService background process is responsible for maintaining the account information. DirectoryService stores user account information in a series of XML-encoded text files located in the /var/db/dslocal/nodes/Default/users folder. This folder is only readable by the System Administrator (root) account, but if you were to directly inspect these files, you would discover that they are organized into lists of user attributes and their associated values. Each user has a variety of attributes used to define the account details. All of the attributes are important, but for the scope of this chapter you need only be familiar with the primary user account attributes:

▶ Full Name—This is the full name of the user. It can be quite long and contain nearly any character. However, no other account on the system can have the same full name. You can easily change the full name later at any point.

▶ MobileMe user name—This is used to associate the Mac user account to a MobileMe subscription service account. This attribute is optional for Mac OS X, but it is required for the MobileMe services Sync, iDisk, and Back to My Mac.

▶ Account Name—Sometimes also referred to as "short name," this is the name used to uniquely identify the account and by default is also used to name the user's home folder. A user can use either the full name or the account name interchangeably to authenticate. However, no other account on the system can have the same account name, and it cannot contain any special characters or spaces.

▶ User ID—This is a numeric attribute used to identify the account with file and folder ownership. This number is almost always unique to each account, though overlaps are possible. User accounts start at 501, while most system accounts are below 100.

▶ Universally Unique ID (UUID)—Sometimes also referred to as "Generated UID" or "GUID," this alphanumeric attribute is generated by the computer during account creation and is unique in both space and time: Once created, no Mac system any- where will ever create an account with the same UUID. It is used to reference the user's password, which is stored in a separate, more secure location. It is also used for group membership and file permissions.

▶ Group—This is a numeric attribute used to associate the user with a default group. As covered previously, the default for most users is 20, which is associated with the staff group. This means that when you create a new file, it belongs to your user account and to the staff group.

► Login Shell—This file path defines the default command-line shell used by the account. Any user who is allowed to use the command line has this set to /bin/bash by default. Both administrative and standard users are allowed command-line access by default.

► Home Directory—This file path defines the location of the user's home folder. All users except for sharing users, who do not have home folders, have this set to /Users/<name>, where <name> is the account name.

NOTE ► Account passwords are stored separately from the rest of the account attributes to enhance security. Password storage is covered in greater detail in "Fundamental Account Security," later in this chapter.

Managing User Accounts

Now that you have a thorough understanding of the user account types and primary attributes used by Mac OS X, it's time to get down to the task of managing user accounts.

Creating New User Accounts

To create new user accounts:

1 Open the Accounts preferences by choosing Apple menu > System Preferences, then clicking the Accounts icon.

2 Click the lock icon in the bottom-left corner and authenticate as an administrative user to unlock the Accounts preferences.

3 Click the plus button below the user list to reveal the account creation dialog.

4 Choose the appropriate account type from the New Account pop-up menu.

At a minimum, complete the Full Name and Account Name fields. A password is not required, but it's highly recommended that you choose a nontrivial password. Passwords and system security are covered in "Fundamental Account Security," later in this chapter.

Password hints are not required either, but they are recommended if you are forgetful of such things. Password hints are revealed at the login screen after three failed attempts.

5   Finally, click the Create Account button to finish the job.

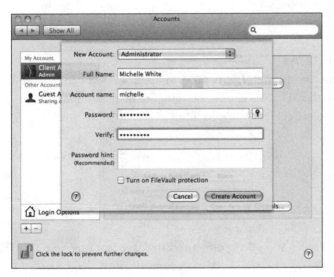

NOTE ▶ If this is the first additional account you've created on a Mac, you will be prompted to turn off automatic login. It is more secure to disable automatic login when your Mac uses multiple accounts.

You can easily modify or add additional attributes at any time by simply selecting the account from the list in the Accounts preferences. Additional configurable attributes here include the user picture, MobileMe subscription account, associated Address Book card, login items, and parental controls. You can also switch an account between standard and administrative at any time with this dialog.

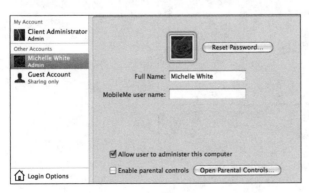

TIP ▶ The guest user account is also enabled and configured from the Accounts preferences.

Managing User Login Items

Some users find it convenient to have their favorite files or applications open automatically as soon as they log in to the Mac. You can easily configure these automatic login items for any account that you are currently logged into:

NOTE ▶ When using the Accounts preferences, even as an administrative user, you cannot configure login items for other user accounts.

To manage login items:

1   Open the Accounts preferences and select your currently logged-in user account. This will appear at the top of the user list under "My Account."

2   Click the Login Items tab.

3   Add login items either by clicking the plus button below the Login Items list to reveal a selection dialog or by simply dragging and dropping items from the Finder into the Login Items list.

4   You can delete login items by selecting them and then clicking the minus button.

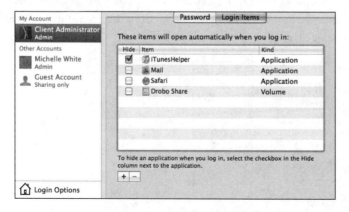

TIP ▶ Drag and drop a shared network volume from the Finder to the Login Items list to have the Mac automatically connect to that shared volume at login.

TIP ▶ You can temporarily disable the login items from automatically opening by holding down the Shift key as you log in to the Mac.

Using Parental Controls

Mac OS X includes an extensive collection of managed preferences that enable you to further restrict what users can and cannot do. Apple puts these managed preferences under the consumer-oriented parental controls moniker, but they are certainly still applicable in a business or institutional setting. As parental controls are designed to further limit standard user accounts, they cannot be applied to an administrative user.

MORE INFO ▶ Parental controls is a limited subset of a much more extensive managed preferences system available when using the Mac OS X Server administration tools. You can find out more about this technology from Apple Training Series: Mac OS X Server Essentials v10.6.

Management options available via parental controls include the following:

▶ Use Simple Finder to simplify the Finder to show only the items most important to your managed user.

▶ Create a list that defines which applications or widgets a user is allowed to open. Users will not be allowed to open any application or widget not specified in the list.

▶ Restrict access to printers, password changes, optical media, and the Dock.

▶ Hide the user from profanity in the built-in Dictionary.

▶ Enable automatic Safari website content filtering, or manually manage a list of permitted websites or a combination of both automatically and manually permitted websites.

▶ Limit Mail and iChat to allow exchanges only with approved addresses.

▶ Set weekday and weekend time usage limits.

▶ Maintain Safari, iChat, and application usage logs. This logs both allowed and attempted but denied access.

NOTE ▶ Most third-party applications will not honor parental controls' content filters and account limit settings. Examples of unsupported applications include the Firefox browser and Entourage email client. This is, however, is easily remedied by using the aforementioned parental controls application restriction list.

To enable and configure parental controls:

1   Open the Accounts preferences and authenticate as an administrative user to unlock its settings.

2   Select the user from the accounts list you wish to manage with parental controls.

3   Ensure that the Enable parental controls checkbox is enabled.

    If not, Click the Enable parental controls checkbox and you will see the user's account type change from Standard to Managed in the accounts list.

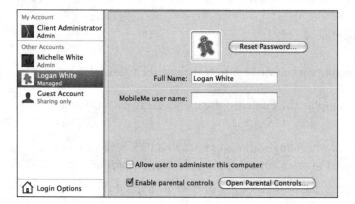

4   Click the Open Parental Controls button. You can also access the Parental Controls preferences directly from the main System Preferences window.

5   Select the user you wish to manage from the accounts list and use the tabs to navigate through all the options.

TIP ▶ Your Mac's Parental Controls preferences can be managed remotely by another Mac running Mac OS X v10.6. To enable this feature in the Parental Controls preferences, click the small gear icon at the bottom of the user list to reveal a pop-up menu allowing you to choose Allow Remote Setup. From another Mac on the local network, open the Parental Controls preferences and any Mac allowing this remote control will automatically appear in the user list. You will have to authenticate using an administrator account on the selected Mac to be granted Parental Controls preferences access.

Managing Additional Account Attributes

From the Accounts preferences, after authenticating as an administrator, you can also access normally hidden user account attributes by right-clicking or Control-clicking on a user account to reveal the Advanced Options dialog. Although you are allowed to manually edit these attributes to make a desired change or fix a problem, you can just as easily break the account by entering improper information. For example, you can restore access to a user's home folder by correcting the Home Directory information; alternately, you can accidentally prevent a user from accessing their home folder by mistyping this information.

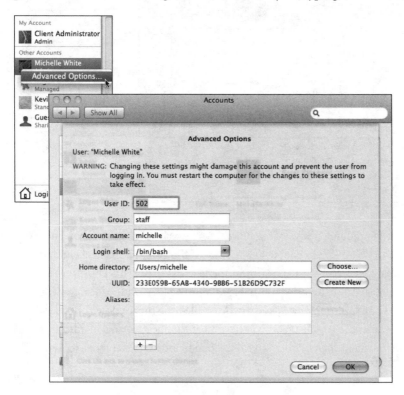

Managing Group Accounts

Essentially, a group account is nothing more than a list of user accounts. Groups are primarily used to allow greater control over file and folder access. Mac OS X uses several dozen built-in groups to facilitate secure system processes and sharing. For instance, all users are members of the "staff" group, administrative users are also members of the "admin" group, and the root user has its own group, known as "wheel." Using groups to manage sharing will be discussed in Chapter 4, "File Systems."

NOTE ▶ Standard accounts are always members of the staff group, and administrative accounts are always members of the admin group regardless of what is shown in the group membership of the Accounts preferences.

NOTE ▶ The Accounts preferences can only be used to manage local non-system users and groups.

Creating new group accounts is similar to creating new user accounts:

1   Open the Accounts preferences and authenticate as an administrative user to unlock its settings.

2   Click the plus button below the user list to reveal the account creation dialog.

3   Choose Group from the New Account pop-up menu.

4   Enter a group name and click the Create Group button. You cannot use the same name for a group that already exists.

5   Add user accounts to the group by selecting the appropriate checkboxes in the
    Membership list.

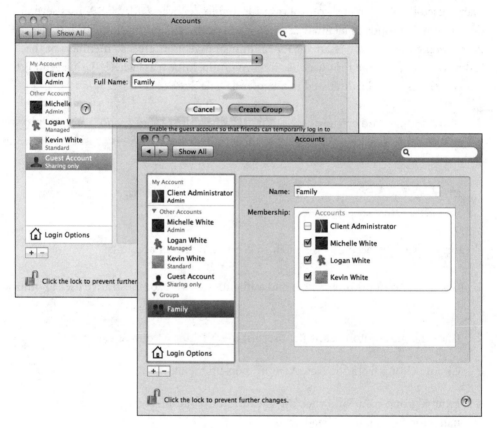

TIP ▶ In Mac OS X, groups can also contain other groups as part of their membership. This feature is known as nested groups.

Managing User Home Folders

If you think of a user's account information as his mailing address, then you can think of his home folder as his house and its contents. The directions to his house are certainly important, but it's the stuff inside the house that's really valuable to the owner. The same is true on the Mac. Aside from the initial account attributes, every other item that the user is likely to create or need is stored in that user's home folder. As mentioned earlier, the default location for a locally stored user home folder is /Users/<name>, where <name> is the account name.

> **NOTE ▶** Network user accounts often have home folders located on a shared server or possibly even a removable disk drive. Network user accounts are briefly covered in Chapter 8, "Network Services."

Understanding Home Folder Contents

Traditional Mac users are notorious for putting personal files anywhere they like with little regard for order. Yet, with every revision of Mac OS X and its included applications, Apple has been coaxing its users into a tidier home folder arrangement. Though users can still create additional folders to store their items, most applications will suggest an appropriate default folder, while other applications won't even ask users and simply use the assigned default folder.

All the contents of the default folders inside a user's home folder are only viewable by the user, with the exception of the Public and Sites folders. Other users are allowed to view the contents of the Public and Sites folders, but they are not allowed to add items or make changes. There is a Drop Box folder inside the Public folder that others are allowed to put files in, but they still cannot see inside this folder. It's important to note that if a user puts other files and folders at the root level of her home folder, by default, other users will be able to view those items. Of course, you can change all of these defaults by adjusting file and folder access permissions as outlined in Chapter 4, "File Systems."

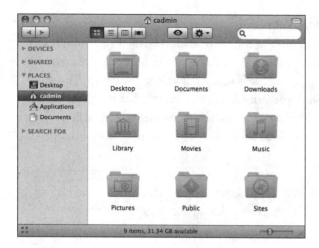

The default items in a Mac user's home folder are:

▶ Desktop—Many an old-school Mac user's files end up right here. This has been the traditional dumping ground for many users' files. Aside from being aesthetically unpleasing, there is no reason to stop users from keeping their items here and having a messy desktop.

▶ Documents—This is the default storage location for any document type that does not have a dedicated folder. Most famously, Microsoft Office prefers this folder as the default location for all its user documents. Certainly putting items here is the best alternative to cluttering up the desktop.

▶ Downloads—This folder made its premiere in Mac OS X v10.5 as part of another solution to prevent desktop clutter. This folder is the default location for all Internet applications to store downloaded files. Sequestering all Internet downloads to this folder also makes it much easier for virus and malware protection utilities to identify potentially harmful files.

▶ Library—Whether a user knows it or not, this is one of the most important folders on a Mac. Nearly all non-document-type resources end up in the user's Library folder. This includes, but certainly isn't limited to, user-specific preference files, fonts, contacts, keychains, mailboxes, favorites, screen savers, widgets, and countless other application resources.

▶ Movies—This is (obviously) the default location for movie files, and therefore is often preferred by applications such as iMovie, iDVD, and iTunes.

▶ Music—This is (obviously) the default location for music files, and therefore is often preferred by applications such as GarageBand, Logic, and iTunes. It is also the default location for iPhone and iPod Touch applications, which are managed by iTunes.

▶ Pictures—This is (obviously) the default location for picture files, and therefore is often preferred by applications such as iPhoto, Aperture, and, once again, iTunes.

▶ Public—This is the default location for users to share files with others. Everyone who has access to a computer locally or via network file sharing can view the contents of this folder. There is a Drop Box folder inside this folder where others can place files that only the owner of the home folder can see.

▶ Sites—This is the default location for personal websites when Web Sharing is enabled. Outside of viewing these files through a web browser, only other local users can actually browse inside this folder.

Deleting a User Account

Deleting a user account on Mac OS X is even easier than creating one. To delete a user account, simply select it from the list of users in the Accounts preferences, and then click the minus button at the bottom of the list. An administrator need only make one choice when deleting a user account: what to do with the user's home folder contents.

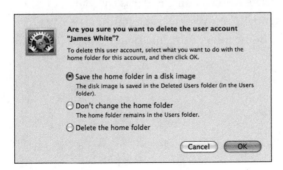

The administrator deleting the user account can choose one of three options:

▶ Save the home folder in a disk image—This option will create an archive of the user's home folder as a disk image file. The disk image file will be saved in the /Users/Deleted Users folder with the account name as the name of the disk image file. Retaining the home folder as a disk image makes it easy to transport to other systems or import archived items to another user's home folder.

Keep in mind you must have enough free disk space available on the local system volume, essentially enough to duplicate the original home folder, in order to create the archive disk image. This process can also take quite a bit of time depending on the size of the user's home folder.

▶ Do not change the home folder—This will leave the user's folder unchanged save for its name. It will simply append "(Deleted)" to the home folder's name, letting you know the user account no longer exists. The deleted user's home folder will maintain the same access restrictions as a normal user home folder. Subsequently, even though this is a much quicker and more space-efficient method when compared to the archival option, you will have to manually adjust file ownership and permissions to access the items.

▶ Delete the home folder—This will delete the home folder contents immediately. The items will not be stored in a "Trash" folder before they are deleted, so they will not be easily recoverable using this method.

NOTE ▶ The default method used to delete a user's home folder is equivalent to a quick erase. Thus, the contents are potentially recoverable using third-party data forensics tools. You can securely erase a home folder using methods outlined in Chapter 4, "File Systems."

Understanding Migration Assistant

The best method to move or restore a user's account and home folder is with Apple's Migration Assistant. This handy application will do all the hard work for you when it comes to properly moving a user account and home folder from one Mac to another. As covered in the previous chapter, "Installation and Initial Setup," the Migration Assistant runs as part of the Mac OS X Setup Assistant on new or newly installed Mac systems. However, you can also run this application at any point by opening /Applications/ Utilities/Migration Assistant. Once open, the Migration Assistant will walk you through a few easy steps to migrate the data.

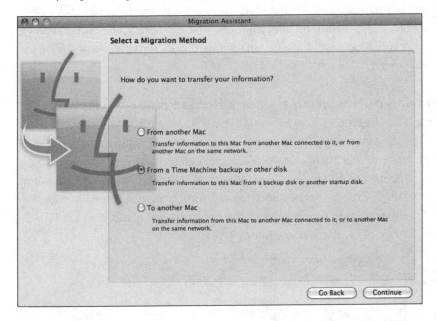

In a nutshell, Migration Assistant automates all the steps necessary to migrate individual user accounts, non-system applications, and other non-system resources from one Mac to another. The migration can occur between two Macs on the same network or directly connected via FireWire. Migration Assistant can also restore user accounts from Time Machine backups, either directly connected or via the network. Lastly, Migration Assistant can copy information from any other volume containing a Mac OS X system. This is useful for when problematic hardware prevents a Mac from starting up, but the system drive itself remains functional. In this case you could physically remove the system drive and connect it to another Mac for migration.

NOTE ▶ Migration Assistant can only migrate FileVault-protected user accounts to a Mac during the initial Setup Assistant process. The Setup Assistant process is covered in the previous chapter, "Installation and Initial Setup." FileVault is covered later in this chapter.

As convenient as Migration Assistant is, there are times when it's not the best solution to move a user account. For example, in certain situations you may need to erase and install a new system to repair or update a Mac. Unfortunately, you can't always count on the user having a recent Time Machine backup of the system. Thus, erasing the system volume would also destroy any user accounts on the Mac. In this case, because you're only working with a single Mac, as opposed to moving from one Mac to another, and you don't have a Time Machine backup, Migration Assistant isn't going to work for you. You will have to manually move the user's home folder.

Manually Moving or Restoring a User's Home Folder

If you find yourself in a situation where Migration Assistant won't fit your needs, then you can manually move the user's home folder data. While this doesn't require another Mac, it does require that you temporarily copy the user's home folder to another "backup" storage volume. Once you have additional backup storage available, log into the user's account and, in the Finder, simply drag his home folder to the backup volume. As long as you copy the root of the user's home, the folder with the user's account name, then the Finder should copy the entirety of the user's home in one move.

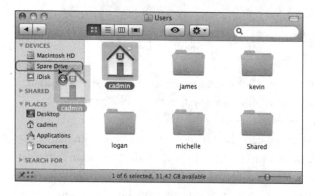

Once you are sure you have a complete copy of the user's home folder on the backup storage, you can erase the system volume and repair it. With the new system working in place, you can follow these steps to manually restore the user's home folder data.

NOTE ► The proper method to restore a user's home folder requires that the user account doesn't yet exist on the system. This is because the system can automatically associate a manually restored home folder with a newly created account.

To manually restore a user's home folder:

1 Log in with an administrative user account that is not associated with the user home folder you're trying to restore.

You can create a temporary administrative user account to perform these steps if you plan to promote the user you're restoring to an administrator as well.

2 In the Finder, copy the user's home folder from its backup location to the Mac system volume. Depending on how the home folder data was originally saved to the backup volume, you will have to complete one of the three following procedures:

► **If the user's home folder is stored normally on another non-system volume:** Simply drag and drop the user's home folder from the backup volume to the root of the /Users folder. Click the Authenticate button and enter your administrator account credentials to complete the copy.

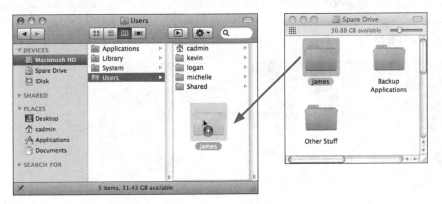

▶ **If the user's home folder is archived as a disk image:** Double-click on the user's disk image file to mount its volume on the desktop. While holding the Option key on the keyboard, drag and drop the mounted disk image volume from the desktop to the root of the /Users folder. Holding the Option key will force the Finder to make a copy of the entire disk image volume. Authenticate as the administrator to complete the copy.

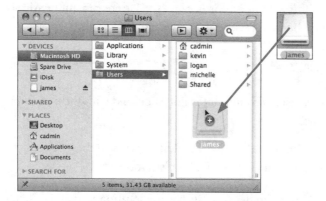

▶ **If the user's home folder was from a previous account on the Mac but the data was never moved off the system volume or archived:** In this case the system left the user's previous home in the /Users folder, but appended the word "(Deleted)" to the name of the home folder. You need to remove the word "(Deleted)," but the Finder won't allow that if the folder is in /Users. The solution is to create a new empty folder on your desktop with the user's account name, then drag that folder to the root of the /Users folder. Next, select all the items (Command-A) in the user's previous (Deleted) home folder and copy all the items to the new properly named home folder. You will have to authenticate as an administrative user twice to accomplish this task.

TIP ► If you are familiar with the command line, there is a much quicker method to change a user's home folder name that doesn't require copying the user's data. From the command line, an administrator can use the mv command to rename any folder. The mv command is covered in Chapter 3, "Command Line and Automation."

3   From the Accounts system preferences, create a new user account using the same account name as the restored user. This is necessary to associate the new account with the restored home folder.

Creating a new user is covered previously in the "Creating New User Accounts" section of this chapter.

4   Assuming you used the same account name as the name of the home folder, the system will recognize this and prompt you to associate the two.

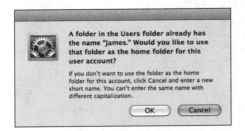

When this dialog appears, click the OK button and the system will automatically resolve any file and folder ownership issues to ensure the new user account can access the restored home folder contents.

5   Log in to the newly restored user account and all the user's settings should take effect.

It would be wise to double-check important settings and application preferences before you erase the backup home folder.

Login Options and Fast User Switching

The login window may look simple, but because it's the front door to your system, there are a variety of security options an administrator should be familiar with. Primarily, these options either provide higher security or greater accessibility. You can adjust the behavior of the login window from the Accounts preferences by authenticating as an administrative user and then clicking the Login Options button at the bottom of the user accounts list.

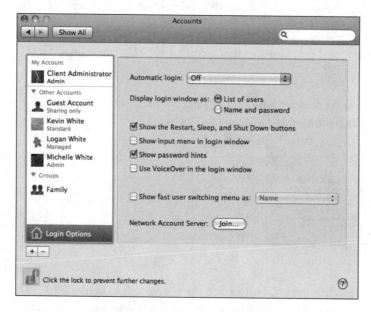

Login window options include:

▶ Enable or disable automatic login as the Mac starts up. Obviously, you can only define one account for automatic login. The Automatic login option is turned on by default if the only account on the Mac is the initial administrative user.

▶ Choose whether the login window shows a list of available users or blank name and password fields. Not only is choosing to have name and password fields more secure, but it's also more appropriate for environments with network user accounts.

▶ Determine the availability of Restart, Sleep, and Shut Down buttons at the login window. Macs in environments that require security will not have these buttons available at the login window.

▶ Specify whether users can use the input menu. This allows users easy access to non-roman characters at the login window.

▶ Determine whether the login window will show password hints after three bad password attempts. This may seem to be an insecure selection, but remember password hints are optional per user account.

▶ Enable users to take advantage of VoiceOver audible assistant technology at the login window.

▶ Enable fast user switching.

▶ Configure the Mac to use accounts hosted from a shared network directory. Network accounts are covered in Chapter 8, "Network Services."

Using Fast User Switching

It's easy to imagine a situation when two users want to use a Mac at the same time. While it's not possible for two users to use the Mac's graphical interface at the same time, it is possible for multiple users to remain logged in to the Mac at the same time. Fast user switching enables you to quickly move between user accounts without logging out or quitting open applications. This allows users to keep their work open in the background while other users are logged in to the computer. A user can later return to his account instantly, right where he left off.

NOTE ▶ Fast user switching is not supported for network accounts.

To enable fast user switching:

1   Open the Accounts preferences and authenticate as an administrative user to unlock its settings.

2   Click the Login Options button below the user list.

3   Select the "Show fast user switching menu as:" checkbox.

4 Optionally you can choose a fast user switching menu style from the adjacent pop-up menu. Your options are name, short name (account name), or a user silhouette icon.

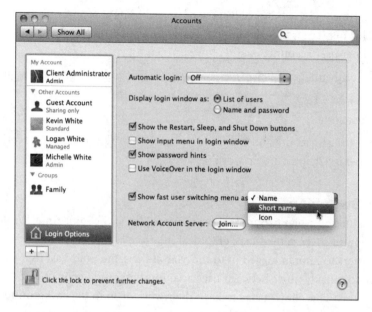

5 The fast user switching menu item will appear on the far right next to the Spotlight search menu. From this menu you can switch to another user simply by choosing her name.

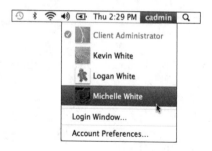

6   If the selected user account has a password, you will be presented with a Login Window dialog. You must authenticate as the selected user in order to switch to that account.

7   Once you're authenticated, the computer will switch to the other account, typically with a cube-spinning transition.

8   Click the fast user switching menu again, and you can verify that other user accounts are still active, as indicated by an orange checkbox next to their names. You can log in or return to any account, at any time, using this menu.

TIP You can move the fast user switching menu item, or any other menu item on the right side of the menu bar, by dragging the menu item while holding down the Command key.

Fast User Switching Issues

Apple has worked hard to make fast user switching a reliable feature. Many of the built-in Mac OS X applications are fast-user-switching savvy. For instance, when you switch between accounts, iTunes will automatically mute or unmute your music, iChat will toggle between available and away chat status, and Mail will continue to check for new messages in the background. However, in some circumstances you will experience resource contention when more than one user attempts to access an item.

Examples of fast user switching resource contention are:

▶   Application contention—Some applications are designed in such a way that only one user can use the application at a time. If other users attempt to open these applications, they are either met with an error dialog or the application simply doesn't open at all. Most of the applications that fall into this category are professional applications, which tend to be resource hogs, so it's advantageous to keep only one copy running at a time.

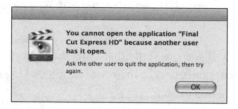

▶ Document contention—These are cases where one user has a document open and remains logged in with fast user switching, often preventing other users from fully accessing the document. As an example, Microsoft Office will allow other users to open the document as read-only and will display an error dialog if the user tries to save changes. In a more extreme example, some applications will not allow other users to open the document at all. Occasionally, in the worst-case scenario, an application will allow two people to edit the file simultaneously, but it will only save changes made by the user who saved last. In this case, the application's developers simply didn't account for the possibility that two users might edit the same document at the same time, so you often won't even see an error message.

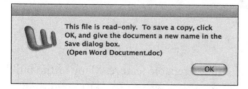

▶ Peripheral contention—Many peripherals can be accessed by only one user at a time. This becomes a fast user switching issue if a user leaves an application running that has attached itself to a peripheral. The peripheral will not become available to other applications until the original application is quit. Examples of this include video cameras, scanners, and audio equipment.

Fast user switching also has interesting ramifications for non-system volumes. For example, if one user attaches an external storage device, the volume is available to all other users on the system, even if they weren't logged in when the storage was attached. Mounted disk image volumes are handled a bit more securely. Only the user who mounted the disk image will have full read/write access to it. However, other users may still have read access to the mounted disk image volume.

Network shares are the only volumes that remain secure in a fast user switching environment. By default, only the user who originally connected to the share can access the share. Even if multiple users attempt to access the same network share, the system will automatically generate multiple mounts with different access for each user. The exception to this rule is network home folders used by network accounts. While one network user can successfully log in, additional network users from the same server will not be able to access their network home folder. For this reason, fast user switching does not support network accounts.

Resolving Fast User Switching Issues

Unfortunately, because each resource and application can act differently, fast user switching issues are not always consistently reported or readily apparent. There is no "fast user switching is causing a problem" dialog in Mac OS X. Still, if you are experiencing access errors to files, applications, or peripherals, your first step should be to check if any other users are still logged in. If so, you should have those other users log out and then reattempt access to the previously inaccessible items.

If you cannot log the other users out—perhaps because they are currently unavailable and you don't know their passwords—then your options are to force the other users' suspect applications to quit or to force the other users to log out by restarting the Mac. Changing a logged-in user's password isn't an option at this point because administrators cannot manage user accounts that are currently still logged in to the Mac. These accounts will be dimmed and not available in the Accounts preferences.

Thus, an administrator will have to force the other users' applications to quit or restart the Mac to free up any contested items or make any changes to the logged-in users. Neither option is ideal because forcing an application to quit with open files often results in data loss. Forcing an open application to quit is covered in Chapter 6, "Applications and Boot Camp."

> **TIP** ▸ If you have already set the master password, then you can reset a currently logged-in user's password from the login window using the master password. Setting the master password and resetting a user's password is covered later in the "Resetting Account Passwords" section of this chapter.

Attempting to restart, though, will reveal another fast user switching issue: If any other users are still logged in, an administrator will have to force those users' open applications to quit in order to restart. The system makes it easy for an administrator to force the other users' applications to quit via an authenticated restart dialog, but once again this will very likely cause data loss to any open files.

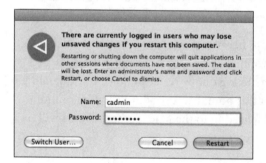

Fundamental Account Security

The primary purpose of a multiple-user operating system is to provide all users with a secure work environment. Mac OS X provides a relatively secure out-of-the box experience for most situations. Yet there are some situations that call for greater security than the defaults afford. Thus, the remainder of this chapter will focus on the built-in advanced security features of Mac OS X, and how best to manage and troubleshoot these features.

Understanding Account Vulnerabilities

As was discussed previously in this chapter, Mac OS X uses a variety of user account types: standard users, administrative users, the guest user, sharing users, and the root user. Apple has made available these different account types to allow greater flexibility for managing user access. Because each account type is designed to allow different levels of access, you should be aware of each account type's potential security risk.

Standard Users

This account type is very secure, assuming an appropriate password is set. This user is allowed to use nearly all the resources and features of the Mac, but he can't change anything that might affect the system software. You can further restrict this account by using managed parental control settings, as discussed previously in this chapter.

Administrative Users

Because this is the initial account created when the Mac is set up for the very first time using the Setup Assistant, many use this as their primary account type. This is necessary and advantageous because it allows the user to literally change anything on the computer as is required for system management. The downside is that the user will be allowed to make changes or install software that can render the system insecure or unstable.

Additional administrative accounts can be used for daily use, but this isn't always the best idea, as all administrative accounts are created equal. In other words, all administrative accounts have the ability to make changes to anything on the system, including deleting or changing the password to other administrative accounts. Administrative users can also change the administrative rights for any other user account, either disabling current administrators or changing standard users into administrators. Further, opening poorly written or intentionally malicious software as an administrative user could seriously harm the system software. Most significantly, though, any administrative user can enable the root account or change the root account password using the Directory Utility application located in the /System/Library/CoreServices folder. For these reasons, you should seriously consider limiting the number of administrative user accounts on your Mac systems.

Guest User

Guest users are allowed, by default, to access your Mac via network file sharing without a password. Additionally, you can allow guests to log in to your Mac's graphical user interface without a password. Even though the guest home folder is deleted every time the guest logs out, the obvious security risk here is that literally anyone has access equivalent to that of a standard user account, including access to the Public, Drop Box, Sites, and Shared folders. This means they could execute some potentially nasty applications or fill your hard drive with unwanted files. The guest user can also restart or shut down your Mac, potentially allowing her to compromise the system during startup.

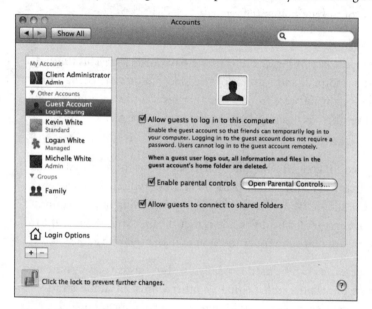

Fortunately, you can restrict the guest account using parental controls to prevent her from running unapproved applications or restarting the Mac. Additionally, you can change the access permissions on the Shared and Drop Box folders so the guest account is not allowed to copy any items to your hard drive. Changing file and folder permissions is covered in Chapter 4, "File Systems."

Sharing Only Users

Sharing users are by default allowed file sharing access to the Public and Drop Box folders, so, like the guest user, they can potentially fill your hard drive with unwanted files. On the other hand, shared users cannot log in to the Mac otherwise and they can be required to use a password, so designating sharing users is generally much safer than using the guest account for file sharing. You can further control sharing users' access to your files by adjusting file and folder permissions. Changing permissions is a two-way street, though, and you could accidentally give a sharing user too much access. Configuring file-sharing services is covered in Chapter 8, "Network Services."

Root User

The root user account, also known as the System Administrator, is disabled by default on Mac OS X clients, and for good reason: The root account has unlimited access to everything on the Mac, and root users can do anything they want with the system. The potential for nefarious activity is literally unlimited with root account access. Remember, though, it only takes an administrative account to initially access the root account, so limiting administrative usage is the key to safeguarding the root account.

Understanding Password Types

Mac OS X relies on passwords as its primary method of verifying a user's authenticity. There are other more elaborate systems for proving a user's identity, such as biometric sensors and two-factor random key authentication, but these require special hardware. It's a pretty safe bet that every Mac is attached to an alphanumeric input device such as a keyboard, so passwords are still the most relevant security authentication method.

If you look closer at the security systems used by Mac OS X, you will discover that there are a variety of passwords at different levels used to secure the computer. Most users are only familiar with their account password, but the Mac can also have a firmware password, a master password, many resource passwords, and several keychain passwords.

Each password type serves a specific purpose:

▶ Account password—Each user account has a variety of attributes that define the account. The account password is the attribute used to authenticate the user so he can log in. For security reasons, a user's account password is stored in a separate file from the other account attributes. User account passwords are stored as encrypted files in a folder that only the root user can access. These password files are located at /var/db/shadow/hash/<UUID>, where <UUID> is the name of the password file that matches the Unique User ID attribute for the particular user account.

▶ Firmware password—The firmware password is used to protect the Mac during startup. By default, anyone can subvert Mac OS X system security settings by simply using one of the commonly known startup-interrupt keyboard combinations. For example, by default anyone can hold down the Option key during startup to select an alternate operating system, thus bypassing your secure system.

Setting the firmware password will prevent unauthorized users from using any startup-interrupt keyboard combinations. The password is saved to the Mac's firmware chip, so this password remains separate from the installed software. You set the firmware password using a utility available when the Mac is booted from the Mac OS X Install DVD. If you require the highest level of security for your Mac, then you must set the firmware password, as any user with access to this DVD can set the password if it hasn't already been set. Once the firmware password is set, only an administrative user or a user who has physical access to the internal hardware can reset the password.

MORE INFO ▶ For more information about the firmware password, reference Knowledge Base article TA22404, "Setting up firmware password protection in Mac OS X 10.1 or later."

▶ Master password—The master password is used to reset standard, administrative, and FileVault user accounts if the user has forgotten his account password. Configuring and troubleshooting FileVault and the master password is covered in greater detail in the "Using FileVault Accounts" section later in this chapter.

▶ Resource password—This is a generic term used to describe a password used by nearly any service that requires you to authenticate. Resource passwords include email, website, file server, application, and encrypted disk image passwords. Many resource passwords are automatically saved for the user by the keychain system.

▶ Keychain password—Mac OS X protects the user's important authentication assets, outside of the account password, in encrypted keychain files. Each keychain file is encrypted with a keychain password. The system will attempt to keep keychain passwords synchronized with the user's account password. However, you can maintain unique keychain passwords separate from an account password as well. Configuring and troubleshooting the keychain security system is covered in greater detail in the "Managing Keychains" section later in this chapter.

Using Security Preferences

In addition to specific user security settings, such as account passwords and keychain items, there are systemwide security preferences that affect all users on the Mac. Many of these security options are disabled by default because the average Mac user would probably consider them inconveniences. However, if your environment requires greater security, these additional security features are indispensable. Open the Security preferences and authenticate as an administrative user to unlock the system security settings.

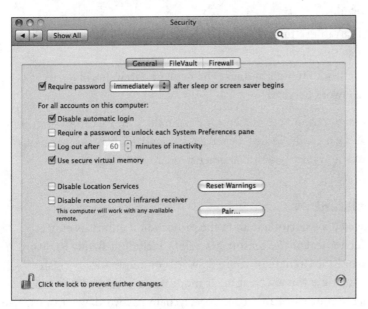

From the Security preferences you can:

▶   Choose to require a password to wake the computer from sleep or screen saver mode. Both standard and administrative users can set this for their account, but an administrator cannot set this for every account from the Security preferences.

▶ Disable automatic login for all accounts.

▶ Require administrative authentication for all lockable system preferences every single time. This way, if a logged-in administrative user leaves her Mac temporarily unattended, anonymous users cannot make any changes to system preferences.

▶ Automatically log out accounts after a certain amount of inactivity.

▶ Enable the use of secure virtual memory. All virtual memory written to disk will be encrypted by the system. This is an important feature for maximum security as passwords and other sensitive data are often temporarily stored in memory.

▶ Disable location services to prevent applications and services from being able to locate the Mac. Any Mac with an AirPort wireless network card can use location services.

▶ Disable the built-in infrared Apple remote sensor on equipped Mac models. By default, unless the Mac has been paired to a specific Apple remote, any Apple remote will be able to affect the Mac.

▶ Enable and configure FileVault settings. FileVault is covered in the "Using FileVault Accounts" section later in this chapter.

▶ Enable and configure network Firewall settings. The network Firewall will be discussed in Chapter 8, "Network Services."

NOTE ▶ Any administrative account can authenticate and unlock the Mac from sleep or screen saver modes if the user who locked the screen is a standard user. This means an administrative user could be granted access to another standard user's logged-in account.

Using Password Assistant

Regardless of how sophisticated a security system is, the protection it affords is only as strong as the password you choose. For this reason, Mac OS X includes a handy Password Assistant utility that will gauge the strength of your passwords or automatically create strong passwords for you. Any time you are creating or modifying a password that will grant access to a substantial resource, like an account or keychain password, you can use the Password Assistant.

TIP You can use the Password Assistant any time you see the small key icon next to a password field.

To use the Password Assistant:

1 Open the Accounts preferences and select your user account; then click the Change Password button.

2 Enter your current account password in the Old Password field.

You can reenter the same password in the New Password field if you just want to test its strength, or you can go ahead and create a new password.

3 Click the key icon next to the New Password field to open the Password Assistant.

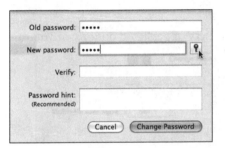

The Quality bar in the Password Assistant dialog will instantly show the strength of your password. If your password is of low strength, the bar will be in shades of red to yellow, and you will be offered some tips as to why your password is a poor choice.

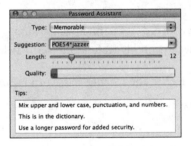

4 Try to find a stronger password by reentering it in the New Password field.

The Password Assistant will automatically gauge your password choices as you enter them. You know you have a strong password when the Quality bar starts turning green.

If you're having a hard time coming up with a good password, the Password Assistant will help you by automatically generating strong passwords. Choose a password type from the Type pop-up menu, and use the Length slider to adjust password length.

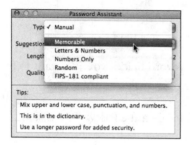

The Suggestion pop-up menu will show a variety of password options, or you can re-roll by choosing More Suggestions.

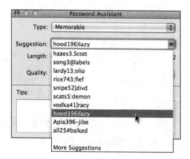

5   Once you have found a strong password with the Password Assistant, it will be auto-entered in the New Password field, but you will have to enter it again in the Verify field.

6   If you are indeed changing your account password, click the Change Password button to finish; otherwise click the Cancel button.

NOTE ▶ If your account password and keychain password are the same, when you change your password using the Accounts preferences it will automatically change both passwords.

Managing Keychains

Mac OS X features a sophisticated system that automatically protects all your authentication assets in encrypted keychain files. Much like service workers might keep a keychain of all the keys needed during their workday, the Mac will keep all your resource passwords, certificates, keys, website forms, and even secure notes in a single secure location. Every time you allow the Mac to remember a password or any other potentially sensitive item, it will save it to a keychain file. Only your account password remains separate from all the other items saved to your keychains.

Because so many important items end up in keychain files, the keychain files themselves are encrypted with a very strong algorithm: They are impenetrable unless you know the keychain's password. In fact, if you forget a keychain's password, its contents are lost forever. Not even the software engineers at Apple can help you—the keychain system is *that* secure. Yet, probably the single best feature of the keychain system is that it's entirely automatic using the default settings. Most users will never know just how secure their saved passwords are because the system is so transparent.

Understanding Keychain Files

There are keychain files stored throughout the system for different users and resources:

▶ /Users/<username>/Library/Keychain/login.keychain—Every standard or administrative user is created with a single login keychain. As a default, the password for this keychain matches the user's account password, so this keychain is automatically unlocked and available when the user logs in. If the user's account password does not match the keychain's password, it will not automatically unlock during login.

Users can create additional keychains if they wish to segregate their authentication assets. For example, you can keep your default login keychain for trivial items, and then create a more secure keychain that does not automatically unlock for more important items.

▶ /Library/Keychain/FileVaultMaster.keychain—This keychain is encrypted with the FileVault master password. Configuring and troubleshooting FileVault and the master password is covered later in greater detail in the "Using FileVault Accounts" section.

▶ /Library/Keychain/System.keychain—This keychain maintains authentication assets that are non-user-specific. Examples of items stored here include AirPort wireless network passwords, 802.1X network passwords, and local Kerberos support items. Although all users benefit from this keychain, only administrative users can make changes to it.

▶ /System/Library/Keychains/—You will find several keychain files in this folder that store root certificates used to help identify trusted network services. Once again, all users benefit from these keychains, but only administrative users can make changes to these keychains.

NOTE ▶ Some websites will remember your password inside a web cookie, so you might not see an entry in a keychain file for every website password you save.

Using Keychain Access

The primary tool you will use to manage keychains is the Keychain Access application found in the /Applications/Utilities folder. With this application you can view and modify any keychain item including saved resource passwords, certificates, keys, website forms, and secure notes. You can also create and delete keychain files, change keychain settings and passwords, and repair corrupted keychains.

Manage Items in a Keychain

To manage keychain items, including saved passwords:

1   As any user, open /Applications/Utilities/Keychain Access.

    The default selection will show the contents of the user's login keychain, but you could select another keychain from the list to view its items.

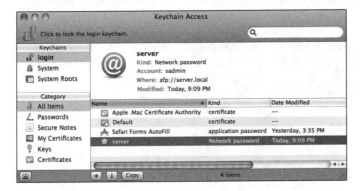

2   Double-click a keychain item to view its attributes.

3   If the item is a password, you can reveal the saved password by selecting the "Show password" checkbox.

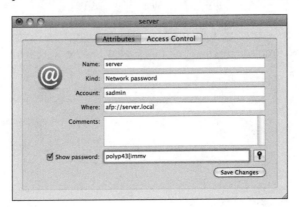

4   When prompted, enter the keychain password once more, and then click the Allow button. It is not advisable to click the Always Allow button.

Once you have authenticated, you can change any attribute in the keychain item dialog.

5   When you have finished making changes, click the Save Changes button.

6   Finally, you can also click the Access Control tab in the keychain item's attributes dialog to adjust application access for the selected item.

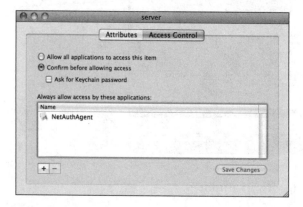

TIP To easily search through all the keychain items, use the Categories views to the left or the Spotlight search in the top-right corner of the toolbar.

TIP The safest place to store secure text on your Mac is in keychains. In Keychain Access, you can create a new secure note by choosing File > New Secure Note Item from the menu bar.

Manage Keychain Files

To manage keychain files, including resetting a keychain's password:

1 As any user, open /Applications/Utilities/Keychain Access.

2 To create a new keychain, choose File > New Keychain from the menu bar. Next, enter a name and location for the new keychain. The default location is the Keychains folder inside your home folder. Finish by entering a nontrivial password that is six characters or longer for the new keychain and click the OK button.

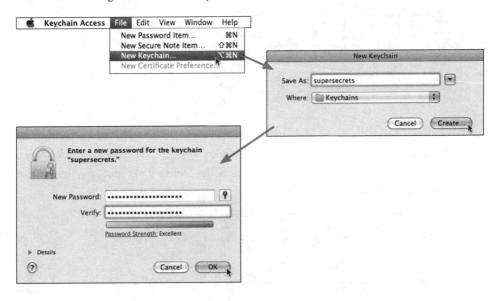

3 To change a keychain's settings, first select it from the list, and then choose Edit > Change Settings for Keychain from the menu bar. You will be able to change automatic keychain locking settings and enable .Mac synchronization. Finish by clicking the Save button.

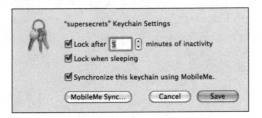

4   To change a keychain's password, first select it from the list, and then choose Edit >
Change Password for Keychain from the menu bar. You will have to enter the keychain's current password first. Finish by entering a nontrivial password that is six
characters or longer and click the OK button.

5   To delete a keychain, select it from the list and choose File > Delete Keychain from
the menu bar. When the Delete Keychain dialog appears, click the Delete References
button to simply ignore the keychain or click the Delete References & Files button to
completely erase the keychain file.

TIP ▶ You can move keychain items between keychains by dragging and dropping
an item from one keychain to another.

TIP ▶ For quick access to your keychains and other security features, you can enable
the security menu item by choosing Keychain Access > Preferences from the menu
bar. Then select the Show Status in Menu Bar checkbox to reveal the security menu
item, as indicated by a small key icon on the right side of the menu bar.

Repair Keychain Files

To verify or repair a keychain file:

1   As any user, open /Applications/Utilities/Keychain Access.

2   If the troublesome keychain is not already in your keychain list, choose File > Add Keychain from the menu bar and you will be able to browse for it.

3   You need to unlock all the keychains you wish to check. Simply select the keychain from the list, then choose File > Unlock Keychain from the menu bar and enter the keychain's password.

4   Choose Keychain Access > Keychain First Aid from the menu bar.

5   You will have to enter your password once more, and then choose the Verify or Repair radio button and finally click the Start button.

    A log will show the keychain verification or repair process.

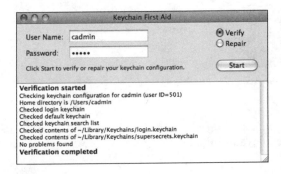

TIP ▶ Additional Keychain First Aid preferences can be found by selecting Keychain Access > Preferences from the menu bar.

Using FileVault Accounts

For the ultimate in account security, Mac OS X includes the FileVault service, which will maintain a user's home folder inside an encrypted disk image. It takes only a few moments for an administrator to initially prepare the Mac for FileVault service by setting a master password. As you'll see later, the master password is used to reset local standard, administrative, and FileVault user accounts should a user forget his account password.

Once the master password has been set, it is easy for users to enable FileVault protection for their home folder. Though initially it may take a while to copy all the user's items into an encrypted disk image, once that is done FileVault protection will remain nearly transparent to the user. When a FileVault user logs in, the system will automatically unlock the encrypted disk image that contains her home folder items and make it available only to that user account. The moment a FileVault user logs out, the system will lock the encrypted disk image so no one else has access to it.

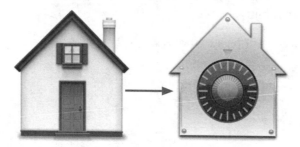

Set Up FileVault

To set the master password and enable FileVault for a user:

1   Log out any other active user accounts, and then log in as the user for whom you're going to enable FileVault protection.

2   Open the Security preferences and authenticate as an administrative user to unlock its settings; then click the FileVault tab.

3   If the master password has not been set, click the Set Master Password button. Otherwise, skip to step 6.

When setting the master password, it's strongly recommend that you choose a high-quality password. Remember, this single master password can be used to reset any other user account password.

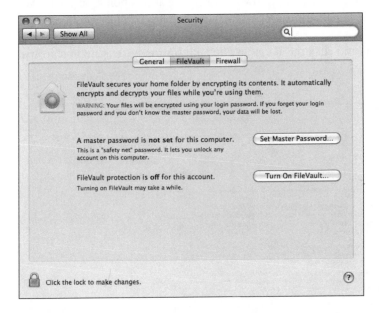

4 Open the Password Assistant by clicking the small key icon to the right of the Password field to gauge the quality of your master password choice.

5 Click the OK button to save the master password.

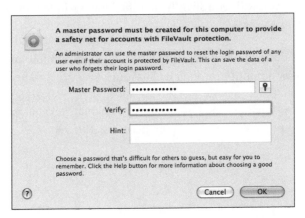

6   Click the Turn On FileVault button, and then enter the user's account password once more.

There is one additional security option you can enable at this point; optionally you can choose to securely erase the previous unencrypted home folder contents.

7   Select your options and click the Turn On FileVault button once again to start the encryption process.

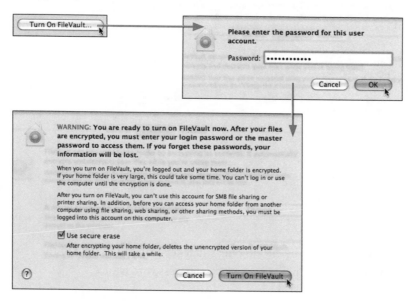

The user will be logged out, and you will see a slightly modified login window showing the home folder encryption process.

8   Once the encryption process is done, you will return to a normal login window and you can now log in with this user account protected by FileVault.

TIP   Once the master password has been set, you can easily enable FileVault as you create new users from the account creation dialog in the Accounts preferences.

FileVault Caveats

Enabling advanced security measures nearly always leads to restricted user access. This applies to FileVault as well. There are several caveats you should be aware of when a user account has FileVault enabled:

▶ Only the FileVault user has access to the contents of his home folder. Thus, the normally shared Public and Sites folders will be inaccessible to all other users.

▶ Several sharing services, such as Windows file sharing, Windows printer sharing, and web sharing, cannot access the FileVault user's home folder.

▶ Even as an administrative user, you must also use the master password to reset a FileVault user account.

▶ The Migration Assistant utility, when started after initial system setup, cannot migrate FileVault users.

▶ Time Machine can only backup FileVault accounts when the user is logged out of his account.

▶ The FileVault encryption process may slow disk access to the point that some high-performance applications cannot function properly. This delay can also be seen at logout, though it won't prevent logout from functioning properly.

Furthermore, you should be aware that FileVault-protected home folders are more likely to become corrupted than other types of accounts. The home folder is stored in an encrypted bundle, which is like a disk image, but the encrypted data is stored inside the bundle as a collection of separate files. If one of those files gets damaged, it's possible that you could lose the portion of your home folder located in that section.

If all these FileVault caveats have you worried, remember you can always disable FileVault from the Security preferences, and protect only your most precious files on a smaller scale. It's relatively easy to manually save your sensitive items into user-created encrypted disk images. Archiving individual files to encrypted disk images is covered in Chapter 5, "Data Management and Backup."

FileVault protection is **on** for this account.   [Turn Off FileVault...]
Turning off FileVault may take a while.

Resetting Account Passwords

A user mistyping or forgetting her password is the primary cause of most login and access issues on any platform. The second most common issue, specific to Mac OS X, is when a user's keychain passwords become out of sync with that user's account password. Fortunately, with a few rare exceptions, Mac OS X provides ways to easily resolve these types of password issues.

> **TIP** ▶ If a user already knows her own password, but she wants to change it, she can do so at any time from the Accounts preferences. She simply selects her account, and then clicks the Change Password button to access a dialog allowing her to change her password. Further, if her account password matches her keychain password this technique will also synchronize the two passwords.

Resetting Regular Account Passwords

By far the most common password issue is when a user simply forgets his account password. Mac OS X provides two methods for easily resetting non-FileVault user account passwords. The first, and most common, method requires administrative authorization. The second method requires configuration and knowledge of the master password and is identical to resetting a FileVault password from the login window.

To reset a non-FileVault account password using administrator authorization:

> **NOTE** ▶ Resetting an account password with this method will not reset the user's keychain passwords. However, by default on Mac OS X v10.6, the next time the user logs in, he will be prompted to fix his login keychain. This process is covered in the "Resetting Keychain Passwords" section later in this chapter.

1 If the inaccessible user account is still logged into the computer because of fast user switching, you will need to restart the computer to forcibly log out the user. Alternatively, you can reset the account password from the login window using the master password, as outlined in the "Resetting FileVault Account Passwords" section.

2 Open the Accounts preferences and authenticate as an administrative user to unlock its settings.

3   Select the inaccessible user account from the list, and then click the Reset Password button. When resetting an account password, it's strongly recommended that you choose a high-quality password.

4   Enter the new account password and verification in the appropriate fields.

5   Click the Reset Password button to save the new account password.

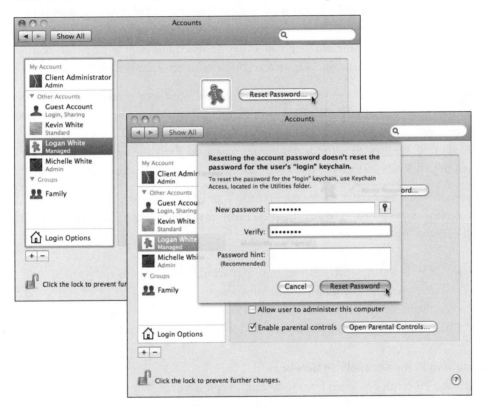

Resetting FileVault Account Passwords

FileVault accounts are unique because the user's home folder is saved inside an encrypted disk image protected by that user's account password. Consequently, it is extremely important for an administrator to have the ability to reset a FileVault user's account password if the user ever wants to access her home folder files again.

A normal administrative user account is not enough to reset a lost FileVault password. Frankly, FileVault wouldn't be very secure if just any old administrative user could come along and break in. Therefore, if a FileVault user has forgotten her account password, the master password is required to reset the account. This is why the Mac forces you to create a master password before you enable any FileVault users.

If you have also lost the master password along with the user's FileVault password, then you are completely out of luck. You must have at least one of these two passwords to recover a FileVault account. Otherwise, you are never, ever going to be able to recover the user's data. Not even Apple can help you—they designed FileVault to be as secure as possible and thus created only one way to reset a FileVault account: the master password.

Obviously, if the master password is lost, an administrative user should reset it immediately for the benefit of other FileVault users. Don't get your hopes up, though; just because you can set a new master password for your Mac doesn't mean you can recover a FileVault account that was created with the old master password. Only the master password created when the FileVault user was enabled can unlock an inaccessible account.

If you do know the master password, Mac OS X provides two methods for easily resetting FileVault user passwords. The first method involves the Accounts preferences, and the second uses the login window.

> **NOTE ▶** Resetting a FileVault account password with the following methods will not reset the user's keychain passwords. However, by default on Mac OS X v10.6, the next time the user logs in, she will be prompted to fix her login keychain. This process is covered in the "Resetting Keychain Passwords" section later in this chapter.

Resetting From Accounts Preferences

To reset a FileVault password from the Accounts preferences:

1   If the inaccessible FileVault user account is still logged into the computer because of fast user switching, you will need to restart the computer to forcibly log out the user. Or, you can reset the FileVault password from the login window, as covered in the next section.

2   Open the Accounts preferences and authenticate as an administrative user to unlock the settings.

3   Select the inaccessible FileVault account from the list; then click the Reset Password button.

4   Enter the master password in the appropriate field.

When resetting a FileVault password, it's strongly recommended that you choose a high-quality password. Open the Password Assistant by clicking the small key icon to the right of the Password field to gauge the quality of your FileVault password choice.

5   Enter the new FileVault password and verification in the appropriate fields.

6   Finish by clicking the Reset Password button to save the new FileVault password.

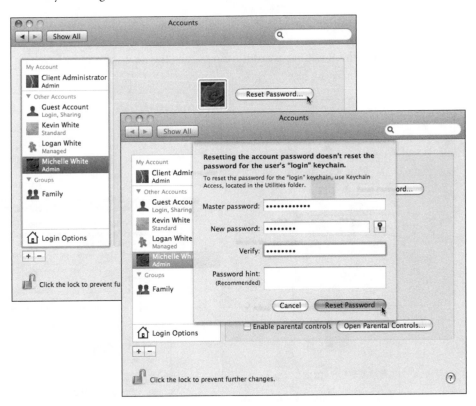

Resetting From Login Window

To reset a FileVault or account password from the login window:

1   Open the login window by logging out, and then select the inaccessible user account. You can also select the inaccessible account from the fast user switching menu if it's enabled.

2   Click the Reset Password button.

3   Enter the master password, and then click the Login button.

You will also have to dismiss a keychain password warning dialog by clicking the OK button.

When resetting an account password, it's strongly recommended that you choose a high-quality password.

4   Enter the new account password and verification in the appropriate fields.

5   Finish by clicking the Reset Password button to save the new account or keychain password and log in as the user.

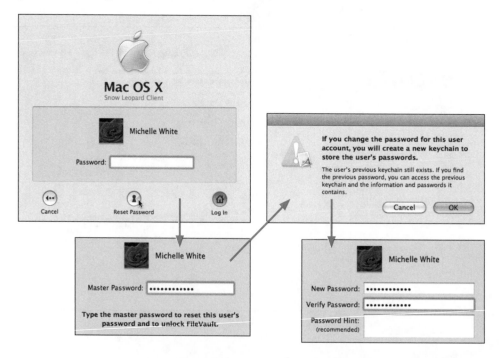

Resetting the Master Password

As mentioned earlier, the master password can be used to reset account passwords and is required to reset FileVault passwords. Thus, it is vital that the master password be properly configured and known by an administrator. There are two distinct situations in which a master password needs to be reset. The first is a situation where the current master password is known, and an administrative user simply wants to reset the password by choice. Changing the master password with this first method is quite easy and will not affect your ability to reset previously enabled FileVault account passwords.

The second situation is when the current master password is lost and a new master password needs to be created. In this case, if you want the new master password to have the ability to reset FileVault account passwords, you will have to reset all FileVault accounts created with the previous master password. Furthermore, because you are dealing with FileVault accounts that were created with a previous unknown master password, you will have to individually log into each account to reset its FileVault encryption. Thus, you must know all the current FileVault account passwords in order to restore the master password reset ability for all accounts. Remember, if both the master password and a user's FileVault password are lost, then that user's home folder contents are lost forever.

Reset a Known Master Password

To reset a known master password:

1   Open the Security preferences and authenticate as an administrative user to unlock its settings; then click the FileVault tab.

2   Click the Change button.

3   Enter the current master password in the appropriate field.

    When resetting the master password, it's strongly recommended that you choose a high-quality password.

4   Enter the new master password and verification in the appropriate fields.

5 Finish by clicking the OK button to save the new master password.

This new master password can be used to reset all accounts, including FileVault accounts.

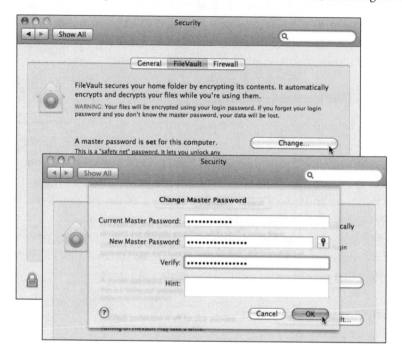

Reset a Lost Master Password

To create a new master password because the previous one was lost:

1 Log out all other users on the system, and then log in as an administrative user.

2 From the Finder, locate and delete the /Library/Keychains/FileVaultMaster.cer and /Library/Keychains/FilevaultMaster.keychain files.

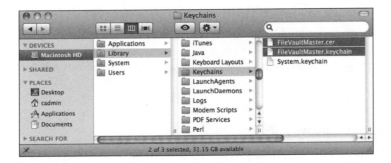

3   Open the Security preferences and authenticate as an administrative user to unlock its settings; then click the FileVault tab.

Note that the computer will think the master password has not been set.

4   Click the Set Master Password button to set a new master password. This will be identical to setting a new master password as outlined earlier in this chapter.

When setting the master password, it's strongly recommended that you choose a high-quality password. Remember, this single master password can be used to reset any other user account password.

5   Click the OK button to save the new master password.

6   Log in using a FileVault account that was created with the previous master password.

7   Open Security preferences and authenticate as an administrative user to unlock its settings; then click the Turn Off FileVault button.

8   You will be prompted to enter the current user's password; do so and then click the OK button.

You will be presented with a final warning dialog reminding you that you are decrypting this user's home folder. Click the Turn Off FileVault button once more to return this user's home folder to a normal account. The user will be logged out and you will see a slightly modified login window showing the home folder decryption process.

9   Once the user's folder is decrypted, log in to the user's account again and re-enable FileVault. This process is outlined in the FileVault section of this chapter.

10 Repeat steps 6 through 9 for each FileVault user created with the previous master password.

Resetting Keychain Passwords

Only if a user knows her current account password and then decides to change her password will the system also change the user's login keychain password. Keychain passwords cannot be changed by any outside password-resetting process so that they remain as secure as possible. Apple did not design the keychain system with a back door, as doing so would render the system less secure.

Consequently, whenever an administrative user resets a user's account or FileVault password, the keychain password will remain unchanged and will not automatically open as the user logs into her account. However, by default in Mac OS X v10.6, when a user with a recently reset password logs in she will be prompted with a dialog to update or reset her login keychain.

TIP ▶ The keychain synchronization dialog can be disabled from the First Aid tab of the Keychain Access application preferences.

The default selection, Update Keychain Password, will work only if the user knows his previous keychain password. This is probably not the case if you just had to reset the password. If so, the user can click the Create New Keychain button to create a new login keychain. The system will rename his old login keychain and leave it in the user's ~/Library/ Keychains folder in case he ever remembers his old password. Finally, the user can simply choose to ignore the warning by clicking the "Continue log in" button.

If the automatic keychain synchronization dialog does not appear, you can still reset the user's login keychain password from the Keychain Access utility, assuming the previous keychain password is known. As you'd expect, if you do not know the user's previous keychain password, then the contents of that keychain are lost forever. Using Keychain Access to manage a user's keychain is covered previously in this chapter.

Resetting the Primary Account Password

Many Macs intended for personal use have only the single primary administrator user account that was created when the Mac was initially set up with the Setup Assistant. Even if more than one person uses this Mac, quite often its owner is not very concerned about security. Thus, it's also likely that the primary user account is automatically logged in during startup and the owner has never enabled the master password. All this results in a high likelihood that Mac owners end up forgetting their primary administrator account password and don't have any way to reset this password because they never enabled the master password or created another administrator account.

Fortunately, Apple has prepared for these occasions by including a password-resetting utility on the Mac OS X Install DVD. The Reset Password utility will allow you to reset the password of any local user account on the selected system volume.

To reset the primary account password:

1   Boot the Mac from the Mac OS X Install DVD by turning on the Mac while holding down the C key, and as soon as possible, insert the DVD. The computer will boot from it.

2   Once the Installer has started, choose Utilities > Reset Password from the menu bar.

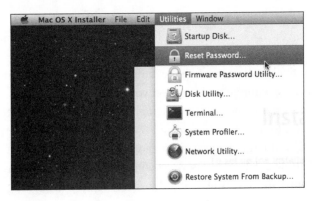

3   Select the system volume containing the inaccessible primary account you wish to reset from the row of system volume icons.

4   Choose the name of the inaccessible primary account from the pop-up menu.

5   Enter and reenter a new password in the appropriate fields.

6   Click the Save button to save the new password.

7   Quit the Reset Password utility to return to the Mac OS X Installer.

8   Quit the Mac OS X Installer to restart the Mac.

TIP   You can also use the Reset Password utility to repair home folder permissions and access control lists (ACLs) for the selected account by clicking the Reset button.

Obviously, the Reset Password utility is a dangerous application that can completely eliminate any of the security settings you've configured to protect your Mac. Because of this, the Reset Password utility will not run if copied off the original media. However, this still doesn't prevent any user with access to the Mac OS X Install DVD from using this utility. Once again, Apple prepared for this situation by providing another utility on the DVD: the Firmware Password utility. Setting a firmware password will prevent any nonauthorized user from booting the computer from a DVD. Using this utility to set a firmware password is covered previously in this chapter.

What You've Learned

▶ There are five types of user accounts, each with its own specific access and capabilities: standard users, administrative users, the guest user, sharing only users, and the root user.

▶ Creating, managing, and deleting users is accomplished from within the Accounts preferences.

▶ A user's home folder can be moved or restored using either the Migration Assistant or by manually moving it to the /Users folder and creating a new account with the same account name.

▶ A variety of login and security options are available within the Accounts and Security preferences.

▶ There are five types of passwords, each with its own specific use: account passwords, the firmware password, the master password, resource passwords, and keychain passwords.

▶ Mac OS X provides robust security for users via technologies such as keychains and FileVault.

▶ There are a variety of password reset methods you may have to use depending on the type of password you are trying to reset.

References

You can check for new and updated Knowledge Base documents at http://www.apple.com/support.

User Account Management

HT1428, "Mac OS X: How to change user short name or home directory name"

HT1528, "Enabling and using the 'root' user in Mac OS X"

Fast User Switching

TA22373, "Mac OS X 10.3 or Later: About Fast User Switching and home folders on servers"

TA22404, "Mac OS X 10.3, 10.4: Some applications only work in one account at a time"

Keychain

HT1060, "Using keychains with MobileMe, troubleshooting keychain issues"

FileVault

TA27532, "iMovie: Using FileVault can affect performance"

TA27530, "Final Cut Pro and Final Cut Express: About using FileVault"

Firmware Password

HT1352, "Setting up firmware password protection in Mac OS X"

Review Quiz

1. What are the five types of user accounts in Mac OS X? How are they different?
2. What are account attributes?
3. How can you limit a user account?
4. What are some security risks associated with each type of user account?
5. What default folders make up a user's home folder?
6. What three types of resource contention issues can occur when fast user switching is enabled?
7. What security risk can occur when fast user switching is enabled?
8. What does a keychain do?
9. How does FileVault secure a user's data?
10. How does resetting the master password affect existing FileVault user accounts?
11. How does resetting a user's password as an administrative user affect that user's keychains?
12. How does the Firmware Password utility help prevent users from making unauthorized password changes?

Answers

1. Standard is the default account type; administrative users can make changes to the system; a guest user does not require a password; sharing only users can access only shared files; and the root user has unlimited access.
2. Account attributes are the individual pieces of information that are used to define a user account. Examples include full name, account name, user ID, unique user ID, group, and home directory.
3. Parental controls can be used to further limit a user account. Examples include enforcing a simple Finder, limiting applications and widgets, setting time limits, and content filtering.

4. Standard user accounts are very secure, assuming they have good passwords. Administrative users can make changes that may negatively affect the system or other user accounts. A guest user could potentially fill your system drive with unwanted files. Sharing only users are generally very secure as long as you don't give them too much access to your items. The potential for mayhem with root user access is nearly unlimited.

5. The default folders in a user's home folder are Desktop, Documents, Downloads, Library, Movies, Music, Pictures, Public, and Sites.

6. Resource contention occurs when fast user switching is enabled and a user tries to access an item that another user already has open in the background. Document contention occurs when a user attempts to open a document that another user has already opened. Peripheral contention occurs when a user attempts to access a peripheral that is already in use by another user's open application. Application contention occurs when the second user attempts to access an application that is designed to run only once on a system.

7. When fast user switching is enabled, all users are allowed to see other users' locally connected volumes.

8. A keychain is an encrypted file that is used to securely save passwords, certificates, or notes. By default, every user has a login keychain that has the same password as his account.

9. FileVault stores the user's home folder in an encrypted disk image. This disk image is accessible only by the FileVault user.

10. If a known master password is reset using the Security preferences, previous FileVault accounts will not be negatively affected. On the other hand, if a master password is reset because it was lost, preexisting FileVault accounts cannot be reset by the new master password until all the old FileVault passwords are reset.

11. If an administrative user resets another user's account or FileVault password, this process will not change any keychain passwords. Therefore, the user's keychains will not automatically open when the user logs in with her new password. The user will have to manually change her keychain passwords using the Keychain Access utility.

12. The Firmware Password utility prevents users from booting off other devices. This in turn prevents them from using the Mac OS X Install DVD to reset local passwords without authorization.

3

Time   This chapter takes approximately 3 hours to complete.

Goals   Become familiar with the command-line environment

Use the command line to perform basic file manipulation and system administration tasks

Understand how Automator and AppleScript can be used to automate tasks in the graphical interface

Understand how scripts can be used to automate tasks at the command-line interface

Chapter 3
Command Line and Automation

The analogy goes like this: You can spend your entire life driving cars without having any idea how to fix them, but if you plan on being a mechanic then you need to know how things work under the hood. The same is true of Mac OS X; you can spend years using Macs without having any idea how to fix them, but if you plan to administer and troubleshoot issues you need to know how things work "under the hood." In the case of Mac OS X, because UNIX is what provides the foundational technologies, "under the hood" means working with the command-line interface.

First, there are a great many indispensable management and troubleshooting tools that are available only at the command line. And once you become comfortable with the command line, you'll find many tasks are actually much more quickly done there than in the graphical interface—especially if you learn how to create scripts. Scripts can be used to automate repetitive tasks and do them much faster than any human can. Mac OS X includes scripting technologies in both the command line and graphical environments.

In this chapter you will be introduced to the Mac OS X command-line environment. You will learn the basics of using commands and command-line navigation, along with other general use commands. In the later parts of this chapter you will also explore the command-line scripting and graphical automation technologies in Mac OS X. You'll see how these tools can save you and your users a lot of time when trying to complete repetitive tasks.

Command-Line Essentials

Aside from impressing all your geek friends, there are several legitimate advantages to using the command line:

▶   Additional options—Many additional administrative and troubleshooting options are available from the command line that are not available from the graphical interface. For example, the following applications have command-line equivalents with more options (commands in parenthesis); System Profiler (`system_profiler`), Installer (`installer`), Software Update (`softwareupdate`), Disk Utility (`diskutil`), and Spotlight (`mdfind`). These are just a few of the examples, as nearly every administrative function has both a graphical and a command-line tool.

▶   Finder limitations—From the command line you have unfettered access to the file system, unlike with the Finder, which intentionally limits a user's ability to access the full file system. For example, the Finder hides many files and folders that are easily visible at the command line. Also, there are many file system permissions settings that the Finder is incapable of displaying properly. File system permissions are detailed in Chapter 4, "File Systems."

▶   "Invisible" remote access—You can remotely log into a Mac's command-line environment, using the secure shell (SSH) protocol, without the currently logged-in graphical user knowing you're there. This allows administrators to make changes at the command line without alerting the user to their work. Using SSH remote login is detailed in Chapter 8, "Network Services."

▶   System user (root) access for administrators—By using the `sudo` command, any administrator can masquerade as the system user, also known as root. This allows for great administrative flexibility at the command line, as covered later in this chapter.

▶ Easily scriptable—If you understand how to interactively work at the command line, then you can apply the same syntax to a command-line script. This allows you to easily automate repetitive tasks, as covered later in this chapter.

▶ Administer multiple Macs simultaneously—If you combine command-line instructions with Apple Remote Desktop (ARD), you can remotely administer multiple, even thousands, of Macs simultaneously. Essentially the ARD application allows you to remotely send the same command to any number of Mac computers with the click of a button. Obviously, this can save a tremendous amount of time for anyone who has to administer multiple Macs.

> **MORE INFO** ▶ The ARD application is not included with Mac OS X, but your Mac does include the client-side half of ARD with the Remote Management service. You can find out more about ARD in Chapter 8, "Network Services," or at www.apple.com/remotedesktop.

Accessing the Command Line

You may hear the term "shell" kicked around when the command line is discussed. A shell is the first command that runs automatically when you access the command line, and it provides you with the actual interactive command-line interface. Many types of shells are available, but Mac OS X will start the bash shell by default.

Although most people access the Mac OS X command line using the Terminal application, there are multiple methods for accessing it:

▶ Terminal application—The main application on Mac OS X for accessing the command line is /Applications/Utilities/Terminal. The Mac's Terminal application is quite sophisticated and has gained many convenient features over the years, including highly customizable interface settings, a tabbed interface for quickly handling multiple command-line sessions, and multiple split panes for easily viewing your history.

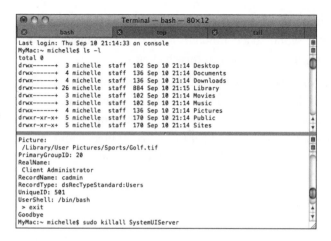

▶ Enter ">console" at the login screen—This method bypasses the graphical interface entirely and takes over the whole screen with a simple black background and white text. You will still have to log in with a user account, but this is a convenient method for testing login issues as the standard login screen doesn't provide much in the way of error reporting. When you want to log out of this mode, simply use the exit command to return to the standard login screen.

NOTE ▶ Only if you can manually enter a user name at the login screen will you be able to use console mode. You can make the login screen default to the "show name and password" mode from the login options of Accounts preferences. Alternately, you can change the login screen to this mode by pressing the Command-Option-Arrow-Enter keyboard combination.

▶ Startup in single-user mode—This is a troubleshooting mode enabled by holding the Command-S keyboard combination at system startup. This mode starts the minimum system required to provide you with a command-line prompt so you can enter commands in attempt to repair a system that cannot fully start up. Using single-user mode is detailed in Chapter 10, "System Startup."

▶ SSH remote login—This allows you to securely log in from a remote computer to access your Mac's command line. SSH is a common standard, so any operating system that supports SSH can remotely log into your Mac. Using SSH remote login is detailed in Chapter 8, "Network Services."

Working at the Command Line

When opening the Terminal for the first time, many approach the command line with unnecessary caution. Even though the command line offers nearly limitless capability, getting started with the basics is not that complicated.

Command-Line Prompt

The first thing you'll see at the command line is the *prompt*. The prompt is presented to you by the computer to let you know that it's ready for your command. By default, the prompt will always show you the name of the computer you're using, followed by where you are in the computer's file system, followed by your current user account name, and ending with a $. The use of $ at the end of the prompt is an indication that you are using the standard bash shell. Where you are in the computer's file system is referred to as the *working directory*, and it will change as you navigate through the file system.

> **NOTE** ▶ While the Mac OS has traditionally called file system containers "folders," the command line's UNIX heritage prefers to use the word "directory." In the context of this chapter these two words are synonymous.

At the prompt you enter your command string, often more than one word, and then press the Return key to initiate or execute the command you entered. Depending on the command entry you chose it will either take over the Terminal window with a text interface, or show the results of the command and then return to the prompt, or simply perform some work and then return to the prompt when the command is complete. Many commands display results only if there was a problem; it's worth reading what the command returns to make sure it doesn't indicate that something went wrong.

NOTE ► Some commands can take a while to execute and may not give any sort of progress indication. Generally, if you don't see a new prompt, you should assume your last command is still running.

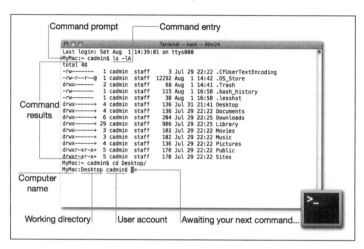

Command String

As for the command string, it is generally composed of only a few parts:

- ► Command name—Commands are just like applications, but they are more focused; many commands provide very specific functionality. Some commands just need you to enter their name to execute.

- ► Command options (sometimes called "flags")—After the command you may specify some options that will change the command's default behavior. These items, being optional, are not required and can be different for every command. Options start with one or two dashes to distinguish them from arguments. Many commands allow several single-letter options to be combined after a single dash. For example ls -1A is the same as ls -1 -A.

- ► Arguments (sometimes called "parameters")—After the command and its options, you will typically specify the argument, or the item that you want the command to modify. Again, this is only necessary if the command requires an item to act upon.

- ► Extras—Extras are not necessary, but they can greatly enhance the capabilities of your command. For example you could add items that redirect the command output, or include other commands, or generate a document.

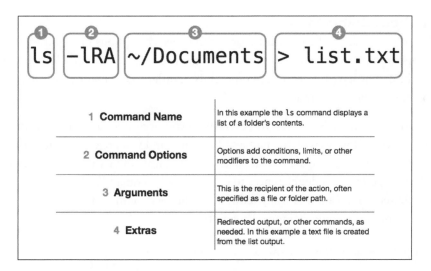

1 **Command Name**	In this example the ls command displays a list of a folder's contents.
2 **Command Options**	Options add conditions, limits, or other modifiers to the command.
3 **Arguments**	This is the recipient of the action, often specified as a file or folder path.
4 **Extras**	Redirected output, or other commands, as needed. In this example a text file is created from the list output.

A Simple Command-Line Example

Here is an example in which the user Michelle is working on a computer called MyMac and her working directory is Documents. She is deleting an application called Junk inside the /Applications folder. It is assumed that Michelle will press the Return or Enter key once she has entered her command.

```
MyMac:Documents michelle$ rm -R /Applications/Junk.app
MyMac:Documents michelle$
```

NOTE ▶ Throughout this guide, highlighted text indicates something the user enters. This makes user-entered text easy to differentiate from text the computer generates. It's important to note that these are merely example commands; it is highly likely that you will have to modify the command string to match your environment.

In this case the command was entered and executed properly, and the computer simply returns to a new prompt. This is an example of a command that only returns information if the command didn't execute properly. The computer will usually let you know if you entered something improperly by returning some sort of error message or help text. Nevertheless, the computer will not prevent you from doing something stupid at the command line, such as accidentally deleting your home folder. If you remember only one rule about using the command line, it should be this one: Always double-check your typing.

Learning About Commands

There are literally thousands of commands, each with dozens of options or requirements for proper usage. In fact, most users are overwhelmed by the command line simply because they think they have to memorize commands in order to use them. In reality, all you need to know is one command: man.

Most commands have manuals that tell you everything you need to know about a command. Simply enter man followed by the name of the command you are curious about, and you will be shown its manual page. Manual pages include command usage and, at the very bottom of the page, often include references to other related commands. Once inside the manual page viewer (which automatically redirects to the less command), you can use a few navigation shortcuts to quickly move through the manual:

▶ Use the Up Arrow and Down Arrow keys to scroll through the manual.

▶ Use the Space bar to move down one screen at a time.

▶ Search through the manual page by entering / and then a keyword.

▶ Exit the manual page by simply pressing the Q key.

What if you don't even know the name of the command you're looking for? Simply enter man -k and then a keyword to search the command manual database. For example, entering man -k owner will return a short list of the commands used for changing file and folder ownership, including the proper command, chown. Using the chown command to change file and folder ownership is covered in Chapter 4, "File Systems."

> **NOTE** ▶ In addition to commands, the manual database also includes scripting and programming functions and file format documentation; hence, a man -k *search* may give results besides the relevant commands.

Command-Line Navigation

If knowing how to use commands is the first part of conquering the command line, the second part is learning how to navigate the file system effectively at the command line. Once again, by the time you master navigation at the command line you'll find that it can be much faster than navigation using the Finder.

NOTE ▸ The command line is case-sensitive and requires that you use full filenames with filename extensions. In other words, the command line will not be able to locate the "itunes" application, but it will easily locate the "iTunes.app" application.

Understanding Navigation Concepts

First, a few common navigation terms must be clearly defined. While the Mac OS has traditionally called file system containers "folders," the command line's UNIX heritage prefers to use the word "directory." Though the terms can be used interchangeably, this book will continue to favor the word "folder" to describe file system containers, as the word "directory" is often used for other non-folder-like items. For example, network databases used to store user information are often referred to as "directories." Furthermore, the process in Mac OS X for accessing these user databases is called DirectoryService.

A new term you'll see in this chapter is *path*. A path represents a file or folder's location in the file system described by the path taken to reach it. You have already seen paths in this book used to describe the specific location of an application or utility. For instance, the Disk Utility application's file system path is /Applications/Utilities/Disk Utility. The command line uses pathnames exclusively for navigating and locating items in the file system.

There are two types of file system pathnames: absolute paths and relative paths. Either type is valid for navigating or locating items at the command line, but they differ in where they start:

▸ Absolute paths—Absolute paths are full descriptions of an item's location starting from the root, or beginning, of the system (startup) volume. Thus, an absolute path will always begin with a forward slash to indicate the beginning of the file system. This book uses absolute paths to describe the location of items. An example of the absolute path to the user Michelle's Drop Box folder would be /Users/michelle/Public/Drop Box. A plain English translation of this path would be, "starting from the startup volume, go into the Users folder, then into the michelle subfolder, then the Public subfolder, and select the item named Drop Box."

▸ Relative paths—Relative paths are partial descriptions of an item's location based on where you're currently working in the file system from the command line. When you first open the Terminal application, your command-line session starts out working from your home folder. Therefore, the relative path from your home folder to your Drop Box would be Public/Drop Box. A plain English translation of this would be, "from where you are now, go into the Public subfolder, and then select the item named Drop Box."

Using Navigation Commands

You will use three basic commands for navigating the file system at the command line:
pwd, ls, and cd.

pwd

Short for "print working directory," this command will report the absolute path of your
current working location in the file system:

```
MyMac:~ michelle$ pwd
/Users/michelle
```

ls

Short for "list," ls will list the folder contents of your current working location. Entering
a pathname following the ls command will list the contents of the specified item. The ls
command has many additional options for listing file and folder information that will be
covered throughout this book.

```
MyMac:~ michelle$ ls
Desktop Library Pictures
Documents Movies Public
Downloads Music Sites
MyMac:~ michelle$ ls Public
Drop Box
```

cd

Short for "change directory," cd is the command you will use to navigate at the command
line. Entering a pathname following the cd command will change your current working
location to the specified folder. Entering cd without specifying a path will always return
you to your home folder. In the following example, Michelle will use the cd command to
navigate to her Drop Box folder, and then she will navigate back to her home folder:

```
MyMac:~ michelle$ cd Public/Drop\ Box/
MyMac:Drop Box michelle$ pwd
/Users/michelle/Public/Drop Box
MyMac:Drop Box michelle$ cd
MyMac:~ michelle$ pwd
/Users/michelle
```

Using Special Characters

At this point you may have noticed that the command line uses special characters in the command prompt and pathnames. Many of these special characters are used as shortcuts to save time. On the other hand, one special character isn't a time-saver; it's an unfortunate necessity. The backslash character "\" is used before a space in a path or filename. This practice is necessary because the command line uses the spaces between items to parse the command entry into separate logical pieces. A space in a filename without the backslash will confuse the command line, and your command will not execute properly.

There are other methods for entering filenames and paths with spaces. One alternative is to surround filenames and paths with quotation marks:

```
MyMac:~ michelle$ cd "Public/Drop Box"
MyMac:Drop Box michelle$ pwd
/Users/michelle/Public/Drop Box
```

Another solution involves dragging and dropping items from the Finder to the Terminal window. The Terminal automatically enters the item's absolute path with the appropriate backslash characters before spaces in names. The most efficient solution, though, is to use the tab complete feature built into Mac OS X's command line to automatically complete file and pathnames for you. Saving time by using tab completion is covered next in this section of the chapter, so be sure to check it out.

> **NOTE** ▶ The space is not the only character that needs to be treated specially at the command line. Others include !, $, &, *, ;, |, and \, as well as parentheses and all types of quotes and brackets. Both Finder's drag-and-drop capability and tab completion deal with these characters appropriately.

When navigating the file system, you can also save time by using the double period ".." shortcut to indicate the parent folder. In other words, if you were working in your home folder located at /Users/username, entering cd .. would tell the command line that you want to navigate to the /Users folder. In the following example, Michelle navigates to her Drop Box folder, backs up to her Public folder, and then finally backs up twice to the /Users folder:

```
MyMac:~ michelle$ cd Public/Drop\ Box/
MyMac:Drop Box michelle$ pwd
/Users/michelle/Public/Drop Box
```

```
MyMac:Drop Box michelle$ cd ..
MyMac:Public michelle$ pwd
/Users/michelle/Public
MyMac:Public michelle$ cd ../..
MyMac:Users michelle$ pwd
/Users
```

Finally, there is the tilde (~). This little guy is used as shorthand to describe the current user's home folder in a pathname. Once again using the example from earlier, the current user's Drop Box is located at ~/Public/Drop Box. This also helps to explain the tilde you see in the default command prompt. For example, if Michelle opened the Terminal on a computer called MyMac, the following would be the command prompt:

```
MyMac:~ michelle$
```

TIP ▶ You can also use the tilde to specify another user's home folder. For example ~logan/Public would specify Logan's Public folder.

If Michelle navigated to her Drop Box, the command prompt would change. Note that the prompt only shows the current working location and not an absolute or even relative path:

```
MyMac:Drop Box michelle$
```

Using Tab Completion

Tab completion is the command line's absolute top time-saving feature. Not only does using tab completion save time by automatically finishing filenames, pathnames, and command names for you, it also prevents you from making typographical errors and verifies that the item you're entering exists.

Using tab completion couldn't be simpler. Start from your home folder by entering cd, then P, and then press the Tab key. The Terminal window will flash quickly and you may hear an audible error sound, letting you know there is more than one choice for items that begin with "P" in your home folder. Press the Tab key again, and the computer will display your two choices, Pictures and Public. Now, enter a u after the initial P, then press the Tab key again and the computer will automatically finish Public/ for you. Finally, enter a D and press the Tab key one last time, and the computer will finish the path with Public/Drop\ Box/.

NOTE ▶ When tab completion fills in a folder name, it automatically puts a forward slash (/) at the end (assuming you want to continue the path from there). Most commands will ignore this trailing slash, but a few will behave differently if it's there. When in doubt, it's usually safest to delete a leftover / at the end of a path.

Even in this small example, tab completion turned a pathname that would take 17 keystrokes (`Public/Drop\ Box/`) into just 5 (`Pu<tab>D<tab>`). Further, tab completion helped you avoid mistakes by essentially spell-checking your typing and verifying the item is where you expected it to be. Making tab completion a habit when using the command line can easily shave hours off the time you have to spend there. Thus, if you remember only two rules about using the command line, it should be these two: Always double-check your typing, and always use tab completion to help make sure you spell correctly and save time.

Viewing Invisible Items

To simplify navigation in the file system, both the command line and the Finder hide many files and folders from your view. Often these are system support items that are hidden for good reason. While there is no easy way to make the Finder reveal hidden items, it is quite simple to view hidden items at the command line. The first reason for this is that many items hidden by the Finder are set this way via the hidden file flag. The command line ignores the hidden file flag, so it will show these items regardless. However, the `ls` command will hide items that have a filename that begins with a period, but even these items can be easily revealed.

To view hidden items at the command line, simply add the `-a` option to the `-l` option when using the `ls` command:

```
MyMac:~ michelle$ ls -la
total 32
drwxr-xr-x  15 michelle  staff   510 Aug 20 17:33 .
drwxr-xr-x   8 root      admin   272 Aug 20 17:05 ..
-rw-------   1 michelle  staff     3 Aug 20 01:08 CFUserTextEncoding
-rw-------   1 michelle  staff  2666 Aug 20 16:42 .bash_history
-rw-------   1 michelle  staff    48 Aug 20 17:19 .lesshst
-rw-------   1 root      staff   632 Aug 20 14:25 .viminfo
drwx------+  5 michelle  staff   170 Aug 20 15:49 Desktop
```

```
drwx------+   3 michelle  staff   102 Aug 20 01:08 Documents
drwx------+   3 michelle  staff   102 Aug 20 01:08 Downloads
drwx------   19 michelle  staff   646 Aug 20 01:08 Library
drwx------+   3 michelle  staff   102 Aug 20 01:08 Movies
drwx------+   3 michelle  staff   102 Aug 20 01:08 Music
drwx------+   4 michelle  staff   136 Aug 20 01:08 Pictures
drwxr-xr-x+   7 michelle  staff   238 Aug 20 15:29 Public
drwxr-xr-x    5 michelle  staff   170 Aug 20 01:08 Sites
```

NOTE ▶ While ls -a shows all items in the folder, including ".." (a shortcut to the parent folder) and "." (a shortcut to the current folder). Another option, ls -A, shows all invisible items except for these two folder shortcuts.

As you can see from Michelle's home folder, any item that has a period at the beginning of its name will be hidden by default in both the command line and the Finder. These items are created and used by the operating system, so they should be left alone.

MORE INFO ▶ Managing hidden items is detailed in Chapter 5, "Data Management and Backup."

Navigating to Other Volumes

At the command line, the system volume is also known as the root volume, and it's identified by the lone forward slash. It may come as a surprise to you, however, that at the command line other nonroot volumes appear as part of the main file system in a folder called Volumes. In the following example, Michelle will start in her home folder, navigate to and list the items in the /Volumes folder, and then finally navigate into a volume named "Backup Drive" that is connected to this Mac via FireWire:

```
MyMac:~ michelle$ pwd
/Users/michelle
MyMac:~ michelle$ cd /Volumes/
MyMac:Volumes michelle$ pwd
/Volumes
MyMac:Volumes michelle$ ls
Backup Drive           Macintosh HD
Mac OS X Install DVD
```

```
MyMac:Volumes michelle$ cd Backup\ Drive/
MyMac:Backup Drive michelle$ pwd
/Volumes/Backup Drive
```

Command-Line File Manipulation

Basic file management is also a much richer experience from the command line than it is from the Finder. Consequently, basic file management from the command line can lead to increased opportunities for user error. Once again, always make sure to thoroughly check your typing before you execute a command.

File Examination Commands

There are a variety of basic commands for locating and examining files and folders from the command line, including cat, less, which, file, and find. As always, you can get more detailed information about each one of these commands by reading their manual entries.

cat

Short for "concatenate," this command will read a file sequentially to the standard output, often the Terminal window. The syntax is cat followed by the path to the item you wish to view. The cat command can also be used to append to text files using the >> redirect operator. In the following example, Michelle uses the cat command to view the content of two text files in her Desktop folder, TextDocOne.txt and TextDocTwo.txt. Then she uses the cat command with the >> redirect operator to append the second text file to the end of the first text file.

```
MyMac:~ michelle$ cat Desktop/TextDocOne.txt
This is the contents of the first plain text document.
MyMac:~ michelle$ cat Desktop/TextDocTwo.txt
This is the contents of the second plain text document.
MyMac:~ michelle$ cat Desktop/TextDocTwo.txt >> Desktop/TextDocOne.txt
MyMac:~ michelle$ cat Desktop/TextDocOne.txt
This is the contents of the first plain text document.
This is the contents of the second plain text document.
```

MORE INFO ▶ Command-line extras, like the >> redirect operator, are covered in the "Basic Command-Line Scripting" section later in this chapter.

less

A play on words from the previously popular text-viewing command more, the less command is much better for viewing long text files, as it will let you interactively browse and search through the text. The syntax is less followed by the path to the item you wish to view. The less viewer command is actually the same interface used to view manual pages, so the navigation shortcuts are identical to what you find when you use the man command:

▶ Use the Up and Down Arrow keys to scroll through the text.

▶ Use the Space bar to move down one screen at a time.

▶ Search through the text by entering /, then a keyword.

▶ Type the "v" key to automatically redirect the text file to the vi text editor. Using vi is covered later in this chapter.

▶ Exit the less viewer command by simply pressing the Q key.

> **NOTE** ▶ In Mac OS X, attempting to run the more command will actually run the less command instead, but with slightly different options. For example, the more command will automatically quit when it gets to the end of a document, while the less command requires you to explicitly quit.

which

This command will locate the file path of a specified command. In other words, it will show you which file you're actually using when you enter a specific command. The syntax is which followed by the commands you wish to locate. In the following example, Michelle uses the which command to locate the file path of the man, ls, pwd, and cd commands:

```
MyMac:~ michelle$ which man ls pwd cd
/usr/bin/man
/bin/ls
/bin/pwd
/usr/bin/cd
```

Using this command, you'll notice that most commands are found in one of four folders; "/usr/bin" for most commands, "/usr/sbin" for system-oriented commands, "/bin" for critical commands the system needs during the startup process, and "/sbin" for critical system-oriented commands.

file

This command will attempt to determine a file's type based on its content. This is a useful command for identifying files that do not have a filename extension. The syntax is `file` followed by the path to the file you're attempting to identify. In the following example, Michelle uses the `file` command to locate the file type of two documents in her Desktop folder, PictureDocument and TextDocument:

```
MyMac:~ michelle$ ls Desktop/
PictureDocument TextDocument
MyMac:~ michelle$ file Desktop/PictureDocument
Desktop/PictureDocument: TIFF image data, big-endian
MyMac:~ michelle$ file Desktop/TextDocument
Desktop/TextDocument: ASCII English text
```

find

This command is used to locate items in the file system based on search criteria. The `find` command does not use the Spotlight search service, but it does allow you to set very specific search criteria and use filename wildcards. (Filename wildcards are covered in the next section.) The syntax is `find` followed by the beginning path of the search, then an option defining your search criteria, and then the search criteria within quotation marks. In the following example, Michelle uses the `find` command to locate any picture files in her home folder by searching only for files with names ending in *.tiff*:

```
MyMac:~ michelle$ find /Users/michelle -name "*.tiff"
/Users/michelle/Desktop/PictureDocument.tiff
/Users/michelle/Pictures/FamilyPict.tiff
/Users/michelle/Pictures/MyPhoto.tiff
```

TIP When using the `find` command to start a search at the root of the system drive, you should also use the `-x` option to avoid searching through the /Volumes folder.

TIP To use the Spotlight search service from the command line, use the `mdfind` command. The syntax is simply `mdfind` followed by your search criteria.

Using Wildcard Characters

One of the most powerful features of the command line is the ability to use wildcard characters, also known as "globs," to define path name and search criteria. Here are three of the most commonly used wildcard characters:

▶ Asterisk (*)—The asterisk wildcard is used to match any string of characters. For instance, entering * matches all files, while entering *.tiff matches all files ending in *.tiff.*

▶ Question mark (?)—The question mark wildcard is used to match any single character. For example, entering b?ok matches *book* but not *brook.*

▶ Square brackets ([ ])—Square brackets are used to define a range of characters to match in that specific space. For example, [Dd]ocument would locate any item named "Document" or "document," and doc[1-9] matches any file named "doc#" where # is any number between 1 and 9.

Combining filename wildcards can be used to great effect. Consider a collection of five files with the names "ReadMe.rtf", "ReadMe.txt", "read.rtf", "read.txt", and "It's All About Me.rtf". Using wildcards among these files:

▶ *.rtf matches ReadMe.rtf, read.rtf, and It's All About Me.rtf

▶ ????.* matches read.rtf and read.txt

▶ [Rr]*.rtf matches ReadMe.rtf and read.rtf

▶ [A-Z].* matches ReadMe.rtf, ReadMe.txt, and It's All About Me.rtf

Using Recursive Commands

When you direct a command to execute some task on an item at the command line, it will touch only the specified item. If the specified item is a folder, the command line will not automatically navigate inside the folder to execute the command on the enclosed items. If you require that a command be executed on a folder and its contents, you have to tell the command to run recursively. "Recursive" is a fancy way of saying, "Execute the task on every item inside every folder starting from the path I specify." Most commands accept -r or -R as the option to indicate that you want the command to run recursively.

In the following example, Michelle will list the contents of her Public folder normally, and then recursively using the -R option. Notice that when she lists the contents of the Public folder recursively, the system also lists the contents of the Drop Box and Drop Folder:

```
MyMac:~ michelle$ ls Public
Drop Box PublicFile1 PublicFile2 PublicFile3
MyMac:~ michelle$ ls -R Public
Drop Box PublicFile1 PublicFile2 PublicFile3

Public/Drop Box:
Drop Folder DroppedFile1 DroppedFile2

Public/Drop Box/Drop Folder:
DropFolderFile1 DropFolderFile2
```

Modifying Files and Folders

There are a variety of basic commands for modifying files and folders from the command line, including mkdir, cp, mv, rm, rmdir, and vi.

mkdir

Short for "make directory," this command is used to create new folders. The syntax is mkdir followed by the paths of the new folders you want to create. An often-used option is -p, which will tell mkdir to create intermediate folders that don't already exist in the paths you specify. In the following example, Michelle uses the mkdir command with the -p option to create a folder called Private with two folders inside it called Stocks and Bonds:

```
MyMac:~ michelle$ ls
Desktop Downloads Movies Pictures Sites
Documents Library Music Public
MyMac:~ michelle$ mkdir -p Private/Stocks Private/Bonds
MyMac:~ michelle$ ls
Desktop Downloads Movies Pictures Public
Documents Library Music Private Sites
MyMac:~ michelle$ cd Private/
MyMac:Private michelle$ ls
Bonds Stocks
```

> **TIP** ▸ You can use the `mkdir` command to quickly create temporary folders for command-line testing. You can also use the `touch` command followed by a filename to quickly create temporary files for command-line testing. While the original purpose of the `touch` command is to update the modification date of the specified item, it will also create an empty file if it doesn't already exist.

cp

Short for "copy," this command will copy items from one location to another. The syntax is `cp` followed by the path to the original item, and ending with the destination path for the copy. In the following example, Michelle uses the `cp` command to create a copy of testfile located at the root of her home folder and place the copy, testfile2, in her Desktop folder.

> **NOTE** ▸ Remember, if you want to copy a folder and its entire contents you must tell the `cp` command to run recursively by adding the `-R` option.

```
MyMac:~ michelle$ ls
Desktop Library Pictures testfile
Documents Movies Public
Downloads Music Sites
MyMac:~ michelle$ cp testfile Desktop/testfile2
MyMac:~ michelle$ ls Desktop/
testfile2
```

When working with the `cd` command, specifying a destination folder but no filename will make a copy with the same name as the original. Specifying a destination filename but not a destination folder will make a copy in your current working folder. Further, unlike copying with the Finder, the `cp` command will not warn you if your copy will replace an existing file. It will simply delete the existing file and replace it with the copy you told it to create. This behavior is true of most commands.

> **TIP** ▸ You can use the secure copy command `scp` to copy files between networked Macs via SSH remote login. Enabling SSH remote login is covered in Chapter 8, "Network Services."

mv

Short for "move," this command will move items from one location to another. The syntax is mv followed by the path to the original item, and ending with the new destination path for the item. In the following example, Michelle uses the mv command to move testfile2 from her Desktop folder to the root of her home folder:

```
MyMac:~ michelle$ ls Desktop/
testfile2
MyMac:~ michelle$ ls
Desktop Library Pictures testfile
Documents Movies Public
Downloads Music Sites
MyMac:~ michelle$ mv Desktop/testfile2 testfile2
MyMac:~ michelle$ ls
Desktop Library Pictures testfile
Documents Movies Public testfile2
Downloads Music Sites
```

The mv command uses the same destination rules as the cp command. Since the destination filename was specified without a folder, it moves it into the current working folder. The mv command also happens to be the rename command. After all, moving an item into the same folder with a different name is the same as renaming it. In the following example, Michelle, working in her home folder, uses the mv command to rename testfile to testfile1:

```
MyMac:~ michelle$ ls
Desktop Library Pictures testfile
Documents Movies Public testfile2
Downloads Music Sites
MyMac:~ michelle$ mv testfile testfile1
MyMac:~ michelle$ ls
Desktop Library Pictures testfile1
Documents Movies Public testfile2
Downloads Music Sites
```

rm

Short for "remove," this command will permanently delete items. There is no Trash folder at the command line. The rm command is forever. The syntax is rm followed by the paths of the items you wish to delete. In the following example, Michelle uses the rm command to delete testifile1 and testfile2.

NOTE ▶ Remember, if you want to delete a folder and its entire contents you must tell the rm command to run recursively by adding the -R option.

```
MyMac:~ michelle$ ls
Desktop Library Pictures testfile1
Documents Movies Public testfile2
Downloads Music Sites
MyMac:~ michelle$ rm testfile1 testfile2
MyMac:~ michelle$ ls
Desktop Downloads Movies Pictures Sites
Documents Library Music Public
```

TIP Items deleted with the rm command are recoverable to a degree using drive recovery tools. Thus to securely erase an item you can use the srm command. Secure erasure is further detailed in Chapter 4, "File Systems."

rmdir and rm -R

Short for "remove directory," this command will permanently delete folders. Again, there is no Trash folder in the CLI. The rmdir command is forever. The syntax is rmdir followed by the paths of the folders you want to delete. The rmdir command cannot remove folders with any items in them, so in many ways the rmdir command is superfluous, as you can easily remove folders and their contents by using the rm command with the recursive option.

In the following example, Michelle tries to use the rmdir command to delete the Private folder but is unable to because it contains items. She then attempts to use the rm command, but again she is unable to because the folder contains items. Finally, she uses the rm command with the recursive option, -R, to remove the Private folder and all its contents.

```
MyMac:~ michelle$ rmdir Private/
rmdir: Private/: Directory not empty
MyMac:~ michelle$ rm Private/
```

```
rm: Private/: is a directory
MyMac:~ michelle$ rm -R Private/
MyMac:~ michelle$ ls
Desktop Downloads Movies Pictures Sites
Documents Library Music Public
```

vi

For many this command, short for "visual," has the most ironic of names, as it's probably the least visually engaging text editor they have ever come across. However, vi is the most common text editor you'll find at the command line. To open a text document for editing with this command simply enter vi followed by the path or name of a text file.

> **TIP** Mac OS X automatically redirects vi to the newer improved version, vim. However, for basic functionality you probably won't notice the difference.

> **TIP** Mac OS X includes nano, a more modern, and by many accounts easier to use, text editor. For example, it features a cheat sheet of commonly used commands at the bottom of the screen. However, vi is the default editor in some situations, as when editing some system files, so it behooves you to learn at least basic vi techniques.

Much like the less command, vi takes over the entire Terminal window with the content of the text file. When vi first opens it's in command mode. In command mode vi is expecting you to type predefined characters that tell vi which operation you want to complete next. You can also browse through the file in command mode by using the arrow keys. When starting out with vi, simply enter the letter a to begin editing the text.

In this mode vi will insert new text into the document wherever the cursor is. You can move the cursor using the arrow keys. When you are done with your edits, you then need to save the changes. This requires you to get back to vi command mode first. You can re-enter vi command mode at any time by pressing the Escape key. Once in command mode you can simultaneously save changes and quit vi by entering ZZ.

In summary, you really only need to know three keyboard commands to get by in the vi text editor; a to begin inserting text, "Esc" to re-enter command mode, and ZZ to save your changes and quit (think, "a to z"). There is one more vi command you should learn in case you make serious mistakes while editing text. In command mode you can quit vi without saving any changes by entering :quit! (think, "quit now!").

Command-Line Administration

Perhaps the most powerful feature at the command line is the ability to quickly invoke the access of another user account or even the system root user account. In this section you will look at a few commands that are very useful to administrators, as they allow you to access items normally restricted by file system permissions.

MORE INFO ▸ A full discussion of file system permissions is available in Chapter 4, "File Systems."

Using su

The su command, short for "substitute user identity," will allow you to easily switch to another user account at the command line. Simply enter su followed by the short name of the user you want to switch to, and then enter the account password (the command line will not show the password in the Terminal). The command prompt will change, indicating that you have the access privileges of a different user. You can easily verify your currently logged-on identity by entering who -m at the command line. You will remain logged on as the substitute user until you quit the Terminal or enter the exit command. In the following example, Michelle will use the su command to change her shell to Kevin's account, and then she will exit back to her account:

```
MyMac:~ michelle$ who -m
michelle ttys001 Aug 20 14:06
MyMac:~ michelle$ su kevin
Password:
bash-3.2$ who -m
kevin ttys001 Aug 20 14:06
bash-3.2$ exit
exit
MyMac:~ michelle$ who -m
michelle ttys001 Aug 20 14:06
```

Using sudo

An even more powerful command is sudo, which is short for "substitute user do," or more appropriately, "super user do." Preceding a command with sudo instructs the computer to execute the command that follows using root account access. The only requirements to use sudo on Mac OS X are that it's initiated and authenticated from an administrative account (again, the command line will not show the password in the Terminal).

In other words, by default on Mac OS X, any administrative user can use sudo to evoke root access at the command line. Further, sudo works even if the root user account is disabled in the graphical interface. This access is one of the primary reasons why, in many environments, granting administrative access to every user is insecure. You can, however, adjust the sudo command's configuration file to further restrict its usage, as described later in this section.

> **TIP** ▶ The sudo command can also be used to execute a command as a specific nonroot user. Before a command, simply enter sudo -u username, where username is the short name of the user you wish to execute the command as.

In the following example, Michelle is not normally allowed to read the text file named Secrets, using the standard command-line text reader command cat. She then uses the sudo command to enable root access for the cat command so she can see the contents of the Secrets text file:

```
MyMac:~ michelle$ cat Secrets.txt
cat: Secrets.txt: Permission denied
MyMac:~ michelle$ sudo cat Secrets.txt
Password:
This is the contents of the Secrets.txt text file that the user account Michelle
does not normally have access permissions to read. However, because she is an
administrative user, she can use the sudo command to envoke root user access and thus
read the contents of this file.
```

> **TIP** ▶ If the command line returns an error because you forgot to use sudo, at the next prompt simply enter sudo !! to run the previous command entry preceded by sudo.

Remember, with great power comes great responsibility. Using the power of sudo with an improperly typed command can easily wreak havoc on your operating system. The command line will only warn you the first time you attempt to use sudo that you could cause serious damage. After that, the command line assumes you know what you're doing. If you remember only three rules about using the command line, it should be these: Always double-check your typing, always use tab completion to help make sure you spell correctly and save time, and, when using sudo, always triple-check your typing.

Switching the Shell with sudo

If, as an administrative user, you need to execute more than one command with root account access, you can temporarily switch the entire command-line shell to have root level access. Simply enter sudo -s, and then your password to switch the shell to have root access. You can easily verify your currently logged-on identity by entering who -m at the command line. You will remain logged on as the root user until you quit the Terminal or enter the exit command. In the following example, Michelle will use the sudo command to switch her shell to the root user, and then she will exit back to her own account:

```
MyMac:~ michelle$ who -m
michelle ttys001 Aug 20 14:31
MyMac:~ michelle$ sudo -s
Password:
bash-3.2# who -m
root ttys001 Aug 20 14:31
bash-3.2# exit
exit
MyMac:~ michelle$ who -m
michelle ttys001 Aug 20 14:31
```

Managing sudo Access

Again, by default, any administrative user can use the sudo command to access resources as the system administrator (root). Additionally, once you initially authenticate the sudo command, it will remain "open" for five minutes, so you do not have to reauthenticate subsequent sudo usage during that time. Further, using sudo -s could leave an open Terminal with root access indefinitely.

For these reasons you should consider limiting sudo access. You can, of course, choose to allow only standard user accounts on your Mac system. This would limit more than sudo access, but as covered in Chapter 2, "User Accounts," this is the safest general-use account for users.

> **TIP**   All usage of the sudo command is written to the system.log, so you can check in to see if a user is improperly wielding his administrative power. You can view the system.log from the /Applications/Utilities/Console application.

Alternately you can manage the sudo configuration file /etc/sudoers. This file contains the rules by which the sudo command determines allowable actions. As an administrative user you can read this configuration file using the cat or less commands. In the following example, Michelle uses cat to read the sudo configuration file. Note that she must preface the cat command with sudo because the sudoers file is protected by root access. Also, the output of the less command has been truncated to show only the most interesting bits of the sudoers file.

```
MyMac:~ michelle$ sudo cat /etc/suders
Password:
# sudoers file.
#
# This file MUST be edited with the 'visudo' command as root.
# Failure to use 'visudo' may result in syntax or file permission errors
# that prevent sudo from running.
#
# See the sudoers man page for the details on how to write a sudoers file.
#
...
# User privilege specification
root          ALL=(ALL) ALL
%admin        ALL=(ALL) ALL
...
```

As you can see from the "User privilege specification" section of this file, the root user or anyone in the admin group is allowed unrestricted sudo access to all commands. You can edit this file, but note that the document states you must use a special version of the vi command known as visudo. Using vi to edit text files is covered earlier in this chapter.

Once you are familiar with vi usage, editing the sudoers file with visudo is quite easy. To disable administrative user sudo access, simply add a hash mark (#) to the beginning of the %admin line, and the sudo command will ignore that line. You can add additional users or groups for sudo access by duplicating the existing user privilege lines with alternate account names. Just remember to use only the account's "short" name and to use the percent symbol (%) to specify any group names.

Command-Line Tips and Tricks

Here are a few command-line tips that will help you customize your experience and save a lot of time typing:

▶ The single best command-line tip is to always use tab completion when entering file paths. Tab completion was covered previously in this chapter.

▶ Drag and drop files and folders from the Finder to the Terminal window to automatically enter their locations at the command line.

▶ Use open . at the prompt to open your current command-line location in the Finder.

▶ Thoroughly explore the Terminal's preferences (Terminal > Preferences from the menu bar) to customize the look and feel of your command line.

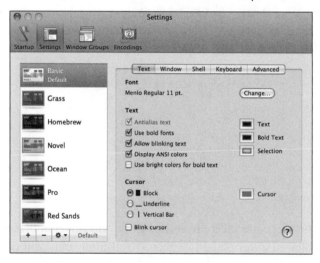

▶ To cancel a command gone awry or clear your current command entry, use the Control-c keyboard combination.

▶ You can edit commands before submitting them. The left and right arrows and the Delete key work as you would expect, but the mouse will not.

▶ At the command prompt, use the Up Arrow and Down Arrow keys to travel through and reuse your command history. This also includes the ability to edit old commands before rerunning them. You can also simply enter the history command to see your recent command history.

▶ To clear the Terminal screen enter the clear command or use the Control-l (lowercase L, not a numeral) keyboard combination.

▶ To move the cursor to the beginning of the current line use the Control-a keyboard combination.

▶ To move the cursor to the end of the current line use the Control-e keyboard combination.

▶ To move the cursor forward one word use the Esc-f keyboard combination.

▶ To move the cursor back one word of the line use the Esc-b keyboard combination.

Using Automator and AppleScript

Mac OS X includes two primary technologies for automating tasks in the graphical interface: Automator and AppleScript. The Automator application, located in the /Applications folder, allows you to easily build workflows from actions in order to automate repetitive tasks. The Automator technology is actually based on AppleScript, which is an older technology. AppleScript is a very powerful English-like application scripting language, but like any computer programming language, it does have a learning curve.

Mastering Automator and AppleScript techniques is well beyond the scope of this guide. The goal here is to help you understand what these automation tools are capable of accomplishing and to provide you with enough information to get started working on your own automated solutions. As is common with many development technologies, there is a huge library of existing Automator and AppleScript examples that you can pull from. Often learning from these examples is the quickest way to accomplish your automation goals.

Mac OS X Automation Results

Perhaps the best way to start learning about Automator and AppleScript is to examine how a user would ultimately take advantage of the automation tools you created. Mac OS X provides a variety of methods for accessing or initiating automated solutions.

With Automator or AppleScript you can create:

▶ Applications—These items are accessed just like a normal application in that the user can open them from the Finder or Dock.

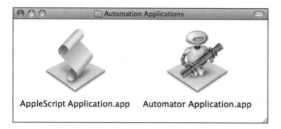

▶ Items for the Scripts menu—Automation items can be quickly opened from the Script menu extra, which can be enabled from the /Applications/Utilities/AppleScript Editor application preferences. This menu is populated from the contents of the /Library/ Scripts and ~/Library/Scripts folders. The Scripts menu allows quick access to open Automator workflow files, AppleScript files, and automated applications.

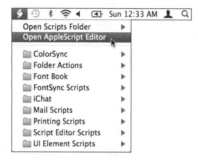

▶ Applets—These items are similar to applications except that instead of the user double-clicking on the icon, the user drags and drops files or folders on top of the applet icon in the Finder or Dock. The automation will act upon the dropped items and when complete the applet will simply quit.

▶ Finder Folder Actions—These are attached to folders that are being watched by the Finder for new content. If something appears in a folder configured with a Folder Action, the system will automatically send those items to an applet for processing. You can configure Folder Actions from the Finder by right-clicking on a folder and from the pop-up menu choosing Folder Actions Setup. This will open the /System/Library/ CoreServices/Folder Actions Setup application, where you can associate an automation with a folder to be watched.

- ▶ Plug-ins—These are items that are designed to accept input from a specific application. Automator has templates for creating printer dialog and Image Capture scanner plug-ins, though plug-ins for other applications are possible, if supported by the application.

- ▶ Services—The services technology allows you to access features of one application from within another application. Within the context of automation, you can create automation services that can be accessed from within the menus of supported applications. Using Services is detailed in the "Combining Automation Techniques" section of this chapter.

Getting Started with Automator

With Automator, even novice computer users can take advantage of AppleScript's powerful automation features without having to know how to write code. Automator accomplishes its work through Automator actions, which each present a small graphical interface that allows you to perform a very specific automated task in a specific application. You can use these actions as building blocks, combining multiple Automator actions into an ordered list to build an Automator workflow that can be used to perform a repetitive task.

Automator.app

To get started with Automator, simply open the application and a new workflow project will open. You can choose to start with a template or simply choose "Workflow" to start with a blank template. To the left you will see the actions library, which lists all available actions.

Selecting an action will display its function at the bottom of the library list. Automator is an extensible technology that allows anyone to develop additional actions. Additional actions can be located in /Library/Actions/, ~/Library/Actions, or even inside an application.

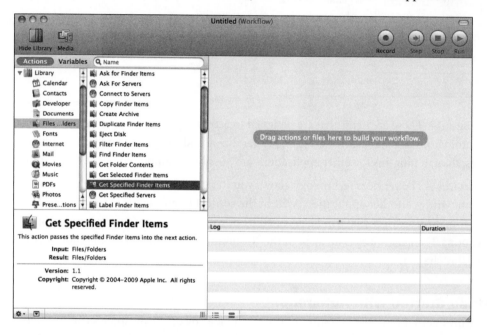

On the right side of the Automator window is the workflow area where you drag your actions to create a workflow. Once the action is in the workflow area you can modify the action details to meet your needs. In many cases the order of the Automator actions in a workflow matters, not only because it defines the order in which actions take place, but also because adjacent actions can communicate to one another though inputs and outputs. For example, an Automator action for the Finder can mount a disk image volume, but first it requires input from another action that identifies the specific disk image to mount. The first action selects the disk image file and outputs that information so the action that mounts the disk image knows which image to mount. The following figure shows a simple example of an Automator workflow. Notice the input-output connection between the two actions.

TIP ▶ You can also use the Automator record feature, initiated with the Record button in the toolbar, to automatically create workflows based on your interaction with the computer.

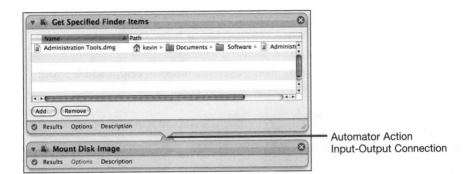

Automator Action
Input-Output Connection

Creating a reliable automation solution often involves testing your work. You can run an Automator workflow using the Step, Stop, and Run buttons to the right in the toolbar. Workflow progress, both positive and negative, will be reported in the Log area of the Automator window. Once you get a workable solution you can save it as a workflow for archiving or later editing. Alternately, if you want the workflow to run without the aid of the Automator application, you can save your workflow as a standalone application or one of the template formats selected when Automator was opened.

> **MORE INFO** ▶ Automator has excellent built-in help, accessed from the Help menu, that includes both documentation and examples. Also, you can find additional Automator actions and example workflows on www.macosxautomation.com and http://macscripter.net.

Getting Started with AppleScript

AppleScript not only provides the foundation for Automator, it can also be used by itself to automate tasks among different applications. AppleScript is an English-like scripting language that was originally created for the classic Mac OS. The primary interface for creating and editing AppleScript scripts is the /Applications/Utilities/AppleScript Editor application.

AppleScript Editor.app

You could certainly start by opening the AppleScript Editor from the Finder, but that will open a blank document. You'll be much better served by browsing through the various /Library/Scripts folders and finding an interesting or related script to start with, and then modifying it to fit your needs. The following example shows a script included with Mac OS X that converts a PostScript file to PDF.

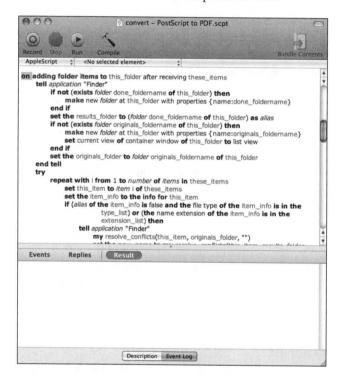

As AppleScript is a full scripting language there is a learning curve to begin working with it. Again, a good place to start is the Help menu inside the AppleScript Editor, which provides extensive general AppleScript documentation. Another local resource is the AppleScript dictionary browser, accessed by selecting File > Open Dictionary from the menu bar. This will open a list of AppleScript dictionaries. Most applications that support AppleScript have a dictionary file that explains the various terms you can use to control the application. Selecting the dictionary for a specific application will open the dictionary browser, allowing you to search through the AppleScript terms used by the application.

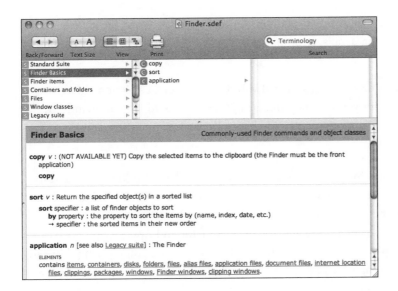

TIP You can also use the AppleScript Editor record feature, initiated with the Record button in the toolbar, to automatically create scripts based on your interaction with the computer.

Again, creating a reliable automation solution often involves testing your work. You can run a script using the Stop and Run buttons in the toolbar. Script progress, both positive and negative, will be reported in the Event Log area of the bottom of the AppleScript Editor window. Once you get a workable solution you can save it as a script for archival and later editing. Alternately, if you want the script to run without the aid of AppleScript Editor, you can save it as a standalone application.

MORE INFO ▶ AppleScript Editor has excellent built-in help, accessed from the Help menu, that includes both documentation and examples. Also, you can find additional AppleScript examples on www.macosxautomation.com/ and http://macscripter.net.

Basic Command-Line Scripting

If you can enter a command in the Terminal then you can script it. The same "language" you use for interacting with the command line is also used for command-line, or more appropriately, shell scripting. After all, the interactive command line is being managed by a shell process; this same shell process can interpret commands in a text file as well. Thus, aside from a few formatting details, a command line script is basically a text file containing a list of commands.

As simple as command-line scripting seems, if you read the previous section about Automator and AppleScript you may be wondering why you would use command-line scripting over the graphical automation technologies. As it turns out, there are several reasons why you would do this:

▶ System administration focus—As you become more familiar with Mac OS X and its various command-line tools, you'll find that many graphical administration tools are based on their command-line equivalents. Likewise, you'll note that most administration tasks are supported poorly, if at all, by Automator and AppleScript. Whereas Automator and AppleScript are primarily used for automating graphical applications, command-line scripting is primarily used for automating system administration tasks.

▶ System administrator (root) access—Most graphical automation runs as a normal user; therefore it cannot modify system resources. On the other hand, it's trivial to run a command-line script with root access. The most common method is to simply precede your script with the sudo command.

▶ No user interface—When graphical applications are controlled by automation, they still "show their work" to the display. This is not the case with command-line scripts, as they essentially run "behind" the user interface.

▶ Higher performance—If you only need to get work done, updating a graphical interface introduces overhead. Tasks that require a high level of repetition are almost always faster at the command line because there is usually less overhead.

▶ More development options—Command-line scripting isn't limited to just what's available in the Terminal shell. In addition to shell scripts, you can create scripts using a wide variety of development languages. For example, Mac OS X also includes built-in support for Perl, Python, PHP, Tcl, and Ruby, to name a few.

Again, mastering command-line scripting techniques is well beyond the scope of this guide. The goal here is to help you understand how to take advantage of command-line scripts and to provide you with enough information to get started working on your own scripts. As is common with many development technologies, there is a huge library of existing script examples that you can pull from. Often learning from these examples is the quickest way to accomplish your command-line scripting goals.

Command-Line "Helpers"

Before you begin command-line scripting proper, there are a few special characters and commands that help facilitate automation at the command line. Examples include grep, | (pipe), and > (redirect).

grep

This command, short for Global Regular Expression Print, searches for patterns (using regular expressions) in text and outputs only the lines that match. This is not only useful for filtering out specific information in an existing large file; it's also useful to filter the output of other commands, as you'll see in the description of pipe later in this section. To filter through an existing file enter grep, followed by the search expression, and then the path to the file.

> **MORE INFO** ▶ The grep command uses regular expressions as filter criteria, which are similar to the wildcard characters covered previously in this chapter. You can find out more about regular expressions by entering man re_format at the command line.

In the following example Michelle uses grep to filter for the phrase "afp" in the /etc/services file. This file lists all the common network ports and services, but it's over 14,000 lines long. The grep command finds the two requested lines almost instantly, which is obviously much faster than a human could.

```
MyMac:~ michelle$ grep "afp" /etc/services
afpovertcp        548/udp      # AFP over TCP
afpovertcp        548/tcp      # AFP over TCP
```

| (pipe)

The special character "|", entered via Shift-Backslash on U.S. keyboards, is called a pipe. As its name implies, it pipes the output of one command to the input of another command. This is can be used to great effect when combining command features. For example the system_profiler command is equivalent to the System Profiler application, but instead it defaults to outputting the information as plain text to the Terminal window. This makes it extremely inconvenient to read the output from this command, much less find exactly what you're looking for.

One solution would be to pipe the output of `system_profiler` to the text reader `less` so you can scroll through the information. You would do this by entering `system_profiler | less`. Another solution would be to use the `grep` command to filter the `system_profiler` output for just the specific information you're looking for. In the following example Michelle does just that using `grep` to filter the output of `system_profiler` for the system version.

```
MyMac:~ michelle$ system_profiler | grep "System Version"
      System Version: Mac OS X 10.6 (10A432)
```

TIP ▶ You can use multiple pipes in one command string to move output from one command to another, in a sense creating a command-line workflow.

> and >>

The special character ">" is commonly known as greater than but is also sometimes called a redirect. At the command line this character can take the output of a command and redirect it to a text file. If the file doesn't exist, the redirect will create a new one. If the file does exist, the redirect will replace it. Using two greater-than characters, ">>", will append to an existing file.

The syntax for redirect is simply the command, followed by a redirect, and then a path to a file. Again, using system_profiler as an example, you can use the redirect character to save the output of system_profiler to a text file. In the following example Michelle creates a system profiler report on her desktop.

```
MyMac:~ michelle$ system_profiler > Desktop/SystemReport.txt
```

Basic Script Construction

Again, a command-line script is nothing more than a text file containing the appropriate syntax. You can use any plain text editor you choose to create your scripts including TextEdit, vi, or nano. However, all text editors are not created equal. Some text editors are "script friendly" in that they have special features that help you develop scripts. A common scripting feature is to color-code different words based on their meaning in the script. The main Xcode application, included with the optional Xcode developer tools installation from the Mac OS X Install DVD, has many features that help with scripting.

NOTE ▶ Command-line scripts must be in plain text format, not RTF or any other formatted text file.

As for the script's name, you could technically choose any name that you like without using any file type name extension. After all, most commands are just the name of the command; there is no file type needed. However, a better approach would be to append the ".sh" file type extension, short for "shell script," to the name of your command. If you were going to use an alternate scripting language, the file type extension would represent that.

On Mac OS X, you also have the option of using the ".command" file type extension. With this extension, when a user double-clicks on your script from the Finder it will automatically open and run in the Terminal. Thus a user can easily run your script without having to know anything about how to start something at the command line.

MORE INFO ▶ An excellent third-party (freeware) application for scripting is TextWrangler by BareBones software, www.barebones.com.

Script Content

Once you have decided on a text editor and started a new appropriately named text file, it's time to create a script. A basic command-line script contains only a few items:

▶ #!/bin/bash—This is the very first line of your script, and it essentially tells the command that this text file is a script. More specifically, it tells the command line to use the bash shell command to interpret the text file and execute its instructions. If the script uses another scripting language the first line needs to indicate that language.

▶ Comments—Any line beginning with a hash mark, "#", will be ignored in most scripting languages. This is the space for you to leave comments in your script. Comments help you and others understand the script's content without having to read the full script. You should make it a habit to leave comments in your scripts so when you return to the script months later, you don't have to remember what you were thinking when you wrote some particularly obtuse scripting code.

▶ Commands—This is the meat of your script. In a bash shell script, you simply type in the commands as you would at the command line. A "return" in the text file acts the same as a "return" at the command line, so enter each command on a separate line. The order of the commands in your script determines the order in which they run.

NOTE ▶ To keep your script files portable, always use absolute paths in scripts.

NOTE ▶ While bash shell scripts can interpret script commands similar to the interactive command line, other scripting languages use different commands and syntax.

Here is an example script that uses a few new commands. The pbpaste and pbcopy commands are used to access the Clipboard contents. The Clipboard is the temporary space used to save whatever you copy from an application. The sort command is used to sort lists of items. This command will take the contents of the Clipboard, sort them alphabetically, and then place the results back in the clipboard. As you can see pipes were used to move the data from one command to another.

```
#!/bin/bash

# Sorts the Clipboard contents, providing the content is a text list.

pbpaste | sort | pbcopy
```

Script Feedback

Implementing feedback into your script helps you identify what parts of your script are executing and when. Two commands that can help provide feedback in your script are echo and date.

The echo command simply repeats what you just entered at the command line. While this may seem trivial when working in the Terminal, this is extremely useful for providing feedback from a command script. For example, placing the line echo "Operation complete." at the end of your script will display the quoted text in the Terminal when your script is complete.

This command can also be combined with a double redirect as an easy way for your script to keep a log file. For example, placing the line echo "Operation complete" >> scriptlog.txt will append the quoted text to the scriptlog.txt file whenever your script reaches that point. By adding the date command with a double redirect, your script's log file will also include the date and time. In this case you would simply include date >> scriptlog.txt in your script.

Using Variables

There are many special characters and syntax options for adding logic to your script. After all, if your script can make decisions and dynamically react to changes, it can do more for you. The most common form of scripting logic is the use of variables. A variable is simply a stand-in value for a potentially dynamic item. For example, say your script uses a specific absolute path multiple times. Instead of typing that path in multiple times, you can set that path as a variable and use the variable's name in its place. Thus, if the path needs to change, you only have to change it once where the variable is set.

The syntax for defining a variable is `variablename="variable value"`. Any time you wish to use the value of the variable in your script simply use `"$variablename"`. The following is an extremely rudimentary example script that shows a variable being used with the `echo` command. The variable name is extremely long in this example; many variable names are much shorter to save on typing. It's not uncommon to see variables named with single letters of the alphabet. This script will simply output "Hello world!" to the Terminal.

```
#!/bin/bash

# Test for echo.

myfirstvariable="Hello world!"

echo "$myfirstvariable"
```

Variables can also be used to implement arguments in your script. Remember, arguments are what you enter after a command as the items for the command to act upon. Your script can also accept arguments in the form of numbered variables. The `"$0"` variable is always the command name (or path to the script) used to invoke the script. Every variable after that is an argument entered after your script's name at the command line, `"$1"`, `"$2"`, `"$3"`, and so on. The following script is designed to accept two arguments and then repeat those arguments back to the Terminal. Thus, to use the script you would enter `scriptname argument1 argument2`.

```
#!/bin/bash

# Test for echo, part two.

echo "$1"

echo "$2"
```

Finally, you can use the output of other commands as variables. The syntax is simply `$(command string)`. This will tell the script to run the command inside the parenthesis first and then place the results where the variable lies. In this last example, the `echo` command is again used to output text to the Terminal. However, this time the text is dynamically generated by the `hostname` command, which returns the computer's DNS hostname, and the `date` command, which again returns the date and time.

```
#!/bin/bash

# Test for echo, the third.

echo "This computer is named: $(hostname)"

echo "Today's date is: $(date)"
```

Running Command-Line Scripts

Once you have completed and saved your text file script, you must first set the script as executable before the command line will allow you to run it. You will use the chmod command to change the script's file system permissions, thus making the script executable. In the following example, Michelle will use chmod +x to make the script named "myscript. command" executable for all users.

```
MyMac:Desktop michelle$ chmod +x myscript.command
```

MORE INFO ▶ A full discussion of file system permissions can be found in Chapter 4, "File Systems."

Once your script has been set to be executable, you can run it by entering an absolute path to your script, or if the script is in the same folder that you are working on at the command line, you will have to enter ./ then the script's filename. This may seem inconvenient, but it is a UNIX security convention to prevent nefarious code from executing. Alternately, you could place your script in the /usr/local/bin folder, which will place the script in one of the default path folders. Items in these folders need only be called by their filename to run at the command line.

Combining Automation Techniques

While the graphical interface and command line automation tools are fundamentally separate, they can be combined to form hybrid automation solutions. This section will introduce you to the basic techniques for integrating these seemingly disparate automation technologies. This section will also introduce a final automation technology, services, which allows you to add custom automated tasks to menu options inside existing applications.

Integrating Automator

As covered previously in this chapter, Automator workflows are built from actions. Thus, you must use actions to integrate with other automation technologies. First, the Run AppleScript action can be used to run AppleScript code. Simply paste the script contents into the action interface in your Automator workflow.

Next, the Run Shell Script action can be used to execute command-line scripts from many different languages including bash, perl, python, ruby, and several variants of the shell environment. In the action interface you can paste the script contents, or enter a path to an executable script, or simply enter a single command string.

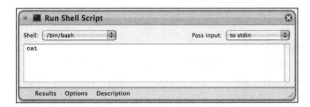

Integrating AppleScript

As covered previously in this chapter, AppleScript text scripts are built using the AppleScript language. Thus, you must use AppleScript syntax within your script to integrate with other automation technologies. With Automator being based on AppleScript, there is a full dictionary of AppleScript terms that can reference Automator actions or workflows. Again, you can access AppleScript dictionaries by selecting File > Open Dictionary while in the AppleScript Editor application. Then select Automator from the dictionary listing.

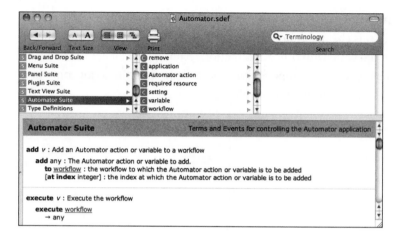

To run a command-line script or command from an AppleScript script, simply enter do shell script followed by a path to your command-line script surrounded by quotes. You cannot simply paste the script contents, or reliably enter a command string, into the AppleScript script because AppleScript can mistake quotes in the middle of the command for the end of the command string. This problem can be avoided by escaping quotes inside the command with the \ character, for example: do shell script "echo \"Hello world!\"". However, this means you will have to deviate from standard bash shell scripting, which doesn't have this requirement.

Integrating Command-Line Scripts

As covered previously in this chapter, command-line scripts are built using a scripting language and commands. Thus, you must use command-line syntax within your script to integrate with other automation technologies. First, anything you can double-click on in the Finder can be executed by the command line using the open command. Simply enter open followed by the path to the item you wish to open in the graphical interface. This includes Automator workflows or AppleScript scripts that have been saved as applications.

You can also use the osascript command (followed by a path to the script) to run AppleScript scripts in their text format. The distinction is that the open command would act similar to double-clicking on the script file from the Finder, which would open the script in AppleScript Editor instead of running the script. In addition, it's possible to specify AppleScript commands directly in a command-line script using the -e option. For example, osascript -e "tell application \"Finder\" to activate".

NOTE ▸ Similar to using AppleScript's do shell script command, controlling which quotes are interpreted by the shell and which by AppleScript can be complex. In the example the quotes preceded by \ are ignored by the shell and interpreted by AppleScript.

Using Custom Services

Essentially, services allow you to access the features of one application from within the menus of another application. The Services menu items can be accessed from the application (name) menu or by right-clicking on a selected item from an application. The Services menu is automatic and dynamic, as it will automatically find new services as they are added to your computer and it will show only services that can be applied to the currently selected item. The following screen shot shows the Services menu from the Finder when an image file is selected.

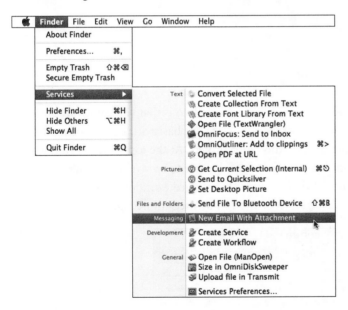

NOTE ▸ This screen shot of the Service menu shows built-in and third-party services.

Services have been around for a while in Mac OS X, but they received a substantial upgrade in Mac OS X v10.6. First the Services menu has been redesigned to more clearly show which applications are offering services. Also individual services can now be manually enabled or disabled, and more importantly can have custom keyboard combinations set for their activation. These new service settings can be found under the Keyboard Shortcuts tab of the Keyboard preferences.

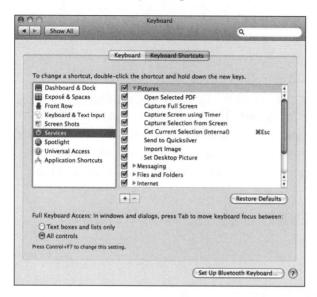

However, the biggest news about services in Mac OS X v10.6 is that you can easily create new custom services using an Automator workflow as your basis. Start by choosing the Service template when you open a new Automator project. At the top of the workflow you define the type of selected item that the service will be able to receive. From there you create your custom service workflow. When you save the service workflow, it will automatically be added to the list of available services and can be used immediately.

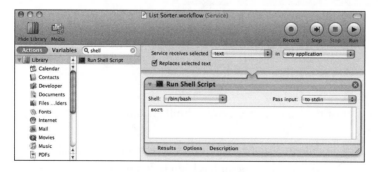

This figure shows a useful custom service that took almost 30 seconds to create. The service will accept the selected text from any application, then sort each line of the text alphabetically, and then replace the text. As it turns out there is no "sort" Automator action for selected text, but there is a sort command. Thus, the Run Shell Script action was added and needed only the name of the command entered in the shell script field. The result is that the core functionally of the sort command has been integrated into any graphical application that can select and replace text.

> **MORE INFO** ▶ Additional service examples and documentation are also well represented at www.macosxautomation.com.

What You've Learned

▶   The command line is a valid method for working on the Mac because it's the only method to accomplish certain administrative tasks efficiently.

▶   You can use the ls, pwd, and cd commands to navigate the file system at the command-line interface.

▶   You have learned fundamental command-line techniques and shortcuts to save time and avoid mistakes, like using tab completion to automatically enter path names.

▶   Administrative users can act as system administrator (root) at the command line using the sudo command.

▶   Automator and AppleScript can be used to automate tasks in graphical applications, while command-line scripting can be used to automate system administration tasks.

▶   All three automation techniques, Automator, AppleScript, and command-line scripts, can be combined to automate nearly any task.

References

You can check for new and updated Knowledge Base documents at www.apple.com/support.

URLs

Apple Remote Desktop network client management software: www.apple.com/remotedesktop

Mac OS X automation resources: www.macosxautomation.com

Mac OS X automation resources: http//macscripter.net

Apple's AppleScript developer site: http://developer.apple.com/applescript

TextWrangler by BareBones software: www.barebones.com

The Advanced Bash-Scripting Guide: http://tldp.org/LDP/abs/html

Bash Pitfalls (a list of common mistakes in shell scripting): http://mywiki.wooledge.org/BashPitfalls

Review Quiz

1. What are six reasons for using the command-line environment?

2. What four methods can be used to access the command-line environment?

3. What three items are in the default command-line user prompt?

4. What are the three main components of a typical command?

5. What do the following terms describe: folder, directory, path, absolute path, and relative path?

6. What is the difference between absolute and relative paths?

7. Which command is used to list items in a folder?

8. Which two commands can be used to read text files?

9. What is the sudo command used for?

10. What are the two primary automation technologies for the graphical interface? How do they differ?

11. What are the three minimal steps required for creating a command-line script?

Answers

1. Six reasons for using the command line are: it gives you access options not available in the graphical interface; it lets you bypass Finder restrictions; administrators can act as root at the command line; remote SSH access is invisible to the user; it makes automation easy using scripting; and you can combine the command line with ARD to send administrative commands remotely to multiple Macs at the same time.

2. Four methods that can be used to access the command line are: the Terminal application, ">console" at the login screen, single-user mode startup, and remotely via SSH.

3. The three items in the default command-line user prompt are, from left to right: computer hostname, working directory, and user account.

4. The three main components of a typical command are: the command's name, command options, and command arguments.

5. Folders and directories are both terms used to describe containers in the file system. A path defines directions to a specific item in the file system. Absolute paths are full directions to a specific item, whereas relative paths are partial directions to a specific item based on the user's current working location.

6. Absolute paths always start from the root, or beginning, of the file system, whereas relative paths start from the user's current working location. The default working location of users is at the root of their home folder.

7. The ls command is used to list items in a folder.

8. Two commands used to read text files are cat and less.

9. The sudo command is used to allow administrators to run commands with root privileges.

10. Automator is an easy-to-use application that can create workflows based on predefined actions. AppleScript is an English-like scripting language that allows you to script graphical applications.

11. Three minimal steps required for creating a command-line script are: create a plain text file containing a list of commands, make the first line "#!/bin/bash", and change the file's permissions to allow execution.

4

Time This chapter takes approximately 2 hours to complete.

Goals Recognize the various file systems supported by Mac OS X

Manage and troubleshoot file systems using a variety of tools

Understand and manage file ownership and permissions

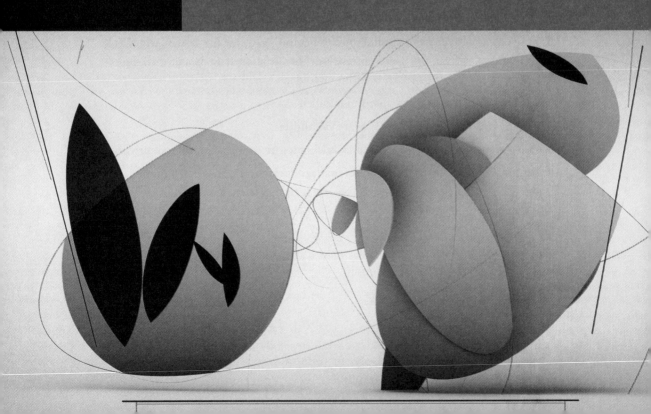

Chapter 4
File Systems

Although personal computer processor speed has increased around one-thousandfold since the first Mac was introduced in 1984, storage capacity has easily increased a million times over. Compare 1984's 400 KB floppy to today's average desktop drive at 500 GB, which is roughly equivalent to 524,288,000 KB, or 1.4 million 400 KB floppies. Users have responded by moving thousands of pictures and hundreds of hours of music and video, historically stored in analog form, to the convenience and dynamism of digital storage. Likewise, enterprise customers have replaced filing cabinets and storage rooms with Redundant Array of Independent Disks (RAID) arrays and backup tapes. Even though the Internet recently changed our perception of what a computer is used for, it's clear that the computer's primary task is still that of a tool to organize, access, and store our stuff.

In this chapter, you will examine the storage technology used by Mac OS X. Storage hardware like disk drives and RAID will be covered alongside logical storage concepts like partitions and volumes. Naturally, you will learn how to properly manage and troubleshoot these storage assets as well. Finally, you will also learn to manage storage security through ownership, permissions, and access control lists (ACLs).

File System Components

Before you begin managing storage on Mac OS X, it is important to understand the distinction between storage, partitions, and volumes. Traditionally, computer storage has been defined by disk drive hardware. After all these years, disk drive hardware still maintains the storage lead, as it has moved from removable floppy disks to enclosed hard disks. However, other more convenient removable formats have become extremely popular as they have increased in capacity. This includes optical media like CDs and DVDs and solid-state storage like SSD, USB key drives, and CompactFlash cards. All are equally viable storage destinations for Mac OS X.

Without proper formatting, though, any storage technology is nothing more than a big empty bucket of ones and zeros, and consequently not very useful to the Mac. Formatting is the process of applying logic to storage in the form of partitions and volumes. Partitions are used to define boundaries on a storage device. You can define multiple partitions if you want the physical storage to appear as multiple separate storage destinations. Even if you want to use the entire space available on a device as a single contiguous storage location, the area must still be defined by a partition.

Once partitions have been established, the system can create usable volumes inside the partition areas. Volumes define how the files and folders are actually stored on the hardware. In fact, it's the volume that is ultimately mounted by the file system and then represented as a usable storage icon in the Finder. Obviously, a storage device with several partitions, each containing a separate volume, will appear as several storage location icons in the Finder.

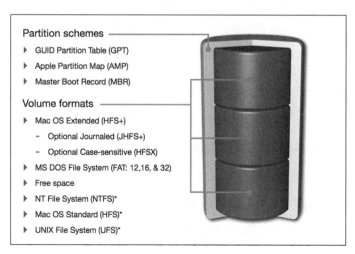

Partition schemes

▶ GUID Partition Table (GPT)

▶ Apple Partition Map (AMP)

▶ Master Boot Record (MBR)

Volume formats

▶ Mac OS Extended (HFS+)

  – Optional Journaled (JHFS+)

  – Optional Case-sensitive (HFSX)

▶ MS DOS File System (FAT: 12,16, & 32)

▶ Free space

▶ NT File System (NTFS)*

▶ Mac OS Standard (HFS)*

▶ UNIX File System (UFS)*

Partition Schemes

As mentioned earlier, drives must be partitioned in order to define and possibly segregate the drive's usable space. Every disk requires at least one partition, but Mac OS X can support up to 16 partitions per disk. You learned the advantages and disadvantages of using single or multiple partitions in Chapter 1, "Installation and Initial Setup."

Mac OS X supports three different types of partition schemes. This may seem excessive, but it's necessary for Macs to support multiple partition schemes in order to boot computers using modern Intel processors, support older Mac drives, and use standard PC-compatible volumes.

The three partition schemes supported by Mac OS X are:

▶   GUID Partition Table (GPT)—This is the default partition scheme used by Intel-based Macs. This is also the only partition scheme supported for Intel-based Macs to start up using disk-based storage. However, PowerPC-based Macs running Mac OS X version 10.4.6 or later can also access this type of partitioning, but they will not be able to boot from it.

▶   Apple Partition Map (APM)—This is the default partition scheme used by older PowerPC-based Macs. This is also the only partition scheme that PowerPC-based Macs can start up from. However, all Intel-based Macs can also access this type of partitioning.

▶   Master Boot Record (MBR)—This is the default partition scheme used by most non-Mac computers, including Windows-compatible PCs. Consequently, this is the default partition scheme you will find on most new preformatted storage drives. This partition scheme is also commonly used by peripherals that store to flash drives such as digital cameras or smart phones. Even though no Mac can boot from this type of partitioning, all Macs can access MBR partitioning.

Obviously, if you have any additional drives formatted with APM or MBR, you will have to repartition those drives in order for them to be bootable on an Intel-based Mac. But if you don't plan on ever using the additional drives as a system disk, there is no advantage to repartitioning. Also, you should keep MBR drives unmodified if you intend to keep those drives backward-compatible with generic PCs or peripherals.

TIP   Intel-based Macs can start up from both USB and FireWire external drives.

Volume Formats

The volume format defines how the files and folders are saved to the drive. To maintain compatibility with other operating systems and provide advanced features for newer Mac systems, Mac OS X supports a variety of storage volume formats.

Volume formats supported as startup volumes for Mac OS X:

▶   Mac OS Extended (Hierarchical File System Plus, HFS+)—Mac OS Extended, also known as HFS+, is the legacy volume format designed and supported by Apple for Macintosh computers. HFS+ itself is an update from the earlier Mac OS Standard (HFS) format. HFS+ supports all the advanced features required by Mac OS X, including Unicode filenames, rich metadata, POSIX Permissions, access control lists (ACLs), UNIX-style links, and aliases.

▶   Mac OS Extended, Case-Sensitive (HFSX)—This Mac OS Extended format adds case sensitivity to the file system. Normally Mac OS Extended is case-preserving but case-insensitive. This means that a normally formatted Mac volume will remember what case you chose for the characters of a file's name, but it cannot differentiate between similar filenames where the only difference is the case. In other words, it would not recognize "MYfile" and "myfile" as different filenames. By adding support for case sensitivity, Apple resolved this issue. However, this is generally an issue only for volumes that need to support traditional UNIX clients, like those shared from Macs or Xserves running Mac OS X Server.

▶   Mac OS Extended, Journaled (JHFS+) or Mac OS Extended, Case-Sensitive, Journaled (JHFSX)—This feature, enabled by default on Mac OS X, is an option for the Mac OS Extended format that adds advanced file system journaling to help preserve volume structure integrity. The journal records what file operations (creation, expansion, deletion, and so on) are in progress at any given moment. If the system crashes or loses power, the journal can be "replayed" to make sure operations in progress are completed, rather than being left in a half-completed, inconsistent state. This avoids both the possibility of volume corruption and the need to run a lengthy check-and-repair process on the volume after a crash.

NOTE ▶ While journaling protects the file structure, it cannot protect the contents of files themselves against corruption. If a large file was half-written when the system crashed, the journal will make sure that half-file is consistently entered in the volume's file-tracking databases, but it's still only half a file.

Volume formats supported as read/write in Mac OS X:

▶ Mac OS Standard (HFS)—This is the legacy volume format used by the classic Mac OS. This format, though a precursor to HFS+, is not supported as a startup volume for Mac OS X.

▶ File Allocation Table (FAT)—FAT is the legacy volume format used by Windows PCs and still used by many peripherals. This format has evolved over the years, with each progressive version supporting larger volumes; FAT12, FAT16, FAT32. Apple's Boot Camp supports running Windows from a FAT32 volume, but Mac OS X itself cannot start up from such a volume. Boot Camp is covered in Chapter 6, "Applications and Boot Camp."

▶ UNIX File System (UFS)—UFS is the legacy native volume format supported by Mac OS X. UFS served as the default UNIX file system for decades. Starting with Mac OS X v10.5, though, UFS volumes are no longer supported as startup volumes. Further, Disk Utility does not support the creation of UFS volumes.

Volume formats supported as read-only in Mac OS X:

▶ NT File System (NTFS)—Windows 7, Windows Vista, Windows XP, and Windows Server all use this as their native volume format. Once again Boot Camp supports running Windows from an NTFS volume, but Mac OS X itself cannot write to or start up from such a volume. Further, Disk Utility does not support the creation of NTFS volumes.

> **TIP** ▶ You can add NTFS volume write support to Mac OS X by installing the free and open source NTFS-3G and MacFUSE software bundle: http://macntfs-3g. blogspot.com.

▶ ISO 9660 or Compact Disk File System (CDFS)—This is a common standard for read-only CD media. Note, however, that "Mac formatted" CD media can contain HFS-formatted volumes.

▶ Universal Disk Format (UDF)—This is a common standard for read-only DVD media. Again, note that "Mac formatted" DVD media can contain HFS-formatted volumes.

> **MORE INFO** ▶ A wide variety of file systems are out there. Wikipedia has a great comparison of all file systems: http://en.wikipedia.org/wiki/Comparison_of_file_systems.

File System Management

The internal disk drive originally included with your Mac is probably the only new storage device you will ever come across that is already properly formatted for full Mac compatibility. Most new storage devices are either completely blank or formatted for Windows. For the most part, you will still be able to use Windows-formatted drives on the Mac without reformatting. Conversely, if you want to install the Mac operating system on a drive or you have a new drive that is completely blank, you will have to reformat the drive.

The primary storage management tool included with Mac OS X is /Applications/Utilities/ Disk Utility. You may have already used this utility from the Mac OS X Install DVD to reformat the system drive before you installed the operating system. Here you are going to explore all the aspects of this tool for managing disk and flash drives.

Disk Utility.app

MORE INFO ▶ If you prefer the flexibility of a command-line tool, then you can perform all the same actions of Disk Utility, plus a few more, with the diskutil command. You can also gather disk-capacity information with the df command and disk-utilization information with the du command. As always, you can find out more about these commands by reading their man pages from the command line.

Though disk-based and solid-state drives are technologically different storage mediums, Mac OS X treats the two similarly because they both provide dynamically writable storage. Optical media, on the other hand, is handled differently by the Mac because it's sequentially written storage. Using optical media is covered in the "Using Optical Media" section later in this chapter.

Macintosh HD

FireWire Drive

USB Key

Formatting or Reformatting a Drive

Despite all the choices Mac OS X gives you for configuring storage, actually formatting a drive is quite easy. In fact, if you attach an unformatted device, the Mac will automatically prompt you to open Disk Utility. On the other hand, if you have a drive that is already formatted and you want to change the partition scheme or the volume structure, you can just as easily reformat the drive using the same steps.

It is important to remember that reformatting a drive will destroy any formatting that is already there; essentially, a reformatted drive is losing its contents. The drive will not technically be erased—all the bits are still stored on the device. Reformatting will simply replace the previously populated volume structure with an empty volume structure. Truly erasing the contents of a drive is covered in the "Securely Erasing Files" section later in this chapter.

To format a drive:

1   Make sure the drive you wish to format is currently attached to the computer, and then open /Applications/Utilities/Disk Utility.

2   Select the drive you wish to format from the column on the left.

The size, manufacturer, and model number is usually the name of the drive. If a drive has any volumes, they will appear directly below and indented from the drive entry. If you want to reformat the entire drive, be sure to select the drive, not a volume.

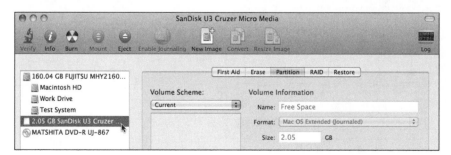

3 Click the Partition tab to the right. This is the only section in Disk Utility that will allow you to change both the partition scheme and the volume format.

4 From the Volume Scheme pop-up menu, choose the number of partitions you want for this drive. You must choose at least one partition.

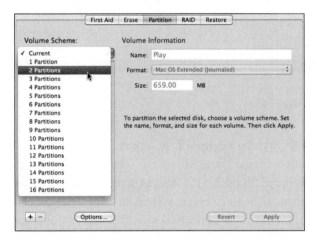

5 Once you have selected the number of partitions you desire, click the Options button at the bottom of the partition diagram to set the partition scheme.

A dialog appears allowing you to select an appropriate partition scheme.

6 Select your partition scheme, and then click the OK button to return.

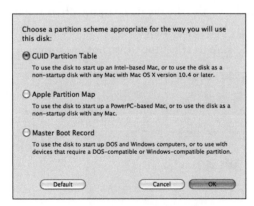

If you have chosen multiple partitions, you can adjust their sizes by clicking and dragging the line between partitions in the partition diagram. You can also specify a precise size by clicking in a partition area and then entering a specific size in the Size entry field to the right.

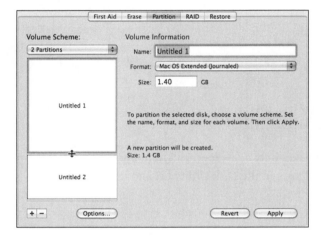

7   Choose a name and volume format for each partition.

If you have only one partition, enter an appropriate name and choose the volume format from the Format pop-up menu. If you have chosen multiple partitions, select each partition from the partition dialog first and then set the name and volume structure.

> **TIP** ▸ You can always change the name of a volume later in the Finder.

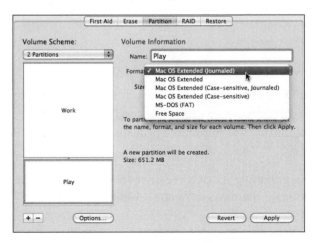

8   Once you have double-checked all your choices, click the Apply button.

You will be presented with a summary dialog, reminding you once again that continuing may destroy any previous volumes. If you are sure this is what you want to do, click the Partition button once more.

Partitioning and formatting takes only a few moments, and once the process is complete, you should see new volumes in the Disk Utility list and in the Finder.

Repartitioning a Drive

The previous system version, Mac OS X v10.5, introduced a new feature in Disk Utility that enables you to dynamically repartition a drive without destroying any currently stored data on the drive. This functionality was introduced primarily to facilitate the Boot Camp setup process.

The only downside to dynamic repartitioning is that some drives may not support the partition changes that you want to make. For instance, some drives may be too full for you to repartition. Also, Disk Utility does not support dynamically repartitioning drives formatted with the Master Boot Record partition scheme. If you come across any of these issues, you can resort to using the old method for repartitioning a drive, which does erase any previous formatting, as outlined in the prior section of this chapter.

NOTE ▶ Always back up important data before making changes to a drive's file system.

To dynamically repartition a drive:

1   Quit all open applications, as they may crash while the file system is being changed and consequently cause data corruption or loss.

2   Make sure the drive you wish to change is currently attached to the computer, and then open /Applications/Utilities/Disk Utility.

3   Select the drive you wish to change from the column on the left.

The size, manufacturer, and model number is usually the name of the drive. Do not select any of the drive's volumes.

4   Click the Partition tab to the right.

Any data currently on the drive will appear as a light blue area in the partition diagram. White areas indicate free space.

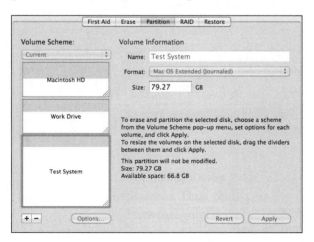

5 Resize any volume, or add new volumes, or delete any volume that isn't the current system drive.

▶ To resize a current volume, click and drag from the bottom-right corner until you reach the desired new size. You will not be allowed to shrink a volume past the light blue that represents data on the drive. You may choose to leave parts of the drive empty if you plan on formatting those parts later using another operating system.

▶ To add a new volume, click the small plus button below the partition diagram. Remember, you can have as many as 16 partitions per drive. Be sure to choose an appropriate name and volume format from the pop-up menu for each new volume.

▶ To delete a volume, select it from the partition diagram and click the minus button below the partition diagram. If you are deleting a preexisting partition, you will be presented with a verification dialog. If you are certain that you want to delete the selected partition, click the Remove button to finish the process. The volume will be deleted immediately, leaving free space where you will be able to resize other volumes or create new volumes.

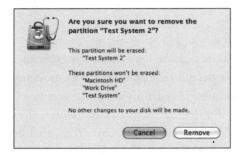

6   Once you have made all your changes and verified your selections, click the Apply button to continue.

7   You will be presented with a summary dialog, listing what changes will be made and which (if any) volumes will be erased. If you are sure this is what you want to do, click the Partition button once more.

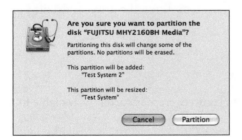

Depending on how much preexisting data must be moved to create your new disk structure, it may take quite a while for the repartitioning process to complete. You should not attempt to interrupt Disk Utility or open any other applications while the system is repartitioning the drive. Doing so may result in catastrophic data loss.

8 Once the process is complete, you should immediately notice the changes in the Disk Utility list and the Finder.

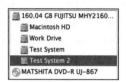

Erasing a Drive or Volume

You have seen earlier in this chapter how Disk Utility can be used to quickly erase an entire drive or volume by reformatting it. Yet the default reformatting process does not actually erase any files from the drive. This is because Disk Utility simply creates new blank volumes by only replacing the file and folder structure data of any volume. The old data files still remain on the drive and can be recovered using third-party recovery tools.

In fact, there is no such thing as erasing data from a drive—all you can do is write new data on top of the old data. Therefore, if you want to truly "erase" a drive or volume, you must somehow write new nonsensitive data on top of it. Disk Utility includes a variety of options that will let you securely erase old data. You can securely erase an entire drive or volume, or just a volume's remaining free space.

NOTE ▶ Erasing or formatting a disk will not change the drive's partition scheme. To change a drive's partition scheme, you must repartition the drive, as detailed previously in this chapter.

To securely erase an entire drive or volume:

1 Make sure the drive or volume you wish to securely erase is currently available to the computer, and then open /Applications/Utilities/Disk Utility.

2 Select the drive or volume you wish to securely erase from the column on the left.

The size, manufacturer, and model number is usually the name of the drive. If a drive has any volumes, they will appear directly below and indented from the drive entry. If you want to reformat the entire drive, be sure to select the drive, not a volume.

3 Click the Erase tab to the right, and then click the Security Options button.

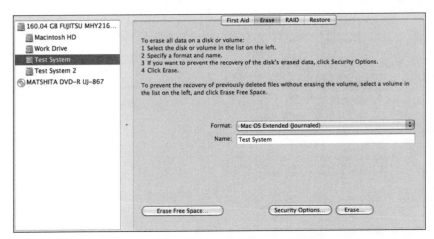

You will be presented with a dialog allowing you to choose one of the four erase options. Select the radio button next to your preferred erase method and click the OK button to continue. The four erase options are:

Don't Erase Data. This is the default action that occurs when you erase or reformat a drive or volume. Obviously, this does not provide any security from drive-recovery utilities. On the other hand, this choice provides a nearly instantaneous erase option.

Zero Out Deleted Files. This option will write zeros over all the data once. This is the quickest of the secure erase options, and for most users provides an adequate level of security.

7-Pass Erase. This is a very secure option that writes seven different passes of random and patterned information to the drive. According to Apple, this option even meets with U.S. Department of Defense standards for securely erasing data. The downside is that this method will take seven times longer than the standard zero-out method.

35-Pass Erase. This is the most secure option, which borders on paranoia. The Mac will write 35 different passes of random and patterned information to the drive. Obviously, this method will take 35 times longer than the standard zero-out method.

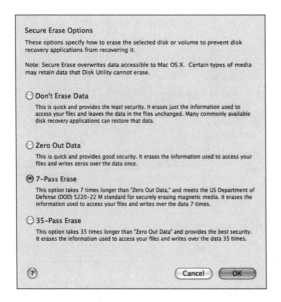

4   At this point you can also change the volume's name or volume format.

5   Double-check all your choices and then click the Erase button.

6   You will be presented with a summary dialog, reminding you once again that you will destroy data on any previous volumes. If you are sure this is what you want to do, click the Erase button once more.

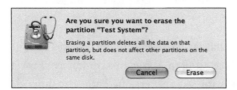

Depending on the size of the selected drive or volume and the erase option you chose, this process can take anywhere from seconds to days. If the process is going to take more than a few seconds, Disk Utility will show a progress indicator with the estimated time required to complete the erase task.

Securely Erasing Files

Because securely erasing an entire drive or volume can take quite a bit of time, you may find it's much quicker to use a more subtle secure erase method. Also, you may not want to erase the entire contents of a volume or disk—you may just want to securely erase a few specific files or only the free space on your drive. Fortunately, Mac OS X provides targeted secure erase options from the Finder and Disk Utility.

Use Finder to Securely Erase Selected Items

To securely erase only select files and folders:

1 In the Finder, move the items you wish to securely erase to the Trash folder.

There are several ways to accomplish this task: You can drag and drop the items into the trash; you can select the items and then choose File > Move to Trash; or you can select the items and use the Command-Delete keyboard shortcut.

2 Choose Finder > Secure Empty Trash from the menu bar.

The Finder's Secure Empty Trash feature is a secure erase method, which writes seven different passes of nonsensical information on top of the erased files. According to Apple, this feature even meets with U.S. Department of Defense standards for securely erasing data.

3 You will be presented with a verification dialog. If you are certain you want to securely erase the items in the Trash forever, click the Secure Empty Trash button to continue.

Depending on the number and size of the files to be erased, this process can take any-where from seconds to days. The Finder will show you a progress indicator, but it will not show an estimated time.

Use Disk Utility to Securely Erase Free Space

If in the past users have neglected to securely erase their files, you can cover their tracks by erasing a volume's free space. To securely erase a volume's remaining free space, including any previously deleted files that were not securely erased:

1   Make sure the volume with the free space you wish to securely erase is available to the system, and then open /Applications/Utilities/Disk Utility.

2   Select the name of the volume with the free space you wish to securely erase from the column on the left. Do not select the drive.

3   Click the Erase tab to the right, and then click the Erase Free Space button.

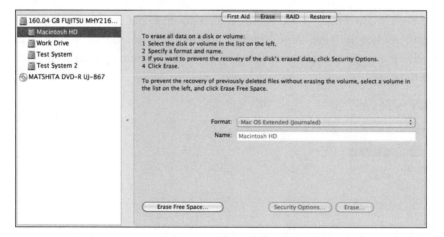

You will be presented with a dialog allowing you to choose one of the three available secure erase options similar to erasing an entire volume or disk: Zero Out Deleted Files, 7-Pass Erase, and 35-Pass Erase.

4 Select the radio button next to your preferred erase method and click the Erase Free
   Space button to continue.

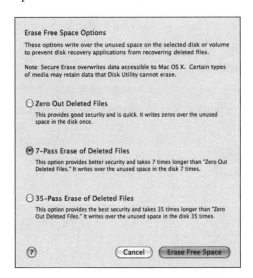

Depending on the amount of free space to erase and the erase option you chose, this
process can take anywhere from seconds to days. If the process is going to take more
than a few seconds, Disk Utility will show a progress indicator with the estimated
time required to complete the erase task.

Mounting, Unmounting, and Ejecting

Mounting a volume is the process by which the system establishes a logical connection to a
storage volume. This is not something users normally concern themselves with on the Mac,
because the system will automatically mount any volume connected to the Mac. Simply plug
a drive in and the drive's volumes will automatically appear in the Finder and Disk Utility.

On the other hand, ensuring users properly unmount and eject volumes is very important to maintaining data integrity. Unmounting is the process of having the Mac cleanly
disconnect from a drive's volumes, whereas ejecting is the process of having the Mac
additionally disconnect electronically from the actual hardware drive or media. When you
choose to eject a drive from the Finder, the computer will actually unmount the volumes
first and then eject the drive.

Ejecting Drives

There are three methods to unmount and eject a drive from the Finder:

▶ Pressing and holding the Eject key, the furthest top-right key on a Mac keyboard, for a few moments will only unmount and eject optical media.

▶ Select the volume you wish to unmount and eject from the Finder's sidebar, and then choose File > Eject from the menu bar.

▶ In the Finder's sidebar, click the small eject button next to the volume you wish to unmount and eject.

TIP If you have more than one optical drive, press Option-Eject to unmount and eject the second optical drive.

When you use the Finder to unmount and eject a single volume that is part of a drive with several mounted volumes, you will be presented with a warning dialog. You will be given the choice to unmount and eject all the volumes on the drive or just the volume you originally selected. You shouldn't experience any problems with a drive by having some volumes mounted while others are unmounted. Just remember to properly unmount the remaining volumes before you disconnect the drive.

TIP ▶ In the Finder you can eject all the volumes of a drive by holding down the Option key while you click the Eject button.

Manage Volume Mounts With Disk Utility

If you need to remount volumes on a connected drive, from the Finder you will have to unmount and eject the remaining volumes on the drive and then physically disconnect and reconnect the drive. Or, you can choose to manually mount, unmount, and eject items using Disk Utility.

To manually mount, unmount, and eject items:

1 Open /Applications/Utilities/Disk Utility.

In this example screenshot, a variety of volumes are shown. Notice the volume names from the second drive appear in dimmed text; those volumes are physically connected to the Mac but not mounted to the file system.

2 Select the volume or drive you wish to unmount or eject from the column on the left.

3 If you have selected a volume to unmount, simply click the Unmount button in the toolbar.

The volume will unmount immediately, disappearing from the Finder, although in Disk Utility the volume's name will remain but appear as dimmed text.

4 To mount an unmounted volume on a connected drive, click on the volume's dimmed name and then click the Mount button in the toolbar.

The volume should immediately mount and appear in the Finder and as normal text in Disk Utility.

5 If you have selected an entire disk to unmount all its volumes and eject, click the Eject button in the toolbar.

All the disk's volumes will be unmounted, and then the disk will be disconnected from the system, disappearing from the Finder and Disk Utility. You will have to physically disconnect and reconnect the drive for its volumes to be remounted.

Ejecting In-Use Volumes

Any volume that contains files currently in use by an application or system process cannot be unmounted or ejected. The obvious reason for this is to avoid data corruption when a process attempts to write to files on that volume. If you attempt to eject a volume with in-use files, the Mac OS X v10.6 Finder will not allow you to eject the volume, but depending on the situation it will try to help you eject the volume. If the application or process using the volume belongs to your account, it will let you know via the following dialog. In this case the resolution is as simple as quitting the suspect application and attempting to eject the volume again.

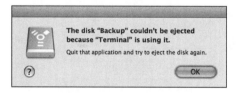

If you don't own the application or process using the volume, the Finder will ask if you want to attempt to forcibly eject the volume. To take this path you will have to click the Force Eject button twice, but the Finder will then try to kill the offending application or process to release the volume you're attempting to eject. If the volume was successfully ejected, you will be notified by the dialog.

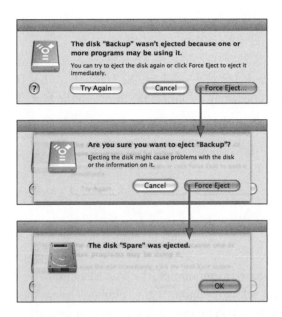

If this doesn't work or the Finder doesn't tell you which application is suspect, you can always log out the current user to quit all their processes and re-log in, or fully restart the Mac to clear the issue. While this may seem excessive, it is not advisable to physically disconnect a volume without first unmounting it, as covered in the next section.

If a volume still refuses to unmount after you've tried the previous troubleshooting steps, or you are unable to restart the computer, you can force a volume to unmount using the diskutil command. Again, it's not advisable to force the system to unmount a volume, but if you need to unmount the volume, this method is better than physically disconnecting the drive from the Mac. The following command-line example shows how to forcibly unmount a volume named "ExternalDrive"; further, using this technique also requires administrator authentication:

```
MyMac:~ michelle$ sudo diskutil unmount force /Volumes/Backup
```

Improperly Unmounting or Ejecting

Disconnecting a volume from the Mac that you did not first unmount can lead to data corruption. If you forcibly eject a drive by physically disconnecting it before you unmount it, or if the system loses contact with the drive due to power failure, the Mac will warn you with a Device Removal dialog. You should immediately reconnect the device so the Mac can attempt to verify or repair its contents.

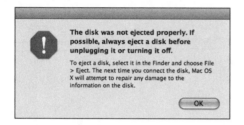

Any time you reconnect a drive that was improperly unmounted, the Mac will automatically run a file system diagnostic on the drive before it remounts any volumes. Depending on the format and size of the drive, it may take anywhere from a few seconds to several hours for the system to verify the contents of the drive. Again, journeyed volumes like JHFS+ should verify quite quickly. So if you connect a drive and notice there is a fair amount of drive activity but the volumes have not mounted yet, the system is probably running a diagnostic on the drive. You can verify that the system is diagnosing a volume by opening the /Applications/Utilities/Activity Monitor application and looking for a background process with fsck in its name. Monitoring processes is covered in Chapter 6, "Applications and Boot Camp."

Using Software RAID

The idea behind RAID (Redundant Array of Independent Disks) is that you can combine similar drives together to form large volumes with increased performance or reliability. The downside is that you have to have special hardware or software to manage the RAID. Hardware-based RAID solutions are often external to the computer because they contain many drives and include specialized hardware to manage the RAID. Conversely, software-based RAID solutions don't require any special hardware as they use software running from the computer's processor to manage the RAID.

MORE INFO ▶ Both Mac Pro and Xserve computers feature optional internal hardware RAID cards. A discussion of these cards is outside the scope of this guide, but you can find out more from the RAID Utility User's Guide available online at http://images.apple.com/xserve/pdf/RAID_Utility_User_Guide.pdf.

Mac OS X includes a software-based RAID solution as part of its file system. The advantage of using the built-in software-based RAID is that no special hardware is required. All you have to do is connect two or more similar drives to the Mac via any compatible hardware interface, and then use Disk Utility to create the RAID set. The main disadvantage is that you cannot use advanced RAID types normally available from a hardware-based RAID solution. Specifically, the popular RAID 5 and 6 implementations, which provide both increased redundancy and performance, are not available using the built-in software-based RAID solution.

TIP ▶ You can use the built-in software-based RAID to further combine hardware-based RAIDs. This technique is often used to combine the two separate sides of an Xserve RAID into a single huge volume.

Mac OS X built-in software-based RAID supports:

▶ RAID 0—Commonly called *striping*, RAID 0 splits up the data into multiple pieces, and then simultaneously writes each piece to a different drive in the set. This yields a single large volume, with dramatically increased read and write performance, equivalent to the cumulative size and performance of all the drives. On the other hand, RAID 0 offers zero increase in reliability since if just one drive in the set fails, then all the data is lost. In fact, RAID 0 increases your chances of data loss because you are introducing more points of failure. In short, RAID 0 is space efficient and fast but provides no redundancy and increased risk.

▶ RAID 1—Commonly called *mirroring*, RAID 1 writes the same data to each drive in the set. This yields a single volume that is the same size as a single drive. Write performance is no faster than a single drive, whereas read performance is increased. The primary advantage to a RAID 1 set is that it can survive and recover from hardware failure. RAID 1 decreases your chances of data loss by providing redundancy. In short, RAID 1 is space-inefficient and partially slower but provides drive redundancy and decreased risk of data loss due to drive failure. Even so, it's very important to remember that mirroring is not a backup solution. Backup solutions create an archive of the data frozen in time and save it to another storage device. If hardware failure occurs, you can recover from a previous backup version of the data. With a mirrored RAID set, all file system changes are applied immediately to all drives in the set and no archival history is maintained.

NOTE ▶ Keep in mind that with a RAID 1 set, if a drive fails your Mac may keep running without warning you. This may leave you with only a single drive in your RAID set, effectively disabling the redundancy. You should periodically check the status of a RAID 1 set from the Disk Utility application.

▶ Nested RAID, 1+0 or 0+1—Because RAID 0 and RAID 1 offer opposed feature sets, nesting one type inside of the other can provide the features of both. In other words, you can stripe data between two mirrors, or you can mirror data on two stripes. These nested configurations are certainly more complicated and require a minimum of four separate drives. However, when you combine their features you get increased performance and redundancy.

▶ Concatenated disk set—This isn't what most would consider a true RAID configuration, as not all drives are being used simultaneously. With a concatenated disk set, the system will simply continue on to the next drive once the previous drive is filled. The only advantage here is that the user will see one large volume instead of several separate drives.

MORE INFO ▶ You can find out more about all the different RAID types by visiting Wikipedia's RAID entry, http://en.wikipedia.org/wiki/RAID.

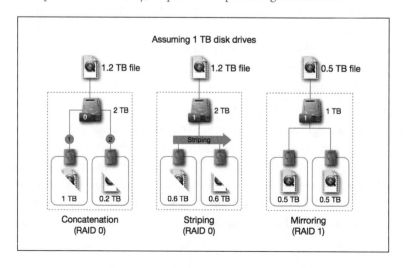

Assuming 1 TB disk drives

1.2 TB file — 2 TB — 1 TB / 0.2 TB
Concatenation (RAID 0)

1.2 TB file — 2 TB — Striping — 0.6 TB / 0.6 TB
Striping (RAID 0)

0.5 TB file — 1 TB — 0.5 TB / 0.5 TB
Mirroring (RAID 1)

Creating a RAID Set

Creating a RAID set with Mac OS X is only slightly more complicated than formatting a standard disk or flash drive. Remember, you can use just about any combination of drives to create a RAID set. Nevertheless, you should follow a couple rules to ensure a healthy RAID set.

Here are some software-based RAID guidelines:

▶ Use identical drives if possible—This will ensure consistent size and performance for all drives in the RAID set. RAID sets are susceptible to performance at the lowest common denominator. In other words, all the drives in a RAID set are treated as large or as fast as your smallest and slowest drives. This is not an issue for a concatenated disk set.

▶ Distribute the drives across multiple interfaces to minimize contention—This often requires extra hardware, but giving the Mac multiple independent paths to the drives can dramatically increase performance.

▶ Make certain that all drives in a set are simultaneously available to the Mac— This may be a difficult criterion if the drives are using different interfaces, but it's necessary to maintain RAID consistency. If a drive in a RAID set is missing for more than a few seconds, the system will assume the drive has failed and the RAID set is damaged. In other words, make sure all the drives are turned on and plugged into the Mac at the same time.

To create a software-based RAID set:

1   Make sure all the drives for the new, unformatted RAID set are connected to the Mac, and then open /Applications/Utilities/Disk Utility.

2   Select any one of the drives from the column on the left, and then click the RAID tab to the right.

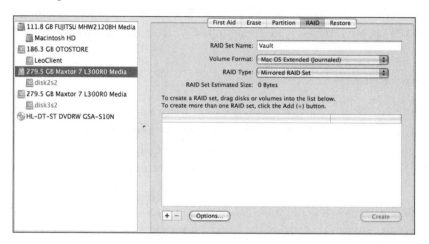

3   Click the small plus button at the bottom of the RAID diagram to create a RAID set. The new RAID set will assume some defaults that you can change at any time before you create the RAID.

4   Configure the newly created RAID set by clicking on its entry in the RAID diagram to select it. For each RAID set, you need to enter a volume name for the RAID set, choose a volume type from the Volume Format pop-up menu, and choose a RAID type from the pop-up menu. Then, click the Options button at the bottom to configure the RAID block size for optimal performance or enable automatic rebuilds if the RAID set is mirrored.

> **NOTE** ▸ Disk Utility will only create RAID sets with one volume. Further, it will not let you repartition the RAID set after it was created.

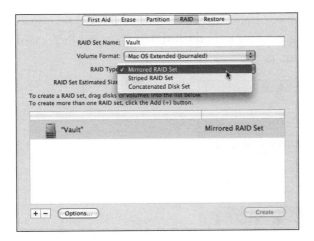

5 If you are creating a nested RAID set, click the small plus button to create additional RAID sets.

Be sure to properly configure each new RAID set. Drag the nested RAIDs on top of the root RAID set to configure the nesting order.

6 Add the drives by dragging the drive icons from the column on the left to the RAID diagram on the right.

Each storage drive you add to your RAID set is considered a "RAID slice." To specify a particular RAID set order, continue to drag drive icons around until you set their appropriate locations in the RAID diagram.

7 Optionally, if you have added three or more drives to a mirrored RAID set, you can define a spare drive by selecting the drive from the RAID diagram and then choosing Spare from the Disk Type pop-up menu.

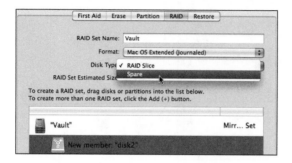

If you set a spare and one of the other drives becomes unreachable during the life of the RAID set, you can have the system automatically rebuild the mirrored RAID. You can enable automatic rebuilding from the RAID options dialog by clicking the Options button below the RAID diagram.

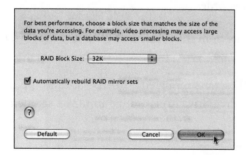

8 If you need to delete items in your RAID, select them from the RAID diagram and then click the small minus button below the diagram.

TIP If you make too many mistakes while designing your RAID, sometimes it's easier to just start over by quitting and then reopening Disk Utility.

9 Double-check all your choices and then click the Create button.

You will be presented with a summary dialog, reminding you once again that continuing may destroy any previous volumes. If you are sure this is what you want to do, click the Create button once more.

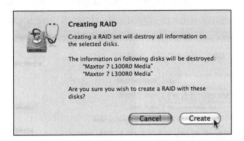

RAID set creation takes only a few moments, and once it's complete, you should see the new RAID set volume in the Disk Utility list and in the Finder. Selecting the newly created RAID set from the column on the left, and then clicking the RAID tab, should reveal that the set is "Online."

Rebuilding a RAID Set

As mentioned earlier, using multiple drives in a RAID set actually introduces more points of storage failure. Fortunately, RAID 1 data mirroring configurations are designed specifically to prevent data loss when a drive fails. Mac OS X even includes the ability to automatically repair mirrored RAID sets if you specified that option during RAID creation.

Before the system mounts a RAID volume, it will check the set for consistency. If the system finds a degraded striped RAID 0 set, you'd better have a good backup because all that data is lost. The system will report the degraded RAID set in Disk Utility, but it will not mount the volume. Only a data recovery service, such as DriveSavers, might have a chance at recovering your data.

On the other hand, if the system finds that a mirrored RAID 1 set is degraded it will either warn you or automatically start rebuilding the RAID set if configured. Either way, the volume will still mount and be accessible to you in the Finder. You should avoid writing new data to a degraded RAID set until you have completed the rebuilding process.

There are two main failure modes for a mirrored RAID 1 set:

▶ One of the drives appears to be responding properly, but the data on the drive is not consistent with the other drives in the set. If configured, the system will automatically start rebuilding the RAID set data by recopying it from a working drive to the apparently corrupted drive. Otherwise, the system will wait for you to manually engage the rebuild process from Disk Utility.

▶ One of the drives in the set is no longer available. If a spare is configured, the system will automatically start rebuilding the RAID set data by copying it from a working drive to the spare drive. Otherwise, the system will wait for you to manually replace the drive and manually engage the rebuild process from Disk Utility.

To manually rebuild a mirrored RAID 1 set:

1 Make sure that all the drives that are part of the RAID set are connected to the Mac, and then open /Applications/Utilities/Disk Utility.

2 Select the degraded RAID set from the column on the left, which should be easy to locate as it will show up onscreen with bright red text for the name. Select the RAID tab to the right if it isn't already selected.

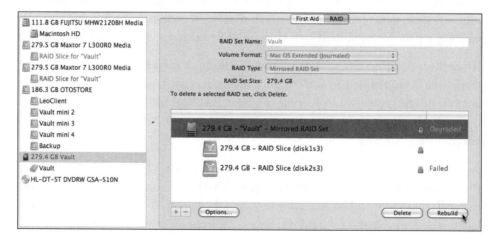

3   Depending on the failure mode of the RAID set, you will need to choose one of two resolutions:

▶   **Inconsistent data.** The system has discovered that one of the drives does not have the same data as the others. You will see the word "Failed" next to the drive with inconsistent data. Simply click the Rebuild button to repair the RAID set.

▶   **Bad or missing drive.** The system can no longer access one of the drives. You will see the word "Offline" next to the missing drive. Select the missing drive from the RAID dialog, and then click the small minus button below the RAID dialog to delete the missing drive. Drag the replacement drive from the column on the left to replace the missing drive from the RAID diagram. Click the Rebuild button to repair the RAID set.

Depending on the size and performance of the RAID set, the rebuild process can take anywhere from seconds to days. Disk Utility will open a progress dialog with the estimated time required to complete the rebuild task.

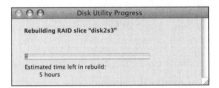

Using Optical Media

Over a decade ago, Apple made headlines by introducing the iMac with only an optical drive, choosing to banish the traditional floppy disk drive from the new computer's revolutionary design. It should come as no surprise, then, that every Mac sold today (except for the super-thin MacBook Air, which has no room for an internal optical drive) includes a CD/DVD writer.

TIP   You can easily identify the capabilities of your Mac's optical drive by opening /Applications/Utilities/System Profiler and viewing the Disc Burning information section.

Obviously, Mac OS X provides support for reading and writing optical media, although the Mac treats optical media differently than disk or flash drives. This is because most optical media formats require that the data be sequentially and permanently written to the disc. This is why the term "burn" is often used to describe the process of writing data to an optical disc. The data is literally burned into the media, and it's common knowledge that you simply can't "un-burn" something once it's been burned.

> **NOTE ▸** As of this writing, no Mac currently shipping includes the ability to write to DVD-RAM. However, Mac OS X supports this hardware. DVD-RAM media is unique among optical media as it provides a dynamically writable volume. Thus, the Mac will treat a DVD-RAM disc just like it treats any other dynamically writable medium.

> **NOTE ▸** As of this writing, no Mac currently shipping includes the ability to write to Blu-ray discs. However, third-party vendors provide both the hardware and software to add this capability to Mac OS X computers.

Several of the applications included with a new Mac are designed to burn specific types of data to optical discs. For example, iTunes can burn audio and MP3 discs, iDVD is used to create video DVDs, and iPhoto can create cross-platform photo discs. Conversely, if you simply want to burn general-purpose data files onto an optical disc, the Finder is your tool. Finally, Disk Utility rounds out the Mac's optical media functionality by providing the means to burn disk images and prepare rewritable discs for reburning.

Burning a Disc via Finder

The Finder provides no less than three different methods for burning data to an optical disc. The first method enables you to quickly select and burn specific items in the Finder to an optical disc. The other two methods involve creating burn folders that let you organize the contents destined for an optical disc before you burn the data to it. This is a convenient way to burn general-purpose data discs, as you cannot change the contents of most optical discs once they have been burned.

> **TIP ▸** The Finder will automatically burn cross-platform optical discs that can be accessed by both Macs and PCs.

Burn Selected Items

To quickly burn specifically selected items:

1 Select the items you wish to burn in the Finder.

You can hold down the Shift key to quickly select contiguous lists of items, or hold down the Command key to quickly select noncontiguous items.

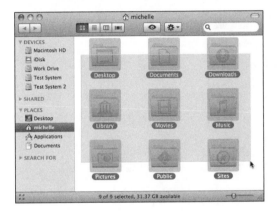

2 Choose File > Burn "Items" to Disc from the menu bar.

The word "Items" in the menu will be replaced by the name of a single item you have selected or the number of items you have selected.

3 The Finder will present you with a dialog asking you to insert a blank disc and letting you know how much storage space will be required. Insert an appropriately sized blank recordable optical disc.

4 Once the system has verified that the inserted optical disc is adequate, it will present a dialog allowing you to select a name for the disc and the burn speed. Stick with the maximum speed unless you are experiencing problems burning discs.

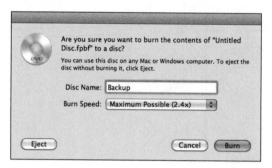

5 Click the Burn button to start the burn and verification process.

Depending on the size of the data and the speed of the drive, the burn and verification process can take anywhere from minutes to hours. The Finder will show a progress dialog that will also allow you to cancel the burn by clicking the small X button on the far right.

6 Once the burn and verification is complete, the Finder will mount the completed disc. Press and hold the Eject key, the furthest top-right key on a Mac keyboard, for a few moments to eject the optical disc.

Using a Burn Folder

To use a burn folder:

1 In the Finder, choose File > New Burn Folder from the menu bar.

This will create a special new folder called "Burn Folder" in the current Finder window or desktop. You can move and rename this folder as you would any other folder.

Burn Folder.fpbf

A burn folder is special because as you drag files and folders inside this folder they will not be moved or copied into the folder. Instead, the system creates aliases to the original items. This allows you to reorganize and rename files and folders inside the burn folder without affecting the originals or wasting drive space. You can even keep burn folders around for future use after you have burned the disc.

2 Once you have perfected the contents of your burn folder, click the Burn button at the top-right corner of the burn folder's Finder window, or select the burn folder and then choose File > Burn "burn folder name" from the menu bar.

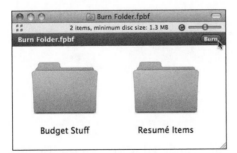

The Finder will present you with a dialog asking you to insert a blank disc and letting you know how much storage space will be required. Insert an appropriately sized blank recordable optical disc.

3 Once the system has verified that the inserted optical is adequate, it will present a dialog allowing you to select a name for the disc and the burn speed. Stick with the maximum speed unless you are experiencing problems burning discs.

4 Click the Burn button to start the burn and verification process.

Depending on the size of the data and the speed of the drive, the burn and verification process can take anywhere from minutes to hours. The Finder will show a progress dialog that will also allow you to cancel the burn by clicking the small X button on the far right.

5 Once the burn and verification is complete, the Finder will mount the completed disc. Press and hold the Eject key, the furthest top-right key on a Mac keyboard, for a few moments to eject the optical disc.

Burning a Specific-Size Disc

To use a burn folder for a specific disc size:

1 From within the Finder, insert a blank recordable optical disc.

If this is the first time you have inserted blank optical media in this Mac, you will be presented with a dialog that will let you choose your preferred action when blank media is inserted. Leave the default action to open the media in the Finder, and then click the OK button.

The Finder will create a new burn folder with an optical disc icon named "Untitled CD" or "Untitled DVD" on your desktop and also create a link to it in the Finder's sidebar. Creating a burn folder this way will cap the size of the burn folder to ensure it will fit once burned to the media you inserted. Note in the following example screenshot that the Finder window shows the Untitled DVD has 8.55 GB available. Also note the Untitled DVD shows up in the Finder's sidebar with a conveniently placed burn button right next to it.

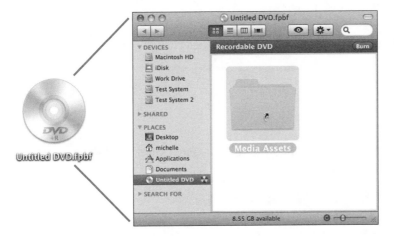

2   Continue to reorganize, move, and ultimately burn this burn folder, as you would use a manually created burn folder outlined in the previous steps.

TIP ▶ You can adjust how the Mac reacts when you insert blank optical media from the CDs & DVDs preferences in System Preferences. For instance, when you insert a blank disc, you can have the Mac automatically open a disc-burning application instead of the Finder.

Burning a Disk Image via Disk Utility

One of Disk Utility's many features is its ability to burn the contents of a disk image to optical discs. This is extremely useful for burning backup copies of disk images you have created from original media. In other words, you can use Disk Utility to create a disk image of an original optical disc, and then burn the contents of the newly created disk image to a recordable optical disc. The burned disc will appear identical to the original media. In fact, Apple uses this technology to distribute system software installers for beta testing. After a tester downloads the latest disk image from one of Apple's servers, she will use Disk Utility to burn the contents of that image to an optical disc.

MORE INFO ▶ Though burning a disk image will be covered here, creating a disk image is discussed in Chapter 5, "Data Management and Backup."

To burn the contents of a disk image:

1 Open /Applications/Utilities/Disk Utility, and then click the Burn button on the toolbar.

A file browser appears that enables you to browse and select the disk image whose contents you wish to burn to an optical disc.

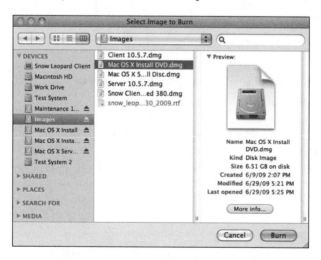

2   A burn options dialog appears. Click the small blue arrow button in the upper-right corner to reveal more burn options.

The default burn options are almost always the best choice, but you can make changes here as you see fit.

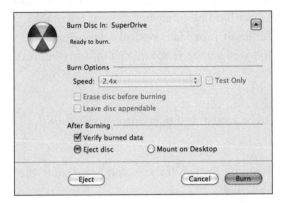

3   Click the Burn button to start the burn and verification process.

Depending on the size of the disk image and the speed of the drive, the burn and verification process can take anywhere from minutes to hours. Disk Utility will open a small progress dialog that will also allow you to cancel the burn by clicking the Cancel button.

4   Once the burn and verification is complete, Disk Utility will either mount or eject the completed disc depending on the options you chose.

Erasing Rewritable Optical Media

One last optical media trick you need to know about Disk Utility is the ability to erase rewritable optical media. Mac OS X requires that you erase rewritable media in order to burn more data to the disc. Most of the time, though, this process takes only a few moments to complete. Only optical media bearing the "RW" initials can be erased and then rewritten again. Also, older optical drive hardware may not support rewritable media. You can easily identify the capabilities of your Mac's optical drive by opening /Applications/Utilities/System Profiler and viewing the Disc Burning information section.

To erase a rewritable optical disc:

1   Insert the rewritable optical media to be erased, and then open /Applications/ Utilities/Disk Utility.

2   Select the optical drive from the column on the left. If there is an Erase tab to the right, select it now if it isn't already selected.

The manufacturer and model number is usually the name of the optical drive. Do not select any disc volumes.

3   Select either the Quickly or the Completely option.

Because erasing completely takes so much longer, you should stick with the Quickly option unless the computer is having problems completing the disc-erase process.

4   Once you have made your choice to quickly or completely erase, click the Erase button to continue.

5   You will be presented with a verification dialog. If you are certain you want to erase the disc, then click the Erase button to start the process.

Depending on the erase option you selected, the erase process will either take a few seconds or up to an hour. If the process is going to take more than a few seconds, Disk Utility will show a progress dialog.

6 Once the erase process is complete, the media will remain in the drive awaiting your next move. Press and hold the Eject key, the furthest top-right key on a Mac keyboard, for a few moments to eject the optical disc.

Understanding File System Permissions

The technologies collectively known as "file system permissions" are used to control file and folder authorization for Mac OS X. File system permissions work alongside the user account technologies, which control user identification and authentication, to provide the Mac's secure multiuser environment. File system permissions—again just like user accounts—permeate every level of the operating system, so a thorough investigation of this system is required to fully understand Mac OS X.

In short, every single item on the system volume has permissions rules applied to it by the operating system. Only users and processes with root account access can ignore file system permissions rules. Thus, these rules are used to define file and folder access for every normal, administrative, guest, and sharing user. Any user can easily identify the permissions of a file or folder with the Finder's Get Info window.

NOTE ▶ The Mac OS X interface sometimes uses the word "privileges" in place of permissions. In general the meaning of these two terms is similar.

Viewing File System Permissions

To identify file system permissions from the Finder:

1 In the Finder, select the file or folder for which you wish to identify the permissions. You can select multiple items to open multiple Get Info windows.

2 Open the Get Info window.

There are several methods for doing this. You can choose File > Get Info from the menu bar; use the Command-I keyboard combination; choose Get Info from the Action pop-up menu in a Finder window toolbar; or in the Finder, right-click or Control-click on an item and choose Get Info.

3   Once you have opened a Get Info window, click the Sharing & Permissions disclosure triangle to reveal the item's permissions.

Note that the permissions list is broken into two columns. To the left is a list of users or groups with access to this item, and to the right is the associated privilege assigned per user or group. Modifying these settings is covered in the "Managing Permissions" sections later in this chapter.

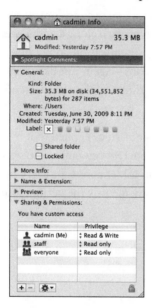

TIP   You can also identify ownership and permissions from the Finder's dynamic Inspector window. This is a single floating window that will automatically refresh as you select different items in the Finder. To open the Inspector window from the Finder, use the Option-Command-I keyboard combination.

Ownership for Permissions

Every file and folder belongs to at least one owner and one group, and also has an owner-ship setting for everyone else. This three-tiered ownership structure provides the basis for file system permissions:

▶ Owner—By default, the owner of an item is the user who created or copied the item to the Mac. For example, the user owns most of the items in his home folder. The system or root user almost always owns system software items, including system resources and applications. Traditionally, only the owner can change the item's owner-ship or permissions. Despite this, Mac OS X makes management easier by giving every administrative user the ability to change ownership and permissions regardless of who the item's owner is.

▶ Group—By default, the group of an item is inherited from the folder it was created in. Thus, most items belong to the staff, wheel, or admin groups. Group ownership is designated to allow users other than the owner to have access to an item. For instance, even though root owns the /Applications folder, the group is set to admin so administrative users can make changes to the contents of this folder.

▶ Everyone—The Everyone setting is used to define access for anyone who isn't the owner and isn't part of the item's group. In other words, this means everyone *else*. This includes local, sharing, and guest users.

The simple three-tiered ownership structure presented here has been part of traditional UNIX operating systems for decades. However, with only three levels of permissions to choose from, it is quite difficult to define appropriate access settings for a computer with many user accounts and shared files, as is the case with many servers. Fortunately, as you'll see later, access control lists (ACLs) were developed to allow for nearly limitless ownership and permissions configurations.

Traditional UNIX Permissions

Mac OS X's basic file system permissions structure is based on decades-old UNIX-style permissions. This system also sometimes goes by POSIX-style permissions. The system may be old, but for most Mac users it is quite adequate because you can define privilege rules separately at each ownership tier. In other words, the owner, the group, and everyone else has individually specified access to each file or folder. Further, because of the inherent hierarchy built into the file system, where folders can reside inside of other folders, you easily create a complex file structure that allows for varying levels of sharing and security.

There is a variety of UNIX privilege combinations available from the command line, as discussed in the "Managing Permissions via Command Line" section later in this chapter. However, Apple has streamlined the Finder to allow only the most common permissions options.

Permissions that you can assign to a file using the Finder are:

▶ Read and Write—The user or group members can open the file and save changes.

▶ Read Only—The user or group members can open the file but cannot save any changes.

▶ No Access—The user or group members have no access to the file at all.
Permissions that you can assign to a folder using the Finder are:

▶ Read and Write—The user or group members can browse and make changes to the contents of the folder.

▶ Read Only—The user or group members can browse the contents of the folder but cannot make changes to the contents of the folder.

▶ Write Only (Drop Box)—The user or group members cannot browse the folder but can copy or move items into it.

▶ No Access—The user or group members have no access to the contents of the folder.

Access Control Lists (ACLs)

Access control lists (ACLs) were developed to expand the traditional UNIX-style permissions architecture to allow more control of file and folder access. Though there is no common standard for ACLs, Mac OS X has adopted a style of ACL similar to that available on Windows-based NTFS file systems and UNIX systems that support NFSv4. This ACL implementation is extremely flexible but increases complexity by adding more than a dozen unique privilege and inheritance attribute types. Further, this implementation supports an unlimited number of ACL attributes for any user or group. Finally, it's important to note that if an ACL rule applies to a user or group, this rule will trump traditional UNIX permissions. However, any users or groups that don't apply to a specific ACL will still be bound by the UNIX permissions currently in place.

Apple does not expect average users to navigate through all the options available using ACLs, so once again the Finder has been streamlined to allow only the most common ACL configurations. In fact, the Finder only allows you to assign ACL attributes that match the most common UNIX permissions configurations that were previously listed in this chapter. The only feature of ACLs that the Finder actually implements is the ability to have an unlimited number of user or group privilege rules. In other words, the Finder uses the ACL architecture to let you configure unique privileges for an unlimited number of users or groups. Prior to Mac OS X v10.5, the Finder would only allow you to assign permissions using the standard three-tiered ownership style, with one owner, one group, and one setting for everyone else.

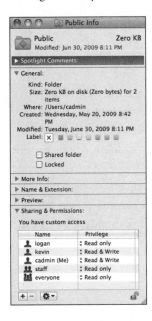

Permissions in a Hierarchical Context

It is important to remember that permissions do not exist in isolation; rather, permissions are applied in the context of folder hierarchy. In other words, your access to an item is based on an item's permissions in combination with the permissions of the folder in which it resides. If you're still confused, it's easiest to think of permissions as defining access to an item's content, not the item itself. Remember the word "content" as you consider the following three simplified examples.

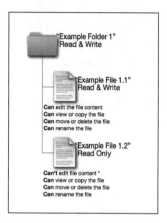

Example 1: Your permissions to Example Folder 1 are read and write. It's obvious that you should have full access to Example File 1.1, as your permissions here are read and write as well. You can also view and copy Example File 1.2, but you can't make changes to the file's content because your permissions are read only. Yet you can still move, delete, or rename File 1.2 because you have read and write access to the folder's contents. Thus, File 1.2 isn't secure in this example because you can make a copy of the original file, change the copied file's content, delete the original file, and finally replace it with the modified copy. In fact, this is how most graphical applications save document changes; thus the file can indeed be edited.

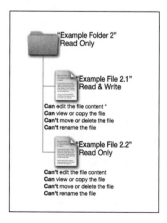

Example 2: You have read-only permission to Example Folder 2. You can edit the content of Example File 2.1 because you have read and write access to it, but you can't move, delete, or rename it because you have read-only access to the folder's contents. On the other hand, you can effectively delete the file by erasing its contents. Example File 2.2 is the only truly secure file, as you're only allowed to view or copy the file. Granted, you can make changes to the contents of a copied file, but you still can't replace the original.

> **NOTE ▶** Many applications cannot save changes to files inside read-only folders, because these applications attempt to replace the original file during the save process, instead of revising the file's content. In other words, you may need read and write access to both the file and the folder it's inside of to save changes to the file.

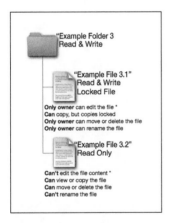

Example 3: Your permissions are identical to the first example, with one significant change. The owner of Example File 3.1 has enabled the locked attribute. Even though you have read and write access to Example Folder 3 and File 3.1, the locked attribute prevents all users who aren't the file's owner from modifying, moving, deleting, or renaming the file. From most applications, only the owner is allowed to change the file's content or delete it, but the owner can also disable the locked attribute to return the file to normal. You can still make a copy of the locked file, but the copy will be locked as well. However, you will own the copy, so you can disable the locked attribute on the copy, but you still can't delete the original locked file unless you're the owner.

> **MORE INFO ▶** The locked attribute is covered in the "Managing Locked Items via Finder" section later in this chapter.

Permissions for Sharing

Once you have an understanding of the permissions options available to you in
Mac OS X, you should explore how the local file system is set up by default to provide a
secure environment that still allows for users to share files.

If you don't have fast user switching enabled as outlined in Chapter 2, "User Accounts,"
you should enable it now to make it easy to test file system permissions as different users.
Further, to aid in your exploration of the file system you should use the Finder's Inspector
window. This single floating window, which automatically refreshes as you select different
items in the Finder, allows you to quickly explore the default permissions settings without
having to open multiple Finder Get Info windows. Open the Inspector from the Finder by
using the Option-Command-I keyboard combination, and then click the disclosure triangle to reveal the Sharing & Permissions section.

NOTE ▶ The Inspector window sports a different title bar than the Get Info window.
Also, the Inspector window will always float on top of all other windows in the Finder.

Home Folder Sharing

Mac OS X protects the user's files by default and allows them to be shared easily when needed. This starts with the user's home folder. You'll notice that users are allowed read and write access to their home folder, while the staff group and everyone is allowed only read access.

This means that every local user or guest can view the first level of every other user's home folder. (As a reminder, guests are allowed access to your computer without a password. This is why you can disable guest access in the Accounts preferences.) The default home folder permissions may seem insecure until you look at the permissions in context. Most user data is actually stored inside a subfolder in the user's home folder, and if you inspect those sub-folders you'll notice that other users are not allowed to access most of them.

There are a few subfolders in a user's home folder, however, that are specifically designed for sharing. The Public and Sites folders remain readable to everyone. A user can easily share files without having to mess with permissions by simply moving the files into those two folders. Others will be able to read those files, but they still cannot make any changes to them.

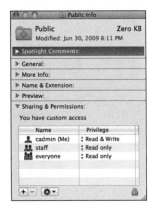 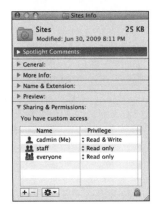

NOTE ▶ User-created files and folders at the root of the home folder will, by default, have permissions like the Public folder's. To secure new items at the root of the home folder, simply change the permissions as outlined in the "Managing Permissions via Finder" section later in this chapter.

Looking deeper, you'll notice a subfolder of the Public folder is the Drop Box. This folder's permissions allow all other users to copy files into the folder even though they cannot actually see other files in the Drop Box folder. This allows other users to discreetly transfer files without others knowing.

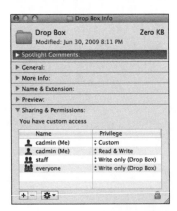

MORE INFO ▶ The permissions used to locally protect the Public and Sites folders are also used to protect these folders as they are shared over the network. Sharing files is covered in Chapter 8, "Network Services."

The Shared Folder

An additional folder set aside for sharing is the /User/Shared folder. You'll notice that this is a general sharing location that allows all users to read and write items to the folder. Normally this permissions setting would also allow any user to delete another user's item in this folder. Yet the Finder's Inspector window is not showing you the full permissions picture here. There is a unique permissions setting on the Shared folder that prevents other users from being able to delete items that they don't own. This permission setting, known as the "sticky bit," can only be set using a command-line tool. Inspecting and changing permissions from the command line is covered in the "Managing Permissions via Command Line" section later in this chapter, and the sticky bit is specifically covered in the "Using the Sticky Bit" section later in this chapter.

Securing New Items

Once you understand how Mac OS X's file system security architecture works with the folder hierarchy, it's time to consider how this technology is used to secure new items. You've learned previously in this chapter that Mac OS X is already preconfigured for secure file and folder sharing, but you will find that new items are created with unrestricted read access.

For example, when a user creates a new file or folder at the root of her home folder, by default all other users, including guest users, are allowed to view this item's contents.

The same is true for new items created by administrators in local areas such as the root of the system volume and the local Library and Applications folders.

New items are created this way to facilitate sharing, so you do not have to change any permissions to share a new item. All that is required of you is to place the new item in a folder that other users can access; like the pre-defined sharing folders covered in the previous section. It's assumed that if you want to secure a new item, you will place it inside a folder that no one else has access to, like your home Desktop or Documents folders.

On the other hand, this default behavior is inconvenient if you want to safely store your items in an otherwise public area, like the root of the system volume. To store items in a public area so they are only accessible to the owner requires you to change the item's permissions using either the Finder or the command line, as outlined later in this chapter.

Specifically, from the Finder's Sharing & Permissions section of the Get Info window, you must remove all other users and all group accounts from the permissions list. You cannot remove the Everyone permission, so you will have to set it to No Access. Once you have made these permissions changes, only the owner will have access to the item.

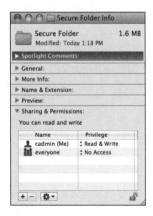

Managing Permissions via Finder

A significantly redesigned Finder was one of the major new features in the previous Mac OS X v10.5. This included a new interface for managing ownership and permissions from the Finder's Get Info window. The redesign was necessary to incorporate support for ACLs. As covered previously in this chapter, the Finder uses the ACL architecture so you can configure unique privileges for an unlimited number of users or groups.

You may find that while the Finder makes permissions management simple, it does so through a form of obfuscation. In other words, the Finder hides the complexity of permissions by intentionally misrepresenting the full permissions of an item. If you're more comfortable with traditional UNIX-style permissions, or you simply require full access to an item's permissions, then you're best served by managing permissions via the command line as covered later in this chapter. However, for the most common permissions settings, the Finder's simplified permissions interface is still the quickest and easiest solution.

Modifying File Permissions via Finder

To change permissions in the Finder:

1   In the Finder, select the file or folder for which you wish to change the permissions, and then open the Get Info window.

2   Once you have opened a Get Info window, click the Sharing & Permissions disclosure triangle to reveal the item's permissions.

3   Click the small lock icon in the bottom-right corner of the Get Info window and authenticate as an administrative user or the owner of the item to unlock the Sharing & Permissions section.

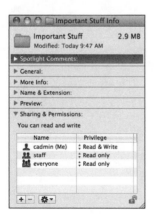

4   To add new users or groups, click the small plus button in the bottom-left corner of the Get Info window.

A dialog will appear, allowing you to select a new user or group. To select an existing user or group, choose his or its name from the list and click the Select button. Alternately, you can create a new Sharing user account by clicking the New Person button or selecting a contact from your Address Book. Creating a new Sharing account in either case requires that you also enter a new password for the account.

MORE INFO ▶ Details about sharing user accounts and how to create additional groups are covered in Chapter 2, "User Accounts."

5 To delete users or groups, select the account from the permission list and click the small minus button in the bottom-left corner of the Get Info window.

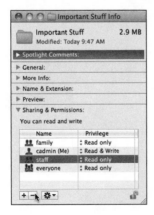

NOTE ▶ The Finder's Get Info window will not allow you to delete or change the original owner, or delete the Everyone privilege of an item. You can use this window to seemingly delete all group privileges, but this isn't truly deleting the group privilege. Instead, it's simply removing all the privileges for the item's original group.

6   To assign different privileges, simply click on any privilege and a pop-up menu will appear, allowing you to choose another access option for that user or group. Details about the privilege options available from the Finder are covered previously in this chapter.

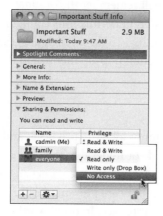

7   If you are changing the permissions of a folder, by default, the Finder will not change the permissions of any items inside the folder. In many cases, you will want to apply the same permissions to the items inside the folder.

You can accomplish this quickly by clicking the gear button at the bottom of the Get Info window to reveal the Action pop-up menu, and then choosing the "Apply to enclosed items" option from this menu.

NOTE ▶ Applying permissions to the enclosed folder items will apply all permissions settings to all enclosed items, not just the changes you recently made.

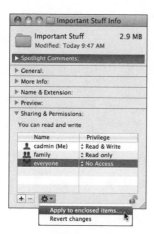

8 Changes made using the Get Info window are applied immediately. When you are done making ownership or permissions changes, close the Get Info window.

As long as you keep the Get Info window open, the Finder will remember the original permissions setting for the item. This is useful for testing different permissions configurations, as you can always revert to the original permissions setting. To do so, click the gear button at the bottom of the Get Info window to reveal the Action pop-up menu, and then choose the "Revert changes" option from this menu.

Managing Locked Items via Finder

Mac OS X includes a special file and folder attribute that trumps all write privileges and even administrative user access. Users can choose to lock a file or folder that they own from the Finder's Get Info window. Locking an item will render it completely unchangeable to all users except the item's owner. Even administrative users are prevented from making changes to another user's locked file in the graphical interface. In other words, a standard user could potentially lock an item that the administrative user would have no ability to change in the graphical interface.

To lock a file or folder in the Finder:

1 In the Finder, select the file or folder you wish to lock, and then open the Get Info window.

2 Once you have opened a Get Info window, click the General disclosure triangle to reveal the Locked checkbox.

3 As long as you are the original owner of the item, you will be allowed to select the Locked checkbox.

Changes made using the Get Info window are applied immediately.

Once an item is locked, no other users can modify, move, delete, or rename it. In the graphi-cal interface the owner can modify the content of the item or delete it, but the Finder still prevents the owner from moving, renaming, or changing ownership and permissions of the locked item. In fact, if you as the owner try to move a locked item, the Finder will default to making a copy. The owner can return the file to the normal state by disabling the locked attribute from the Finder's Get Info window. An administrative user can disable the locked attribute, but only via the command line, as covered later in this chapter.

Permissions for External Volumes

Portable external disk and flash drives are useful tools for transferring files and folders from one computer to another. A downside to this technology, though, is that computers can't prop-erly interpret file ownership because they don't share the same user account database. In other words, most Macs don't have the exact same user accounts, so when a drive is moved from one Mac to another, the file ownership from one Mac is meaningless to another.

> **NOTE ▸** The Mac considers any locally mounted volume that is not the system vol-ume to be an external volume. Thus, other partitions on your internal system disks will still be considered external volumes.

Unless you plan to implement a centralized network user database so all your Macs do share the same user account database, ownership on external volumes will have to be ignored to prevent access issues. This is the default behavior on Mac OS X for all external volumes. Keep in mind, however, that this approach introduces the security risk that all local users will have full access to the contents of external volumes. Because some may find this an unacceptable security risk, you can disable the default behavior and force Mac OS X to honor ownership on external volumes.

To honor ownership on external volumes:

1   In the Finder, select the external volume for which you wish the system to honor the ownership, and then open the Get Info window.

2   Once you have opened a Get Info window, click the Sharing & Permissions disclosure triangle to reveal the item's ownership and permissions.

3   Click the small lock icon in the bottom-right corner of the Get Info window and authenticate as an administrative user to unlock the Sharing & Permissions section.

4   Deselect the "Ignore ownership on this volume" checkbox.

Changes made using the Get Info window are applied immediately.

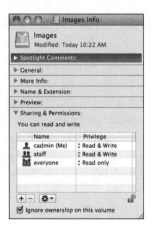

Managing Permissions via Command Line

Viewing and modifying file system permissions in the command line is both much richer and more complicated than in the Finder. The Finder has streamlined ownership, permissions, and ACLs, providing only the most common features that users require. However, the command line offers every conceivable ownership and permissions option. Further, the command line often provides more than one method for performing identical permissions tasks.

> **NOTE ▶** If you aren't already comfortable with navigation in the UNIX command line, then it's strongly recommended that you study the command line concepts in Chapter 3, "Command Line and Automation," before reading the remainder of the section.

Viewing Traditional UNIX Permissions

Once again, the ls command is your primary tool for viewing file and folder information in the command line. The ls command has many options for viewing nearly any file or folder attribute. You can learn more about all the options available to ls from its manual entry page. Here, you will be presented with a few fundamental permissions viewing options.

The most basic ls option for viewing file and folder ownership and permissions is -l:

```
MyMac:~ michelle$ ls -l
total 0
drwx------+ 5 michelle staff 170 Aug 20 15:49 Desktop
drwx------+ 3 michelle staff 102 Aug 20 01:08 Documents
drwx------+ 3 michelle staff 102 Aug 20 01:08 Downloads
drwx------ 19 michelle staff 646 Aug 20 01:08 Library
drwx------+ 3 michelle staff 102 Aug 20 01:08 Movies
drwx------+ 3 michelle staff 102 Aug 20 01:08 Music
drwx------+ 4 michelle staff 136 Aug 20 01:08 Pictures
drwxr-xr-x+ 7 michelle staff 238 Aug 20 15:29 Public
drwxr-xr-x 5 michelle staff 170 Aug 20 01:08 Sites
```

The first string of characters at the beginning of each line is shorthand for the item type and permissions. The following information appears from left to right: the number of hard links associated with the item (for most users, this particular bit will be trivial information), the assigned owner, the assigned group, the last modification date, and finally the item's name.

The syntax for the abbreviated information section is:

▶ The first character is item type: - for file, d for folder, and l for symbolic link.

▶ The next three characters indicate the owner's permissions: - for no access, r for read access, w for write access, and x for file execute access or folder browsing access.

▶ The middle set of three rwx or - characters indicate the group's permissions.

▶ The final set of three rwx or - characters indicate everyone else's permissions.

▶ Optionally, there may be a + at the end to indicate that the item has ACL rules applied to it, or an @ at the end to indicate that the item has extended attributes.

The execute privilege attribute x has not been introduced yet, but it is the third standard UNIX privilege attribute after read and write. The execute privilege is enabled on files that are commands and applications (or folders that contain application bundles), to indicate that the item contains executable software code. The execute privilege is also required on normal folders to access the contents of the folder. The Finder doesn't show you when the execute privilege is used, but it will properly manage the execute privilege when you make permissions changes using the Get Info window.

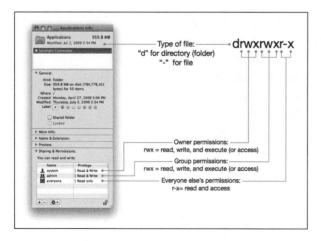

Viewing Access Control Lists (ACLs)

The ACL technology is more advanced than traditional UNIX-style permissions because it allows for an arbitrary number of user and group permissions rules per item. Each permissions rule is known as an Access Control Entry (ACE). Every file and folder on the system can have an unlimited list of ACE rules, hence the "list" in ACLs.

From the command line, Mac OS X's ACL implementation provides more than a dozen unique privilege attribute types and lets you define each as a specific allow or deny rule. In other words, you can assign an item an unlimited number of user or group rules, or ACEs, which can be used to allow or deny any of the following privilege attributes:

▶ Administration—Administration attributes, which define a user's or group's ability to make permissions changes, include change privileges and change ownership.

▶ Read—Read attributes define a user or group's ability to read items and include read attributes, read extended attributes, read file data or list folder contents, execute file or traverse folder, and read permissions.

▶ Write—Write attributes define a user's or group's ability to make changes and include write attributes, write extended attributes, read file data or create files in folder, append file data or create new subfolder inside folder, delete item, and delete subfolders and files.

Furthermore, each ACE for a folder can include a static inheritance rule that defines whether the folder's permissions also apply to new items placed in the folder. Inheritance attributes include the following: no inheritance, apply to just new items in this folder, apply to any new child folders, apply to any new child files, and apply to all descendants of this folder.

To view an item's ACLs alongside their permissions, simply add the -e option to the -l option:

```
MyMac:~ michelle$ ls -le
total 0
drwx------+ 5 michelle staff 170 Aug 20 15:49 Desktop
 0: group:everyone deny delete
drwx------+ 3 michelle staff 102 Aug 20 01:08 Documents
 0: group:everyone deny delete
```

```
drwx------+ 3 michelle staff 102 Aug 20 01:08 Downloads
 0: group:everyone deny delete
drwx------ 19 michelle staff 646 Aug 20 01:08 Library
drwx------+ 3 michelle staff 102 Aug 20 01:08 Movies
 0: group:everyone deny delete
drwx------+ 3 michelle staff 102 Aug 20 01:08 Music
 0: group:everyone deny delete
drwx------+ 4 michelle staff 136 Aug 20 01:08 Pictures
 0: group:everyone deny delete
drwxr-xr-x+ 7 michelle staff 238 Aug 20 15:29 Public
 0: group:everyone deny delete
drwxr-xr-x 5 michelle staff 170 Aug 20 01:08 Sites
```

Modifying File Permissions via Command Line

You will use two primary commands for changing file and folder permissions in the command line: chown for changing ownership and chmod for changing privileges.

Changing Ownership via Command Line

Short for "change ownership," chown will let you change the owner and group associated with a file or folder. Using chown often requires root access, so this command is almost always preceded by the sudo command. To use chown, enter the new owner's name, followed optionally by a colon and the new group name, and then finish with the item's path. In the following example, Michelle will use the chown command to change testfile1's ownership to the user account "kevin" and the group account "admin."

NOTE ▶ Remember that, as covered in Chapter 3, if you want to change the ownership of a folder and its contents, you must tell the chown command to run recursively by adding the -R option.

```
MyMac:~ michelle$ ls -l Desktop/
total 0
-rw-r--r-- 1 michelle staff 0 Aug 20 15:49 testfile1
drwxr-xr-x 4 michelle staff 136 Aug 20 15:47 testfolder
```

```
MyMac:~ michelle$ sudo chown kevin:admin Desktop/testfile1
Password:
MyMac:~ michelle$ ls -l Desktop/
total 0
-rw-r--r-- 1 kevin admin 0 Aug 20 15:49 testfile1
drwxr-xr-x 4 michelle staff 136 Aug 20 15:47 testfolder
```

Changing Privileges via Command Line

Short for "change file mode," chmod will let you change the privileges associated with a file or folder. Using chmod on files you don't own requires root access, so the chmod command is often preceded by the sudo command. To use chmod, enter the new privileges first followed by the item's path.

As for changing privileges, there are two basic methods when using the chmod command:

▶ Using alphanumeric abbreviations—The basic syntax goes: account type, modifier, and then privilege. Account types include u for owner, g for group, and o for everyone else. Modifiers include + for allow, - for deny, and = for exact setting. Privileges are as expected with r for read, w for write, and x for execute or folder access. For example, if you're using this method to allow full access for the owner and group but read-only access for everyone else, you'd enter ug=rwx,o=r.

> **TIP** ▶ As an alternative to x you can also use X for smart execute, which tells chmod to add the x permission only to items for which it makes sense—all folders and files that are already marked executable. This is specially for recursive operation, where x should be added to folders but not (most) files.

▶ Using octal notation—As you can see, chmod extensively uses shortcuts and abbreviations. To save even more keystrokes you can use octal notation, which uses numeric abbreviations for defining privileges. The basic syntax for octal notation is to use a single-digit number for the user first, followed by a single number for the group, and then a last single number for everyone else. Octal notation uses 0, for no access; 1, for execution only; 2, for write-only; and 4, for read-only. To use mixed permissions, simply add the numbers together. For example, if you're using this method to allow for full access to a folder for the owner and group but read-only access for everyone else, you'd type 775.

In the following example, Michelle will use the `chmod` command to change the permissions of testfile1 and testfolder to allow read and write access for the owner and the group but read-only access for everyone else. She will first use alphanumeric abbreviations, and then octal privilege equivalents.

> **NOTE ▶** Remember, if you want to change the privileges of a folder and its contents, you must tell the `chmod` command to run recursively by adding the `-R` option.

```
MyMac:~ michelle$ ls -l Desktop/
total 0
-rw-r--r-- 1 michelle staff 0 Aug 20 15:49 testfile1
drwxr-xr-x 4 michelle staff 136 Aug 20 15:47 testfolder
MyMac:~ michelle$ chmod ug=rw,o=r Desktop/testfile1
MyMac:~ michelle$ ls -l Desktop/
total 0
-rw-rw-r-- 1 michelle staff 0 Aug 20 15:49 testfile1
drwxr-xr-x 4 michelle staff 136 Aug 20 15:47 testfolder
MyMac:~ michelle$ chmod 775 Desktop/testfolder/
MyMac:~ michelle$ ls -l Desktop/
total 0
-rw-rw-r-- 1 michelle staff 0 Aug 20 15:49 testfile1
drwxrwxr-x 4 michelle staff 136 Aug 20 15:47 testfolder
```

> **MORE INFO ▶** The `chmod` command supports many other permissions settings, including full ACL management, which go beyond the scope of this guide. However, you can always find out more about `chmod` by reading its built-in `man` page.

Using the Sticky Bit

As mentioned previously in this chapter, the /Users/Shared folder has a unique permission setting that allows all local users to read and write items into the folder yet prevents other users from being able to delete files that they didn't originally put in this folder. This special permissions configuration is brought to you courtesy of the "sticky bit." Essentially, enabling the sticky bit on a folder defines it as an append-only destination, or, more accurately, a folder in which only the owner of the item can delete the item.

You can clearly see the sticky bit setting of the /Users/Shared folder when you view its ownership and permissions. Note the t on the end of the permissions information, which indicates that the sticky bit is enabled:

```
MyMac:~ michelle$ ls -l /Users/
total 0
drwxrwxrwt   7 root     wheel  238 Aug 10 18:49 Shared
drwxr-xr-x+ 16 cadmin   staff  544 Aug 17 00:10 cadmin
drwxr-xr-x+ 16 logan    staff  544 Aug 19 00:06 logan
drwxr-xr-x+ 17 kevin    staff  578 Aug 17 00:14 kevin
drwxr-xr-x+ 15 michelle staff  510 Aug 20 16:43 michelle
```

You can enable sticky bit functionality similar to the /Users/Shared folder on any other folder using a special octal notation with the chmod command. In the following example, Michelle has already created a new folder named NewShared. She then uses the chmod command with +t to set sharing for all users with sticky bit functionality:

```
MyMac:~ michelle$ chmod -R +t NewShared/
MyMac:~ michelle$ ls -l
total 0
drwx------+ 5 michelle staff 170 Aug 20 15:49 Desktop
...
drwxrwxrwt 2 michelle staff 68 Aug 20 17:20 NewShared
...
```

Managing Locked Items via Command Line

As mentioned previously, Mac OS X includes a special file system lock feature that prevents anyone but the owner of an item from making changes to that item. Any user can easily lock a file or folder he owns from the Finder's Get Info window, also covered earlier in this chapter.

The problem with the file system lock is that the Finder prevents even other administrative users from making changes or even unlocking items they don't own. In fact, this file system lock extends to the command line as well. Even with sudo access, an administrator is not allowed to change a locked item—with one important exception, the chflags command. This command allows the administrator to change file system flags, which among other things allows you to lock or unlock any file or folder on the system.

In the following example, Michelle needs to change the permissions of a folder owned by another user so the folder can be shared. However, even using sudo she is denied access from doing this, indicating the file is locked. She verifies this by using ls -lO to view the file listing with file flags, which indeed returns that the folder is locked, "uchg". She then uses the chflags command with the nouchg option to unlock the folder. Finally, she is able to make changes to the previously locked file.

```
MyMac:Shared michelle$ sudo chmod go+rx SecureFolder/
chmod: Unable to change file mode on SecureFolder/: Operation not permitted
MyMac:Shared michelle$ ls -lO
total 0
drwx------  7 cadmin  wheel  -      238 Jul  7 13:18 AnotherFolder
drwx------  7 cadmin  wheel  uchg  238 Jul  7 13:18 SecureFolder
MyMac:Shared michelle$ sudo chflags nouchg SecureFolder/
MyMac:Shared michelle$ sudo chmod go+rx SecureFolder/
MyMac:Shared michelle$ ls -lO
total 0
drwx------  7 cadmin  wheel  -      238 Jul  7 13:18 AnotherFolder
drwxr-xr-x  7 cadmin  wheel  -      238 Jul  7 13:18 SecureFolder
```

MORE INFO ▶ Using the chflags command with the uchg option will enable the file system lock on an item, thus preventing others from changing that item. Read the man page for chflags to reveal the other types of file flags that it can manipulate.

File System Troubleshooting

Because a functional file system is required by the operating system, the software that drives the file system is very reliable. In fact, most file system failures are due to bad hardware or media. It doesn't matter how good the software is, though; if the hardware is no longer reading or writing bits, it's pretty much useless to the file system. If, during troubleshooting, you determine that catastrophic hardware failure is the problem, there really isn't anything you can do from a software perspective to repair the device. Only a data recovery service, such as DriveSavers, might have a chance at recovering your data.

MORE INFO ▸ When storage hardware suffers from catastrophic failure, DriveSavers is the most popular hard drive recovery service for Macs. You can find out more about its product at www.drivesaversdatarecovery.com.

Conversely, if you're experiencing file system issues but the storage hardware still appears to function, you may be experiencing partial hardware failure or file system corruption. In these cases, there are some steps you can try using built-in Mac OS X utilities to repair the volumes or at least recover data.

Gathering File System Information

Before attempting any fixes, you should become fully familiar with the file system configuration you're dealing with. Once again, the /Applications/Utilities/Disk Utility application will be your main tools for gathering file system information. The availability and status of storage hardware in Disk Utility will help determine if you are indeed experiencing hardware failure.

When you open Disk Utility, it will scan the file system for all attached devices and volumes. To gather detailed information about a specific drive or volume in Disk Utility, simply select the item from the column on the left and then click the Info button in the toolbar. Remember, the drive's name is its size and manufacturer information, whereas a drive's volumes appear directly below the drive name in the list.

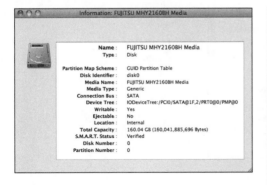

The information gathered from these dialogs will reveal a great deal about the status of a drive or volume. Of most importance for determining hardware failure is a drive's S.M.A.R.T. (Self-Monitoring, Analysis, and Reporting Technology) status. Drives that feature S.M.A.R.T. technology can automatically determine if the drive is suffering from some sort of internal hardware failure.

If a connected drive doesn't even appear in the Disk Utility list, odds are the drive has suffered a catastrophic failure. You should double-check the drive's status using /Applications/Utilities/System Profiler to verify that the drive is unreachable. When you open System Profiler, the drive's information should appear when you select the bus that the drive is connected to, such as Serial-ATA or FireWire. If a drive does not appear in System Profiler either, then it is not available to the Mac in its current state. At this point you should focus your efforts on troubleshooting the drive hardware. This includes simple fixes, such as looking for loose connections or replacing bad cables, as well as more complex fixes, such as having to replace bad hardware.

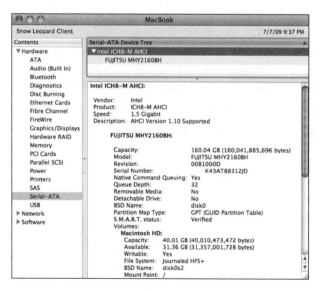

Verify or Repair a Volume

Disk Utility can be used to examine and attempt to repair a volume's directory database. The volume's directory database is used by the file system to catalog where files and folders exist on the drive. To access data on the drive, the file system must first check with the directory database in order to locate the appropriate bits on the drive that make up the requested file. Obviously, any damage to the volume's directory database can lead to serious problems, including data loss.

Before any volume is mounted, the Mac will automatically perform a quick consistency check to verify the volume's directory database. The system will also quickly scan the startup volume during the boot process. However, if the system is unable to mount a volume, you are experiencing issues accessing a volume, or you are booting from the startup disk, you can use Disk Utility to verify and repair a volume's directory database.

To use Disk Utility's verify and repair features:

1   If you're attempting to repair the system drive, you should first boot from the Mac OS X Install DVD and then choose Disk Utility from the Utilities menu.

     If you are on a currently running Mac, make sure the drive you wish to verify or repair is currently attached to the computer, then open /Applications/Utilities/Disk Utility.

2   Select the drive or volume you wish to verify or repair from the column on the left, and then click the First Aid tab to the right.

3   Verify the selected item by clicking the Verify Disk button in the bottom-right corner.

     It may take a few minutes to complete the verification process. During this time Disk Utility will show a progress indicator and log entries in the history area. Click the Show details checkbox to view more detail in the history log. You can stop the process at any time by clicking the Stop button.

4   If no problems were found, you should see an entry in the history log with green text. If problems were uncovered, they will appear in bright red text. If the drive has problems, and you haven't already started the repair process, you should do so now.

The system will continue to run the repair process until no more problems are found. This may take a while because the system may run through the repair process several times.

Using FireWire Target Disk Mode

Mac hardware has a unique ability to share its internal drives via a feature called FireWire target disk mode. Basically, when FireWire target disk mode is engaged, instead of booting normally from the system disk the Mac will bridge any internal drives to the FireWire ports. Because target disk mode is a function built into the Mac's hardware, even if the installed operating system volume is corrupted, you can still use this feature. An administrative user can enable FireWire target disk mode on a currently running Mac by clicking the Target Disk Mode button in the Startup Disk preferences. Alternately, you can engage target disk mode during system startup by holding down the T key while you turn on the Mac.

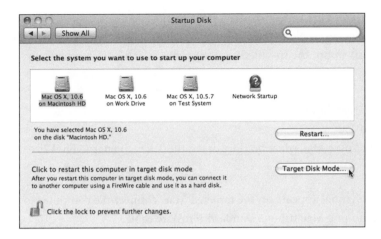

NOTE ▶ FireWire target disk mode is not supported on any Mac that lacks FireWire ports or uses third-party storage interfaces.

NOTE ▶ Target disk mode cannot be engaged during system startup when using a Bluetooth wireless keyboard.

Once target disk mode is engaged, you will see a large FireWire symbol on the screen, and then you can simply plug the targeted Mac into another fully functioning Mac via a FireWire cable. The targeted Mac's internal volumes should mount normally on the other Mac as if you had plugged in a normal external FireWire-based drive. At this point, you can do anything to the targeted Mac's internal drive that you could do to any local drive, including installations, repairs, and data migration.

Recovering Data from an Unbootable System

If you are still stuck with a Mac that refuses to fully boot from its internal system drive, you might be able to recover important data off the drive as long as it's functional. You can use the Mac's built-in FireWire target disk mode to easily access the internal system drive and recover important data from another fully functional Mac.

NOTE ▶ If your Mac doesn't support, or is unable to engage, target disk mode, then your best bet is to visit an Apple authorized repair center. An alternate solution would be to remove the drive from the troubled computer and attach it to another fully functional Mac.

To recover data using target disk mode:

1 Turn on the troublesome Mac while holding down the T key to engage FireWire target disk mode.

2 Once the FireWire symbol appears on the targeted Mac, connect the computer to another fully functioning Mac using a standard FireWire cable.

3 If the targeted Mac's volume appears in the Finder, you should first attempt to repair the volume using Disk Utility, as detailed previously in this chapter.

4 Once repairs have been completed, you have a variety of data recovery options:

▶ **Use the Finder** to manually copy data from the targeted Mac to storage attached to the functioning Mac.

▶ **Use Disk Utility** on the functioning Mac to create a disk image archive of the targeted Mac's system volume. Creating disk images is covered in Chapter 5, "Data Management and Backup."

▶ **Use the Migration Assistant** on a functioning or newly installed Mac to easily migrate user accounts, settings, or applications. The Migration Assistant is covered in Chapter 1, "Installation and Initial Setup."

5 After you have migrated the data, you should use Disk Utility to reformat the targeted Mac's drive and then attempt to reinstall the operating system.

System installation is also covered in Chapter 1, "Installation and Initial Setup."

Depending on the amount of corruption present on the targeted Mac's system drive, you may not be able to use Disk Utility or the Migration Assistant. The drive may simply be too corrupted to recover all that data. In this case, you will have to resort to manually copying data.

In general, the most important items to users are stored in their home folder, so you should start there. This can be a time-consuming process; as the Finder discovers damaged files, you will have to manually restart the copy process and omit the damaged files.

> **TIP** Use the ample spare time between manual file copies to remind the Mac's owner (or yourself) that you wouldn't have to labor over the broken drive if there was a good backup! Using Time Machine to keep backups is covered in Chapter 5, "Data Management and Backup."

Permissions Troubleshooting

Permissions issues can be caused from a variety of situations. Many issues are due to user error, but others can be the result of an unintentional failure elsewhere in the system. For instance, some software installers may improperly change permissions during the installation process. You may also experience permissions issues after restarting from a power loss or system freeze.

System and application errors, such as applications that will not open or an inability to empty the Trash, may occur due to incorrect permissions. Many of these permissions issues can be resolved by utilities that are part of Mac OS X. If you are having trouble accessing an application, you should attempt to resolve the issue using Disk Utility's Repair Disk Permissions feature. Also, if you are experiencing problems trying to access home folders, you can use the Reset Password utility on the Mac OS X Installer DVD to reset home folder permissions. The use of these two utilities for resolving permissions issues is covered later in this section.

Most general permissions issues are revealed in obvious ways. A user attempting to access a file or folder is immediately stopped and presented with a dialog stating that he doesn't have the appropriate permissions. In this case, a permissions change on the item, or the folder it's inside of, is usually all that's needed to resolve the issue. If you are going to attempt to repair the item's permissions manually, you should be familiar with the methods for managing permissions outlined previously in this chapter.

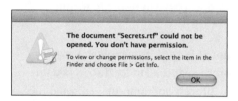

MORE INFO ▶ For further guidance on general permissions troubleshooting you can also refer to Apple Knowledge Base document HT2963, "Troubleshooting permissions issues in Mac OS X."

Clearing ACLs via Command Line

Compared with adjusting traditional UNIX-style permissions, adjusting file and folder ACLs is quite complicated—in fact, such detailed ACL management goes beyond the scope of this guide. Nevertheless, there is one helpful trick for resolving access issues if you think improperly set ACLs are causing the issue. You can, with a single command, clear all the ACLs for a given file or folder using the chmod command with the -N option.

In the following example, Michelle needs to clear the troublesome ACLs of a shared folder named "SharedStuff" and its contents. She first lists the permissions with ACLs using the ls command. Then uses chmod -N to "clear" the folder's ACLs. Finally, Michelle double-checks her work by viewing the permissions again, verifying that the ACL is empty for the SharedStuff folder.

```
MyMac:Shared michelle$ ls -le
total 0
drwxr-xr-x+ 2 cadmin  wheel  68 Jul  7 22:37 SharedStuff
 0: group:family allow add_file,search,add_subdirectory,delete_child,readattr,writeat
tr,writeextattr,readsecurity
MyMac:Shared michelle$ sudo chmod -N SharedStuff/
Password:
MyMac:Shared michelle$ ls -le
total 0
drwxr-xr-x  2 cadmin  wheel  68 Jul  7 22:37 SharedStuff
```

Disk Utility's Repair Permissions

One of the most common troubleshooting techniques for Mac OS X is to use Disk Utility's Repair Disk Permissions feature. Many novice Mac administrators use this technique every time they encounter any problem. The reality is that this process fixes only file permissions issues specific to certain installed Apple software. Further, this process will not touch any incorrect permission settings on personal or user data.

In other words, this process, though a good starting point for addressing system and application issues, will not fix every incorrect permissions issue on a problematic Mac. In fact, you can verify exactly which installed items the repair permissions process will fix from the repair_packages command. In the following example Michelle uses this command to list the packages that will be checked. Note that the output was truncated to save space.

```
MyMac:~ michelle$ sudo /usr/libexec/repair_packages --list-standard-pkgs
Password:
     com.apple.pkg.ServerAdminTools
     com.apple.pkg.ServerSetup
     com.apple.pkg.Rosetta
     com.apple.pkg.X11User
...
```

MORE INFO ▶ For more information, you can also reference Apple Knowledge Base document HT1452, "About Disk Utility's Repair Disk Permissions feature."

The upside is that the repair permissions process is an easy troubleshooting step that could resolve many permissions issues. Keep in mind that many default folders were also installed as part of the operating system. Thus, the repair permissions process will not only repair system items, but also important folders like /Applications and /Library.

To verify or repair disk permissions:

1 Open Disk Utility on a currently running Mac by opening /Applications/Utilities/Disk Utility, or on a Mac booted from the Mac OS X Install DVD by choosing Disk Utility from the Utilities menu.

2 Select the system volume you wish to repair from the column on the left.

3   Select the First Aid tab to the right.

4   Click the Verify Disk Permissions button to view a log of any potential problems.

5   Click the Repair Disk Permissions button to view and fix any permission problems.

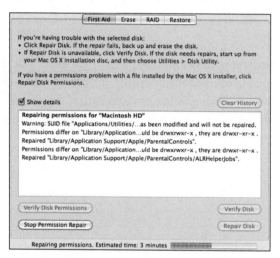

Reset Password's Reset Home Permissions

If a user's home folder becomes inaccessible due to improper permissions, you can attempt to fix the issue by manually adjusting the permissions yourself, or you can try the Reset Password utility found only on the Mac OS X Install DVD. This utility was primarily designed to reset user passwords; nonetheless, this tool also has the ability to reset a user's home folder permissions and ACLs. Keep in mind that this process will reset all home folder permissions, including intentionally changed permissions that may have benefited the user.

To reset home folder permissions and ACLs:

1   Start up the Mac from the Mac OS X Install DVD by turning on the computer while holding down the C key, and as soon as possible, insert the installation disc and the computer will start from it.

2   Once the installer has started, choose Utilities > Reset Password from the menu bar.

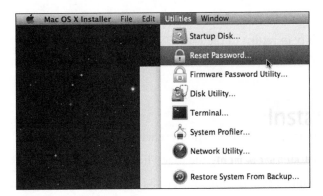

3   Select the system volume containing the home folder you wish to reset from the row of system volume icons.

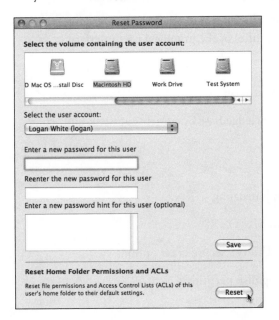

4   Choose the user account whose home folder needs resetting from the user pop-up menu.

5   Click the Reset button at the bottom to reset this user's home folder permissions and ACLs.

6   Quit the Reset Password utility to return to the Mac OS X Installer. Then quit the Mac OS X Installer to restart the Mac.

What You've Learned

▶   Mac OS X's file system supports a variety of partition schemes and volume types.

▶   Disk Utility is your primary tool for managing the Mac's file system.

▶   Mac OS X includes robust built-in support for software-based RAID sets and burning optical media.

▶   File system permissions, in the form of traditional UNIX-style permissions, and access control lists (ACLs) are used to control file and folder access.

▶   There are many useful tools available in the command line for managing the Mac's file system that go beyond the capabilities of the graphical user interface.

References

You can check for new and updated Knowledge Base documents at www.apple.com/support.

General File System

HT2355, "Mac OS X: About file system journaling"

HT1375, "About disk optimization with Mac OS X"

TA24002, "Mac OS X 10.4: About Disk Utility's secure erase options"

HT2374, "Mac OS X 10.5: About resizing disk partitions"

RAID

HT2559, "Mac OS X, Mac OS X Server: How to use Apple-Supplied RAID software"

TA24104, "Intel-based Macs: Flashing question mark when trying to boot from RAID volume"

HT1346, "Mac Pro RAID Card and Xserve RAID Card: Frequently Asked Questions (FAQ)"

Optical Media

TA23505, "Mac OS X 10.4: About improved disc burning and burn folders"

HT2882, "Factors that affect writing to or reading from optical media"

HT2543, "About optical disc drive burning and write speeds"

TA23476, "About default optical drive burning speeds"

HT2446, "Using nonstandard discs in optical drives"

Ownership and Permissions

TS1402, "Unable to move, unlock, modify, or copy an item in Mac OS X"

HT2963, "Troubleshooting permissions issues in Mac OS X"

HT1452, "About Disk Utility's Repair Disk Permissions feature"

File System Troubleshooting

HT1782, "Using Disk Utility in Mac OS X 10.4.3 or later to verify or repair disks"

TS1417, "Resolve startup issues and perform disk maintenance with Disk Utility and fsck"

HT1526, "You can't empty the Trash or move a file to the Trash"

HT2528, "Intel-based Macs: 'You have inserted a disk containing no volumes that Mac OS X can read' alert message"

URLs

NTFS-3G/MacFUSE software bundle provides full support for NTFS: http://macntfs-3g.blogspot.com

Wikipedia entry comparing file systems: http://en.wikipedia.org/wiki/Comparison_of_file_systems

Apple RAID Utility User's Guide: http://images.apple.com/xserve/pdf/RAID_Utility_User_Guide.pdf

Wikipedia entry comparing RAID types: http://en.wikipedia.org/wiki/RAID

DriveSavers data recovery: www.drivesaversdatarecovery.com

Review Quiz

1. What is the difference between disk drives, partitions, and volumes?

2. What are the two primary partition schemes for Mac-formatted drives? What are their differences?

3. What are the six volume formats supported by Mac OS X? How are they different?

4. How does file system journaling work?

5. What are the four erase options available in Disk Utility? What are the differences between them?

6. How does the Finder's Secure Empty Trash feature work?

7. What three methods can be used to eject a volume or drive from the Finder?

8. What is the potential side effect of improperly unmounting or ejecting a drive or volume?

9. What differentiates a RAID 0 set from a RAID 1 set?

10. How do you use the Finder's burn folder feature?

11. How do you use Disk Utility to burn an optical disc?

12. Why is the root, or beginning, level of a user's home folder visible to other users?

13. How are the permissions on the Shared folder set to allow for local user sharing?

14. How does the default organization of the file system allow users to safely share local files and folders?

15. What does it mean when you choose the option to "ignore volume ownership" in the Finder? What are the security ramifications of ignoring volume ownership?

16. How do you identify the ownership and permissions of a file or folder in the Finder? In the Terminal?

17. How do permissions in the Finder appear different than permissions in the Terminal?

18. What is the sticky bit?

19. How is Disk Utility's Verify and Repair feature used?

20. What is target disk mode and how is it engaged?

Answers

1. Disk drives are the actual storage hardware, partitions are logical divisions of a disk drive used to define the storage space, and volumes, contained inside partitions, are used to define how the individual files and folders are saved to the storage.

2. GUID Partition Table is the default partition scheme on Intel-based Macs, and Apple Partition Map is the default partition scheme on PowerPC-based Macs.

3. The volume formats supported as startup volumes for Mac OS X are Mac OS X Extended, the native volume format supported by all Macintosh computers; Mac OS X Extended, Journaled, the default volume format for Mac OS X drives; and Mac OS X Extended, Journaled, Case-Sensitive, the default volume format for Mac OS X Server drives. Volume formats supported as read/write are Mac OS Standard (HFS), a legacy Mac OS volume format; UNIX File System (UFS), a legacy volume format supported by many other UNIX-based systems; and File Allocation Table (FAT32), the volume format used by many peripherals and older Windows-based PCs. Volume formats supported as read-only: NT File System (NTFS), the native volume format used by modern Windows-based operating systems; ISO 9660, a common format for CD media; and Universal Disk Format (UDF), a common format for DVD media.

4. File system journaling records what file operations are in progress at any given moment. This way, if a power failure or system crash occurs, after the system restarts it will be able to quickly verify the integrity of the volume by "replaying" the journal.

5. The four erase options in Disk Utility are Don't Erase Data, which simply replaces the volume's directory structure; Zero Out Data, which provides good security by writing zeros on top of all the previous drive data; 7-Pass Erase, which provides even better security by writing seven separate passes of random information on top of all the previous drive data; and 35-Pass Erase, which provides the best security by writing 35 separate passes of random information on top of all the previous drive data.

6. The Finder's Secure Empty Trash will perform a 7-pass erase on the contents of the Trash folder.

7. The three methods used to eject a volume or drive from the Finder are press and hold the Eject key for a few moments to unmount and eject optical media; select the volume you wish to unmount and eject from the Finder and choose File > Eject from the menu bar; and finally, in the Finder's sidebar, click the small eject button next to the volume you wish to unmount and eject.

8. Improperly unmounting or ejecting a drive or volume may cause data corruption. The system will automatically verify and repair an improperly unmounted or ejected volume the next time it becomes available to the Mac.

9. RAID 0 uses disk striping to simultaneously write data to all drives providing increased performance but increases your chances of data loss due to drive failure. RAID 1 uses disk mirroring to write the same data to multiple drives, which does not increase performance, but it does greatly decrease your chances of data loss due to drive failure.

10. There are two methods for using a burn folder in the Finder. First, you can create a burn folder of any size by choosing File > New Burn Folder from the menu bar. Once you are done adding and arranging items in the burn folder, click the Burn button and then insert a blank recordable optical disc. Or you can create a burn folder of a specific optical disc size by first inserting a blank recordable optical disc; then the Finder will automatically create a burn folder that matches the size of the recordable optical disc.

11. Disk Utility can burn the contents of a disk image to an optical disk. Click the Burn button in Disk Utility's toolbar, select a disk image, and then insert a blank recordable optical disc.

12. The root level of a user's home folder is visible to other users so they can navigate to the Public and Sites shared folders.

13. The Shared folder is set up to allow all users to read and write files, but only the user who owns an item can delete it from the Shared folder. This is accomplished using the sticky bit permissions setting.

14. Every home folder contains a Public folder that other users can read and a Drop Box folder that other users can write to. All other subfolders in a user's home folder (except the Sites folder) have default permissions that do not allow access to other users. The Shared folder is also set for all users to share items.

15. You can choose to ignore ownership on any nonsystem volume. This will ignore any ownership rules and grant any logged-on user unlimited access to the contents of the volume. This is a potential security risk because it will allow any local user account to have full access to the volume even if that user did not originally mount the volume.

16. An item's ownership and permissions can be identified using the Get Info or Inspector windows in the Finder, or by using the ls -l command in the Terminal.

17. The Finder shows only four different permissions options: no access, read and write, read only, and write only. On the other hand, using the options available from the ls command in the Terminal will show you every possible permissions configuration.

18. The sticky bit is a special permission used to define a folder as an append-only destination or, more accurately, a folder in which only the owner of the item can move, rename, or delete the item.

19. The Disk Utility's Verify and Repair feature is used to verify or repair the directory structure of a volume. The directory structure contains all the information used to locate files and folders on the volume.

20. Target disk mode is a Mac-specific hardware feature that, when engaged, will share the Mac's internal disk drives through the FireWire ports. Target disk mode can be engaged from the Startup Disk preferences or by holding down the T key as you turn on the Mac.

5

Time

This chapter takes approximately 2 hours to complete.

Goals

Explore and understand the Mac OS X file layout

Discover common system files, their location, and their purpose

Leverage file metadata by using Spotlight for advanced searching

Learn file management techniques unique to Mac OS X

Archive files and folders using technologies built in to Mac OS X

Use Time Machine to back up and restore important data

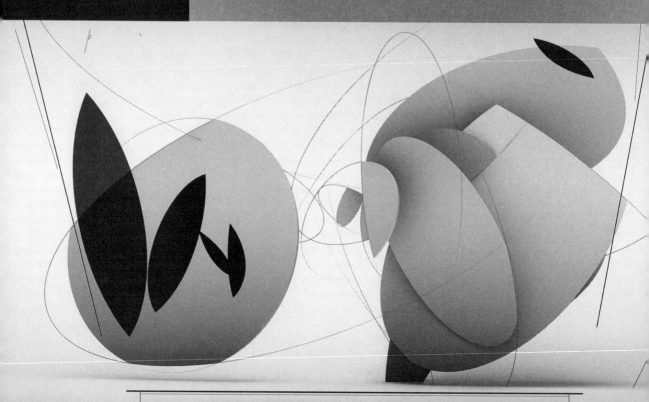

Chapter **5**

Data Management and Backup

It is not unusual for a Mac OS X system volume to contain well over 100,000 folders and 500,000 files just to support the operating system and its applications. As you can imagine, the number of items in a user's home folder varies widely depending on the user, but even the most frugal of users will have thousands of items in his home folder. With this many files on hand, attempting to explore and fully comprehend Mac OS X's file layout may seem like a monumental task. On the contrary, Mac OS X's system files have been streamlined and reorganized into an easy-to-understand layout that provides enhanced security and manageability for the Mac administrator.

This chapter builds on the previous chapter, "File Systems," to focus more specifically on the composition and organization of the files and folders that make up Mac OS X. In this chapter you, acting as an administrator, will use the file layout to strategically allocate resources. You will also work with many Mac-specific file technologies, including resource forks, packages, Quick Look, and Spotlight. Finally, you will use the built-in features for archiving data on the Mac, and learn how to back up and restore data using Time Machine.

Mac OS X Volume Hierarchy

Mac OS X's system layout is designed to strike a balance between ease of use and advanced functionality. For the basic user, looking at the root, or beginning, of the file system from the Finder will reveal only four default folders: Applications, Library, Users, and System. The contents of these four folders represent all that most users, and many administrators, will ever need to access. Yet when advanced users look at the system root from the command-line interface, they will see many more items that the Finder would normally hide. Thus, the complexity and flexibility of a UNIX operating system remains for those users who require it.

Exploring Mac OS X's system layout from the command-line interface is covered previously in Chapter 3 "Command Line and Automation," but for now the following describes the default system root folders you'll see from the Finder:

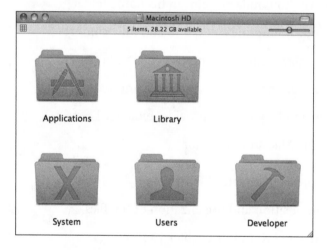

▶ Applications—Often called the local Applications folder, this is the default location for applications available to all local users. Only administrative users can make changes to the contents of this folder.

▶ Library—Often called the local Library folder, this is the default location for ancillary system and application resources available to all local users. Once again, only administrative users can make changes to the contents of this folder.

▶ System—This folder contains resources required by the operating system for primary functionality. Users very rarely have to make changes to the contents of this folder. Even administrative users are unable to make changes to items in the System folder without reauthenticating.

▶ Users—This is the default location for local user home folders. Specific access to home folder items is discussed in Chapter 2, "User Accounts."

▶ Developer (Optional)—This optional folder contains the Apple Xcode Developer Tools. This is not part of the standard installation, but it's still a fundamental part of the system, and its installer can be found on the Mac OS X Install DVD. Similar to the Applications and Library folders, the Developer folder can be changed only by an administrative user.

System Resource Types

All Mac OS X–specific system resources can be found in the various Library folders throughout the system volume. System resources can be generally categorized as any resource that is not a general-use application or user file. That's not to say that applications and user data can't be found in the Library folders. On the contrary, the Library folder is to keep both user and system resources organized and separated from the items you use every day. This keeps the Applications folder and user home folders free from system resource clutter.

Opening any of the Library folders will reveal several dozen categories of items. It is not necessary to explore every single possible Library item, but there are a few system resources you should be familiar with:

▶ Application Support—This folder can be found in both the user and local Libraries. Any ancillary data needed by an application may end up in this folder. For example, it often contains help files or templates for an application. Once again, application resources are placed here to keep the Applications folders tidy.

▶ Extensions—Also called kernel extensions, these items are found only in the system and local Library folders. Extensions are low-level drivers that attach themselves to the kernel, or core, of the operating system. Extensions provide driver support for hardware, networking, and peripherals. Extensions load and unload automatically, so there is little need to manage them, as is common in other operating systems. Extensions are covered to greater detail in Chapter 9, "Peripherals and Printing."

► Fonts—Found in every Library folder, fonts are files that describe typefaces used for both screen display and printing. Font management is covered in the "Managing Font Resources" section later in this chapter.

► Frameworks—Found in every Library folder, frameworks are repositories of shared code used among different parts of the operating system or applications. Frameworks are similar to extensions in that they load and unload automatically, so again there is little need to manage these shared code resources. You can view your Mac's currently loaded frameworks from the /Applications/Utilities/System Profiler application.

► Keychains—Found in every Library folder, keychains are used to securely store sensitive information, including passwords, certificates, keys, website forms, and notes. Keychain technology is covered previously in Chapter 2, "User Accounts."

► LaunchDaemons and LaunchAgents—These items can both be found in the local and system Libraries, and LaunchAgents can also be found in the user's library. These Launch items are used to define processes that start automatically via the launchd process. Mac OS X uses many background processes, which are all started by launchd. Furthermore, every single process is a child of the launchd process. LaunchAgents are for processes that need to start up only when a user is logged in, whereas LaunchDaemons are used to start processes that will always run in the background even when there are no users logged in. More about launchd can be found in Chapter 10, "System Startup."

► Logs—Many system processes and applications archive progress or error messages to log files. Log files can be found in every local Library folder. Log files are viewed using the /Applications/Utilities/Console application.

► PreferencePanes—PreferencePanes can be found in any Library folder. These items are used by the System Preferences application to provide interfaces for system configuration. System Preferences usage is covered in Chapter 1, "Installation and Initial Setup."

► Preferences—Preferences, found in both local and user libraries, are used to store system and application configuration settings. In other words, every time you configure a setting for any application or system function, it is saved to a preference file. Because preferences play such a critical role in system functionality, they are often the cause of software problems. Troubleshooting preference files is covered in Chapter 6, "Applications and Boot Camp."

▶ Startup Items—Startup Items, found in only the local and system Libraries, are pre-cursors to LaunchAgents and LaunchDaemons. Starting with Mac OS X 10.5, Apple is officially discouraging the use of Startup Items. In fact, you will have Startup Items only if you've installed third-party software that hasn't been updated. In Mac OS X 10.6 the launchd process will still support many Startup Items, but this will probably not be true for future versions.

System Resource Hierarchy

Library folders, and thus system resources, are located in each of the four domain areas: user, local, network, and system. Segregating resources into four domains provides increased administrative flexibility, resource security, and system reliability. Resource domains are more flexible because administrators can choose to allocate certain resources to all users or just specific users. Using resource domains is more secure because standard users can add resources only to their own home folder and cannot access other users' resources. Finally, it's more reliable because, in most cases, you don't have to make changes to the core system functionality in order to provide more services.

The four system resource domains are, in order:

▶ User—Each user has his own Library folder in his home folder for resources. When resources are placed here, only the user has access to them. Also, a user can have his own Applications folder in his home folder.

▶ Local—Both the root Applications and root Library folders are part of the local resource domain. This is why they are known as the local Applications and local Library folders. Any resources placed in these two folders are available to all local user accounts. By default, only administrative users can make changes to local resources.

▶ Network—Mac OS X can access system resources and applications from a network file share. Administrators must configure an automounted share in order to enable the Network resource domain. Configuring automounted shares goes beyond the scope of this guide. However, it is covered in another reference guide, *Apple Training Series: Mac OS X Server Essentials v10.6*.

▶ System—Finally, the system domain encompasses all the items necessary to provide core system functionality. There are many hidden items at the root of the system volume that make up the system resource domain, but the only one you will see in the Finder is the root System folder. In many cases, you do not need to add or manage any resources here.

With four different domains containing resources, there is a strong likelihood for overlap in resources, meaning there may be multiple copies of similar resources available to the system and user at any given time. The system is designed to handle this by searching for resources from the most specific, those in the user domain, to the least specific, those in the system domain. If multiple similar resources are discovered, the system will use the resource most specific to the user. For example, if multiple versions of the font Times New Roman are found, one in the local Library and one in the user's Library, the copy of the font in the user's Library will be the one used.

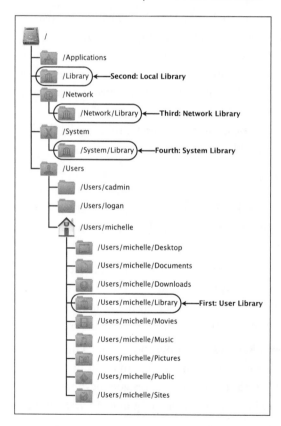

System Resource Troubleshooting

System resource issues are rare, and they are generally easy to identify. You will occasionally see an error message calling out an issue with a specific item, but you may also experience a situation where the item appears to be missing. In some cases, the system resource in question may be missing, but many times the system will simply ignore a system resource if it determines that the resource is in some way corrupted. The solution for both of these situations is to simply replace the missing or suspect item with a known working copy.

When troubleshooting system resources, you must also remember to heed the resource domain hierarchy. Using font resources as an example, you may have loaded a specific version of a font in the local Library that is required by your workflow to operate properly. In spite of this, a user may have loaded another version of the same font in her home folder. In this case, the system will load the user's font and ignore the font you installed. Therefore, this user may experience workflow problems even though it appears that she is using the correct font.

> **TIP** If fonts are missing from within applications but appear to be properly installed, remember to check Font Book as the font may be temporarily disabled. Font Book is covered in the next section of this chapter.

Logging in with another account on the Mac is always a quick way to determine if the problem is in the user's home folder. You can also use /Applications/Utilities/System Profiler to list active system resources. System Profiler will always show the file path of the loaded system resources, so it's easy to spot resources that are loading from the user's Library.

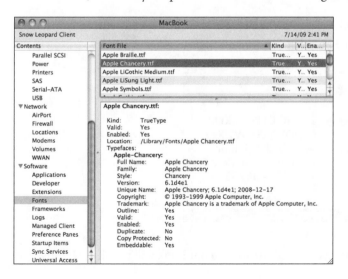

Managing Font Resources

An excellent way to experience the system resource domain hierarchy is by managing fonts. Mac OS X has advanced font-management technology that enables an unlimited number of fonts using nearly any font type, including bitmap, TrueType, OpenType, and all PostScript Type fonts. As mentioned previously, fonts are installed in the various Font folders located in the Library folders throughout the system. A user can manually install fonts simply by dragging them into a Fonts folder.

On the other hand, Mac OS X includes a very nice font-management tool, /Applications/ Font Book, which will automatically install fonts for you. Font Book can also be used to organize fonts into more manageable collections, enable or disable fonts to simplify font lists, and resolve duplicate fonts.

NOTE ▶ Third-party font-management tools, such as Extensis's Suitcase Fusion or Universal Type Server, will interrupt Font Book and take over font management for the system.

To manage fonts with Font Book:

1 Open /Applications/Font Book.

The main Font Book window appears, allowing you to preview any currently installed font by clicking on it in the Font list.

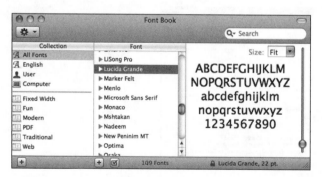

2 Choose Font Book > Preferences to adjust where Font Book will install new fonts.

By default, Font Book will install fonts to the user's Library. If you are an administrative user, you can choose to install fonts to the local Library by choosing Computer from the pop-up menu. Close the Font Book Preferences dialog once you have made your selections.

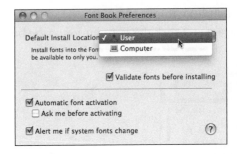

NOTE ▶ Font Book will, by default, automatically validate a font before enabling it. This helps prevent font issues by making sure the font file isn't compromised. Thus, installing fonts via Font Book is favored over manual installation via Finder.

3   From the Finder, simply double-click on the font you wish to install. Font Book will automatically open the font and show you a preview.

4   Click the Install Font button to validate and install the font to your selected default Library folder.

NOTE ▶ Some applications may need to be restarted to take advantage of recently added fonts.

5   If you, or the application you're using, have difficulties choosing fonts from a large list, you can temporarily disable fonts within Font Book by selecting the font and then clicking the small checkbox button at the bottom of the font list. You will also have to verify your choice by clicking the Disable button when a verification dialog appears.

Disabled fonts will appear dimmed in the font list with the word Off next to their name. To enable the font, simply select it again and click the same button at the bottom of the font list.

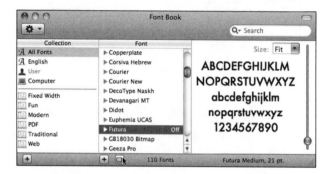

6   Fonts that have multiple copies on your system will show a small dot next to their name in the font list. You can automatically disable fonts that are duplicated in your system with Font Book, by choosing Edit > Resolve Duplicates from the menu bar.

7   To remove a font, select it from the font list and press the Delete key. You will be presented with a summary dialog, reminding you that continuing will move the selected fonts to the Trash folder. If you are sure this is what you want to do, then click the Remove button.

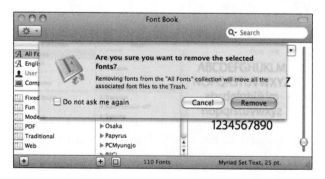

TIP Remember, you can always disable a font instead of deleting it entirely.

8 If you're having font issues you can identify problem fonts by forcing the system to revalidate all the fonts on your system. To do this select All Fonts from the Collection list, then select a single font in the Font list, and finally use the Command-A keyboard combination to select all the fonts. Choose File > Validate Fonts to start the validation process.

The Font Validation window will open and scan all the selected fonts. This window will clearly show problem fonts with a status indicator next to the font's name. To remove a problem font simply select the checkbox next to its name and then click the Removed Checked button.

Managing Hidden Items

Mac OS X is a fully compliant UNIX operating system, and as such requires a number of files that will never be used by the average user. The root level of the Mac's system volume is littered with resources that are required by UNIX processes and expected by UNIX administrators. Apple made the wise choice of configuring the Finder to hide these items from the average user. On a daily basis, the average user—and even most administrative users—do not need to access any of these items from the graphical interface. Realistically, the only people who even care about these normally hidden resources are going to be using the command-line interface to do their work anyway. In other words, keeping these system items hidden in the Finder not only provides a tidier work environment but also prevents average users from poking around in places they don't need to go.

Mac OS X, being a hybrid of UNIX and Mac OS technologies, uses two methods to hide files and folders. The first method is a UNIX tradition; simply using a period at the beginning of the item's name will hide the item. This will hide the item in both the Finder and while using the default options to list items with ls in the command line. The second method is a Mac OS tradition; enable an item's hidden file flag. This method, however, will only hide the item in the Finder.

> NOTE ▶ If you aren't already comfortable with navigation in the UNIX command line, then it's strongly recommended that you study the command line concepts in Chapter 3, "Command Line and Automation," before reading the remainder of the section.

Revealing Hidden Items

From the command line you can easily override both types of hidden items. Again, by default, the ls command ignores the hidden file flag used by the Finder; thus it will simply show these items in the list. However, in its default mode the ls command doesn't show items whose names begin with a period. You can modify this behavior by using the -a option to list all items.

In the following command line example, Michelle will use the ls command with the -a option to reveal all items at the root of a Mac OS X system volume:

```
MyMac:~ michelle$ ls -a /
total 36669
.                                                    Users
..                                                   Volumes
.DS_Store                                            bin
.Spotlight-V100                                      cores
.Trashes                                             dev
.com.apple.timemachine.supported                     etc
```

```
.file                          home
.fseventsd                     mach_kernel
.hotfiles.btree                net
.vol                           private
Applications                   sbin
Developer                      tmp
Library                        usr
Network                        var
System
```

Of the nearly 30 items at the root of the system volume shown in this example, only 5 are shown in the Finder: Applications, Developer, Library, System, and Users. All of these additional items are created and used by the operating system, so they should generally be left alone. Again, for this reason they are hidden to most users by the Finder.

Opening Hidden Items in the Finder

Should you want or need to open normally hidden items in the Finder, there are two methods. The first involves use of the Finder's Go menu to open any folder; the second involves using the open command from the command line to open any file or folder.

Using the Go Menu

To reveal hidden folders in the Finder:

1   From the Finder, choose Go > Go to Folder from the menu bar, or you can use the Command-Shift-G keyboard combination.

    This will reveal a dialog allowing you to enter an absolute path to any folder on the Mac. A good starting place is the /private folder, as many UNIX system configuration files are found in this folder.

2   Click the Go button once you have entered the path.

The Finder will reveal the hidden folder in a window. Note the dimmed folder icon representing the normally hidden folder. To save time for when you return to the Go dialog, the previous path you entered will be there.

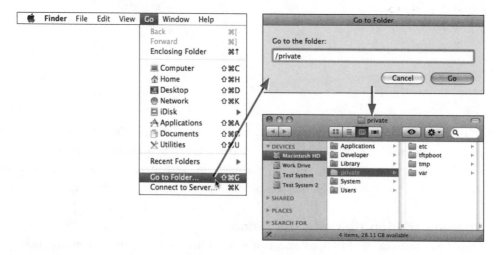

Using the open Command

The open command is a rather unique command that spans the chasm between the command line and the graphical interface. The open command can be used to open files, folders, and URLs from the command line to an application in the graphical interface. Folders are opened in a Finder window, the default web browser opens URLs, and files are opened by the default application for the specified file type. Again, because the command line doesn't respect the hidden file flag, you can use the open command to open any hidden item as well.

> **NOTE ▶** The only caveat when using the open command is that the user who executes the open command must also be logged in to the graphical interface. In other words, the same user account must be logged in to the graphical interface and the command line to use the open command.

The following example will use the open command to open the user's current working folder from the command line to a Finder window. The period used in the command is command-line shorthand for "this folder," thus this example literally translates to "open this folder."

```
MyMac:~ michelle$ open .
```

The next example will open the /private folder, which is normally hidden, in a Finder window:

```
MyMac:~ michelle$ open /private
```

This next example will open a file on Michelle's desktop called Proof.pdf with the default PDF reader, most likely the Preview application:

```
MyMac:~ michelle$ open Desktop/Proof.pdf
```

This final example will open Apple's main website in the default web browser, most likely the Safari application:

```
MyMac:~ michelle$ open http://www.apple.com/
```

> **TIP** Remember, you can automatically enter paths in the command line by dragging a file or folder from the Finder to a Terminal window.

Hiding or "Un-Hiding" Items

The easiest way to hide an item is to simply name it with a period at the beginning of the filename. However, to prevent novice users from accidentally hiding their items, the Finder will not let you save a file with a period at the beginning of its name. Therefore, you must use the command line. Simply use the mv command to rename the item, as covered in Chapter 3, "Command Line and Automation."

If you need to hide an item from the Finder, but you can't change its name to start with a period, then you can enable the hidden file flag. This is also only possible from the command line. You can use the chflags command with the hidden option to hide any item from the Finder. Further, you can use the -0 option, along with the list long option -l, to show any file system flags, verifying which items have the hidden file flag enabled.

In the following example Michelle uses the chflags command to hide a folder named SuperSecrets in her desktop folder. She also uses the ls command before and after to show the file flags, verifying that the folder became hidden after the change.

```
MyMac:Desktop michelle$ ls -lO
total 0
drwx------  2 michelle   staff   - 68 Jul 14 22:00 SuperSecrets
```

```
MyMac:Desktop michelle$ chflags hidden SuperSecrets/
MyMac:Desktop michelle$ ls -lO
total 0
drwx------@ 2 michelle   staff   hidden 68 Jul 14 22:00 SuperSecrets
```

TIP To disable the hidden file flag simply use the nohidden option with the chflags command.

TIP You can use the chflags command to enable or disable any file flag, including the notorious locked file or folder flag, as covered in Chapter 4, "File Systems."

Using Aliases and Links

Another example of Mac OS X being a hybrid of both UNIX and the classic Mac OS is the multiple methods used for file system pointers or shortcuts. Generally speaking, file system shortcuts are files that reference other files or folders. This allows you to have a single item appear in multiple locations or with multiple names without having to create multiple copies of the item. Both the system and users take advantage of file system shortcuts to access items in more convenient locations without having to duplicate those items.

NOTE ▶ Do not confuse the shortcuts found in the Dock or the Finder's sidebar with true file system shortcuts. Both the Dock and Finder save their references to original items as part of their configuration files, whereas file system shortcuts appear as individual files that can be located anywhere on a volume.

Mac OS X uses three primary file system shortcut types:

▶ Aliases—These shortcuts are a holdover from the classic Mac OS but have been updated for Mac OS X duties. Aliases can be created with the Finder but are useless in the command line. Command line tools think that aliases are nothing more than data files and do not know how to follow their references back to the original items. Aliases, however, are more resilient than other shortcut types in that if the original item is replaced or moved, the alias will almost never lose the original item. An example of how aliases are used by the operating system is the Finder's burn folder feature, which allows you to organize files before you burn them to an optical disc. The Finder populates the burn folder with aliases instead of copies of the original items in order to save space.

▶ Symbolic Links—These shortcuts are part of the traditional UNIX file system and are simple pointers to the file system path of the original item. Thus, if you move the original item, the symbolic link will be broken. However, replacing the original item works because the path remains the same. You can create symbolic links with the ln command. The Finder cannot create symbolic links, but it can follow them to the original item. An example use of symbolic links in Mac OS X is the way the system layout stores several fundamental UNIX folders in the /private folder but also makes those items available at the root of the file system using symbolic links.

▶ Hard Links—These shortcuts are also part of the traditional UNIX file system and are actual additional references to the original item. Think of a normal file as two parts; first, the bits on the physical drive that make up the file's actual content, and second, a name that points to those bits. A hard link is an additional name that points to the same bits on the physical drive. You can also use the ln command to create hard links. The Finder cannot create hard links, but it can follow them. An example use of hard links in Mac OS X is for Time Machine backups. Time Machine uses hard links to reference items that have not changed since the previous backup, thus saving a tremendous amount of space. Finally, Mac OS X is unique in its ability to use hard links of both files and folders; again, this is to support Time Machine backups.

Creating Aliases

The Finder provides several methods for creating aliases. Simply select the item you want to create an alias for, and then choose one of the following methods:

▶ Choose File > Make Alias from the menu bar.

▶ Use the Command-L keyboard shortcut.

▶ In a Finder window select the Action (gear) button from the toolbar and then from the pop-up menu select Make Alias.

▶ Right-click or Control-click the item, and then from the pop-up menu select Make Alias.

▶ Click and drag the original item while holding down the Option and Command keys to drop an alias in another location. This is the only method that doesn't append the word "alias" to the new alias filename.

Once you have created the alias, you can rename it or move it anywhere you like. As long as the original item remains somewhere on the original volume, even if it's replaced or its name changes, the Finder will be able to locate the alias. An alias file is easy to recognize given the small curved arrow that appears at the bottom left corner of the icon. From the Finder you can locate the alias's target by right-clicking, or Control-clicking, on the alias and then selecting Show Original from the pop-up menu.

In the rare case that an alias is broken, most likely because the original item was copied to another volume and then deleted off the original volume, you can repair the alias in the Finder. One method is to double-click on the broken alias and the Finder will automatically prompt you to select a new original. Another option, which can also be used to redirect an existing alias, is to open the Finder's Get Info window and then in the General area click the Select New Original button. Both methods will open a browser dialog allowing you to select a new original for the alias.

Creating Symbolic Links

Because UNIX tools do not support aliases, you will need to create links if you wish to use shortcuts at the command line. The `ln` command used with no additional options creates hard links, while using the `-s` option creates symbolic links. In both cases the arguments are the original item's path and name first followed by the new link's path and name.

NOTE ▶ The `ln` command cannot create hard links of folders, even though Mac OS X supports this via Time Machine. In most cases a symbolic link is sufficient as a folder shortcut.

In the following example Michelle has already created a folder named MyFolder and alias to that folder named MyFolderAlias. She first lists the items using `ls -lh` to list in long format with "human readable" file sizes. She then attempts to navigate into the alias folder, but as covered previously, the command line does not understand alias files, so it returns an error. Next, Michelle uses `ln -s` to create a symbolic link of MyFolder with the new link being named MyFolderSymLink. She lists items again to verify the symbolic link was created; note the "l" at the beginning of the permissions string and the arrow after the symbolic link's name pointing to the original item. Finally, she successfully navigates into the symbolic link folder.

```
MyMac:Desktop michelle$ ls -lh
total 2032
drwxr-xr-x  19 michelle  staff    646B Jul 15 21:24 MyFolder
-rw-r--r--@  1 michelle  staff    507K Jul 15 22:39 MyFolderAlias
MyMac:Desktop michelle$ cd MyFolderAlias
-bash: cd: MyFolderAlias: Not a directory
MyMac:Desktop michelle$ ln -s MyFolder MyFolderSymLink
MyMac:Desktop michelle$ ls -lh
total 2040
drwxr-xr-x  19 michelle  staff    646B Jul 15 21:24 MyFolder
-rw-r--r--@  1 michelle  staff    507K Jul 15 22:39 MyFolderAlias
lrwxr-xr-x   1 michelle  staff      8B Jul 15 22:47 MyFolderSymLink -> MyFolder
MyMac:Desktop michelle$ cd MyFolderSymLink
MyMac:MyFolderSymLink michelle$ pwd
/Users/michelle/Desktop/MyFolderSymLink
```

Comparing File System Shortcut Types

This next example shows the differences between aliases, symbolic links, and hard links from the command line. Michelle has already created a rather large disk image file named BigFile and an alias to that item named BigFileAlias. She starts by listing the items showing their size; note that the original file is much larger, measured in megabytes, than the alias, measured in kilobytes. She then makes two links; the first is a hard link named BigFileHardLink, and the second is a symbolic link named BigFileSymLink. Finally, she lists the items to compare their sizes once more.

```
MyMac:Desktop michelle$ ls -lh
total 200512
-rw-r--r--@ 1 michelle  staff     98M Jul 15 21:07 BigFile.dmg
-rw-r--r--@ 1 michelle  staff    109K Jul 15 23:03 BigFileAlias
MyMac:Desktop michelle$ ln BigFile.dmg BigFileHardLink
MyMac:Desktop michelle$ ln -s BigFile.dmg BigFileSymLink
MyMac:Desktop michelle$ ls -lh
total 400584
```

```
-rw-r--r--@ 2 michelle  staff    98M Jul 15 21:07 BigFile.dmg
-rw-r--r--@ 1 michelle  staff   109K Jul 15 23:03 BigFileAlias
-rw-r--r--@ 2 michelle  staff    98M Jul 15 21:07 BigFileHardLink
lrwxr-xr-x  1 michelle  staff    11B Jul 15 23:04 BigFileSymLink -> BigFile.dmg
```

Note in the previous example that the hard link is the exact same size as the original, indicating that they are both pointing to the same bits on the physical drive. Also note that the number between the permissions string and the owner for the original item has increased from 1 to 2. This number represents the number of links to a file, thus creating the new hard link incremented this number by one. Finally, notice how small the symbolic link is, measured in bytes, compared with the alias. The extra information in the alias is what allows the system to keep track of the original item if it should ever change locations.

NOTE ▶ Removing additional hard links will not delete the original item. Furthermore, deleting the original item will not delete the hard links; they still point to the same bits on the disk, which won't be freed until there are no links left to them. This is unlike aliases and symbolic links, where deleting the original item leaves the shortcut pointing at nothing.

Finally, the following screenshot shows multiple Finder Get Info dialogs examining all four of the items created for this example. Specifically, look at what the Get Info dialog reports for the item's "Kind." Both the alias and the symbolic link are reported as an "Alias" despite their size and technology difference. Besides the size, another clue is that the Finder cannot select a new original for the symbolic link. Also notice that the hard link is reporting the exact same information as the original item, again indicating that they share the same bits on the physical drive.

Understanding File System Metadata

Metadata is data about data. More specifically, metadata is information used to describe content. The most basic forms of file and folder metadata employed by nearly every operating system are names, paths, modification dates, and permissions. These metadata objects are not part of the item's content, yet they are necessary to describe the item in the file system. Mac OS X uses several types of additional file system metadata for a variety of technologies that ultimately lead to a richer user experience.

Resource Forks

Resource forks have a long history in the Macintosh operating system, dating back to the original Mac OS. To simplify the user experience, Apple created a forked file system to make complex items, such as applications, appear as a single icon. Forked file systems, like Mac OS Extended, allow multiple pieces of data to appear as a single item in the file system. In this case, a file will appear as a single item, but it is actually composed of two separate pieces, a data fork and a resource fork. This also allows the Mac OS to support standard file types in the data fork, while the extra Mac-specific information resides in the resource fork. For many years the Mac OS has relied on forked files for storing both applications and files.

Mac OS X not only continues but also expands the use of resource forks, even going so far as to allow developers to take advantage of an arbitrary number of additional named forks. This enables Apple, and other developers, to implement unique file system solutions without having to modify the existing file system. For instance, Mac OS X v10.6 features compressed application code, wherein the actual executable program files are all compressed to save space and then when needed automatically decompressed on-the-fly. To prevent previous versions of Mac OS X or older applications from improper handling of these compressed executables, Apple chose to hide the compressed bits in various data forks and the resource fork.

The downside to resource forks, and other types of additional file system metadata, is that many third-party file systems, like FAT, do not know how to properly store the resource fork data. The solution to this issue is addressed with the AppleDouble file format covered later in this chapter.

File Flags and Extended Attributes

Mac OS X also uses file system flags and extended attributes to implement a variety of file system features. In general, file system flags are holdovers from the original Mac OS and are primarily used to control user access. Examples of file system flags include the locked flag covered in Chapter 4, "File Systems," and the hidden flag covered previously in this chapter.

With Mac OS X, Apple needed to expand the range of possible attributes associated with any file or folder, which is where so-called extended attributes come into play. Any process or application can add an arbitrary number of custom attributes to a file or folder. Again, this allows developers to create new forms of metadata without having to modify the existing file system. The Mac OS Extended file system will store any additional attributes as another fork associated with the file.

The Finder uses extended attributes for several general file features, including setting an item's color label, stationary pad option, hide extension option, and Spotlight comments. All of these items can be accessed from the Finder's Get Info window.

Metadata via the Command Line

From the command line you can verify that an item has additional file system metadata present using the ls command with both the long list option, -l, and the -@ option. In the following example, Michelle uses the ls command to view the file system metadata associated with an alias file and the file shown in the previous Get Info window screen shot.

```
MyMac:Desktop michelle$ ls -l@
total 1368
-rw-r--r--@ 1 cadmin   staff    43316 Jul 15 15:49 AliasFile
        com.apple.FinderInfo                         32
        com.apple.ResourceFork                    42950
-rw-------@ 1 michelle  staff   557722 Jul  1 17:16 Document.pdf
        com.apple.FinderInfo                         32
        com.apple.metadata:kMDItemFinderComment     120
```

Note the "@" symbol at the end of the permissions string, which indicates the item has additional metadata. This symbol is shown any time you perform a long listing. For the sake of simplification, using ls -l@ combines the viewing of both resource fork and extended attribute data. The indented lines below the primary listing show the additional metadata that the Finder has added. In the case of the alias file, it's clear from the file sizes that the resource fork is used to store the alias data.

Bundles and Packages

Sometimes forked files aren't the most efficient solution for hiding data, especially if you have a lot of related files that you need to hide. So instead of creating a new container technology, Apple simply modified an existing file system container, the common folder. Bundles and packages are nothing more than common folders that happen to contain related software and resources. This allows software developers to easily organize all the resources needed for a complicated product into a single bundle or package, while discouraging normal users from interfering with the resources.

Bundles and packages use the same technique of combining resources inside special folders. The difference is that the Finder treats packages as opaque objects that, by default, users cannot navigate into. For example, where a user sees only a single icon in the Finder representing an application, in reality it is a folder potentially filled with thousands of resources. The word "package" is also used to describe the archive files used by the installer application to install software—that is, installer packages. This is appropriate, though, as users cannot, by default, navigate into the contents of an installer package because the Finder again displays it as a single opaque object.

The anatomy of an installer package is quite simple; it usually contains only a compressed archive of the software to be installed and a few configuration files used by the installer application. Other software bundles and packages, on the other hand, are often much more complex as they contain all the resources necessary for the application or software.

Software bundles or packages often include:

▶ Executable code for multiple platforms

▶ Document description files

▶ Media resources such as images and sounds

▶ User interface description files

▶ Text resources

▶ Resource forks

▶ Resources localized for specific languages

▶ Private software libraries and frameworks

▶ Plug-ins or other software to expand capability

Although the Finder default is to hide the contents of a package, you can view the contents of a package from the Finder. To access the content of a package in the Finder, simply right-click or Control-click on the item you wish to explore, and then choose View Package Contents from the shortcut menu.

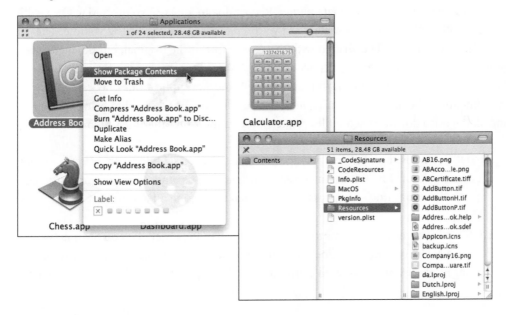

Nevertheless, you should be very careful when exploring this content. Modifying the content of a bundle or package can easily leave the item unstable or unusable. If you can't resist the desire to tinker with a bundle or package, you should always do so from a copy and leave the original safely intact.

> **MORE INFO** ▶ Tools for creating and modifying bundles and packages are included with the optional Xcode Developer Tools package that can be found on the Mac OS X Install DVD.

AppleDouble File Format

While file system metadata helps make the user's experience on Mac OS X richer, compatibility with third-party file systems can be an issue. Only volumes formatted with the Mac OS Extended file system fully support Mac OS X resource forks, data forks, file flags, and extended attributes. Third-party software has been developed for Windows-based operating systems to allow them to access the extended metadata features of Mac OS Extended. More often though, users will use the compatibility software built into Mac OS X to help other file systems cope with these metadata items.

For most non-Mac OS volumes, Mac OS X stores the file system metadata in a separate hidden data file. This technique is commonly referred to as AppleDouble. For example, if you copy a file containing metadata named Report.doc to a FAT32 volume, Mac OS X will automatically split the file and write it as two discrete pieces on the FAT32 volume. The file's internal data would be written with the same name as the original, but the metadata would end up in a file named ._Report.doc, which would remain hidden from the Finder. This works out pretty well for most files because Windows applications only care about the contents of the data fork. Consequently, some files do not take well to being split up and all the extra dot-underscore files create a bit of a mess on other file systems.

> **NOTE** ▶ Because bundles and packages are really just special folders, these items simply copy over to non-Mac OS volumes as regular folders. The Finder will continue to recognize the items as bundles or packages even when they reside on a third-party volume.

Mac OS X 10.5 introduced an improved method for handling metadata on SMB network shares from NTFS volumes that doesn't require the AppleDouble format. The native file system for modern Windows-based computers, NTFS, supports something similar to file forking known as alternative data streams. The Mac's file system will write the metadata to the alternative data stream so the file will appear as a single item on both Windows and Mac systems.

> **NOTE ▶** Mac OS X will always revert to using "dot underscore" files when writing to FAT32 and UFS volumes or older NFS shares.

AppleDouble Files via Command Line

Historically, UNIX operating systems have not used file systems with extensive metadata. As a result, many UNIX commands do not properly support this additional metadata. These commands can manipulate the data fork just fine, but they often ignore the additional metadata, leaving files damaged and possibly unusable. Fortunately, Apple has made some modifications to the most common file management commands, thus allowing them to properly work with all Mac files and support the AppleDouble format when necessary. Metadata–friendly commands on Mac OS X include cp, mv, and rm.

In the following example, Michelle will use the metadata-aware cp command to copy a file on her desktop called ForkedDocument.tiff to a FAT32 volume. Note that the file is a single item on her desktop, but on the FAT32 volume it's in the dual file AppleDouble format. The metadata part is named with a preceding period-underscore. Finally, Michelle will remove the file using the metadata-aware rm command. Note that both the data and the metadata part are removed from the FAT32 volume.

```
MyMac:~ michelle$ ls -a Desktop/
.                           .localized
..                          ForkedDocument.tiff
MyMac:~ michelle$ cp Desktop/ForkedDocument.tiff /Volumes/FAT32VOLUME/
MyMac:~ michelle$ ls -a /Volumes/FAT32VOLUME/
.                           ._.Trashes
..                          ._ForkedDocument.tiff
.DS_Store                   .fseventsd
.Spotlight-V100             ForkedDocument.tiff
.Trashes
MyMac:~ michelle$ rm /Volumes/FAT32VOLUME/ForkedDocument.tiff
```

```
MyMac:~ michelle$ ls -a /Volumes/FAT32VOLUME/
.                        ._.Trashes
..                       .DS_Store
.fseventsd               .Spotlight-V100
.Trashes
```

Managing Launch Services

Aside from a file's name, the most fundamentally important piece of metadata about a file is its type. Identifying a file's type allows Mac OS X to almost always choose the correct application to open when you double-click on a file. Launch Services is the technology responsible for helping Mac OS X make the connection between a file's type and the appropriate application. When you double-click on a file from the Finder, it asks Launch Services to open the file with the appropriate application. Launch Services identifies the file based on its type and then references an application registration database to determine which application should open the file.

File Type Identification

Apple pioneered file type identification when it first introduced the Macintosh operating system. Apple designed the file identification system to use four-character file type and creator signature file attributes, which were normally hidden from the user. This was a brilliant design that separated the file's type and default application binding from the file's name.

Unfortunately, the popularity of other operating systems forced the awkward practice of adding a file type identifier to the end of a file's name, thus complicating the practice of naming files by requiring the user to identify and maintain the appropriate filename extension. You probably recognize many of these extensions, like .mp3 for compressed audio files, .jpg for compressed picture files, or .doc for Microsoft Word files. Using filename extensions has become standard practice, so modern operating systems have been designed to work around this poor design choice by simply hiding the filename extension from the user. For the sake of compatibility, Apple adopted this later method of file type identification as the default for Mac OS X.

> **NOTE ▶** Mac OS X v10.6 still supports the legacy file type attribute but no longer supports the creator code attribute. Thus some files may not default to opening in the application that created them. However, you can change the default behavior as covered later in this section.

Since the Finder hides many file type extensions by default, you can toggle file type extension visibility from the Finder's preferences by choosing Finder > Preferences from the menu bar. Then click the Advanced button and select or deselect the checkbox next to "Show all file extensions."

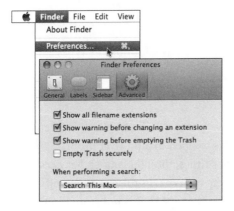

NOTE ▶ Choosing to show all file extensions in the Finder will override the individual file attribute for hiding the extension as configured from the Get Info and Inspector windows in the Finder.

Application Registration

When a user attempts to open a file, Launch Services reads from a database of applications and the types of files each can open to determine a match. After every reboot or login, a background process automatically scans for new applications and updates this database. Further, both the Finder and Installer keep track of new applications as they arrive on your system and add their supported file types to the database.

The application registration system is pretty good at finding matches, so odds are if the system gives you an error message, then you probably don't have the correct application for the file. In Mac OS X v10.6, Launch Services has mapped many common file types to the built-in TextEdit application by default if the primary application is missing. Examples include files created with the iWork or Microsoft Office suites. This presents a problem, though, because TextEdit supports only common text files and Word files. Thus, TextEdit will either present an error dialog or treat the file as plain text, in which case it will usually show a file filled with gibberish.

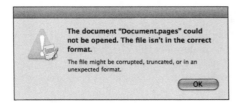

TIP Mac OS X's Quick Look feature can preview many common file types even without the applications installed. This includes both iWork and Microsoft Office documents. Quick Look details are covered later in this chapter.

If TextEdit, or any other application, cannot properly open a specific file type, you can change the Launch Service settings to force those files to open in a more appropriate application, as outlined next in this chapter. Other times, though, Launch Services may not have any idea which application to use for the file type. In this case you will be prompted to find a match. If you attempt to open a file type that is not stored in the Launch Services database, the computer will prompt you to find an application that supports the file.

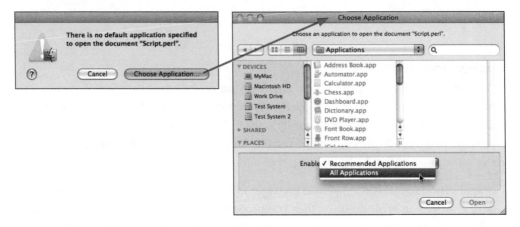

Change Launch Service Settings

From the Finder's Get Info window you can override Launch Service's default application settings for any specific file type. This setting is saved per user, so one user's application preferences will not override another's. These custom settings are saved to the com. apple.LaunchServices.plist preference file in each user's ~/Library/Preferences folder.

To change a user's Launch Services settings in the Finder:

1   In the Finder, select the file or multiple files you wish to change the Launch Service settings for, and then open the Get Info or Inspector window.

2   To open the Get Info window, do one of the following (performing the same tasks while holding the Option key will open an Inspector window):

▶   Choose File > Get Info from the menu bar.

▶   Use the Command-I keyboard combination.

▶   Choose Get Info from the Action (gear icon) pop-up menu in a Finder window toolbar.

▶   Choose Get Info from the Finder's shortcut menu by right-clicking or Control-clicking on an item.

3   Once you have opened a Get Info window, click the "Open with" disclosure triangle to reveal the default application selected by Launch Services.

4   To change just the selected files' default application, simply select another application from the pop-up menu.

5 To change the default application for all files of this type, click the Change All button.

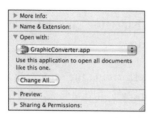

NOTE ▶ If you do not click the Change All button, the Launch Service settings will be saved only for the selected files. These settings will, however, stay with the selected file until changed again.

6 All Launch Service changes take place immediately.

TIP ▶ You can also modify Launch Service settings in the Finder by right-clicking or Control-clicking the selected files and then choosing Open With from the pop-up menu. Additionally, holding down the Option key will change the menu command to Always Open With.

Using Spotlight and Quick Look

Spotlight was a significant new feature in Mac OS X v10.4 that revolutionized the way users searched for files on their Macs. Spotlight enables you to perform nearly instantaneous searches that go wider and deeper than previous desktop search technology. Spotlight has the ability to go beyond simple file system searches and actually search for relevant metadata inside application files and databases. For example, an application like Address Book stores contact information in a database that appears opaque to the file system. Nevertheless, Spotlight can return search results from inside the Address Book database along with results from dozens of other databases and the entire file system hierarchy nearly instantly.

> **NOTE** ▶ In addition to the file system metadata that was covered previously in this chapter, many files also contain internal metadata used to describe the file's content. For example, many digital camera image files contain additional camera setting information embedded as metadata inside the file. Spotlight can search through both file system and internal metadata information.

Though Spotlight was pretty amazing when it debuted in Mac OS X v10.4, Apple added a few more tricks to Spotlight in Mac OS X v10.5. This included adding the ability to search through the contents of shared files from other Mac clients, servers, AirDisk volumes over the network, and Time Machine backups. Apple also added the ability to use advanced search operations while performing Spotlight searches from the Finder or menu bar.

Advanced Spotlight search operations include:

▶ The use of Boolean logic by using AND, OR, or NOT

▶ The use of exact phrases and dates by using quotation marks

▶ The use of search ranges by using greater-than and less-than symbols.

Mac OS X v10.5 also added another new feature called Quick Look that allows you to quickly preview the content of most files even if you don't have the application that created the file installed on your Mac. The combination of Spotlight and Quick Look allows you to locate and preview items with unmatched ease and speed.

Using Spotlight for Searching

You can initiate a Spotlight search any time by clicking the Spotlight icon on the far right of the menu bar or using the Command-Space bar keyboard combination. The Spotlight search is so fast that the results will actually change in real time as you type in your search query. Selecting an item from the results will open it immediately.

TIP Spotlight searches can also be accessed from the command line by using the `mdfind` command.

Selecting Show All from the Spotlight search results menu will open a new Finder window with the results. You could have also arrived at this same window by opening a new Finder window and entering your search in the Spotlight field from the Finder's toolbar, or by selecting File > Find from the menu bar, or using the Command-F keyboard shortcut. Selecting an item from the search results will show you the path to the selected item at the bottom of the Finder window. Selecting an item and then tapping the Space bar will open a Quick Look preview of the selected item.

You can refine your Spotlight search from a Finder search window by clicking the small plus buttons on the right below the search field. This will allow you to add as many specific search attributes as you need. After you add a new search attribute click the first word in the search attribute to choose another type from the pop-up menu.

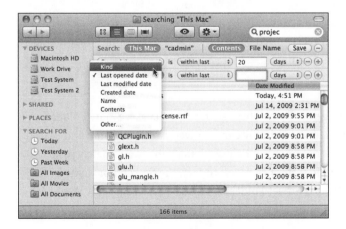

If you don't see the search attribute you're looking for, there are literally dozens of other attributes, which aren't enabled by default, that you can easily add. To enable additional search attributes, select any attribute and from the pop-up menu select the Other option. This will reveal a dialog that allows you to add additional search attributes to the pop-up menu. Two especially useful search attributes for administrators are "File visibility" and "System files," neither of which is shown by default in any Spotlight search.

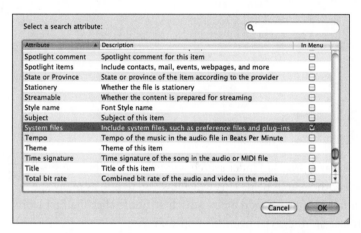

TIP Take some time to explore the additional search attributes; you may be surprised at the depth of Spotlight's search capabilities. Search attributes include specifying audio file tags, digital camera metadata, authorship information, contact information, and many other metadata types.

Clicking the Save button on the right will save these search criteria as a Smart Folder. Smart Folders are like normal folders in that they can be given a unique name and placed anywhere you like, but they are special because their contents will always match your search criteria no matter how the file system changes. In fact, the Search For items in the Finder's sidebar are simply predefined Smart Folders for Today, Yesterday, Past Week, All Images, All Movies, and All Documents.

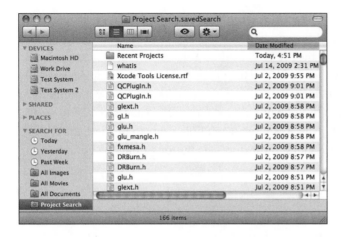

NOTE ▶ Smart Folders do not work from the command line.

Using Quick Look for Previewing

Again, Quick Look allows you to preview nearly any file type without having to open any additional applications, or even having those applications installed on your Mac. This makes Quick Look the most convenient method to view the contents of any file. Quick Look previews can be accessed, or dismissed, by pressing the Space bar from any Finder view, the Time Machine restore interface, most open and save browser dialogs, the Mail application, or any other application that supports Quick Look.

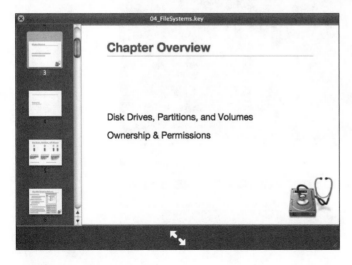

With the Quick Look preview window open you can resize the window by clicking and dragging the bottom right corner of the window, or you can go full-screen by clicking the twin arrow button at the bottom of the preview window. You can also use the arrow keys to navigate and preview through a list of files. If the previewed file has multiple pages you'll be able to scroll through the document. In some cases—Keynote presentations, for example—Quick Look will show a thumbnail preview of each slide allowing you to scroll through the thumbnails as well. Finally, if you select multiple items to preview, the Quick Look window will allow some basic slideshow features via buttons along the bottom of the window.

Quick Look technology is also used to provide the Finder with previews for files in icon view, previews in column view, and the preview section of the Get Info and Inspector windows. Finally, Quick Look also provides previews for the Finder's Cover Flow view. This new view, also added with Mac OS v10.5, allows you to browse folder content similar to that found in iTunes and Apple's other mobile devices. Quick Look can be accessed from any Finder window by selecting its icon in the toolbar.

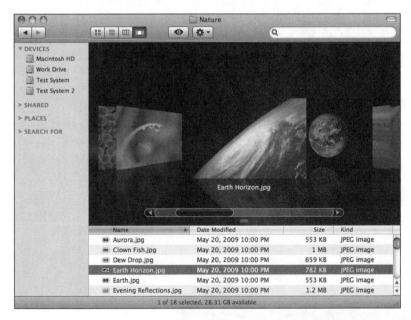

Quick Look Plug-ins

Quick Look is able to preview an ever-growing variety of file types using a plug-in technology. Each Quick Look plug-in is designed to preview specific types of files. Many Quick Look plug-ins are included by default, but Apple and third-party developers can create additional plug-ins to expand Quick Look's preview capabilities.

Included Quick Look plug-ins enable you to:

▶ Preview any audio or video file that can be decoded by QuickTime

▶ Preview a variety of graphics files, including many digital camera files, PDF files, EPS files, and any standard graphics file

▶ Preview a variety of productivity files including standard text files, script files, and files created by the iWork and Microsoft Office suites

▶ Preview a variety of Internet-centric files including mailboxes, iChat transcripts, and web archives

Quick Look plug-ins, like any other system resource, are stored inside the various Library folders. Apple's built-in Quick Look plug-ins are always found in the /System/Library/QuickLook folder, and sometimes appear in the /Library/QuickLook folder. Third-party plug-ins should always be installed in either the /Library/QuickLook or the ~/Library/QuickLook folder, depending on who needs access to it.

Understanding the Spotlight Service

Spotlight is able to perform wide and deep searches quickly because it works in the background to maintain highly optimized databases of indexed metadata for each local volume. When you first set up Mac OS X, it will create these databases by indexing all the available local volumes. Mac OS X will also index new local volumes when they are first attached.

On your Mac, a background process called mds, short for metadata server, will automatically update the index databases on the fly as changes are made throughout the file system. Because these indexes are kept current, the Spotlight process need only search through the databases to return thorough results. Essentially, Spotlight preemptively searches everything for you in the background so you don't have to wait for the results when you need them.

> **NOTE** ▶ Spotlight does not create index databases on read-only volumes or write-once media such as optical discs.

NOTE ▶ Your Mac's Spotlight service will index Time Machine and AirDisk volumes directly, but it will not index shared volumes from other computers. However, Spotlight can connect to indexes on shared volumes from other Mac OS X Server computers.

You can find the Spotlight general index databases at the root level of every volume in a folder named .Spotlight-V100. A few applications maintain their own databases separate from these general index databases. One example is the built-in email application Mail. It maintains its own optimized email database in each user's folder at ~/Library/Mail/ Envelope Index. Also, the Spotlight index database for a FileVault user is stored at the root level inside his encrypted home folder for enhanced security. If you are experiencing problems with Spotlight, you can force it to rebuild the index databases by deleting them and restarting your Mac, or by managing the Spotlight settings as covered later in this chapter.

Spotlight Security

In order to provide security on par with the rest of the file system, Spotlight also indexes every item's permissions. Even though Spotlight indexes every item on a volume, it will automatically filter search results to show only items that the current user has permissions to access. There is still a security concern, though, when users search through locally attached non-system volumes because they can choose to ignore ownership on these volumes. In other words, all users can search through locally attached non-system volumes, including mounted disk images, even if another user attached the device.

Spotlight Plug-ins

Spotlight is able to create indexes, and thus search, from an ever-growing variety of metadata using a plug-in technology. Each Spotlight plug-in is designed to examine specific types of files or databases. Many Spotlight plug-ins are included by default, but Apple and third-party developers can create additional plug-ins to expand Spotlight's search capabilities.

Included Spotlight plug-ins enable you to:

▶   Search via basic file metadata, including name, file size, creation date, and modification date

▶   Search via media-specific metadata from picture, music, and video files, including time code, creator information, and hardware capture information

▶   Search through the contents of a variety of file types, including text files, iLife related files and databases, Photoshop files, PDF files, iWork files, and Microsoft Office files

▶ Search through personal information like Address Book contacts and iCal calendar events

▶ Search for correspondence information like the contents of Mail emails and iChat chat transcripts

▶ Search for highly relevant information like your favorites or web browser bookmarks and history

Spotlight plug-ins, like any other system resource, are stored inside the various Library folders. Apple's built-in Spotlight plug-ins are always found in the /System/Library/Spotlight folder and sometimes appear in the /Library/Spotlight folder. Third-party plug-ins should always be installed in either the /Library/Spotlight or the ~/Library/Spotlight folder, depending on who needs access to it.

TIP You can create custom metadata for Spotlight by entering Spotlight comments in the Get Info and Inspector windows from the Finder.

Managing Spotlight Settings

From the Spotlight preferences, any user can choose to disable specific categories from appearing in Spotlight searches. A user can also prevent volumes from being indexed by specifying those volumes in the privacy list. However, by default all new volumes are automatically indexed, so a user must manually configure Spotlight to ignore a volume.

The Spotlight privacy list is a computer-level setting that remains the same across all user accounts, but it's not protected by administrative access, which means any user can change the privacy list. In this case, the Spotlight privacy list isn't any less secure than the rest of the file system, as any user can still have full access to locally connected non-system volumes because the system defaults to ignoring ownership on those volumes.

To change Spotlight settings:

1 Open the Spotlight preferences by choosing Apple menu > System Preferences, and then click the Spotlight icon.

The Spotlight preferences will open to the Search Results tab, allowing you to disable specific categories from the search results.

2   Simply deselect the checkboxes next to the categories you wish to ignore.

You can also drag categories to change their order in the search results. Each user has her own separate Search Results settings.

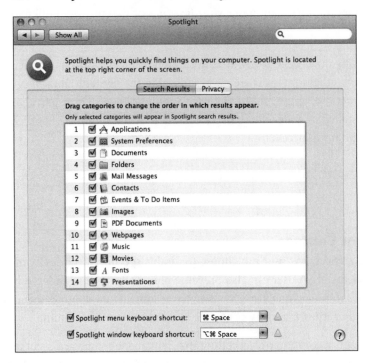

3   To prevent Spotlight from indexing specific items, click the Privacy tab to reveal the list of items for Spotlight to ignore.

To add new items click the small plus icon at the bottom of the privacy list and choose the items from a browser dialog, or simply drag and drop items into the privacy list.

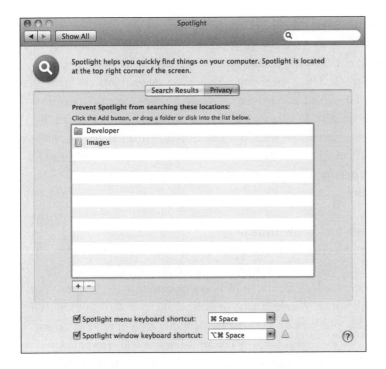

4   You can delete an item from the privacy list by selecting it and then clicking the
minus icon at the bottom of the privacy list.

All Spotlight settings are applied immediately. If you add an entire volume to the privacy
list, then the system will delete the Spotlight index database from that volume. In turn,
removing a volume from the privacy list will rebuild the Spotlight index database on that
volume. This technique, to rebuild the Spotlight index databases by adding, then removing, a volume from the privacy list, is the most common method to resolve problematic
Spotlight performance.

Using File Archives and Disk Images

Archiving and backup are both synonymous with copying data to another location for safekeeping, yet in the context of this chapter and Mac OS X, they are different processes serving different purposes. In Mac OS X, archiving is typically a manual process that involves creating compressed copies of selected data. Archive formats are efficient from a storage and data transfer perspective, but they generally require user interaction. On the other hand, the backup service introduced with Mac OS X v10.5, Time Machine, is an automated process that allows users to easily browse the backup history of their entire file system. As you can imagine, maintaining a history of your file system is not space efficient, but it is extremely useful.

Understanding Archive vs. Disk Image

At its essence, archiving is the practice of saving copies of important information to another location or format better suited for long-term storage or network transfer. Large amounts of hard disk drive storage have become much less expensive in the last few years, but this type of storage is still not as reliable as tape or optical media in terms of longevity. This type of archival media has not kept up with the tremendous growth of hard drives, so storing archival data in a more efficient form by compressing it is still relevant. Also, no matter how robust your Internet connection is, there never seems to be enough bandwidth, so compressing items in preparation for data transfer is almost always a time-saver. Mac OS X includes two archival technologies, archives and disk images, that allow you to combine multiple files and compress the data into a more efficient file suited for long-term storage or network data transfer.

First, the Mac's Finder will allow you to create zip archives from a selection of files or folders. This is an efficient method for archiving relatively small amounts of data quickly. The zip archive format is also widely compatible, as many operating systems include software to decompress zip archives back to their original items. However, zip archives on Mac OS X do not offer the flexibility provided by disk images.

Disk images, created using Disk Utility, are more widely used in Mac OS X for archival purposes because they offer many features not available from zip archives. Primarily, disk images allow you to archive the contents of an entire file system into a single file that can be compressed, encrypted, or both. Disk images can also be created read/write so you can easily make changes to them over time. The only downside to disk images created using Disk Utility is that, by default, only Macs can access the content—other systems require third-party software to access Mac disk image content.

Creating Zip Archives

Mac OS X's Finder allows you to quickly create a compressed zip archive from any number of selected items. By default, creating a zip archive in the Finder will not delete the original items you've selected to compress.

To create a zip archive in the Finder:

1 Select the items you wish to archive and compress in the Finder.

You can hold down the Shift key to quickly select contiguous lists of items, or hold down the Command key to quickly select noncontiguous items. It's best to put all of the items in one folder and then compress that, as opposed to selecting multiple items.

2 Choose File > Compress "Items" from the menu bar.

The word "Items" in the menu will be replaced by the name of a single item you have selected or the number of items you have selected.

If the archival process is going to take more than a few seconds, the Finder will show a progress dialog with the estimated time required to complete the erase task. You can also choose to cancel the archive by clicking the small X button on the far right.

3 When the archival process has completed, you will be left with a zip archive named either Archive.zip or Item.zip, where Item is the name of the single item you chose to archive and compress.

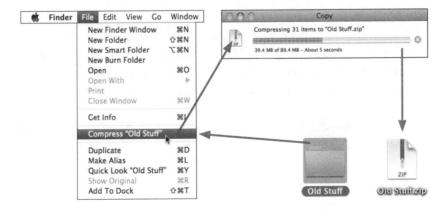

TIP ▶ You can also archive and compress items in the Finder by right-clicking or Control-clicking the selected files and then choosing Compress "Items" from the shortcut menu.

TIP ▶ From the command line you have more options when using the zip command to create compressed archives.

Once the archive process is complete, it's always interesting to compare the original items' size with the archive's size using the Get Info or Inspector windows in the Finder. In many cases you can expect at least a 50 percent decrease in file size. On the other hand, many media formats are already quite compressed in their original form, so you may not experience very good results when compressing these types of files.

Expanding Zip Archives

Expanding a zip archive in the Finder is as simple as double-clicking on the zip archive file. The Finder will decompress the entire archive file and place the resulting files and folders in the same folder as the original zip archive. The Finder cannot list or extract individual items from a zip archive. By default, the Finder will not delete the original zip archive.

TIP ▶ From the command line you have more options when using the unzip command to expand the contents of compressed archives.

Understanding Disk Images

Disk images are files that contain entire virtual drives and volumes. Mac OS X relies on disk images for several core technologies, including software distribution, system imaging, NetBoot, FileVault, and network Time Machine backups. Disk images are also useful as a personal archive tool. Though Mac-created disk images work only on Mac computers by default, they are much more flexible to use than zip archives. Disk images provide advanced compression and encryption, but their greatest benefit is that they can be treated like a removable volume.

To access the contents of a disk image, you simply double-click on the disk image file in the Finder. This will mount the volume inside the disk image file as if you had just connected a normal storage device. Even if the disk image file is located on a remote file server, you can still mount it as if it was a local drive. You can treat the mounted disk image volume as you would any other storage device by navigating through its hierarchy and selecting files and folders as you need them. Further, if the disk image is read/write you can add to the contents of the disk image by simply dragging items to the volume.

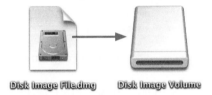

Disk Image File.dmg   Disk Image Volume

NOTE ▶ When you are done with a disk image volume, be sure to properly unmount and eject it as you would any other removable volume.

Using /Applications/Utilities/Disk Utility to make disk images allows you to create blank images or images containing copies of selected folders or even entire file systems. Mac OS X supports disk images up to at least 2 terabytes. Disk images also feature a number of configuration options, including:

▶ Image format—Disk images can be read-only or read/write. They can also be a set size or expandable as a sparse disk image. Sparse disk images will take up only as much space as necessary and automatically grow as you add items to them.

▶ Compression—Read-only disk images can be compressed to save space. With a compressed disk image, any free space becomes negligible in size, and most other files average a 50 percent reduction in size.

▶ Encryption—Any disk image can be protected with a password and encrypted with strong 128-bit or 256-bit AES encryption. Choosing a higher bit rate is more secure but degrades performance. This feature is useful for securing data stored on otherwise unsecure volumes like removable drives and network shares. The encryption always happens on the local computer, so even if the disk image file is physically stored externally, as on a network file share, the data is always encrypted as it travels across the connection.

▶ File system—Disk images can contain any partition scheme or volume format that Mac OS X supports, including optical media formats. Details regarding the differences between file system options are covered in Chapter 4, "File Systems."

MORE INFO ▶ Advanced disk image management is covered in another reference guide, *Apple Training Series: Mac OS X Deployment v10.6.*

Creating Empty Disk Images

To create an automatically resizing empty disk image that you can fill with content over time:

1 Open /Applications/Utilities/Disk Utility, and then choose File > New > Blank Disk Image from the menu bar. Or with nothing selected in the drives list, you can click the New Image button in the toolbar.

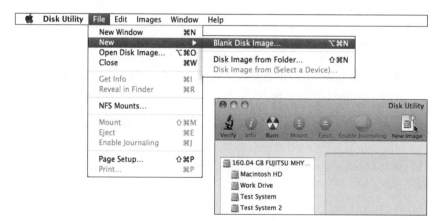

2 Enter a name for the disk image file, and then select a destination for the disk image file from the Where pop-up menu. Also enter a name for the volume inside the disk image.

The disk image file and volume names do not have to match but should be similar so that you can recognize their relationship.

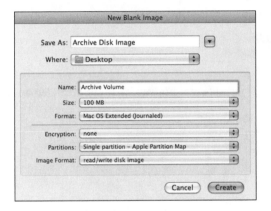

3 Select a volume size from the pop-up menu, or select Custom to specify a disk image of arbitrary size.

Remember this disk image will occupy only as much space as the files you copy inside it. Obviously if this disk image is going to be saved on an external volume of limited size that should define your maximum size.

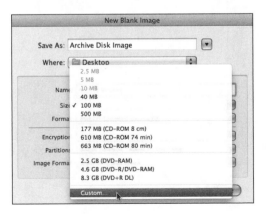

4 You can select a different volume format or partition scheme from the pop-up menus, but in most cases you will want to stick with the default Mac OS Extended (Journaled) and Apple Partition Map selections.

5 You can also select an encryption at this point from the pop-up menu. For most uses, 128-bit AES is secure enough and still provides good performance.

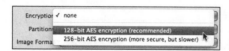

6 Choose "sparse disk image" from the Image Format pop-up menu to create an automatically resizable disk image.

7 Click the Create button to create the disk image.

8 If you have selected an encrypted disk image you will be prompted to enter a password for the disk image. After you have selected a secure password, click the OK button to finish the disk image creation process.

After the system has created the new blank disk image, it will automatically mount it. From the Finder, you can open Get Info windows on both the disk image file and the disk image volume to verify that the volume size is much larger than the image size. As you copy files to the volume, the disk image file will grow accordingly.

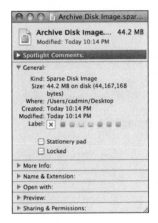 

TIP ▶ You can change the format of a disk image at any time in Disk Utility by choosing Images > Convert from the menu bar. This will open a dialog allowing you to select the image you want to change and save a copy of the image with new options.

TIP ▶ From the command line you have more options when using the `hdiutil` command to manage disk images.

Creating Disk Images from Items

To create a disk image that contains copies of selected items:

1   Open /Applications/Utilities/Disk Utility.

2   At this point you can choose to create a new disk image from the contents of a folder or the contents of a volume:

To create a disk image from the contents of a folder, choose File > New > Disk Image From Folder from the menu bar, and then select the folder you wish to copy into a new disk image from the file browser window. Once you have made your selection, click the Image button to continue.

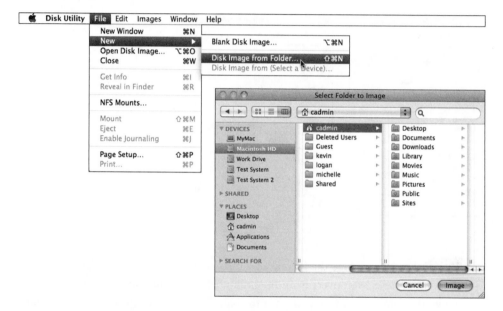

To create a disk image from the contents of an entire volume, select the volume you wish to copy into a new disk image from the Disk image column on the left, and then choose File > New > Disk Image from disk *volumename*, where *volumename* is the name of the selected volume, or click the New Image button in the toolbar.

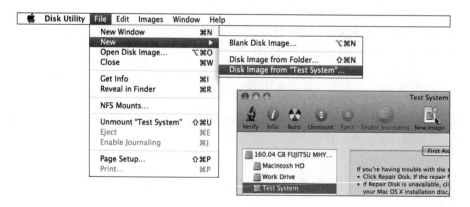

NOTE ▸ Disk Utility can only make disk images of volumes that it can temporarily unmount. Thus, you cannot make a disk image of the currently running system volume.

3 Enter a name for the disk image file, and then choose a destination for the disk image file from the Where pop-up menu.

Again, the disk image file and volume names do not have to match but should be similar so that you can recognize their relationship.

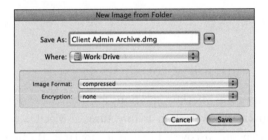

NOTE ▸ Make sure you have enough free space on the destination volume where you plan to save your disk image file.

4 Choose an image format from the pop-up menu. Remember, compressed images are also read-only.

NOTE ▸ It takes nearly twice as much free space to create a compressed disk image— the system must create a noncompressed image first and then convert the first image to a compressed image.

5 You can also choose an encryption at this point from the pop-up menu.

For most uses, 128-bit AES is secure enough and still provides good performance.

6 Click the Save button to create the disk image.

If you have selected an encrypted disk image, you will be prompted to enter a password for the disk image. After you have selected a secure password, click the OK button to start the disk image creation process.

Depending on the amount of data that has to be copied and the image format you chose, it can take anywhere from minutes to hours for the disk image copy process to complete. Disk Utility will open a small progress dialog that will also allow you to cancel the disk image copy by clicking the Cancel button.

Managing Time Machine

There are several mature and relatively easy-to-use backup solutions for the Mac, so you may be wondering why Apple chose to invent a new backup architecture for Mac OS v10.5. The folks at Apple did a little research and discovered that, prior to Time Machine's introduction, only 4 percent of Mac users back up their data on a regular basis. This is an unacceptable number, so Apple decided that the only way to convince users to do so on a regular basis was to create a new backup process that's as easy as possible and also surprisingly fun to use. Apple's solution was Time Machine.

Aside from being built into the operating system, Time Machine has two features that make it fundamentally different than any other solution currently out there. First, configuring Time Machine is so easy it's nearly automatic. The system practically begs you to set up Time Machine if you haven't already, and with as little as one click the system is configured.

The second, more significant feature is that Time Machine is so tightly integrated with the operating system that users don't even have to exit the application they are currently using to recover data. Applications, both built-in and third party, can tie directly into the Time Machine backup system. From applications supporting Time Machine, a user can activate the visually striking Time Machine interface and travel back through time to see the application's data as it was in the past. If an application doesn't yet support Time Machine, you can use the Finder while in Time Machine's interface to browse the entire file system through time.

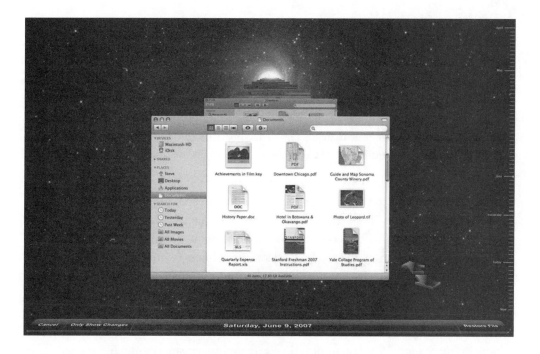

Understanding Time Machine Backups

Time Machine can save backup archives to any locally connected Mac OS X Extended volume that is not the startup volume. You are allowed to select a backup destination volume that resides as another partition on the system disk drive, but this is an incredibly bad idea—if the system drive dies, so does your backup. If you don't have a local volume suited for backup, you can also select a shared network volume as your backup destination. Time Machine supports network shares by creating a disk image on the share to store the backups. Time Machine currently only supports backing up to Apple Filing Protocol (AFP) network shares hosted from Mac OS X Servers or Time Capsule wireless base stations.

> **MORE INFO ▶** You can find out more about Apple's Time Capsule wireless base station at Apple's website, www.apple.com/timecapsule.

Logistically, Time Machine uses a sophisticated background process, named backupd, to automatically create new backups of the entire file system every hour. Obviously, Time Machine employs some tricks to keep these backups as small as possible so that you can maintain a deep history. The initial Time Machine backup will copy almost the entire contents of your file system to the specified backup volume. In order to provide fast backups and convenient restores, Time Machine does not use a compressed archive format common to many other backup systems. Instead, Time Machine simply copies the items as is to the backup destination. As you'll see later, this allows for easy access to the backup items.

The space saving comes into play with each subsequent backup. Between backups, a background process, similar to the one used by the Spotlight search service, will automatically track any changes to the file system. When the next scheduled backup occurs, only the items that have changed will be copied to the backup volume. Time Machine will then combine this new content with hard link file system pointers (which occupy nearly zero disk space) to the previous backup content, and create a simulated view of the entire file system at that point in time.

NOTE ▶ Do not confuse Time Machine with snapshot technology common on other operating systems. While snapshots do create multiple instances of a file system through time, they do not provide you with a backup, as they don't actually copy data to another storage device. In other words, if a drive containing file system snapshots dies, those snapshots are just as lost as the current data on the dead drive.

Time Machine also saves space by ignoring files that do not need to be backed up, as they can be re-created after a restoration. Generally speaking, Time Machine ignores temporary files, Spotlight indexes, items in the Trash, and anything that can be considered a cache. Software developers can also tell Time Machine to ignore specific application data that does not need to be backed up.

MORE INFO ▶ Specifically, Time Machine always ignores files as defined by a configuration file that lives at /System/Library/CoreServices/backupd.bundle/Contents/Resources/StdExclusions.plist. Of particular note, this configuration file tells Time Machine to ignore system log files, which you could need for later troubleshooting. Thus you may find it beneficial to modify this file to suite your own backup needs.

Eventually, so as not to waste space on your backup volume with historical data that has outlived its usefulness, Time Machine will start "aging out" backups. Time Machine will only keep hourly backups for a day, daily backups for a week, and weekly backups until your backup volume is full. After your backup volume is full, Time Machine will start deleting the oldest items first. However, Time Machine will always keep at least one copy of every item that is still also on your current file system.

> **NOTE ▶** If the backup volume isn't available when a backup is scheduled to execute, Time Machine will continue to keep track of all the changes to the file system and then save them to the backup volume once it becomes available again.

Configuring Time Machine

Despite the rather complex process going on behind the scenes to make Time Machine possible, configuration couldn't be easier. In fact, Time Machine is enabled by default and simply waiting for you to pick a backup destination. If you haven't configured a Time Machine backup destination, the system will automatically scan the network for a Time Machine network share or wait for you to attach an external drive. If the system locates either, you will be prompted to select it as your backup destination. If you select your backup destination with this method, after you click the Use as Backup Disk button Time Machine is fully configured. It's just that easy.

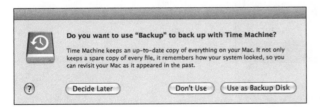

On the other hand, you can choose to manually configure Time Machine settings to better suit your needs:

1   Open the Time Machine preferences by choosing Apple menu > System Preferences, and then click the Time Machine icon.

> **TIP ▶** You can also access the Time Machine preferences by clicking on its icon in the Dock.

2   Enable Time Machine by sliding the switch to the On position, and then click the Choose Backup Disk button.

This will reveal a dialog allowing you to select a backup destination. Once you have selected an appropriate volume, click the Use for Backup button.

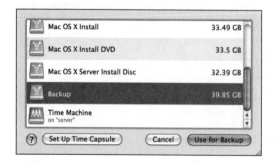

TIP   If Time Machine ever "loses" its backup volume, simply select it again from this interface.

At this point Time Machine will wait two minutes, allowing you to make further configuration changes, before it starts the first backup.

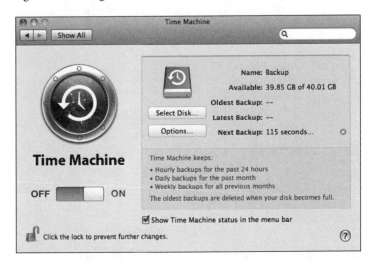

3   Click the Options button to reveal a dialog allowing you to adjust a few Time Machine settings.

4   The most important configuration choice you can make with Time Machine is to exclude items from the backup. Excluding items will obviously reduce the amount of space required to maintain your backups. It's not uncommon for users to leave only the /Users folder as the single item to back up; after all, that's where all the important user items reside.

You can drag and drop items into the list field, or you can click the small plus button at the bottom of the list to reveal a file browser, allowing you to select specific folders or volumes to exclude.

NOTE ▶ If you're going to save space by excluding system items, simply add the /System folder to the exclude list and you will be prompted to exclude all system files or just the /System folder. It's best to exclude all system files.

NOTE ▶ If you do not perform a full backup of your system volume, then you will not be able to perform a full restoration of it. Instead, you will have to install Mac OS X first and then restore the remainder using Migration Assistant, as covered later in this chapter.

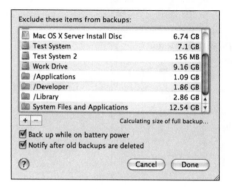

5 Click the Done button when you are ready to commence with the backup.

The two-minute timer will reset every time you make a Time Machine configuration change. Once you are done, simply wait two minutes and the initial Time Machine backup will commence.

Depending on the amount of data that has to be backed up, it can take from minutes to hours for the initial backup to complete. Time Machine will open a small progress dialog that will also allow you to cancel the backup by clicking the small "X" button to the right of the progress bar. The Time Machine preferences has a similar progress bar.

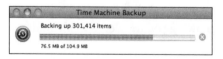

Subsequent backups will occur automatically in the background. Revisiting the Time Machine preferences will show you the time and date of the oldest, last, and next backup. You can also verify the last backup and force an immediate backup from the Time Machine menu extra (or icon) near the clock in the menu bar.

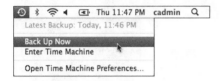

> **TIP** If you only want Time Machine to back up when you say so, then simply turn it off in the Time Machine preferences and use the Time Machine menu extra to initiate manual backups. You can also postpone backups by disconnecting from the backup volume, though this works only for locally attached backup volumes.

Restore from Time Machine

Using Time Machine to restore data is what many will consider the best part because of the dynamic interface Apple has created to "look through time." Clicking the Time Machine icon in the Dock, or using the Time Machine menu extra, will enter the Time Machine history browser. Few applications currently support the Time Machine interface, so in most cases you will be presented with a historical view in the Finder.

> **TIP** Right-click or Control-click the Time Machine icon in the Dock to reveal a shortcut menu allowing you to adjust Time Machine preferences, start a backup immediately, or browse another Time Machine backup.

The Finder windows will let you browse as usual with one significant addition. You can use the navigation arrows on the bottom right, or the navigation timeline on the right side, to view Finder contents as they change through time. To aid in your search through time, the Spotlight search field remains active, and you can quickly preview any item using the Finder's Quick Look feature. Once you have found the item you were looking for, simply click the Restore button at the bottom-right corner and the Finder will return to "the present" with your recovered file intact where it once was.

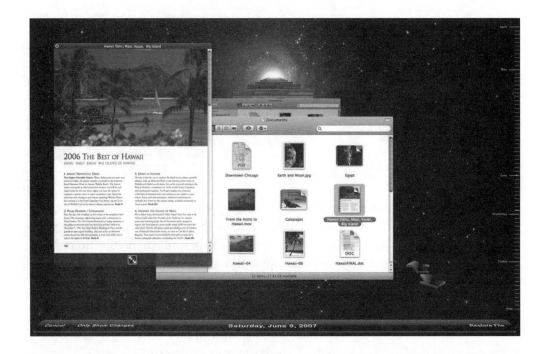

NOTE ▶ FileVault users cannot access their home folder backup via the standard Time Machine interface. They can, however, use the following three methods to access their home folder in a Time Machine backup.

Restoring with Migration Assistant

You can also restore a complete user home folder or other non-system data from a Time Machine archive using the Migration Assistant. You can use this technique if you choose not to perform full system backups, if your system is already running and you want to migrate specific information from a backup. First, make sure the Time Machine backup volume is available to the destination Mac, then open /Applications/Utilities/Migration Assistant. When the Migration Assistant opens, simply choose to restore from a Time Machine backup. The remainder of the Migration Assistant process is identical to the standard migration process covered in Chapter 1, "Installation and Initial Setup," for system items or Chapter 2, "User Accounts," for user home folders.

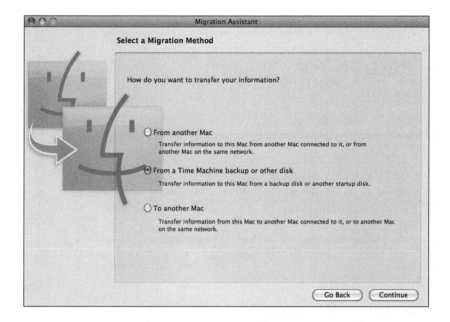

NOTE ▶ FileVault user accounts can only be fully restored when using the Migration Assistant during the Mac OS X initial system setup.

Restoring an Entire System

You can restore an entire system volume when booted from the Mac OS X Install DVD. This technique assumes you did not exclude any items from your system volume; thus you have backed up the entire system volume. When booted from the Mac OS X Install DVD, as covered in Chapter 1, "Installation and Initial Setup," once the installer has started, choose Utilities > Restore System From Backup from the menu bar. This will open the Time Machine system restore assistant. The assistant will first scan for local and network Time Machine backup volumes. Once you have selected the Time Machine volume, you can restore the entire system from any backup instance on that volume to your new system drive.

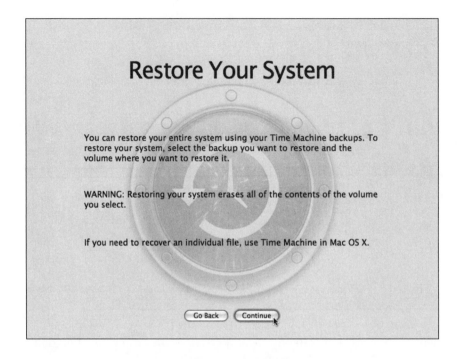

Manually Restoring from Time Machine

If you are experiencing problems using one of the Time Machine restoration interfaces, you can always browse the backup from the Finder. Time Machine's backup technology uses file system features that are part of standard Mac OS X Extended volumes, so no special software is needed to browse through backup contents.

> **NOTE** ▶ You should not directly modify the contents of a Time Machine backup, as doing so could damage the backup hierarchy. The default file system permissions will not give you write access to these items.

> **NOTE** ▶ FileVault home folders will remain inside an encrypted disk image in the Time Machine backup. Thus you will need the user's password to access the secure home folder contents.

If you're using a locally attached drive for Time Machine, then the backups are located on the root of your backup volume in a folder named Backups.backupdb. Once inside the backup database folder, you will see folders with the name of each computer that is backed up to that volume. Inside each computer folder you will see folders named with a date and time indicating each backup. Finally, inside each dated folder you will see folders representing each volume that was backed up.

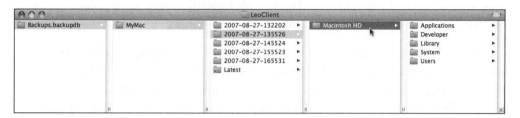

If you're backing up Time Machine over a network, you will need to manually connect to the Time Machine share point first. Connecting to share points is covered in Chapter 8, "Network Services." Once connected, you will need to locate the Time Machine backup disk images. They will be at the root of the Time Machine share point and named with the computer's name, followed by the computer's MAC address, followed by the ".sparse-bundle" extension. Double-click to mount the Time Machine backup disk image volume, which will be named "Backup of" followed by the computer's name. Inside this volume you will find the same Backups.backupdb folder and contents that you would find on a directly connected Time Machine backup.

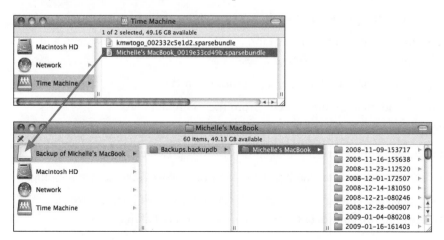

Time Machine Caveats

Though Time Machine is revolutionary, it is not without flaws. Time Machine's backup architecture does not lend itself well to large files that change often. For example, many database files appear as large, single files to the file system. While the database application may be able to change just a few bytes of the large file as a user edits the database, Time Machine will not recognize this, and it will have to create another copy of the entire database file during the next backup. This will obviously fill your backup volume much quicker than if the database had been stored as many smaller files.

This leads to the next Time Machine issue: running out of backup space. Once Time Machine fills up the backup volume, it will begin deleting older items to make room for newer ones. Therefore, the depth of your backup history will vary based not only on the size of your backup volume, but also on how often you change your files and how Time Machine recognizes those changes. Because you cannot change how Time Machine chooses to delete older items, you may discover that items you thought would still be on the backup volume have already been deleted.

TIP By default, Time Machine will let you know if it needs to delete older items to make space for new backups.

What You've Learned

▶ Mac OS X's file system is laid out to enhance ease of use and administration.

▶ System resources are stored in various Library folders throughout the system, and these folders provide different levels of access.

▶ Font Book is the primary tool for managing font resources.

▶ You can reveal and manage hidden items from the command line.

▶ Mac OS X provides aliases and links as methods to provide file system shortcuts.

▶ You can override Launch Services to open files in your preferred applications.

▶ Mac OS X uses extensive metadata to provide robust file system searches with Spotlight.

▶ Time Machine backup, along with other archival tools like disk images, provides ample means to secure your data from human or hardware failure.

References

You can check for new and updated Knowledge Base documents at www.apple.com/support.

Font Management

▶ HT2435, "Mac OS X: Font locations and their purposes"

▶ TA22195, "Mac OS X: Font file formats"

Spotlight

▶ TA23187, "Mac OS X 10.4: Where does Spotlight search?"

▶ HT2409, "Spotlight: How to re-index folders or volumes"

Time Machine

▶ HT1770, "Mac OS X 10.5: Using Time Machine and troubleshooting Time Machine issues"

▶ HT3446, "Mac OS X 10.5: Security tips for using Time Machine over a network"

▶ HT1175, "Backing up with Time Capsule for the first time"

▶ HT1177, "Restoring files from a Time Capsule backup"

▶ HT1170, "Time Capsule: Time Machine backups do not mount"

▶ TS2986, "Mac OS X v10.6: Cannot install Mac OS X v10.6 on a volume used by Time Machine for backups"

URLs

Apple's Time Capsule wireless base station: www.apple.com/timecapsule

Review Quiz

1. What are the four default top-level folders visible in the Finder?

2. What are six common system resources? What purpose does each resource serve? Where are they located in the file hierarchy?

3. What are the four system resource domains? What purpose does each domain serve?

4. Why does the Finder hide certain folders at the root of the system volume?

5. What two methods can be used to hide items from the Finder?

6. What are resource forks and why have they fallen out of favor?

7 What are some of the common file flags and extended attributes used by Mac OS X?

8. What does Mac OS X use bundles or packages for?

9. How does the system identify which application to open when a user double-clicks on a file?

10. What three common UNIX commands support Mac file system metadata?

11. What are the differences between zip archives and disk images?

12. How does the Spotlight search service use metadata?

13. Where does Spotlight store its metadata index databases? How about the Spotlight plug-ins?

14. What backup destinations does Time Machine support?

15. How does Time Machine maintain a backup history of the file system?

16. What are some privacy and security concerns with the Spotlight service?

17. What types of files are omitted from Time Machine backups?

18. Why is Time Machine inefficient at backing up large databases?

19. Why might a previously backed-up item be no longer available in Time Machine?

Answers

1. The four default top-level folders visible in the Finder are: Applications, containing applications all local users have access to; Library, containing system resources all local users have access to; System, containing necessary system resources; and finally, Users, containing all the local user home folders.

2. Six common system resources are: extensions, which attach themselves to the system kernel to provide hardware and peripheral driver support; frameworks, which are shared code libraries that provide additional software resources for both applications and system processes; fonts; preference files, which contain application and system configuration information; LaunchAgents and LaunchDaemons, used by `launchd` to provide services that automatically start when they are needed or at system startup; and finally, logs, which are text files that contain error and progress entries from nearly any application or system service.

3. The four system resource domains are: User, containing applications and system resources specific to each user account; Local, containing applications and system resources available to all users on the local Mac; Network (optional), containing applications and system resources available to any Mac that has an automated network share; and finally, System, containing applications and system resources required to provide basic system functionality.

4. The Finder hides traditional UNIX resources from average users because they don't need to have access to those items. If users do need access to these UNIX items, they can access them from the Terminal.

5. The Finder will not show items with periods at the beginning of their filename, or items with the hidden file flag enabled.

6. Resource forks are used to make the file system appear less complex. Data forks and resource forks are combined to appear as one single item in the file system. They have fallen out of favor because they are not directly compatible with non-Mac OS volumes, nor are they extensible.

7. Common file flags include the locked flag, which locks files from changes, and the hidden flag, which hides the item in the Finder. Common extended attributes used in the Finder are setting an item's color label, stationary pad option, hide extension option, and Spotlight comments.

8. Bundles and packages are used to combine complex items into individual folders. Packages have the additional advantage of appearing as a single item in the Finder. This allows software developers to combine resources into a single item and prevents users from messing with those resources.

9. Files are identified either by their file type attributes or their filename extension. Launch Services maintains a database of known applications and which file types they can open. When you double-click on a file in the Finder, Launch Services tries to find an appropriate match. You can override the default application selection in the Finder.

10. Three common UNIX commands that have been updated to support Mac file system metadata are cp, mv, and rm.

11. Zip archives are created with the Finder from a specific selection of items. Zip archives are compatible with many operating systems. On the other hand, disk images are created using Disk Utility and allow you to create highly flexible archive volumes that can contain nearly anything.

12. The Spotlight search service creates index databases of file system metadata so that it can perform normally time-intensive searches nearly instantly.

13. Spotlight metadata index databases are stored at the root of every volume in a /.Spotlight-V100 folder. However, a FileVault user's database is stored in his encrypted home folder. Also, the Mail application maintains its own database in each user's home folder at ~/Library/Mail/Envelope Index. Spotlight plug-ins can be located in any Library in a folder named Spotlight.

14. Time Machine can back up to any Mac OS X Extended volume, including volumes from disk images stored on an AFP share from a Mac OS X or Mac OS X Server.

15. Time Machine starts with a full copy of the file system; then it records any changes to the file system and only copies the changes. It creates a simulation of the full file system using hard links for files that have not changed.

16. Though Spotlight indexes file and folder permissions, it will allow other users to search the contents of locally attached nonsystem volumes when ownership is ignored on those volumes.

17. Time Machine always ignores temporary files, Spotlight indexes, items in the Trash, and anything else that can be considered a cache. Time Machine will also ignore any files an application has defined as exempt, or any files you have defined as exempt in the Time Machine preferences.

18. Time Machine is inefficient at backing up large databases because it must back up the entire database file every time any change, no matter how small, is made to the database.

19. A previously backed-up item will not be available if your backup volume has become full and Time Machine has had to start deleting older items to make room for newer items.

6

Time This chapter takes approximately 4 hours to complete.

Goals Understand and support the various application types
Monitor and control processes and applications
Locate and manage application preferences
Configure and administer Boot Camp for Windows compatibility

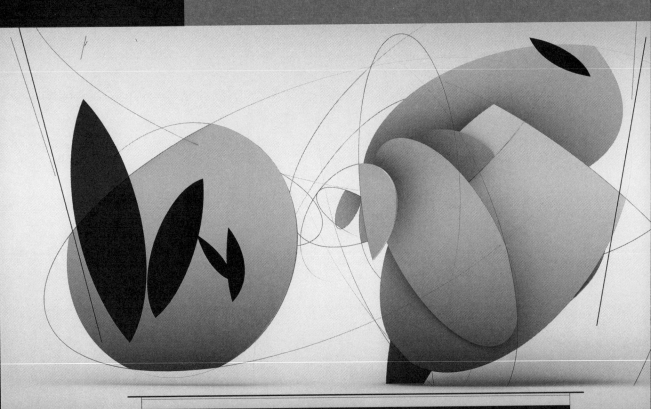

Chapter **6**

Applications and Boot Camp

People acquire computers because they want to run applications, not operating systems. Most users don't care about the technologies underneath as long as the applications they want run smoothly. This is why, despite Mac OS X's growing popularity, non-Mac users are apprehensive about switching. It cannot be ignored that there are many applications that run only on Windows-based computers.

Yet, many Mac-only applications tempt non-Mac users because they represent the best solutions available. For several years now, Apple has held a strong lead on media creation applications with the iLife and Pro production suites. Third-party developers have stepped up their game in the last few years as well, as Mac OS X provides a robust development platform with many unique features. For hundreds of examples, look no further than the Apple Products Guide, http://guide.apple.com.

Ultimately, with Apple's move to Intel processors for Mac hardware, users can finally have one computer that runs Mac OS X, UNIX/Linux, and Windows applications. This means that modern Macs have the unique ability to run nearly every application available today.

In this chapter you will explore the application environments available to Mac OS X, and you will learn how to monitor and control applications and processes. You will also learn proper application configuration and troubleshooting techniques. Finally, this chapter will walk you through the configuration of Apple's Boot Camp technology, which facilitates running Windows natively on Mac hardware.

Understanding Applications and Processes

A process is any instance of executable code that is currently activated and addressed in system memory. In other words, a process is anything that is currently "running" or "open" on a Mac. Mac OS X handles processes very efficiently, so although an idle process will likely consume zero processor resources, it's still considered an active process because it has dedicated address space in system memory. The four general process types are applications, commands, agents, and daemons.

Applications are a specific category of process that is generally identified as something the user opened in the graphical interface. *Commands* are also normally opened by the user but are only available at the command-line interface. *Agents* are background processes that run on behalf of a certain user to provide a service that generally doesn't require user interaction. Agents are always started automatically for the user, but both applications and commands can also be opened automatically. Most important, all three of these process types are considered part of the user's space because they are executed with the same access privileges the user has.

Processes that run on behalf of the system fall into the final category, *daemons*, which are also background processes because they rarely have any user interface. Daemons usually launch during system startup and remain active the entire time the Mac is up and running. These background daemons are responsible for most of the automatic Mac OS X system features like detecting network changes and maintaining the Spotlight search metadata index.

Mac OS X Process Features

Mac OS X is a desirable platform for running applications and other processes because it combines a rock-solid UNIX foundation with an advanced graphical user interface. Users will most likely recognize the graphical interface elements right away, but it's the underlying foundation that keeps things running so smoothly. Specifically, a few fundamental features of Mac OS X are responsible for providing a high level of performance and reliability.

Mac OS X Process Performance Features

▶ Preemptive multitasking—This gives Mac OS X the ability to balance computing resources without letting any single process take over. It allows the system to maintain dozens of background processes without significantly slowing down user applications.

▶ Symmetric multiprocessing—Whenever possible the system will use all available computing resources to provide the best performance. This is a key feature since every currently shipping Mac includes at least two processor cores. Mac OS X v10.6 introduces two new unique multiprocessing features, Grand Central Dispatch and OpenCL, which provide for even greater performance than previous versions of Mac OS X. Grand Central Dispatch makes it much easier for application developers to take full advantage of not just multiprocessor systems, but also multicore processors. OpenCL takes this even further by allowing applications to use your Mac's powerful graphics processor to accelerate general computing tasks.

▶ Simultaneous 32-bit and 64-bit support—Mac OS X is one of the few operating systems that supports both 32-bit and 64-bit modes simultaneously. A process running in 64-bit mode has the ability to individually access more than 4 GB of system memory, can perform higher-precision computational functions much faster, and can take advantage of Intel's updated x86-64 architecture for improved performance and security. Only Macs featuring 64 bit–capable processors can take advantage of 64-bit system features. Currently, Macs with Intel Core2Duo or Intel Xenon processors include 64-bit support. Mac OS X v10.5 improved 64-bit support by allowing both command-line and graphical interface applications to access 64-bit resources. With Mac OS X v10.6, Apple updated nearly all included software to take advantage of 64-bit resources, including the core of Mac OS X, the system kernel.

NOTE ▶ Mac OS X always defaults to a 32-bit kernel for compatibility with older kernel extensions. More about the 64-bit kernel is covered in Chapter 10, "System Startup."

Mac OS X Memory Management Features

▶ Protected memory—Similar to how the file system prevents users from meddling with items they shouldn't, processes are also kept separate and secure in system memory. The system manages all memory allocation so processes are not allowed to interfere with each other's system memory space. In other words, an ill-behaved or crashed application will not affect any other process on the system.

▶ Dynamic memory allocation—The operating system will automatically manage system memory for processes at their request. Though real system memory is clearly limited by hardware, the system will dynamically allocate both real and virtual memory when needed. Thus, the only memory limitation in Mac OS X is the amount of free space you have available on your system volume.

Mac OS X Process Security Features

▶ Security architecture—At both the command line and graphical interface, processes are not allowed to access resources unless they are authorized. Again, access restrictions at the file system are responsible for much of the security here. However, system privileges are allowed when needed. The most obvious example of this is the Installer application, which requires administrative authorization to install software that affects more than one user. The security architecture built into Mac OS X is one of the primary reasons Macs remain relatively free of malware.

▶ Code signing—Mac OS X v10.5 introduced support for secure signed application and process code. Signed applications and processes include a digital signature, which is used by the system to verify the authenticity and integrity of the software code and resources. Code is verified not only on disk but also as it is running. Therefore, even if some part of the application's or process's code is inappropriately changed while it's active, the system can automatically quit it. Code signing is also used by the Keychain, the personal application firewall, Parental Controls preferences, and Managed Client settings to verify applications after they have been updated.

▶ Application quarantine—Mac OS X v10.5 also introduced an application quarantine service that displays a warning when you attempt to open an application downloaded from an external source. This gives you the chance to verify your intent to open a new application, or cancel if you have any suspicions about the safety of an item. Mac OS X v10.6 further enhances this feature by maintaining a list of known malicious software. If you attempt to open any software on this list, the system will present a warning dialog suggesting that the item should be moved to the Trash.

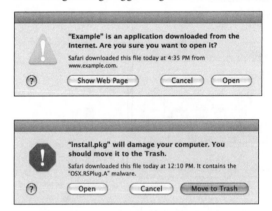

MORE INFO ▶ The list of malicious software can be updated by Software Update and is located on your Mac at /System/Library/CoreServices/CoreTypes.bundle/Contents/Resources/XProtect.plist.

Application Environments

Mac OS X supports a wide range of application environments. Several of them are required solely to provide backward compatibility for legacy Mac applications, while others add support for popular UNIX-based tools. Most important, though, average users do not need to concern themselves about which environment their application is using—the system will provide the appropriate resources automatically. The five primary application environments in Mac OS X are Cocoa, Carbon, Java, BSD, and X11.

NOTE ▶ The Classic compatibility environment, which enables users to run software created for Mac OS 9, is no longer supported as of Mac OS X v10.5.

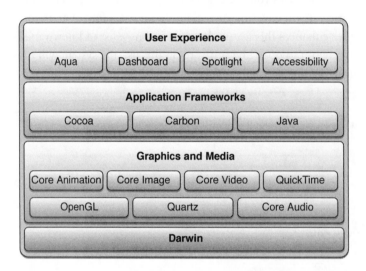

MORE INFO ▶ To learn more about Mac OS X system architecture and application environments, see Apple's development resources, http://developer.apple.com/macosx/architecture/index.html.

Cocoa

Cocoa is the application environment most specific to Mac OS X, as Cocoa-based applications run only on Mac OS X. Cocoa is based on the Objective-C object-oriented programming language. Often, developers must use the Cocoa environment if they want to take advantage of the latest Mac features. As an example, only Cocoa applications can both have a graphical interface and take advantage of 64-bit services. For this reason, most of the built-in system software and new third-party software is developed for the Cocoa environment.

MORE INFO ▶ To learn more about the Cocoa application environment, refer to Apple's own development resources, http://developer.apple.com/cocoa.

Carbon

The Carbon application environment is a streamlined and updated version of the previous Mac OS 9 environment. Developers can update their legacy Mac applications, often with little work, to run natively in Mac OS X. Carbon is based on the industry-standard C and C++ programming languages. On the surface, it's hard to identify any differences between Carbon and Cocoa applications. With every new version of Mac OS X, Apple has further blurred the lines between Cocoa and Carbon. In fact, many modern applications contain code that takes advantage of both environments.

> **MORE INFO** ▶ To learn more about Carbon, see Apple's development resources, http://developer.apple.com/carbon.

Java

Java is an application environment developed by Sun Microsystems with the goal of creating non-platform-specific applications. This means a developer can create software code once and it can run on many different environments. Mac OS X includes both 32-bit and 64-bit Java SE 6 (Standard Edition). This implementation supports Java in two ways: Java applets and full Java applications.

Most full Java applications are also delivered via a web download from a small Java Web Start (.jnlp) file. Double-clicking on a .jnlp file opens /System/Library/CoreServices/Java Web Start, which downloads the remainder of the Java application to ~/Library/Caches/Java/cache. Once the download is complete, the Java application runs in its own environment alongside your other Mac applications. When you open a Java application the second time, the Java Web Start application automatically converts the small .jnlp file to a stand-alone Java application. You can further adjust Java applications by opening the /Utilities/Java Preferences application.

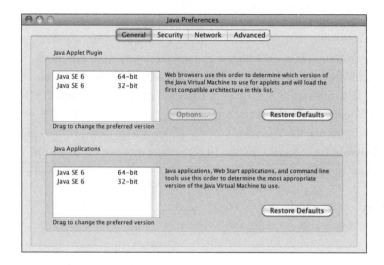

MORE INFO ▶ To learn more about Java on Mac OS X, see Apple's development resources, http://developer.apple.com/java.

BSD

Since the introduction of Mac OS X v10.5, the system has been both Posix- and UNIX 03-compliant. Thus, Mac OS X is compatible with most UNIX software. Mac OS X's system foundation, named Darwin, is based on the open source Free Berkeley Software Distribution (FreeBSD) UNIX command-line interface. The command line is most often accessed via the /Applications/Utilities/Terminal application. Various command line utilities are covered throughout this guide, but Chapter 3, "Command Line and Automation," serves as an introduction to this environment.

MORE INFO ▶ To learn more about Darwin, see Apple's development resources, http://developer.apple.com/Darwin.

X11

X11 is an extension of the BSD environment that provides a common graphical applications platform for UNIX workstations. Apple's implementation of X11 is based on the popular open source XFree86 project. You can access X11 applications by simply double-clicking on their executable binary file or by opening the X11 interface located at /Applications/Utilities/X11.

> **MORE INFO** ▶ To learn more, visit Apple's X11 resource website, http://developer.
> apple.com/opensource/tools/X11.html.

Open Source Software

By now you may have noticed that quite a bit of Mac OS X is based on something called open source software. Generally speaking, open source is a method of software creation based on the free distribution and contribution of software source code. In other words, it's software whose code is freely available to anyone for general use or further modification. Interested individuals are expected and usually encouraged to provide improvements to open source software by adding to the software's code. It's expected that over time this community involvement will yield software products of exceptional quality often free of cost.

Apple is deeply involved with many open source projects; this includes not just borrowing from open source but also contributing to existing projects and creating entirely new open source projects as well. In fact, the core of Mac OS X, Darwin, is an entirely open source operating system that includes more than 200 individual open source projects. Keep in mind, though, that Apple maintains proprietary closed software solutions as part of Mac OS X as well. The creation of the proprietary parts of Mac OS X necessitates Apple charging for them, but this also allows Apple to employ hundreds of talented developers to create exceptional software.

> **MORE INFO** ▶ To learn more about Apple's open source involvement visit,
> www.opensource.apple.com.

The astounding growth of open source software in the last decade has not only produced some great software but also led to the rise of an entirely new operating system, Linux. With the growing popularity of Linux, high-quality open source applications have taken off as well. Because of Mac OS X's open source and UNIX heritage, you can also take advantage of many of these open source applications on your Mac. Some open source applications run in the command line, others through X11, and some have even been converted to full-fledged Mac applications. In summary, you should take some time to explore these free open source solutions for your Mac, as they may be suitable replacements for commercially purchased software.

> **MORE INFO ▶** Apple maintains a collection of popular open source applications at www.apple.com/downloads/macosx/unix_open_source.

> **MORE INFO ▶** The MacPorts project hosts over 5,900 open source software titles for Mac OS X at www.macports.org.

64-bit vs. 32-bit Mode

As covered previously, one of the main improvements in Mac OS X v10.6 is that nearly all of the operating system and included applications support both 32-bit and 64-bit modes. In fact, only four of the main built-in applications are still limited to 32-bit mode: DVD Player, Front Row, Grapher, and iTunes.

While moving most of the applications to support 64-bit mode will generally improve performance, this advancement is not without drawbacks. Namely, applications that run in 64-bit mode can't take advantage of any 32-bit code. This means any application that uses plug-in technology may suffer from compatibility issues with third-party plug-ins that have not been updated to support 64-bit mode.

Examples of plug-in software affected by this issue include:

▶ Printer drivers that add additional interfaces for the printer dialog

▶ Screen savers

▶ Audio device drivers known as Audio Units

▶ Spotlight metadata import plug-ins

▶ Dashboard Widgets that require plug-in code, though most Widgets don't use extra code, so they should work without issue

▶ Safari plug-ins

In short, applications running in 64-bit mode will not load 32-bit plug-ins. If you need to use a third-party 32-bit plug-in with a 64-bit capable application, then you will have to force the application to run in 32-bit mode on most Macs. This can be accomplished from the Finder's Get Info or Inspector windows by simply selecting the "Open in 32-bit mode" checkbox. Obviously, forcing 32-bit mode may make the application run slower, but this is required to use non-updated plug-ins.

There is one system application that will automatically switch modes for you, System Preferences. When a user tries to open a third-party 32-bit System Preferences plug-in, often called a System Preferences pane, it will prompt the user to restart System Preferences. If the user selects the default OK button, then System Preferences will restart in 32-bit mode and load the selected pane.

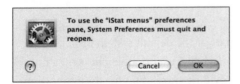

NOTE ▶ The process that handles the Dashboard will automatically run both 64-bit and 32-bit widgets. Dashboard is detailed in the "Managing Dashboard" section later in this chapter

NOTE ▶ With the exception of Dashboard and System Preferences, third-party plug-ins that tie into a system resource or background process must support 64-bit mode in order to work with Mac OS X v10.6.

Universal vs. Rosetta

In 2006 Apple moved the entire Mac product line from PowerPC processors to Intel processors. With the move to Intel-based Macs, Apple had to introduce an entirely new code base to Mac OS X. At the hardware level, PowerPC and Intel processors are so different that they require their own separate versions of software. Apple had been secretly maintaining an Intel-compatible version of Mac OS X since its inception, so when Apple announced the move to Intel processors, Mac OS X and all its included applications were already Intel native.

However, every other Mac application was not Intel native. Apple did preannounce the arrival of Intel-based Macs six months early to allow software developers to create Universal applications. Universal applications contain software code that runs on both PowerPC and Intel-based Macs. Yet for some third-party developers, updating software to Universal proved more difficult than others. There are still many older Mac applications that have not made the move to Universal.

So as not to leave both users and developers stranded with new hardware that couldn't run their old software, Mac OS X includes the Rosetta compatibility environment for Intel-based Macs. Rosetta is software that efficiently translates PowerPC code to Intel code on the fly. Most users will never even know that their application is running through the Rosetta translation process.

Using Rosetta

Starting with Mac OS X v10.6, Rosetta is no longer part of the default system installation. If Rosetta was installed when the system was installed, when a user double-clicks on a non-Universal application, Rosetta automatically starts providing translation for the application. The user probably won't notice, because the application should open and run as normal.

If Rosetta was not installed during the system installation, when an administrative user double-clicks on a non-Universal application, he will be prompted to install Rosetta. Non-administrative users will be presented with an authentication dialog requesting administrative authentication. Once an administrative user chooses to install Rosetta, the Software

Update application will open and automatically download the Rosetta installer from Apple's website and install it on the Mac. Once Rosetta is installed, the non-Universal application should open and run normally.

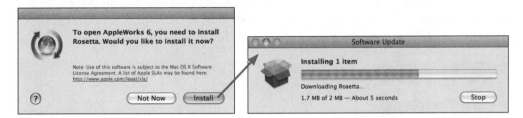

TIP ▶ The Rosetta installer is also part of the Optional Installs package found on the Mac OS X Install DVD.

Rosetta Caveats

Rosetta, like many compatibility solutions, is not without flaws. Much like the move from 32-bit to 64-bit applications, there will be some incompatibility. In certain cases, there simply isn't an Intel equivalent for PowerPC software code. In other cases, such as support for Classic, it was simply prudent for Apple to stop supporting such old technology.

Rosetta does not support the following software:

▶ Applications created for any version of the Mac OS earlier than Mac OS X

▶ The Classic compatibility environment

▶ Screen savers written for PowerPC architecture

▶ Software that inserts PowerPC preference panes in System Preferences

▶ Applications that specifically require a PowerPC G5 processor

▶ Applications that depend on one or more PowerPC-only kernel extensions

▶ Kernel extensions or hardware drivers written for the PowerPC architecture

▶ Java applications with JNI libraries

▶ Java in applications that Rosetta can translate (this means a web browser that Rosetta can run translated will not be able to load Java applets)

▶ Plug-ins written for the PowerPC architecture if the software they tie into runs as Intel native

There is, however, a solution if you need to use older PowerPC plug-ins with a Universal application. You will have to force the application to run in Rosetta compatibility mode. This can be accomplished from the Finder's Get Info or Inspector windows by selecting the "Open in 32-bit mode" checkbox, if available, and then selecting the "Open using Rosetta" checkbox. Obviously, forcing Rosetta compatibility mode may make the application run considerably slower, but this is required to use non-updated plug-ins.

Application Accessibility

Apple has worked hard to ensure that Mac OS X remains approachable for all users, including those who have trouble using the standard Mac interface via keyboard, mouse, and video display. Apple has built an extensive accessibility architecture into Mac OS X called Universal Access. Universal Access enables assistive interaction features for Apple and many third-party applications.

You can enable these features from the Universal Access preferences by choosing Apple menu > System Preferences, then click the Universal Access icon. General preferences include showing the Universal Access menu item and enabling access for assistive devices like electronic Braille interfaces. The remaining Universal Access preferences are presented in four separate tabs representing different assistance features:

▶ Seeing—The accessibility features in this section are designed to assist those who have difficulty viewing the screen or who are unable to view the screen at all. Options include enabling dynamic screen zooming and adjusting display settings to enhance clarity. The VoiceOver spoken-word interface, covered next in this section, is also enabled here.

▶ Hearing—The accessibility features in this section are designed to assist those who have difficulty hearing or who cannot hear sound. The primary option here is to enable screen flashing as an alternative to the alert sound.

▶ Keyboard—The accessibility features in this section are designed to assist those who have difficulty using a keyboard. Options include enabling sticky keys to assist with using keyboard combinations and slow keys to help with initial or repeated keystrokes.

▶ Mouse & Trackpad—The accessibility features in this section are designed to assist those who have difficulty using or who cannot use a mouse or trackpad. Options include increasing the cursor size so it's easier to see and enabling mouse keys that allow you to use the keyboard arrow keys in place of a mouse or trackpad.

MORE INFO ▶ To learn more, visit Apple's Accessibility resource website, www.apple. com/accessibility.

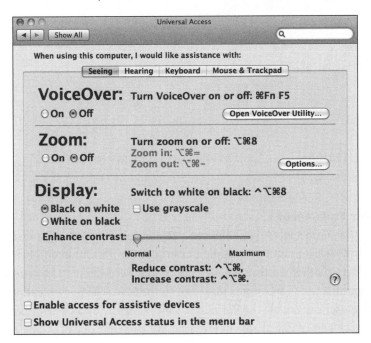

Using VoiceOver

VoiceOver is an interface mode that enables you to navigate the Mac OS X user interface using only keyboard control and spoken English descriptions of what's happening onscreen. You enable VoiceOver from the Seeing section of the Universal Access preferences. The first time you enable VoiceOver it will automatically launch an interactive tour of the VoiceOver interface. This spoken tour teaches the user how to use the various VoiceOver keyboard shortcuts. Learning these shortcuts is necessary to use VoiceOver. A highly customizable interface, VoiceOver allows the user to adjust almost every interaction parameter by opening the /Applications/Utilities/VoiceOver Utility application.

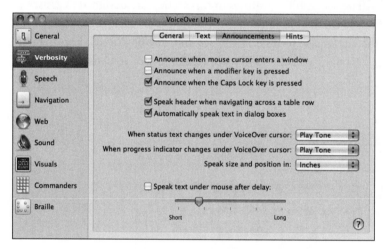

MORE INFO ▶ To learn more, visit Apple's VoiceOver resource website, www.apple. com/accessibility/voiceover.

Managing Accessibility Preferences

It is important to note that almost all Universal Access preferences are saved on a per-user basis. Thus, each user will have a unique com.apple.universalaccess.plist located in her ~/ Library/Preferences folder. In other words, each user has unique accessibility preferences that are active only when that user's account is logged in to the Mac. The one exception is that an administrative user can enable the VoiceOver feature for use by all accounts at the login window. This preference is available in the Accounts preferences by clicking the Login Options button.

The VoiceOver system includes a portable preferences feature that helps a user move his VoiceOver settings between multiple Macs. From the /Applications/Utilities/VoiceOver Utility application the user can define an external storage device as a location to save his VoiceOver settings. This will place a VoiceOver folder at the root of the external volume that contains all the user's VoiceOver preferences. As he moves to a new Mac he need only attach the external storage device, and if VoiceOver is enabled it will automatically detect his preferences.

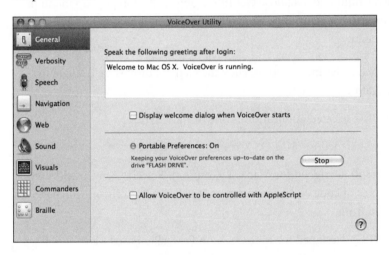

Monitoring Applications and Processes

Mac OS X provides several methods for identifying and managing applications and processes. You can use the Finder or System Profiler to identify application and command information, including what processor architectures the item supports. The Activity Monitor application and the ps and top commands are used for viewing and managing all processes as they are running on your Mac.

Application Identification

To quickly locate basic application information from the Finder:

1 In the Finder select the application you wish to identify, and then open the Get Info or Inspector window.

There are several ways to open the Get Info window: choose File > Get Info from the menu bar; press Command-I; choose Get Info from the Action pop-up menu in a Finder window toolbar; or right-click/Control-click an item and choose Get Info from the shortcut menu.

2 Once you have opened a Get Info window, click the General disclosure triangle to reveal general application information.

This will reveal that the selected application is one of three types:

Application (Intel). Designed for Mac OS X on Intel-based Macs.

Application (Universal). Designed for Mac OS X on both PowerPC and Intel-based Macs. It has both types of code embedded in it, so it will run natively on whichever platform it is opened from.

Application (PowerPC). Designed for Mac OS X on PowerPC-based Macs, it will open on Intel-based Macs using the Rosetta translation service.

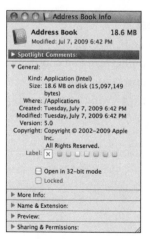 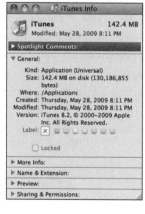 

NOTE ▶ Classic applications, though identifiable from the Get Info dialog, are not compatible with Mac OS X v10.6.

If you want to quickly gather information about all the applications on your Mac, try the /Applications/Utilities/System Profiler application. Upon opening, System Profiler scans the contents of all available Application folders. This includes /Applications, /Applications/Utilities, ~/Applications, /System/Library/CoreServices, and any other "Applications" folders at the root of any mounted volumes. Select Applications from the Contents list to see which applications System Profiler found. Selecting an application from the list reveals its name, version number, modification date, and application type.

Monitoring Processes via Activity Monitor

The primary Mac OS X application for monitoring processes as they are running is Activity Monitor. This extremely useful tool shows you the vital signs of any currently running process and the system as a whole. If an application has stopped responding or has become noticeably slow, check Activity Monitor. Also check here if the overall system is running noticeably slower. Activity Monitor will help you identify an application or background process that is using a significant percentage of system memory or processor resources.

To view your Mac's currently running processes with Activity Monitor:

1 Open /Applications/Utilities/Activity Monitor.

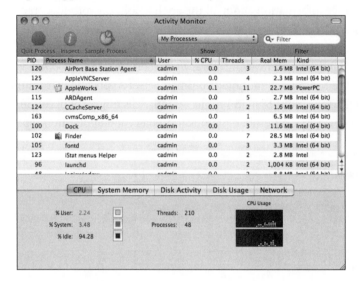

Process Identification (PID). Each process has a unique identifier that is chosen based on the order in which it was opened since system startup.

Process Name. This is the human name of the running process, as chosen by its creator.

User. Each process is opened on behalf of a particular user. Thus, each application has file system access based on the assigned user account.

% CPU. This number is the percentage of total CPU usage the process is consuming. Note that the maximum percentage possible is 100 percent times the number of processor cores.

Threads. Each process is further broken down into the number of thread operations. Multithreading a process helps increase responsiveness by enabling the process to perform multiple simultaneous tasks. Multithreading also increases performance as each thread of a single process can run on a separate processor core.

Real Mem. This represents the amount of physical memory that the process is currently occupying.

Kind. This shows what processor architecture the application is currently using: Intel (64 bit), Intel, or PowerPC.

2 Click a column title to sort the process list by that column.

Click the column title again to toggle between ascending and descending sorts. You can also adjust the number of statistics shown in the columns and the update frequency from the View menu.

PID	Process Name	User	% CPU	Threads	Real Mem	Kind
125	AppleVNCServer	cadmin	1.0	7	18.2 MB	Intel (64 bit)
165	Activity Monitor	cadmin	0.9	2	21.1 MB	Intel (64 bit)
101	SystemUIServer	cadmin	0.1	3	11.1 MB	Intel (64 bit)
48	loginwindow	cadmin	0.0	2	8.8 MB	Intel (64 bit)
113	UserEventAgent	cadmin	0.0	3	5.4 MB	Intel (64 bit)
96	launchd	cadmin	0.0	2	1,004 KB	Intel (64 bit)
102	Finder	cadmin	0.0	4	27.1 MB	Intel (64 bit)
120	AirPort Base Station Agent	cadmin	0.0	3	1.6 MB	Intel (64 bit)
150	mdworker	cadmin	0.0	3	6.0 MB	Intel (64 bit)
174	AppleWorks	cadmin	0.0	8	22.8 MB	PowerPC
115	ARDAgent	cadmin	0.0	5	2.7 MB	Intel (64 bit)

3 By default, Activity Monitor will only show processes running for the currently logged-in user. To view all active processes, choose All Processes from the Show pop-up menu.

Use the Spotlight search filter in the upper-right corner of the Activity Monitor window to quickly pare down the list of running processes.

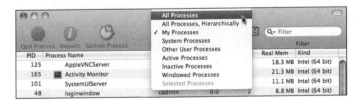

By viewing all processes and then re-sorting the list by either % CPU or Real Mem, you can determine whether any process is using excessive resources.

4 To further inspect a process, double-click its name in the Activity Monitor list. This reveals a window showing detailed process information.

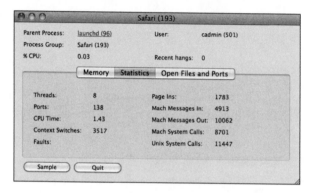

5 Finally, to inspect overall system information click through the tabs at the bottom of the Activity Monitor window.

These monitoring features are invaluable for troubleshooting as they show you real-time system statistics.

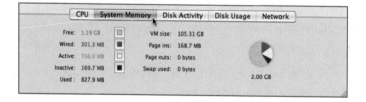

TIP Take time to explore all the features available from the Activity Monitor menu options. For an even more detailed process inspector, check out the /Developer/Applications/Instruments application installed as part of the optional Xcode Developer Tools package that can be found on the Mac OS X Install DVD.

Monitoring Processes via Command Line

Two primary commands exist for viewing active processes from the command-line interface, top and ps.

> **NOTE** ▸ If you aren't already comfortable with navigation in the UNIX command line, then it's strongly recommended that you study the command line concepts in Chapter 3, "Command Line and Automation," before reading the remainder of section.

top

The top command is so named because it's typically used to show the "top" processes that are taking up the most processor resources. However, by default with Mac OS X, top lists commands in reverse order based on their process ID number. To have top sort by processor usage, include the -u option. The top command takes over the Terminal window when you open it. To return to the command prompt, press the Q key. The following code shows the default output of the top command. Notice the similarities to Activity Monitor.

```
Processes: 51 total, 2 running, 49 sleeping, 216 threads          16:56:52
Load Avg: 0.12, 0.07, 0.13  CPU usage: 1.46% user, 2.43% sys, 96.9% idle
SharedLibs: 10M resident, 6936K data, 0B linkedit.
MemRegions: 5649 total, 185M resident, 12M private, 140M shared.
PhysMem: 330M wired, 387M active, 440M inactive, 1158M used, 890M free.
VM: 119G vsize, 1041M framework vsize, 72392(0) pageins, 0(0) pageouts.
Networks: packets: 208547/32M in, 544054/595M out.
Disks: 26496/931M read, 19094/513M written.


PID  COMMAND   %CPU TIME     #TH #WQ #POR #MRE RPRVT RSHRD RSIZE VPRVT
751  top       3.3  00:02.69 1/1 0   24   34   844K  264K  1416K 17M
741  mdworker  0.0  00:00.04 3   1   48   84   1360K 11M   3288K 23M
737  bash      0.0  00:00.01 1   0   17   25   348K  856K  1008K 17M
736  login     0.0  00:00.01 1   0   22   54   436K  312K  1572K 10M
...
```

ps

Short for "process status," the ps command lists active processes, but it does not take over the Terminal window as the top command does. Sometimes you have so many active processes that the top command simply can't show them all on your monitor, and this is where the ps command comes in handy. The syntax is ps, followed by any listing options you specify. The most useful options are -ax (to show all processes), -c (to only show the process name instead of the absolute path to the process), and -u followed by a user's short name (to list only processes belonging to that user). In the following example, Michelle first uses the ps command with the -c and -u options to shorten the process name and list active processes belonging to her user account. She then uses the ps command with only the -ax options to view all active processes with full pathnames. The results were too long to print, so they have been cut off at process 10 in this example.

```
MyMac:~ michelle$ ps -cu michelle
 UID PID TTY TIME CMD
 502 922 ?? 0:00.05 launchd
 502 1113 ?? 0:00.65 sshd
 502 1205 ?? 0:00.35 Spotlight
 502 1206 ?? 0:00.17 UserEventAgent
 502 1208 ?? 0:00.13 Dock
 502 1210 ?? 0:00.76 SystemUIServer
 502 1211 ?? 0:00.00 pboard
 502 1212 ?? 0:01.18 Finder
 502 1214 ?? 0:00.12 ATSServer
 502 1367 ?? 0:00.58 ScreenSaverEngine
 502 1369 ?? 0:00.14 mdworker
 502 1115 ttys001 0:00.12 -bash
 0 1371 ttys001 0:00.00 ps
MyMac:~ michelle$ ps -ax
 PID TTY TIME CMD
 1 ?? 0:03.65 /sbin/launchd
 9 ?? 0:00.86 /usr/libexec/kextd
 10 ?? 0:05.01 /usr/sbin/DirectoryService
 ...
```

Application Troubleshooting

Application issues are as diverse as the applications themselves. Just as each application is designed to provide unique features, problems often manifest in unique ways as well. Fortunately, there several general troubleshooting steps you can take when diagnosing and resolving an application issue. The actions in the following list are presented from the least invasive and time-consuming to the most invasive and time-consuming. Actions are also generally presented by the likelihood of their success in resolving the issue, from most to least likely.

> **NOTE** ▶ Some software is simply just incompatible with Mac OS X v10.6. Apple maintains a list of software known to be incompatible at Knowledge Base article HT3258, "Mac OS X v10.6: About incompatible software."

General application troubleshooting methods include:

▶ Restart the application—Often restarting an application will resolve the issue, or at least resolve application responsiveness. In some cases, the application may become unresponsive and you have to forcibly quit it to restart it, as detailed later in this section.

▶ Try another known working document—This is an excellent method to determine if a document has become corrupted and is the cause of the problem. If you discover that the problem's source is a corrupted document file, usually the best solution is to restore the document from an earlier backup. Mac OS X includes a sophisticated and yet easy-to-use backup system called Time Machine. Time Machine is covered previously in Chapter 5, "Data Management and Backup."

▶ Try another application—Many common document types can be opened by multiple Mac applications. Try opening the troublesome document in another application. If this works, save a new "clean" version of the document from the alternate application.

▶ Try another user account—Use this method to determine if a user-specific resource file is the cause of the problem. If the application problem doesn't appear when using another account, you should search for corrupted application caches, preferences, and resource files in the suspect user's Library folder. Creating a temporary account to test and then delete is quite easy, as covered previously in Chapter 2, "User Accounts."

▶ Check diagnostic reports and log files—This is the last information-gathering step to take before you start replacing items. Few applications keep detailed log files; however, every time an application crashes, the Mac OS X problem-reporting feature saves a diagnostic report of the crash information. Problem reports are detailed later in this chapter.

▶ Delete cache files—To increase performance, many applications create cache folders in the /Library/Caches and ~/Library/Caches folders. A specific application's cache folder almost always matches the application's name. While not the most likely application resource to cause problems, cache folders can be easily deleted without affecting the user's information. Once you delete an application's cache folder, the application will create a new one the next time you open it. One cache type that can't be removed easily from the Finder is the various font caches. However, they can be removed by using the `atsutil` command. At the command line, to delete user font caches enter `sudo atsutil databases -removeUser`; to delete system font caches enter `sudo atsutil databases -remove`. You should restart the Mac after you remove these font caches.

▶ Replace preference files—Corrupted preference files are the most likely of all application resources to cause problems, as they change often and are required for the application to function properly. Application preference troubleshooting is detailed later in this chapter.

▶ Replace application resources—Although corrupted application resources can certainly cause problems, they are the least likely source of problems, since application resources are rarely changed. Application resource troubleshooting is also detailed later in this chapter.

Forcibly Quit via Graphical Interface

It's pretty easy to tell when an application becomes unresponsive—it stops reacting to your mouse clicks and the cursor often changes to a spinning beach ball for more than a minute. Hence, the term "beach-balling" has become slang for a frozen Mac application. Because the forward-most application controls the menu bar, it may seem as if the application has locked you out of the Mac entirely. But this simply isn't so, because moving the cursor from the frozen application window to another application window or the desktop usually returns the cursor to normal—and you can then click another application or the desktop to regain control of your Mac.

Mac OS X provides no less than three methods for forcibly quitting applications from the graphical interface:

▶ From the Force Quit Applications dialog—Choose Apple menu > Force Quit or use the Option-Command-Escape keyboard combination to open the Force Quit Applications dialog. A frozen application will appear in red text with "(not responding)" next to it. To forcibly quit, select any application and click the Force Quit button. Note that you can only restart the Finder from this dialog.

▶ From the Dock—Control-click, right-click, or click and hold the application's icon in the Dock to display the Dock's application shortcut menu. If the Dock has recognized that the application is frozen, simply choose Force Quit from this menu. Otherwise, hold down the Option key to change the Quit menu command to Force Quit.

▶ From Activity Monitor—Open /Applications/Utilities/Activity Monitor and select the application you wish to quit from the process list. Next, click the Quit Process button in Activity Monitor's toolbar, and then click the Force Quit button. Activity Monitor is the only built-in graphical application that will also allow administrative users to quit or forcibly quit any other user processes or background system process.

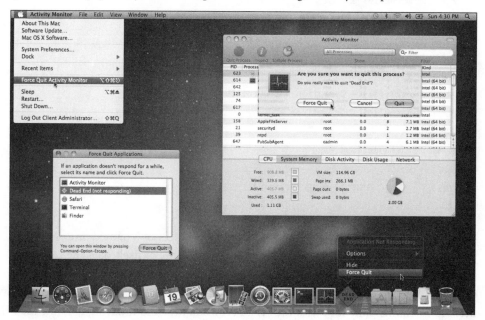

Forcibly Quit via Command Line

Two primary commands exist for viewing and forcibly quitting processes from the command-line interface, kill and killall.

The intent of the kill command is clear by its name. This command is used to forcibly quit processes. The syntax is kill, followed by the process identification number (PID) of the process you wish to forcibly quit. As covered previously, you can identify a process's PID from the Activity Monitor application or the top and ps commands.

In the following example, Michelle attempts to use the kill command to kill the DirectoryService process, which happens to be process 11 and is always owned by the system. Initially she isn't allowed because the process belongs to the system, so being an administrative user, she uses the sudo command to execute the kill command as the root user. Michelle uses ps -axc to verify the DirectoryService process before and after the kill command. Notice that the DirectoryService process has a new PID after the kill command, indicating that it has been restarted by the system. The full output of the ps command has been truncated for this example.

```
MyMac:~ michelle$ ps -axc
...
11 ??          0:00.99 DirectoryService
...
MyMac:~ michelle$ kill 11
-bash: kill: (11) - Operation not permitted
MyMac:~ michelle$ sudo kill 11
Password:
MyMac:~ michelle$$ ps -axc
...
705 ??         0:00.13 DirectoryService
...
```

The killall command was invented to kill all the instances of a named process. This is especially useful when a process spawns multiple instances of itself, as is the case with some network service processes. In the previous example, Michelle had to locate the PID of the DirectoryService process to forcibly quit it with the kill command. She could have accomplished this same task with the killall command without having to know the PID.

She would, however, have to enter the exact spelling of the running process. In this case Michelle would simply enter:

```
LeoClient:~ michelle$ sudo killall DirectoryService
```

Problem Reports

To help diagnose persistent issues, Mac OS X's problem-reporting feature springs into action any time an application quits unexpectedly, commonly known as a *crash*, or stops functioning and you have to forcibly quit it, commonly known as a *hang*. This process displays a warning dialog to the user letting her know a problem has occurred. More important, this process records log files that detail the circumstances surrounding the application's crash or hang. If you click the Report button when the warning dialog appears, then you can see the problem report or automatically send it to Apple via the Internet.

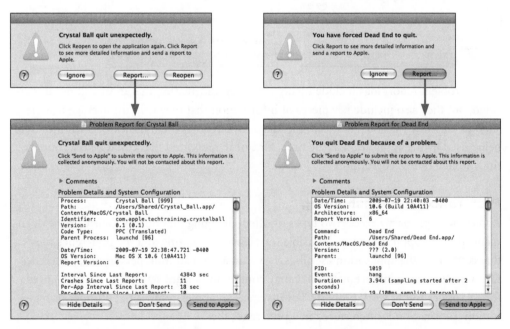

Even if you don't send the report to Apple, you can revisit problem reports again, as they are always saved to the system volume. If the application crashed, a problem report log with the name of the application followed by ".crash" is saved in the user's ~/Library/Logs/DiagnosticReports folder. However, if the application hung, a problem report log with the name of the application followed by ".hung" is saved in the local /Library/Logs/ DiagnosticReports folder. The easiest way to view these reports is to open the /Applications/ Utilities/Console application, and then click the Show Log List button in the toolbar. The problem reports will be chronologically listed in the Diagnostic Information section.

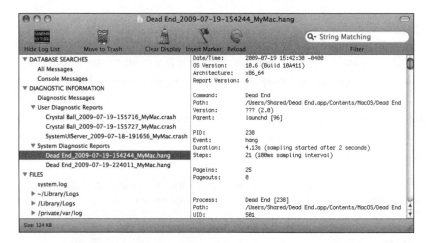

These problem report logs include highly technical information that most will not understand, but they also include key pieces of information that may help the average troubleshooter diagnose the issue. For example, diagnostic reports often indicate which files were being used by the application at the time. One of the reported files could be the source of the problem due to corruption.

Preference Troubleshooting

Applications primarily access two types of often-changing files during their use: the documents that the application is responsible for viewing or editing and the preference files that contain all the application's settings. From an administration perspective, preference files are often more important, as they may contain important settings that are required for an application to work properly. For instance, an application's serial number or registration information is often stored in a preference file.

Preference files can be found in any Library folder, but most application preferences end up in the user's Library, specifically in the ~/Library/Preferences folder. This is because the local Library should only be used for system preferences. More important, it enables each user to have his own application settings that do not interfere with other users' application settings. By this logic, it's clear that if you're troubleshooting a system process, then you should look for its preferences in the /Library folder.

Most application and system preference files are saved as a property list file. The naming scheme for a property list file is usually in the form of a reverse domain name, followed by the program name, ending with the file type .plist. For example, the Finder's preference file is named com.apple.finder.plist. This naming scheme may seem strange at first, but it helps avoid confusion by identifying the software's maker along with the application.

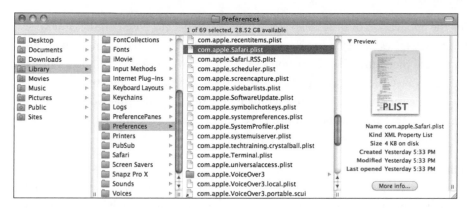

Application preference files are one of the most common application resources to cause problems. Because these files can contain both internal application configuration information and user-configured preferences, even if you haven't changed any preferences, odds are the application is constantly storing new information in this file. It is the only file required by most applications that is constantly being rewritten, so it's ripe for corruption.

Apple has worked hard to make its own applications and the user preference system wary of corrupt preference files. Many applications, including third-party applications, that use Apple's preference model will simply recognize the corrupt preference file, ignore it, and create a new one. On the other hand, many third-party applications use their own proprietary preference models that are not as resilient. If this is the case, corrupted preferences typically result in an application that crashes frequently or during startup.

Resolving Corrupted Preferences

The most convenient method of isolating a corrupted preference in this case is to rename the suspect preference file. If any part of the preference file name is different than expected, the application will ignore it and create a new preference file. In the Finder add an identifier to the end of the suspect preference file name—something like ".bad." Alternately you could simply put a tilde, or "~" character, at the beginning of the preference file, which will cause the Finder to put it at the beginning of the file listing when sorted alphabetically.

Restarting the application or process creates a new preference file based on the code's defaults. If this resolves the issue and doesn't remove any irreplaceable settings, go ahead and trash the old preference file; if not, you should move on to resource troubleshooting. If you eventually resolve the problem elsewhere, you can then restore the previous settings by deleting the newer preference file and removing the filename identifier you added to the original preference file. The benefit is that you didn't lose any of the settings or custom configuration from the previous preference file.

Viewing and Editing Preferences

One of the primary advantages of using the property list file format is that it can generally be understood by humans. During your troubleshooting, you may find it advantageous to verify settings by directly viewing the contents of the configuration property list file. Many applications and processes keep additional settings items in these files that may not have a graphical interface for configuration.

> **NOTE** ▶ A few third-party applications do not store their preference files as property lists. Thus, they will likely sport a different naming convention, and you will probably not be able to view or edit the file's contents.

The content of a property list file is formatted either as plain-text Extensible Markup Language (XML) or binary. The XML format is relatively human-readable with normal text interspersed alongside special text tags that define the data structure for the information. Thus, you can view and attempt to decipher the XML code of plain-text-formatted property list files using any text-reading application. Binary-encoded files are only readable using special tools designed to convert the binary code into human-readable format. Fortunately, Mac OS X includes a Quick Look plug-in that will allow you to easily view the contents of either type of property list file by simply hitting the Space bar while you have the file selected in the Finder.

If you determine that you need to edit a property list file, the most complete graphical application for doing so is Property List Editor. Not only does this application decode binary property list files, but it also enables you to view and edit any property list in an easy-to-read hierarchical format. The Property List Editor application is installed as part of the optional Xcode Developer Tools package on the Mac OS X Install DVD.

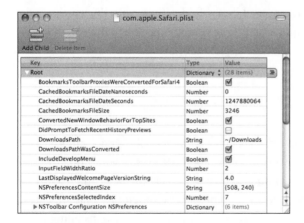

Resource Troubleshooting

Although rare, corrupted application software and associated non-preference resources can be a source of application problems. These types of files rarely, if ever, change after the initial application installation, so the likelihood that such a resource is the cause of a problem is low. However, keep in mind that many applications use *other* resources from the local and user Library folders, such as fonts, plug-ins, and keychains, as well as items in the Application Support folder. The hard part is locating the suspect resource; once you have, the fix is to simply remove or replace the corrupted resource and restart the application.

NOTE ▶ Applications running in 64-bit mode will not load plug-in resources that only support 32-bit mode. This compatibility issue is covered in the "64-bit vs. 32-bit Applications" section previously in this chapter.

NOTE ▶ Applications running native on Intel will not load plug-in resources that only support PowerPC. This compatibility issue is covered in the "Universal vs. Rosetta" section previously in this chapter.

Remember that corrupted resources in the user's home folder Library will affect only that user, while corrupted resources in the local Library affect all users. Use this fact to narrow your search when looking for a corrupted resource. Further, application and problem report logs, covered previously in this section, may tell you which resources the application was attempting to access when it crashed. Obviously, those resources should be your primary suspects.

If the application exhibits problems with only one user, attempt to locate the specific resource at the root of the problem in the user's Library folder. Start with the usual suspects; if you find a resource that you think could be causing the problem, move that resource out of the user's Library and restart the application.

NOTE ▶ Some older applications have a bad habit of storing their resources in the user's Documents folder, so you may have to check there as well.

If you've determined that the application issue is persistent across all user accounts, start by reinstalling or upgrading to the latest version of the application. You will probably find that there is a newer version of the application available that likely includes bug fixes. At the very least, by reinstalling you will replace any potentially corrupted files that are part of the standard application. If you continue to experience problems after reinstalling the application, search through the local Library resources to find and remove or replace the corrupted resource.

NOTE ▶ If you are discovering a large number of corrupted files, this is probably indicative of a much more serious file system or storage hardware issue. Troubleshooting these items is covered in Chapter 4, "File Systems."

Managing Dashboard

Mac OS X v10.4 introduced the Dashboard as a new interface concept that provides instant access to narrowly focused, but usually very attractive, mini-applications called widgets. When the Dashboard is activated, your chosen mini-applications will instantly spring to life and appear "on top" of the Mac's normal interface. A simple click on the Mac's normal interface will dismiss the Dashboard just as quickly. The convenience of using these mini-applications from the Dashboard caught on quickly, and within a few months after its introduction hundreds of new third-party widgets were available.

Apple added a few new tricks for Dashboard with Mac OS X v10.5, including the ability for any user to quickly make new widgets from any website using the Safari Web Clip button. Apple has also completely reworked the widget runtime architecture to run more efficiently and securely than before. To help increase the number of third-party widgets, Apple formalized the widget creation process by introducing a full widget development environment called Dashcode. Dashcode is installed as part of the optional Xcode Developer Tools package on the Mac OS X Install DVD. Finally, with Mac OS X v10.6 the Dashboard process made the move to 64-bit mode for improved performance.

Adding More Widgets

By default, the Dashboard is activated by clicking the Dashboard icon in the Dock, pressing the F12 key on older Macs, pressing the F4 key on current Macs, or using the scroll wheel button on a compatible mouse. If you don't like the default shortcuts, you can adjust the Dashboard keyboard key and activate an Active Screen Corner for Dashboard from the Exposé & Spaces preferences. Further, you can adjust the Dashboard mouse button from the Keyboard & Mouse preferences.

Dashboard

Built-in Apple widgets are located in /Library/Widgets, while third-party widgets are typically installed in ~/Library/Widgets in the user's home folder. Most users will use the automatic widget install mechanisms in Mac OS X to add new widgets to their Dashboard.

To easily locate, test, and install a new widget:

1   Open the Dashboard using one of the methods outlined previously. The default method on all Macs is to click on the Dashboard icon in the Dock.

2   Once in Dashboard, click the small plus button at the bottom corner of the screen to reveal the widget bar.

The widget bar allows you to add currently installed widgets to your dashboard area by simply clicking on the widget's icon.

3 With the widget bar open, click the Manage Widgets button or the Widgets icon in the bottom right corner of the screen.

This will open the widget manager that allows you to disable installed widgets or download new widgets from Apple's website.

4 From the widget manager click the More Widgets button, and it will automatically open the default web browser and take you to Apple's online widget repository.

At this point you can browse and download any additional widgets that strike your fancy. Alternately you can acquire widgets using any method you like including other websites or file sharing.

TIP You can also create your own custom widgets from web pages in Safari by selecting File > Open in Dashboard from the menu bar.

5 If you downloaded the widget with Safari, it will automatically prompt for installation. However, if you acquired the widget through other means you will have to double-click on the widget file in the Finder to start the widget installer.

6 When the Widget Installer dialog appears, click the Install button to open the widget in the Dashboard for installation.

The Dashboard will open the new widget in a test environment.

7 Thoroughly explore the widget and, if you like it, click the Keep button to complete the installation process.

The widget will be installed in the currently logged-in user's home folder, in the ~/Library/Widgets folder, and will always be available to that user in the Dashboard from the widget bar.

Manually Manage Widgets

You can also manually install widgets by simply dragging them into one of the Widgets folders. This is necessary if you want to install a widget for all users of the system. Similar to other system resources, widgets installed in the user's home folder will only be available to that user, and widgets installed in the local Library folder will be available to all local users. If you manually install a widget, thus bypassing the automatic widget installer, users will still have to manually add that widget to their Dashboard from the widget bar.

To remove a widget, locate it in either the local or user library Widgets folder and drag it to the trash. If the widget is still active in the Dashboard after you have removed it from the Widgets folder, log the user out and then back in again to restart the Dashboard process.

Understanding Widget Architecture

The widget runtime architecture was reworked for Mac OS X v10.5 to provide a more efficient and secure Dashboard environment. When a user logs in, the `launchd` process starts the `Dock` process. The first time a user attempts to access the Dashboard, the `Dock` process starts the `DashboardClient` process. The `DashboardClient` process is responsible for running the Dashboard environment, including all widgets. The included Apple widgets run in 64-bit mode, but if you install any third-party widgets it's likely you'll have some widgets that only support 32-bit mode. If this is the case the system will automatically launch an additional `DashboardClient` process in 32-bit mode to handle these older widgets. This means that even if you have dozens of widgets open, you will still have only two active processes handling all those widgets.

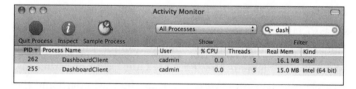

The `DashboardClient` process maintains two general Dashboard preference files in the ~/Library/Preferences folder: com.apple.dashboard.client.plist, and com.apple.dashboard.plist. Each open widget also maintains its own preference file in the user Preferences folder named widget-com.*widgetmaker*.widget.*widgetname*.plist, where *widgetmaker* is the name of the software developer who created the widget, and *widgetname* is the name of the widget.

The `DashboardClient` process has the same access privileges as the user. So generally, widgets are as secure as any other normal application. Nevertheless, it is possible for someone to create and distribute widgets that have a negative effect. Widgets are basically miniature specialized web browsers, so just about any data transfer or software that can run from a web browser can also be run by a widget. The Dashboard is only as safe as the widgets a user chooses to run. If you are at all suspicious of a third-party widget, simply avoid using it.

> **TIP** Although an administrator can't prevent a user from downloading third-party widgets, she can limit a user's ability to use third-party widgets with the Parental Controls preferences, as covered in Chapter 2, "User Accounts."

Troubleshooting Widgets

If a widget appears to stop working or becomes unresponsive, your first step should be to attempt to reset the widget. From the Dashboard, click once on the widget, then press Command-R to reset the widget. Widgets use a swirling animation to indicate that they have reset.

If the widget is still having problems, or you're having trouble using all the widgets, restart all the DashboardClient processes associated with the user account. You can forcibly quit the DashboardClient processes by using /Applications/Utilities/Activity Monitor. More information about forcibly quitting processes is available in the "Forcibly Quit" sections earlier in this chapter. After you quit the DashboardClient processes, reactivate the Dashboard and the DashboardClient processes, and all open widgets will reopen. Another method is to restart all user processes by logging the user out and then back in again.

If restarting the widget and the DashboardClient processes doesn't work, you may have a corrupted widget or widget preference file. Widgets are similar to other applications in that they are susceptible to errors from corrupted files. Start by removing the specific widget preference file, and then restart the DashboardClient processes. If you're having trouble with a third-party widget, download a new copy and replace the widget itself. Finally, you can reset the entire Dashboard system by removing all Dashboard and widget preference files and then logging the user out and back in again.

Understanding Boot Camp

Mac hardware, aside from generally having more appealing industrial design, higher build quality, and the unique ability to run Mac OS X, isn't that much different than other Intel-based PCs. In fact, Apple hardware is a great platform for running Windows or any other operating system that supports the Intel chipset.

When Apple introduced the first Intel-based Macs, users were scrambling for solutions to run Windows on Mac hardware. For several months, dedicated hackers attempted to get Windows working on Mac hardware; Apple, however, had already been working on the problem and eventually introduced the Boot Camp Public Beta. With the introduction of Mac OS X v10.5, the testing was done and Boot Camp became a complete product that provides users with full support for running Windows natively on their Mac.

> **NOTE ▶** Although it is possible to run any Intel-compatible operating system on Intel-based Macs, at the time of this writing Boot Camp provides only setup and hardware driver support for Windows XP SP2+ and various versions of Windows Vista.

Mac OS X v10.6 introduces Boot Camp 3.0, which includes several significant updates, including:

▶ Drivers that allow the Windows Boot Camp system read-only access to Mac OS X formatted volumes

▶ Improved Windows Boot Camp system support for the buttons on Apple Cinema displays

▶ Improved Windows Boot Camp system support for tap-to-click on Macs with trackpads

▶ The ability to restart into Mac OS X from the Windows Boot Camp system command line

Your Mac's Intel-based hardware is what primarily enables Windows to run natively. Boot Camp simply provides the means for you to easily prepare the Mac's system drive for Windows installation and provides the appropriate hardware drivers for Windows systems. The Boot Camp Assistant will quickly partition and prepare your Mac OS X system drive to accept a Windows installation. You then install Windows from optical media as you would on any other PC hardware. Finally, the Mac OS X Install DVD includes

Windows drivers for your Mac's hardware, including support for Mac-specific features such as integrated iSight cameras and Apple keyboards, mice, and track pads.

> **MORE INFO** ▶ A very popular alternative to Boot Camp is running Windows in a virtual environment that allows you to use both Mac OS X and another operating system simultaneously. Two solutions for this are Parallels Desktop, www.parallels.com/products/desktop/, and VMware Fusion, www.vmware.com/products/fusion.

Boot Camp Requirements

The following is required to install and set up Windows on your Mac:

▶ An Intel-based Mac computer—If you're already running Mac OS X v10.6 this shouldn't be an issue because it has the same requirement.

▶ Directly attached input devices—The Windows installation process does not support Bluetooth wireless input devices, which means you must use either a USB keyboard and mouse, or a built-in keyboard and track pad.

▶ Mac OS X v10.6 or later—The latest version of Mac OS X is strongly recommended. You can check for Apple software updates if your Mac is connected to the Internet by choosing Apple menu > Software Update to launch the Software Update application. You can also check Apple's Support Download website at www.apple.com/support/downloads.

▶ All firmware updates for your Mac—The latest version of firmware is strongly recommended. Again, you can check for Apple firmware updates by using the Software Update application. Another source is the Apple Knowledge Base document HT1237, "EFI and SMC firmware updates for Intel-based Macs."

▶ A Mac OS X v10.6 installation disc—You can use either a store-purchased "box copy" Mac OS X Install DVD or, if your Mac came with OS X v10.6 preinstalled, you can use the Mac OS X Install Disc 1 that came with your Mac.

▶ At least 10 GB of free disk space to dedicate to Windows—Remember that Windows cannot natively access other Mac-formatted volumes, so you should probably carve out more than the minimum amount of disk space. If you have a Mac Pro with multiple drives, you can dedicate an entire drive to Windows.

► 2 GB or more of RAM when running Windows Vista on a Mac Pro—Windows Vista is a notorious resource hog. Mac Pros require more memory when used by Windows Vista because they use Intel Xeon processors.

► Boot Camp Assistant—Included with Mac OS X, Boot Camp Assistant is located at /Applications/Utilities/Boot Camp Assistant.

► A single full-install Windows install disc—At the time of this writing, Boot Camp supports full installations of Windows XP Home Edition or Professional with Service Pack 2 or later, or Windows Vista Home Basic, Home Premium, Business, and Ultimate including both 32-bit and 64-bit versions.

Boot Camp Caveats

Before installing Windows using Boot Camp, be aware of its known limitations:

► The Boot Camp Assistant cannot be used on drives containing more than one partition.

   TIP You can dynamically repartition your Mac's internal hard drive to restore it to a single partition using Disk Utility, as covered in Chapter 4, "File Systems."

   TIP Though not supported by Apple, as an alternative you can set as many partitions as you want using Disk Utility as covered in Chapter 4, "File Systems." However, Boot Camp will only work from the last Windows-formatted partition of the drive.

► Boot Camp does not work with external hard drives.

► If you are installing Windows on a portable computer, always connect the power adapter to ensure that the laptop remains on during the entire Windows installation process.

► Do not use Windows-based tools to create or modify partitions on drives containing Mac volumes. Doing so may delete Mac-formatted volumes or render your system drive unbootable. However, you can use Windows-based tools to modify individual volume formatting.

► Mac OS X includes support for mounting NTFS volumes as read only. So, while using Mac OS X you'll be able to view and copy the contents of Windows volumes, but you won't be able to write changes.

> TIP▶ You can add NTFS volume write support to Mac OS X by installing the free and open source NTFS-3G and MacFUSE software bundle: http://macntfs-3g.blogspot.com.

▶ The Boot Camp 3.0 drivers for Windows offer read-only support for Mac OS X Extended volumes.

> TIP▶ You can add read/write Mac OS X Extended volume support to Windows by installing the MacDrive software package by Mediafour: www.mediafour.com/products/macdrive.

▶ Finally, just because you're using Mac hardware doesn't mean Windows is any less susceptible to viruses, spyware, and malware. Keep Windows updated at all times with the latest security updates and be sure to install Windows protection software.

Configuring Boot Camp

Setting up Boot Camp is a significant process that can take up to several hours. Apple has worked hard to make the setup process as easy as possible, but there isn't much Apple can do to make the Windows system installation and setup process any less complex or time consuming. In fact, the majority of setup time is spent with Windows setup.

Here are a few things to do before setting up Boot Camp:

▶ Always back up important items before making any significant changes to the Mac. Needless to say, setting up Boot Camp is a very significant change.

▶ Print out the Boot Camp Installation & Setup Guide accessible from the Boot Camp Assistant introduction screen.

▶ Update to the latest version of Mac OS X v10.6 and to the latest firmware for your Mac. You can use the built-in Software Update or visit the Apple Support Downloads website at www.apple.com/support/downloads.

The three primary steps for setting up Boot Camp are:

▶ Use Boot Camp Assistant—This assistant will create a new partition on your internal startup disk for the Windows system. If you have multiple internal disks, you can use this assistant to prepare a specific disk for Windows. This assistant will automatically restart the Mac from the Windows installation disc.

▶ Install and set up Windows—In addition to correctly choosing and possibly reformatting the Windows partition, you will have to complete the standard Windows installation and setup process.

▶ Install Boot Camp drivers for Windows—These drivers add support for Mac-specific hardware like the built-in iSight camera and Apple input devices.

Boot Camp Assistant

The Boot Camp Assistant process is used to start the Boot Camp setup process. It's easy to follow and takes only a few minutes to complete.

To start the Boot Camp setup process with Boot Camp Assistant:

1 Quit all currently running applications, as they may stop responding and lose data during the repartitioning process.

2 As an administrative user, open /Applications/Utilities/Boot Camp Assistant and click the Continue button after you heed the Introduction warning.

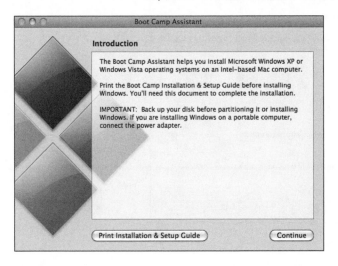

3 Depending on your hardware situation, you'll see one of two options. If you have only a single internal drive, click and drag the divider to specify the size of the Windows partition. You can also use the two buttons below the partition diagram to make a quick choice.

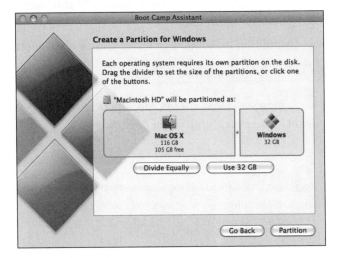

If you have multiple internal drives, you'll be able to select any drive for the Windows partition. You can dedicate an entire drive to Windows, or you can choose to create a second partition.

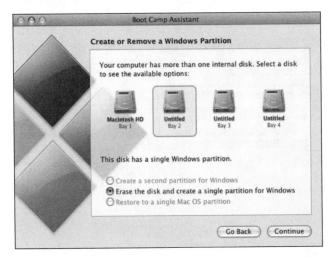

The Boot Camp Assistant won't let you choose a partition size larger than the amount of free space your drive has available. If you're installing Windows Vista, it's strongly advised that you choose a minimum partition size of 32 GB.

4 Click the Partition or Continue button to repartition the drive and create the Windows volume.

It may take several minutes for this process to complete; the system will have to verify the integrity of the volume and possibly move any data that would interfere with the new partition space. It's important that you do not open any other applications while the repartition process is under way.

When the repartition process is complete, the Boot Camp Assistant will format the new Windows partition as a FAT32 volume named BOOTCAMP. In most cases, you will have to reformat this volume later using the Windows installer.

Once the Windows partition has been created, you will be prompted to start the Windows installation process.

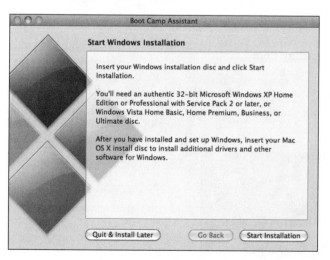

5 Insert a compatible Windows installation disc and click the Start Installation button.

The Mac will restart from the inserted disc, which should start the Windows installation process.

If you want to install Windows later, simply click the Quit & Install Later button. The next time you open the Boot Camp Assistant, it will automatically detect the Windows partition and again prompt you to start the Windows installation process.

NOTE ▶ If the Boot Camp Assistant cannot complete the repartition process, you have a few solutions to try. First, you should repair the disk as outlined in Chapter 4, "File Systems." You can also restart the Mac and try the Boot Camp Assistant again.

Install and Set Up Windows

The installation and setup process for Windows on a Mac using Boot Camp is nearly identical to the process used on a standard Windows-compatible PC. The Windows installation and setup process isn't difficult, but it does require quite a bit of time, an Internet connection, and several restarts.

NOTE ▶ The following installation and setup overview assumes you're installing Windows Vista, but the main points still apply to installing Windows XP. Windows 7 was not supported by Boot Camp at the time of this writing.

To install and set up Windows using Boot Camp:

1 The Mac will take a few minutes to boot from the Windows installation disc. Once the installer begins, advance through the language, Windows activation, and license terms screens.

2 Because no previous version of Windows exists on your Mac, the installer forces you to choose a Custom (Advanced) installation process. Click anywhere in the Custom (Advanced) area to continue.

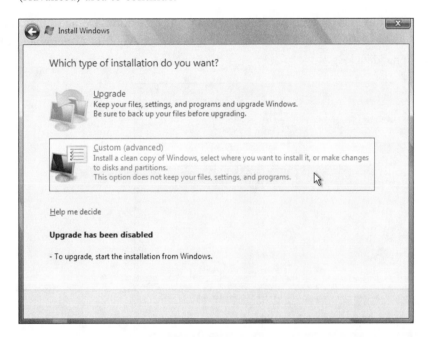

3 The Windows installation process will scan the Mac's local drives for any available volumes.

Because Windows doesn't fully comprehend the GUID partitioning scheme, you may see several "Unallocated Space" or unnamed partitions listed. It's critical that you choose the correct Windows partition that you created earlier for Boot Camp. The partition created by the Boot Camp Assistant should appear as "BOOTCAMP," but Windows can also identify the Boot Camp partition by its size.

4 Once you have selected the correct partition, you have to reformat it with the NTFS file system. Click "Drive options (advanced)" below the partition list. Then click Format to reformat the selected partition.

You will have to dismiss a final dialog by clicking OK to format the partition. By default, Windows will not name formatted volumes, so they will show up in Mac OS X as "Untitled."

Do not attempt to format other partitions or extend any partition. Doing so may corrupt the drive's partition structure or erase the Mac's system volume. Either will result in catastrophic data loss.

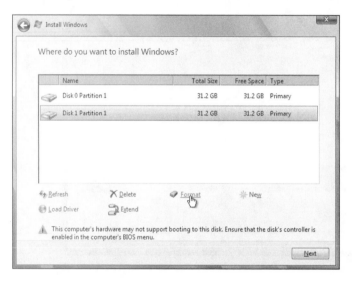

5   Once you have selected and reformatted the Windows partition, click the Next button to start the installation process. This process may take several hours, and the Mac will restart several times.

6   Finally, work through the Windows first-run setup, complete any Windows activation, and make sure to check for any Windows updates.

The Windows Update system is managed from the Windows Update Control Panel.

NOTE ▶ You may not be able to initially check for Windows updates until you install the appropriate network drivers via the Boot Camp drivers for Windows.

Install Boot Camp Drivers for Windows

You could theoretically continue to use Windows without installing the Boot Camp drivers, but the generic drivers included with Windows do not fully support all of your Mac's advanced hardware. Most important, though, installing the Boot Camp drivers allows you to restart into Mac OS X from Windows.

NOTE ▶ Again, the following instructions assume you're installing Windows Vista, but the main points still apply to installing Windows XP.

To install the Boot Camp drivers for Windows:

1   Once you have Windows installed and set up, you need to eject the Windows installation disc, but because you haven't installed the proper drivers yet, the Mac's keyboard Eject key will be useless.

    To eject the Windows installation disc, choose Computer from the Windows Start menu, select the Windows install disc icon, and click the Eject button.

TIP ▶ From the Computer view you can also rename the Local Disk (C:) volume to something more recognizable for when you're using Mac OS X, as demonstrated in the previous screen shot.

2 Insert the Mac OS X Install DVD, and the Windows AutoPlay service automatically opens the Boot Camp Installer.

Windows Vista requires that you click "Run setup.exe" to validate that you want to run the Boot Camp Installer.

3 Proceed through the Boot Camp Installer welcome, license agreement, and install screens.

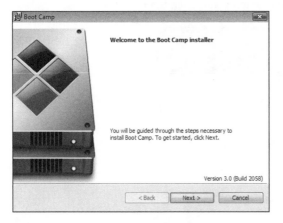

When the installer is done, you will be prompted to restart Windows. Click the Yes button to restart immediately.

4 After Windows restarts, you should have full access to all the Mac's hardware features. You will also have access to the Boot Camp system tray item in the Windows Taskbar, the Boot Camp Control Panel, Apple Software Update for Windows, and the Boot Camp Help system.

TIP ▶ Apple Software Update for Windows, available from the All Programs section of the Start menu, allows you to download and install all Apple software for windows including iTunes and Safari.

TIP ▶ The Mac OS X Install DVD will also allow you to install "Remote Install Mac OS X and DVD" or "CD Sharing" on Windows systems. This software provides support for sharing a computer's optical drive to MacBook Air laptops.

Removing Windows

If for some reason you decide to remove Windows from your Mac, the Boot Camp Assistant makes quick work of the process.

To remove Windows:

1   While in Mac OS X, as an administrative user open /Applications/Utilities/Boot Camp Assistant, and then click the Continue button to advance past the Introduction screen.

2   The Boot Camp Assistant will automatically recognize that Windows is already installed and present you with the choice to "Create or remove a Windows partition." Click Continue once more.

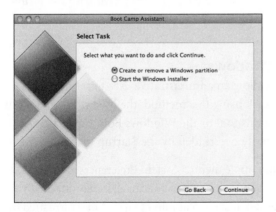

The next screen shows the final size of the Mac volume once the Windows partition has been removed.

3   Click the Restore button to remove the Windows partition and reclaim the storage space into a single Mac volume.

Switching Between Systems

Although switching between Mac OS X and Windows requires a full restart of the Mac, there are several convenient methods for choosing which operating system you want to engage:

▶ The Startup Manager allows you to temporarily select the operating system before the computer fully starts up.

▶ The Mac OS X Startup Disk preferences allow you to set the Mac's startup disk.

▶ The Windows Boot Camp Control Panel allows you to set the Mac's startup disk.

Boot Camp via Startup Manager

The Startup Manager is a feature built into the Mac's firmware that allows you to temporarily select the startup disk. This selection is considered temporary because as soon as you restart the Mac, it reverts to the startup disk that was selected by one of the other two methods.

Holding down the Option key during the first moments when the Mac is starting up activates the Startup Manager. It scans all locally attached volumes and the network for valid operating systems, and displays those choices to you using a Mac-like graphical interface. You can use the arrow and Return keys or the mouse to select a startup disk from multiple choices.

> **NOTE** ▶ Access to the Startup Manager can be password protected with the Firmware Password Utility, as covered in Chapter 2, "User Accounts."

Switching from Mac OS X to Windows

The Mac OS X Startup Disk preferences allow an administrative user to set the Mac's startup disk. When you select a startup disk using this method, the Mac will adhere to the selection until you change it again using this tool or the Windows Boot Camp Control Panel. This selection can also be temporarily overridden by the Startup Manager.

To use the Startup Disk preferences, choose Apple menu > System Preferences and then select the Startup Disk preferences icon. The Startup Disk preferences scan all locally attached volumes and the network for valid operating systems. Keep in mind that volumes formatted by Windows will, by default, be named "Untitled." Select the operating system you wish to set as the startup disk from the list, and then click the Restart button to restart the Mac.

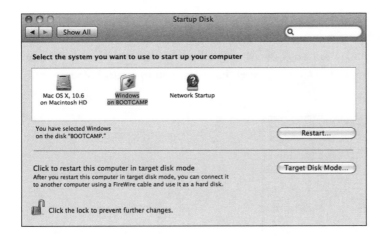

TIP Alternately, from the Mac OS X command line you can select the Windows volume for startup using the `bless` command. You can find out more about the `bless` command by reading its manual page.

Switching from Windows to Mac OS X

The Windows Boot Camp Control Panel also allows an administrative user to set the Mac's startup disk. Additionally, when you select a startup disk using this method the Mac will adhere to the selection until you change it again using this tool or the Mac OS X Startup Disk preferences. Once more, this selection can be temporarily overridden by the Startup Manager.

The quickest route to the Boot Camp Control Panel is clicking on the Boot Camp system tray item, which looks like a gray diamond, in the Windows Taskbar. This reveals a pop-up menu allowing you to open the Boot Camp Control Panel. Notice this pop-up menu also allows you to access the Boot Camp Help system and, with one click, restart back into Mac OS X.

The Boot Camp Control Panel will open to the Startup Disk section, which scans all locally attached volumes and the network for valid operating systems. Mac OS X volumes appear with their given name, but the Windows volume always appear as simply "Windows." Select the operating system you wish to set as the startup disk from the list, and then click the Restart button to restart the Mac. Finally, take a few minutes to explore the other sections of the Boot Camp Control Panel that allow you to control Mac-specific hardware functions.

TIP Alternately, from the Windows command line you can select the Mac volume for startup using the instructions outlined in Apple Knowledge Base article HT3802, "Boot Camp: Restarting into Mac OS X using the command line."

What You've Learned

▶   Mac OS X supports a variety of new and old applications on both 32-bit and 64-bit Intel-based Mac systems.

▶   Mac OS X includes application accessibility interfaces via Universal Access and VoiceOver.

▶   You can use Activity Monitor in the graphical interface or top and ps in the command-line interface to monitor applications and processes.

▶   Application troubleshooting involves locating the problem source by taking steps from the least invasive and time-consuming action to the most invasive and time-consuming action.

▶   The Dashboard provides instantaneous access to useful mini-applications called widgets.

▶   Boot Camp allows Intel-based Macs to natively run Windows XP SP2 or Windows Vista.

References

You can check for new and updated Knowledge Base documents at www.apple.com/support.

Rosetta

TS1963, "Intel-based Mac: Some migrated applications may need to be updated"

TS1966, "Safari, Intel-based Macs: Internet plug-in not installed alert or blank page when loading plug-in content"

TA24166, "Some QuickTime components may display white instead of video on Intel-based Macintosh computers"

Application Accessibility

HT1343, "Mac OS X keyboard shortcuts"

TA23838, "Mac OS X 10.4: Computer Speaks unexpectedly, or a black box unexpectedly appears around a file, folder, or other item"

HT3786, "VoiceOver command differences between Mac OS X v10.6 and Mac OS X v10.5"

Application Troubleshooting

HT3258, "Mac OS X v10.6: About incompatible software"

HT1342, "Mac OS X: Reading system memory usage in Activity Monitor"

TA20517, "Mac OS X: How to View Memory Usage With the 'top' Utility"

HT1199, "Mac OS X: How to troubleshoot a software issue"

HT3662, "About file quarantine in Mac OS X v10.5 and v10.6"

Dashboard

HT2254, "Mac OS X 10.4.2 or later: Installing and removing Dashboard widgets"

TS1549, "Mac OS X 10.5: Dashboard widgets issues with Parental Controls and Fast User Switching enabled"

Boot Camp

HT1237, "EFI and SMC firmware updates for Intel-based Macs"

HT1899, "Boot Camp: System requirements for Microsoft Windows"

HT1461, "Mac 101: Using Windows via Boot Camp with Mac OS X 10.5 Leopard"

HT3777, "Boot Camp 3.0, Mac OS X 10.6: Frequently asked questions"

TS1978, "Intel-based Mac: Startup issues after using unsupported version of Windows installer via Boot Camp"

HT2587, "Mac OS X 10.5, Boot Camp: Understanding how Apple localized keyboard character combinations are mapped in Windows"

TS1606, "Mac OS X 10.5, Boot Camp: Windows Vista 'Problem Reports and Solutions' indicates compatibility issues before Boot Camp drivers installation"

HT3841, "Boot Camp 3.0: Cannot Install Windows XP Service Pack 3"

HT3802, "Boot Camp: Restarting into Mac OS X using the command line"

URLs

Apple's product guide: http://guide.apple.com

Mac OS X architectural overview: http://developer.apple.com/macosx/architecture/index.html

Cocoa application environment: http://developer.apple.com/cocoa/

Carbon application environment: http://developer.apple.com/carbon/

Apple's Java implementation: http://developer.apple.com/java/

Apple's UNIX implementation, Darwin: http://developer.apple.com/Darwin/

Apple's X11 implementation: http://developer.apple.com/opensource/tools/X11.html

Apple's open source software initiatives: www.opensource.apple.com/

Apple's list of popular open source software: www.apple.com/downloads/macosx/unix_open_source/

The MacPorts project open source collection: www.macports.org/

Apple's Accessibility resource: www.apple.com/accessibility/

Apple's VoiceOver resource: www.apple.com/accessibility/voiceover/

Apple's online widget site: www.apple.com/downloads/dashboard/

NTFS-3G/MacFUSE software bundle provides full support for NTFS:
http://macntfs-3g.blogspot.com/

Mediafour's MacDrive, which provides Mac OS Extended file system support for
Windows: www.mediafour.com/products/macdrive/

Parallels Desktop virtualization software: www.parallels.com/products/desktop/

VMware Fusion virtualization software: www.vmware.com/products/fusion/

Apple's Support Downloads: http://support.apple.com/downloads/

Review Quiz

1. What is protected memory? What is 64-bit memory addressing?

2. What are the five application environments supported by Mac OS X? What is each
    one used for?

3. What are the advantages of code signing?

4. What is Rosetta? What types of items are not supported by Rosetta?

5. What system preference enables the accessibility features in Mac OS X? What accessi-
    bility features are available in Mac OS X? Finally, where is the preference file for these
    features located?

6. How can you identify the type of a particular application?

7. How can you identify which applications are installed on your Mac?

8. What steps should you use when troubleshooting application issues?

9. What three ways can you forcibly quit an application from the graphical interface?

10. What does the problem-reporting feature do?

11. Where are application preferences stored? What format is often used for preference files?

12. What process or processes are responsible for Dashboard widgets?

13. How does Boot Camp work?

14. What are the minimum system requirements for Boot Camp?

15. What are the three primary steps for setting up Boot Camp with Windows?

16. What three methods can be used for selecting the startup disk on a Mac with
    Windows installed?

Answers

1. The system keeps applications from interfering with one another by segregating their memory usage using protected memory. Macs with 64-bit-capable processors allow processes to run in 64-bit mode, which allows them to individually access more than 4 GB of memory.

2. The five application environments supported by Mac OS X are: Cocoa, the native application environment for Mac OS X; Carbon, which is based on Mac OS 9 but still provides native Mac OS X performance; BSD, which is Mac OS X's command-line interface (CLI) and is based on Berkeley Software Distribution (BSD) UNIX; X11, which is a popular UNIX windowing environment; and Java, which was originally created by Sun Microsystems.

3. Code signed items include a digital signature that the system can use to verify the authenticity and integrity of the application or process and its resources.

4. Rosetta is translation software optionally installed with Mac OS X that allows Intel-based Macs to use software originally designed for PowerPC-based Macs. Rosetta does not support applications created for any version of the Mac OS earlier than Mac OS X, the Classic compatibility environment, screen savers written for the PowerPC architecture, software that inserts PowerPC preference panes in System Preferences, applications that specifically require a PowerPC G5 processor, applications that depend on one or more PowerPC-only kernel extensions, kernel extensions or hardware drivers written for the PowerPC architecture, Java applications with JNI libraries, Java in applications that Rosetta can translate, or plug-ins written for the PowerPC architecture if the software they tie into runs as Intel native.

5. Mac OS X's accessibility features are available from the Universal Access preferences. Universal Access includes options to assist users who have difficulty seeing, hearing, using the keyboard, or using the mouse and trackpad. The Universal Access preference file is com.apple.universalaccess.plist, located in ~/Library/Preferences.

6. You can identify an application's type with the Get Info or Inspector window in the Finder or with System Profiler.

7. You can use the System Profiler application to easily scan all the appropriate application locations and return a list of installed applications.

8. General application troubleshooting steps include restarting the application, trying another known working document, trying another user account, checking log files, deleting cache files, replacing preference files, and replacing application resources.

9. The three ways to forcibly quit an application from the graphical interface are from the Force Quit Application dialog accessed from the Apple menu, from the Dock's application shortcut menu accessed by Control-clicking or right-clicking on the application's icon, or from the /Applications/Utilities/Activity Monitor application.

10. The problem-reporting feature automatically springs into action any time an application crashes or hangs. This process creates a problem report log that can be viewed immediately, reported to Apple via the Internet, or viewed later in the /Applications/Utilities/Console application.

11. Application preferences are almost always stored in the user's Library folder in the ~/Library/Preferences folder. Most application preferences are property lists, which are XML-formatted files that use the ".plist" filename extension.

12. The Dock process starts the `DashboardClient` processes on behalf of the currently logged-in user. All open widgets run inside one of the two `DashboardClient` processes.

13. At the time of this writing Boot Camp allows Windows XP SP2+ or Windows Vista to run natively on Mac hardware. The Boot Camp Setup Assistant automatically repartitions the system volume in preparation for the Windows installation. Users install Windows as they would on any other PC, and then load Mac hardware drivers for Windows from the Mac OS X Install DVD.

14. The minimum system requirements for Boot Camp are:

    An Intel-based Mac computer

    Directly attached input devices

    Mac OS X v10.5 or later

    All firmware updates for your Mac

    A Mac OS X v10.5 installation disc

    At least 10 GB of free disk space for installing Windows

    2 GB or more of RAM when running Windows Vista on a Mac Pro

    Boot Camp Assistant

    A single full-install Windows Installation disc

15. To set up Boot Camp, you must start with the Boot Camp Assistant, then install and set up Windows from the Windows installation disc, and finally install the Boot Camp drivers for Windows from the Mac OS X Install DVD.

16. If you have both Mac OS X and Windows installed, you can select the startup disk from the Startup Manager as soon as you turn on the Mac, from the Mac OS X Startup Disk preferences, or from the Windows Boot Camp Control Panel.

7

Time   This chapter takes approximately 3 hours to complete.

Goals   Understand fundamental TCP/IP network concepts

Configure Mac OS X networking

Manage multiple network locations and interfaces

Identify and resolve network connectivity issues

Chapter 7

Network Configuration

The capability to share information between computers across a network has always been paramount. During the early years of personal computer development, vendors designed their own proprietary local network systems. Apple was no exception with its implementation of AppleTalk and LocalTalk network standards for file sharing and network printing. Yet although these vendor-specific technologies were suitable for smaller networks, they didn't scale very well once customers wanted to create more complicated networks with large numbers of computers over long distances. Further, special hardware or software had to be put in place to translate from one vendor's network to another.

Around the same time, researchers were working at the behest of the United States Department of Defense to create a wide area network standard for military and governmental use. From this research was born the Internet protocol suite known as TCP/IP. The marriage of the Transmission Control Protocol (TCP) and the Internet Protocol (IP) became the universal language that allows computers to communicate on the Internet. This standard became so pervasive that nearly every network today, including small local networks all the way up to the largest long-distance network on Earth, the Internet, is based on the TCP/IP suite.

It should come as no surprise, then, that Mac OS X includes a robust TCP/IP implementation. In fact, the first computer systems to popularize the use of TCP/IP were UNIX systems. Thus, much of the TCP/IP software built into Mac OS X is based on open source UNIX software that was established long before Mac OS X ever existed as a product from Apple.

In this chapter, you will configure network settings and troubleshoot network connectivity issues using Mac OS X. Before that, though, you must have a fundamental understanding of core network concepts. Accordingly, the first part of this chapter is devoted to those concepts.

Fundamental Network Concepts

Properly configuring and troubleshooting networking on any operating system requires a basic understanding of fundamental network concepts. Due to the widespread adoption of standardized network technology, the following network overview applies to nearly any operating system, Mac OS X included. Basic network terminology is covered first, followed by an overview of the processes involved in actual data delivery across a network.

Fundamental Network Terminology

It's best to explore networking from a layered perspective. In fact, there is an established seven-layer model used to describe network technologies, the Open Systems Interconnection Reference Model (known as the OSI model). Exploring networking using the OSI model goes well beyond the scope of this text. Consequently, networking concepts will be presented in a more simplistic abstraction of three basic elements:

▶ Network interface—The network interface is the medium through which the network data flows. Network interfaces can be physical or virtual. The most common physical network interfaces for computers are Ethernet and 802.11 wireless Ethernet, which is known in the Apple world as AirPort. Virtual network interfaces are also available that can be used to secure otherwise insecure network connections by creating a virtual private network (VPN) riding on top of a standard network interface.

▶ Network protocol—A protocol defines a set of standard rules used for data representation, signaling, authentication, or error detection across network interfaces. Primarily, protocols are designed to ensure that all data is communicated properly and completely. Specific protocols have a narrow focus, so often multiple protocols are combined or layered to provide a complete network solution. For example, the combined TCP/IP protocol suite provides only for the addressing and end-to-end transport of data across the Internet; dozens of other protocols are required for something as simple as checking your email or browsing a website.

▶ Network service—In the context of the Network preferences, the term *network service* describes a network interface's settings, which are necessary to define a network connection. A fundamental feature of Mac OS X is the ability to support multiple network services, or connections, per each individual network interface. A different definition of the term network service is used in Chapter 8, "Network Services," wherein a network service is information provided on the network by a server for use by clients. Common examples in Chapter 8 include file-sharing services, messaging services, and collaboration services. Often a specific set of protocols is used to define how the particular service works.

MORE INFO ▶ For more information regarding the OSI model for describing computer networks, refer to this Wikipedia entry: http://en.wikipedia.org/wiki/OSI_model.

Simplifying computer network technology to only three distinct elements does not provide a detailed abstraction, but it still shows clearly how each is related. When a network interface, service, or protocol is created, it is often put through a review process before it's deemed a network standard. Standards committees are formed with members from multiple network organizations and vendors to ensure that new network standards remain interoperable with existing network standards. Most networking technologies in use today have been ratified by some standards body, so you may often come across an interface, protocol, or service labeled as a "standard."

Media Access Control (MAC) Address

The Media Access Control (MAC) address is used to uniquely identify a physical network interface on a local network. Each physical network interface has at least one MAC address associated with it.

NOTE ▶ The Intel-based Xserve has two MAC addresses per Ethernet interface to provide functionality for lights-out management.

Because the most common network interface is Ethernet, people often refer to MAC addresses as *Ethernet addresses*. Still, nearly every other network interface type also uses some type of MAC address for unique identification. This includes, but isn't limited to, AirPort, Bluetooth, FireWire, and Fibre Channel.

A MAC address is usually a 48-bit number represented by six groups of two-digit hexadecimal numbers, known as octets, each separated by colons. For example, a typical MAC address would look something like this: 00:1C:B3:D7:2F:99. The first three octets are the Organizationally Unique Identifier (OUI), and the last three octets identify the network device itself. In other words, you can use the first three octets of a MAC address to identify who made the network device.

> **MORE INFO** ▶ The Institute of Electrical and Electronics Engineers (IEEE) maintains a searchable database of publicly listed OUIs at its website: http://standards.ieee.org/regauth/oui/index.shtml.

Internet Protocol (IP) Address

Communicating with computers on both local and remote networks requires an Internet Protocol (IP) address. IP addresses, unlike MAC addresses, are not permanently tied to a network interface. Instead, IP addresses are assigned to the network interface based on the local network it's connected to. This means if you have a portable computer, every new network you connect to will probably require a new IP address. If necessary, you can assign multiple IP addresses to each network interface, but this approach is often only used for computers that are providing network services.

There are currently two standards for IP addresses: IPv4 and IPv6. IPv4 was the first widely used IP addressing scheme and is by far the most common today. An IPv4 address is a 32-bit number that is represented by four groups of three-digit numbers, also known as octets, separated by periods. Each octet has a value between 0 and 255. For example, a typical IPv4 address would look something like this: 10.1.45.186.

With IPv4 there are a little over 4 billion unique addresses. This may seem like a lot, but considering every new network-ready gadget that comes out and the number of people who want to own multiple network-ready gadgets, this number isn't really big enough. For the time being, the available IPv4 addresses are extended by using network routers that can share a single real IPv4 address to a range of reusable private network addresses.

This is how most home networks are configured, but it is only a temporary solution for what's to come next.

The successor to IPv4 is IPv6, but because IPv4 is so entrenched in the backbone of the Internet, the transition to IPv6 has been slow. The main advantage to IPv6 is a much larger address space—so large in fact, every person on Earth could have roughly 1.2x1019 copies of the entire IPv4 address range. This may appear to be a ridiculous amount of IP addresses, but the design goal of IPv6 was to eliminate the need for private addressing and allow for easier address reassignment and changing to a new network. An IPv6 address is a 128-bit number that is presented in eight groups of four-digit hexadecimal numbers separated by colons. Hexadecimal numbers use a base-16 digit system, so after the number 9 you use the letters A through F. For example, a typical IPv6 address would look something like this: 2C01:0EF9:0000:0000:0000:0000:142D:57AB. Large strings of zeros in an IPv6 address can be abbreviated using a double colon, resulting in an address more like this: 2C01:0EF9::142D:57AB.

Subnet Mask

The computer uses the subnet mask to determine the IPv4 address range of the local network. Networks based on the IPv6 protocol do not require subnet masks. A subnet mask is similar to an IPv4 address in that it's a 32-bit number arranged in four groups of octets. The computer applies the subnet mask to its own IP address to determine the local network's address range. The nonzero bits in a subnet mask (typically 255) correspond to the portion of the IP address that determines which network the address is on. The zero bits correspond to the portion of the IP address that differs between hosts on the same network. For example, assuming your computer has an IP address of 10.1.5.3 and a commonly used subnet mask of 255.255.255.0, the local network is defined as hosts that have IP addresses that range from 10.1.5.1 to 10.1.5.254.

> **MORE INFO** ▶ Another way of writing the subnet mask is known as CIDR notation. This is written as the IP address, a slash, and then the number of 1 bits in the subnet mask. The previous subnet example would be 10.1.5.3/24. You can find out more about CIDR notation from Wikipedia: http://en.wikipedia.org/wiki/Classless_Inter-Domain_Routing.

Whenever the computer attempts to communicate with another network device, it applies the subnet mask to the destination IP address of the other device to determine if it's on the local network as well. If so, the computer will attempt to directly access the other network device. If not, the other device is clearly on another network and the computer will send all communications bound for that other device to the router address.

Router Address

Routers are network devices that manage connections between separate networks. Routers, as their given name implies, route network traffic between the networks they bridge. Routing tables are maintained by routers to determine where network traffic goes. Even if a router is presented with traffic destined for a network that the router is unaware of, it will still route the traffic to another router that it thinks is closer to the final destination. Thus, routers literally are the brains of the Internet.

In order to be able to reach computers beyond the local network, your computer needs to be configured with the IP address of the router that connects the local network with another network, or more commonly in residential situations, an Internet service provider. Typically the router's address is at the beginning of the local address range, and it's always in the same subnet. Using the previous example, assuming your computer has an IP address of 10.1.5.3 and a commonly used subnet mask of 255.255.255.0, the local network IP address range would be 10.1.5.0 to 10.1.5.255 and the router address would most likely be 10.1.5.1.

Transmission Control Protocol (TCP)

The Transmission Control Protocol (TCP) is the primary protocol used to facilitate end-to-end data connectivity between two IP devices. TCP is the preferred transport mechanism for many Internet services because it guarantees reliable and in-order delivery of data. In other words, IP provides network addressing and data routing, and TCP ensures that the data arrives at its destination complete. The combination of these two protocols encompasses the TCP/IP suite, commonly known as the Internet protocol suite.

The TCP/IP protocol suite chops continuous data streams into many individual packets of information before they are sent across the network. This is because IP networks use packet-switching technology to route and transmit data. Almost all digital networking technologies are packet-based because this provides efficient transport for network connections that aren't always reliable. Remember, the TCP/IP protocol was originally designed with the military in mind, so packet-based network technology is ideal because it's designed to work around communications link failure. This is why sophisticated routing hardware was originally developed for TCP/IP networks, so data could be literally rerouted and re-sent should a network link go down.

A lesser-used protocol known as User Datagram Protocol (UDP) is also attached to the TCP/IP suite. UDP is a simpler protocol that does not guarantee the reliability or ordering of data sent across networks. This may seem like a poor choice for networking, but in some cases UDP is preferred because it provides better performance than TCP. Examples of network services that use UDP include the Domain Name System (DNS), media streaming, voice over IP (VoIP), and online gaming. These services have been designed to tolerate lost or out-of-order data so they can benefit from UDP's increased performance.

> **MORE INFO ▸** For more information regarding the Internet protocol suite, refer to this Wikipedia entry: http://en.wikipedia.org/wiki/internet_protocol_suite.

Networks in Action

Manually assigning an IP address, a subnet mask, and a router address is technically all that is needed to configure a computer to use TCP/IP-based networking on both local area networks (LANs) and wide area networks (WANs). Yet there are two other network services that are almost always involved in basic network functionality: Dynamic Host Configuration Protocol (DHCP) and the Domain Name System (DNS). These two services, combined with TCP/IP, characterize core network functionality that provides the foundation for nearly any network service.

Local Area Network (LAN) Traffic

Most local area networks (LANs) use some form of wired or wireless connection. Once the network interface has been established, TCP/IP networking must be configured, either manually or via DHCP. Once both these steps are complete, network communication can begin.

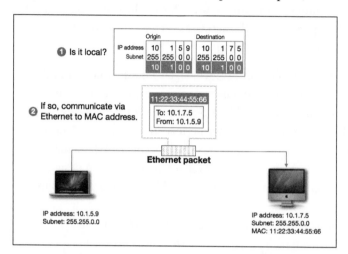

TCP/IP packets are encased inside Ethernet frames to travel across the local network. The TCP/IP packet includes the originating IP and destination IP addresses along with the data to be sent. The network device applies the subnet mask setting to determine if the destination IP address is on the local network. If so, it will consult its Address Resolution Protocol (ARP) table to see if it knows the MAC address corresponding to the destination IP address. Each network host maintains and continuously updates an "ARP table" of known MAC addresses that correspond to IP addresses on the local network. If the MAC address is not listed yet, it broadcasts an ARP request to the local network asking the destination device to reply with its MAC address, and adds the reply to its ARP table for next time. Once the MAC address is determined, an outgoing Ethernet packet, encasing the TCP/IP packet, will be sent using the destination MAC address.

The other network device will likely return some information as well using the same technique of transferring TCP/IP packets inside of MAC-addressed Ethernet packets. This goes on and on for thousands of packets every second to complete a data stream. The standard Ethernet packet size is only 1,500 bytes (that's roughly 1.5 kilobytes or 0.0015 megabytes) so you can imagine how many packets are necessary to transmit even a small file.

Wide Area Network (WAN) Traffic

Sending data over a wide area network (WAN) differs only in that data is sent through one or more network routers to reach its intended destination. WANs exist in all shapes and sizes, from a small WAN perhaps used to connect separate LANs in a large building, all the way up to the biggest and most popular WAN, the Internet.

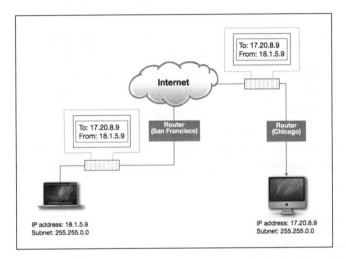

Initially transferring data across a WAN is similar to transferring data on a LAN. After all, the first stop for the data destined for the WAN is to the network router on the local network. The network device will prepare the packets as before by encasing the TCP/IP packets inside Ethernet frames. Once again, the subnet mask will be applied to the destination IP address to determine if the address is on the local network. In this case, the network device determines that the destination is not on the local network, so it sends the data to the router. Because the router is on the local network, the transmission between the local network client and the router is identical to standard LAN traffic.

Once the router receives the Ethernet-encased TCP/IP packets, it will examine the destination IP address and use a routing table to determine the next closest destination for this packet. This almost always involves sending the packet to another router closer to the destination. In fact, only the very last router in the path will send the data to the destination network device.

Network routers also often perform some sort of repackaging and readdressing of the data because WAN network links are rarely standard Ethernet connections. The router will strip the Ethernet container away from the original TCP/IP packet and then rewrap it in another container that is appropriate for the WAN connection. Obviously, the final router will have to prepare the TCP/IP packet for the last leg of the journey on the destination device's local network by rewrapping it in an Ethernet frame addressed to the destination's MAC address.

In most cases, network data will be transferred back and forth several times to establish a complete connection. Remember, these packet sizes are very small. The default packet size for Internet traffic is also 1,500 bytes with a maximum packet size of 65,535 bytes for most TCP/IP connections. Network routers are highly optimized devices that can easily handle thousands of data packets every second, so for small amounts of data many WAN connections "feel" as fast as LAN connections. Conversely, a lot of latency is introduced from all the different routers and network connections involved in transferring data across a WAN, so often sending large amounts of data across a WAN is much slower than across a LAN. Thus, many a user's favorite time-wasting computer practice was born: waiting for an Internet download or upload.

Domain Name System (DNS)

Most people are notoriously bad at remembering strings of seemingly arbitrary numbers used to define addresses, so additional technology is often implemented to help users find addresses. Even the most humble of cell phones features a contact list so users don't have to remember phone numbers. For TCP/IP networks, the Domain Name System (DNS) makes network addressing much more approachable to normal humans.

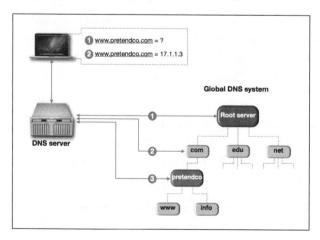

In essence, the DNS is a worldwide network of domain servers with the task of maintaining human-friendly host names used to easily locate specific network IP addresses. If you've spent any time at all on the Internet, you're already familiar with the DNS naming convention. For example, Apple's main website is located at www.apple.com. Any network device can have a host name, but only those network devices providing a service that needs to be easily located on the Internet need to have host name entries on a DNS server. Websites and mail servers are the most common devices to have DNS entries.

The hierarchical DNS naming convention relates directly to the hierarchical structure of the DNS domain architecture. As you know, DNS names are broken into labels separated by periods. Each label represents a different level, or domain, of the DNS hierarchy. The very top of the DNS hierarchy is the "root" or "." domain. The names that are part of the root domain are the familiar abbreviations at the end of nearly every Internet resource. Common examples are .com, .edu, .gov, and others, including various country codes. These top-level domains (TLDs) are hosted by a consortium of commercial and governmental organizations.

Below the TLDs, individual organizations or users host or rent their own DNS domain. For example, Apple hosts several DNS servers that are known by the TLD servers in order to maintain the apple.com domain. Apple can host an unlimited number of host names inside the apple.com domain. Apple can create unlimited domain names by preceding any text before apple.com. Examples include www.apple.com, training.apple.com, and developer.apple.com.

When a local network device needs to resolve a DNS name into the corresponding IP address, it sends the name query to the IP address of a DNS server. The IP address for a DNS server is usually configured along with the other TCP/IP address information for the network device. The DNS server will search its local and cached name records first. If the requested name isn't found locally, the server will query other domain servers in the DNS hierarchy. This process may take a while, so DNS servers will temporarily cache any names they have recently resolved to provide a quicker response for future requests. Querying a DNS server to resolve an IP address given a known host name is called a forward lookup, whereas querying a DNS server to resolve a host name from a known IP address is called a reverse lookup. When initially configured, network clients will query the DNS server with a reverse lookup of its own IP address to determine if the network client has its own DNS name.

MORE INFO ▸ For more information regarding DNS, refer to this Wikipedia entry: http://en.wikipedia.org/wiki/Domain_Name_System.

MORE INFO ▸ Bonjour is a name discovery service that uses a name space similar to DNS. Bonjour is covered in Chapter 8, "Network Services."

Dynamic Host Configuration Protocol (DHCP)

Although not required to provide network functionality, the Dynamic Host Configuration Protocol (DHCP) is used by nearly all network clients to automatically acquire preliminary TCP/IP configuration. In some situations, an administrative user may still choose to manually enter TCP/IP networking configuration information. This is often the case with network devices that are providing network services. However, manually configuring multitudes of network clients is tedious work that is prone to human error. Thus, even on rigorously managed networks, DHCP is still widely used to configure network clients.

NOTE ▸ A precursor to DHCP is the Bootstrap Protocol (BOOTP). DHCP is backward compatible with BOOTP but provides greater functionality and reliability.

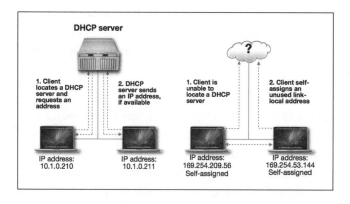

A DHCP server is required to provide the service. On many networks, the network routers provide the DHCP service, but in some cases a dedicated server can be used for this purpose. When a network device becomes active on the network, it first negotiates a link with the hardware interface, and then it sends out a broadcast to the local network requesting DHCP information. Because the new network client doesn't yet have an IP address, it uses the network interface's MAC address for identification. If a DHCP server that is listening has available addresses, it will send back a reply to the client with TCP/IP configuration information. At a minimum, this information includes IP address, subnet mask, router, and a DHCP lease time that defines how long the client can retain the address before it's given away. Ancillary DHCP information can include DNS information, directory service information, and NetBoot information.

If the DHCP server has run out of available network addresses, or there is no DHCP service available, as is the case with small ad hoc networks, the client will automatically generate a self-assigned link-local address. Link-local addresses are always in the IP address range of 169.254.xxx.xxx with a subnet mask of 255.255.0.0. The network client will automatically generate a random link-local address and then check the local network to make sure no other network device is using that address. Once a unique link-local address is established, the network client will only be able to establish connections with other network devices on the local network.

MORE INFO ▶ For more information regarding DHCP, refer to this Wikipedia entry: http://en.wikipedia.org/wiki/Dhcp.

Basic Network Configuration

Initial networking configuration is handled by the Setup Assistant, which runs the first time you start up a new Mac or a fresh Mac OS X system installation. The Setup Assistant makes it easy for even a novice user to configure Mac OS X's network settings. Yet even if you choose to not set up networking during the initial system setup process, the Mac will automatically enable any active network interface, including connecting to unrestricted wireless networks, and attempt to configure TCP/IP via DHCP. Consequently, for many users Mac OS X does not require any initial network configuration at all.

If network changes are required after initial setup, you can still use the Network Setup Assistant to help guide you through the network configuration process. You can access the Network Setup Assistant by clicking the "Assist me" button at the bottom of the Network preferences.

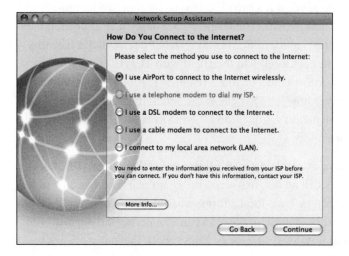

Although this assistant is helpful for novice users, you should be familiar with all network configuration options so you're prepared for any potential network situation or troubleshooting issue. With the previous version, Mac OS X v10.5, Apple introduced a consolidation of previously separate network configuration windows into a new, unified Network preferences. Thus, all network settings can be found in the Network preferences. You'll note that the Network preferences are locked, indicating that only administrative users have access to these settings and that DHCP is enabled by default for Ethernet and AirPort interfaces.

NOTE ▶ In the screen shot above, note that DHCP is also providing configuration for the DNS server. The light-gray color of the DNS server IP address indicates that you can manually enter the IP address of an alternate DNS server. Most importantly, if there is no DNS server IP address configured, your Mac will not be able to resolve DNS hostnames.

As a convenience, many network settings are also available outside the Network preferences as menu items near the top right corner of the screen. These network menu items also give non-administrative users access to the most commonly needed network settings. An example of this is the frequently used AirPort menu item, which allows you to select from the wireless networks within range of your Mac.

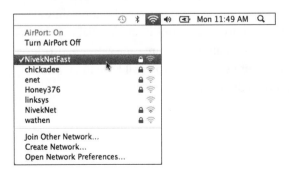

Using Network Locations

Similar to how applications are designed to save information to any number of individual documents, Mac OS X allows you to save network settings to any number of individual network configurations known as network locations. A network location contains all network interface, service, and protocol settings, allowing you to configure as many unique network locations as you need for different situations. For example, you could create one network location for home and a different network location for work. Each location would contain all the appropriate settings for that location's network situation.

A network location can contain any number of active network interfaces or services. This allows you to define a single location with multiple network connections. The system will automatically prioritize multiple interfaces based on a service order that you set. Details about using multiple network interfaces are covered in the "Using Multiple Simultaneous Interfaces" section later in this chapter.

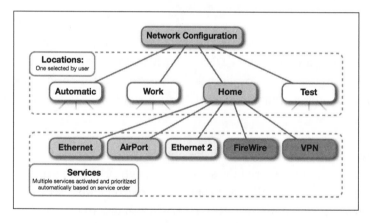

It is not necessary to add new network locations to change network settings, but it is more convenient as you can easily switch back to the previous network location should you make a mistake. Thus, creating additional network locations is an essential network troubleshooting technique. Also, because Mac OS X always requires one active network location, if you ever want to temporarily turn off networking, you will have to create a new location with all the interfaces and services disabled.

Configuring Network Locations

The default network location on Mac OS X is called Automatic. In spite of this, this first location is no more automatic than any other network location you create. The initial location is simply called Automatic to indicate that it will attempt to automatically initialize any network interface to establish a TCP/IP connection via DHCP, but all network locations regardless of their name attempt this as well.

To configure network locations:

1   Open the Network preferences by choosing Apple menu > System Preferences, then clicking the Network icon.

You may have to click the lock icon in the bottom-left corner and authenticate as an administrative user to unlock the Network preferences.

2   Choose Edit Locations from the Location pop-up menu.

This will reveal the interface for editing network locations.

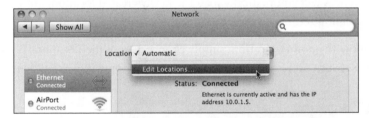

3   To add a new location with default settings, click the small plus button at the bottom of the locations list, and then enter a new name for the location.

Or, you can duplicate an existing location by selecting its name from the locations list and clicking the gear icon at the bottom of the list and then choosing Duplicate Location from the pop-up menu.

Finally, double-clicking on a location name will allow you to rename any location.

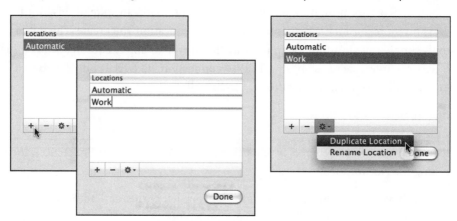

4 When you are finished making location changes, click the Done button to return to the Network preferences.

The Network preferences will automatically load the newly created location, but it will not apply the location settings to the system.

If you want to work with another location, simply choose it from the Locations pop-up menu, and the Network preferences will load it but won't apply it to the system.

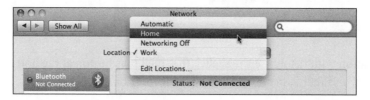

5 Once you have completed all the necessary network location changes, click the Apply button at the bottom-right corner of the Network preferences to activate the currently selected network location.

> **TIP** If you make a mistake at any time using Network preferences, click the Revert button in the bottom-right corner to return to the current active network configuration.

You may have noticed that the Network preferences is different from all the other system preferences in that you must click the Apply button to activate the new settings. This allows you to easily prepare new network locations and settings without disrupting the current network configuration.

Changing Network Locations

Though you can certainly choose and apply a different network location from the Network preferences, only administrative users have this ability, as normal users do not have access to the Network preferences. Conversely, all users who can log in to the Mac OS X graphical user interface can quickly and easily change the network location by choosing Apple menu > Locations > *location name* from the menu bar. This will apply the selected network location. Keep in mind that changing locations may interrupt network connections. Once a network location is selected, it will remain active until another location is selected. Even as other users log in to the Mac, or the Mac is restarted, the selected network location will remain active.

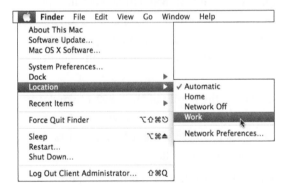

Using Hardware Network Interfaces

Mac hardware has a long history of providing built-in network connectivity. Apple started including Ethernet on Macs as early as 1991 and was the first manufacturer to have wireless as a built-in option when it introduced the iBook in 1999. Mac models have varied over the years as network technologies have grown increasingly faster and more affordable. You can identify the hardware network interfaces and services available to your Mac from the /Applications/Utilities/System Profiler application. Detecting network information and troubleshooting with the Network Utility will be covered later in this chapter. Virtual network interfaces, like those used for virtual private networks (VPNs) or link aggregation, will also be covered later in this chapter.

Mac OS X includes built-in support for the following hardware network interfaces:

▶ Ethernet—Ethernet is the family of IEEE 802.3 standards that define most modern wired LANs. Every Mac since 1997 has included standard built-in Ethernet connectivity, with some models even featuring multiple Ethernet ports. The lone exception to this rule is the current MacBook Air, which requires an optional Apple USB Ethernet Adapter.

▶ FireWire—FireWire is Apple's marketing name for the IEEE 1394 connection standard. Though not a common network standard, Mac OS X includes software that allows you to create small ad hoc networks using daisy-chained FireWire cables. FireWire 400 is standard on many Macs, with some models featuring FireWire 800.

▶ External (analog) Modem—Although no currently shipping Mac includes an analog modem, it's available via an optional Apple External USB Modem and is still supported by Mac OS X. For many years the analog modem was the standard method for home users to connect to the Internet. With the proliferation of high-speed and wireless Internet connections, analog modems are usually only necessary from the most remote of locations or to provide fax services.

▶ AirPort—AirPort is Apple's marketing name for the family of IEEE 802.11 wireless standards, which has become the default implementation for most wireless LANs. Every desktop and portable Mac since 2006 has included standard built-in AirPort connectivity. AirPort remains an option for MacPro as well.

▶ Bluetooth DUN—This relatively low-speed wireless interface has become popular as a short-range connectivity standard. Every recent Mac that includes AirPort also includes Bluetooth. Mac OS X supports Bluetooth as a network bridge to some mobile phones that can provide Internet connectivity via a cell phone network.

Using Multiple Simultaneous Interfaces

Mac OS X supports these network interfaces via a multilink networking architecture. This means that Mac OS X supports multiple simultaneous network interfaces. For example, you can have both an active wired Ethernet connection and an active AirPort, or wireless Ethernet, connection at the same time. Typically, having multiple active network interfaces means you will also have multiple active IP addresses. To handle multiple IP addresses, Mac OS X also features IP network multihoming. In fact, Mac OS X supports multiple IP addresses for each network interface.

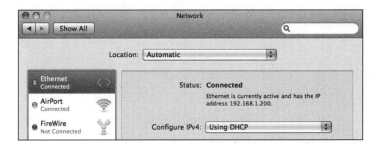

In other words, you can configure as many separate network interfaces with as many unique IP addresses as you need. This may seem like overkill for most Mac clients, but remember Mac OS X and Mac OS X Server share the same underlying architecture. For some servers, multilink multihoming networking is a requirement, but Mac clients can also benefit from this technology. You may have a work environment where you have one insecure network for general Internet traffic and another network for secure internal transactions. With Mac OS X you can be on both of these networks at the same time.

When multiple IP addresses are available, the system can communicate via any of those interfaces but will attempt to pick the most appropriate route for every network connection. As described earlier, a network client will use the subnet mask to determine if an outgoing transmission is on the LAN. Mac OS X takes this a step further by examining all active LANs when determining a destination for outgoing transmission. Because a LAN connection is always faster than a WAN connection, Mac OS X will always route outgoing transmissions to the most appropriate LAN.

Any network connections that are not destined for a LAN that your Mac is connected to will be sent to the router address of the primary active network interface. Therefore, all Internet traffic will also connect via the primary active network interface. Any active network interface with a valid TCP/IP setting will be considered, but the primary active network interface is automatically selected based on the network service order. You can manually configure the network service order, as outlined in the next section of this chapter.

Using the previous example where you have a Mac active on both wired and wireless Ethernet, the default network service order prioritizes wired over wireless Ethernet because wired is almost always faster. Thus, in this example, even though you have two active valid network interfaces, the primary active interface will be the wired Ethernet connection.

NOTE ▶ All DNS hostname resolution is handled by the DNS server specified in the primary active interface configuration.

NOTE ▶ Mac OS X v10.6 now includes automatic source routing. This means incoming connections to your Mac over a specific interface will always be responded to on the same interface, regardless of the service order.

Configuring Hardware Network Interfaces

Every time you open the Network preferences, the system identifies all available network interfaces. Even if an interface is not connected or properly configured, it will create a service for that interface, which will show up in the network services list. In the Network preferences, each network interface is tied to one or more network services.

A quick glance at the network services list clearly shows the status of all network interfaces and their configured services. Network services with a red indicator are not connected, a yellow indicator shows services that are connected but not properly configured, and a green indicator shows connected and configured network services. The active service at the top of this list is the primary network service as defined by the network service order. This list updates dynamically as new interfaces become active or as active interfaces become disconnected, so it's always the first place you should check when attempting to troubleshoot a network issue.

To manage network interfaces and their configured services:

1   Open and unlock the Network preferences.

Choose the network location you wish to edit from the Locations pop-up menu, or configure a new network location, as detailed previously in this chapter.

2   To configure a particular network service, simply select it from the network services list.

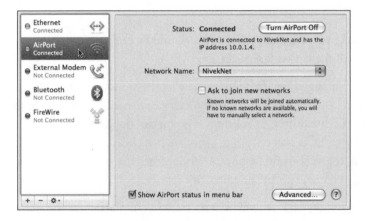

Remember, each network service has its own settings separate from the other services. The configuration area to the right of the list will change to reflect primary options available to the selected service. Clicking the Advanced button in the bottom-right corner of the Network preferences will reveal all the network protocol options available to the selected network service. Network protocol configuration will be covered later in this chapter.

3   To make a service inactive, select it from the services list, click the gear icon at the bottom of the list, and then choose Make Service Inactive from the pop-up menu.

An inactive service will never activate even if connected and properly configured. You can also delete an existing network service by selecting its name from the services list and then clicking the minus button at the bottom of the list.

Inactivating or deleting a network service from this list is the only way to disable a hardware network interface in Mac OS X.

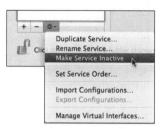

4   To create another configurable instance of a network interface, click the small plus button at the bottom of the network services list.

This reveals a dialog that allows you to choose a new interface instance from the Interface pop-up menu and then assign it a unique service name to identify it in the services list. Click the Create button to continue. Or you can duplicate an existing network service by selecting its name from the services list, clicking the gear icon at the bottom of the list, then choosing Duplicate Service from the pop-up menu. Using this menu you can also rename an existing network service.

Creating additional instances of a network service allows you to assign multiple IP addresses to a single network interface.

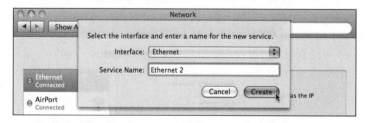

5   To change the network service order, click the gear icon at the bottom of the network services list, and then choose Set Service Order from the pop-up menu.

This reveals a dialog that allows you to click and drag network services into your preferred order for selection as the primary network interface. Click the OK button when you have finished reordering.

6   Once you have completed all the necessary network interface and service changes, click the Apply button at the bottom-right corner of the Network preferences to activate the currently selected network location.

TIP If you make a mistake at any time using the Network preferences, click the Revert button in the bottom-right corner to return to the current active network configuration.

Using Virtual Network Interfaces

Virtual network interfaces are logical networks within a hardware network interface. Think of a virtual network interface as providing another unique network interface by carving out a section of an established network connection.

Some virtual network services are used to increase security by encrypting data before it travels across an IP network, and others are used to segregate or aggregate network traffic across LAN connections. Mac OS X includes the necessary client software that will allow you to connect to many common virtual network services and establish a virtual network interface.

If necessary, you can define multiple separate virtual network interfaces for each network location. Virtual network interfaces are not always tied to a specific hardware network interface, as the system will attempt to seek out the most appropriate route when there are multiple active connections. Likewise, any virtual network interface that is not destined for a LAN connection will always be routed to the primary active network interface.

NOTE ▶ Third-party virtualization tools, like Parallels Desktop and VMware Fusion, also use virtual network interfaces to provide networking for multiple simultaneous operating systems.

Mac OS X includes built-in support for the following virtual network interfaces:

▶ Virtual private network (VPN)—By far the most commonly used virtual network service, VPNs are primarily used to create secure virtual connections to private LANs over the Internet.

▶ Point-to-Point Protocol over Ethernet (PPPoE)—Used by some service providers for directly connecting your Mac to a modem providing a high-speed Digital Subscriber Line (DSL) Internet connection.

▶ 6 to 4—Creates a VPN of sorts to transfer IPv6 packets across an IPv4 network. There is no enhanced security when using a 6 to 4 connection, but your Mac will appear to be directly connected to a remote IPv6 LAN. The differences between IPv4 and IPv6 were covered earlier in this chapter.

▶ Virtual local area network (VLAN)—Mac OS X's VLAN implementation allows you to define separate independent LANs on a single network hardware interface.

▶ Link aggregation—Allows you to define a single virtual LAN interface using multiple network hardware interfaces.

Configuring PPPoE

PPPoE is a connection protocol that encapsulates PPP packets inside standard Ethernet packets. This protocol is primarily used by high-speed Digital Subscriber Line (DSL) providers. You may or may not need to use PPPoE for your DSL connection.

To manage PPPoE connections:

1   Open and unlock the Network preferences.

Choose the network location you wish to edit from the Locations pop-up menu, or configure a new network location, as detailed previously in this chapter.

2 Click the small plus button at the bottom of the services list to add a PPPoE virtual network interface.

This will reveal a dialog allowing you to add a new network interface and service.

3 Choose PPPoE from the Interface pop-up menu.

PPPoE is tied to a specific Ethernet interface, so you must choose the specific interface that will be used for the PPPoE connection from the Ethernet pop-up menu. Finally, enter a descriptive name and click the Create button to make a new PPPoE virtual network interface and service.

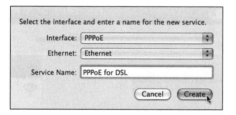

4 Select the PPPoE service from the network services list to configure PPPoE settings.

Basic PPPoE configuration settings will appear to the right of the services list. At a minimum you will need to enter the account name and password given by the service provider. You should also probably check the "Remember this password" checkbox to save the PPPoE authentication information to the system keychain so other users don't have to remember it.

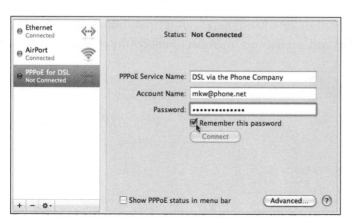

5   To configure advanced PPPoE settings, click the Advanced button in the bottom-right corner of the Network preferences.

This reveals the advanced settings dialog. Click the PPP tab to view PPP-specific settings.

Because PPPoE is based on PPP, they share similar advanced configuration options. Probably the most significant settings are to optionally connect automatically when needed and to not disconnect when switching to another user account. Click the OK button when you have made all your selections.

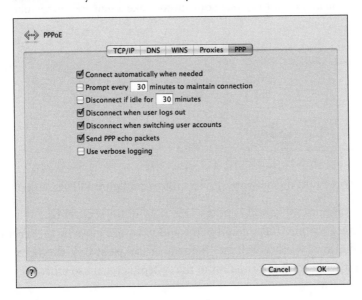

6   Once you have completed all PPPoE settings, click the Apply button at the bottom-right corner of the Network preferences to save and activate the changes.

7   You can make accessing PPPoE connectivity options much easier by clicking the "Show PPPoE status in menu bar" checkbox. The PPPoE menu bar item allows you to easily connect, disconnect, and monitor PPPoE connections.

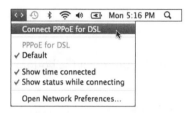

As you can see, PPPoE connections are not always on like other high-speed services. Mac OS X supports automatically connecting PPPoE when needed, but you can also manually connect and disconnect the PPPoE link from the PPPoE menu bar item or by clicking the Connect button in the Network preferences. Once the connection is established, the PPP process automatically configures TCP/IP and DNS settings. You can also manually configure these settings, as outlined later in this chapter. PPPoE services are automatically placed above all other services in the network service order, so as soon as the PPPoE service is connected and completely configured it will be the primary network interface for all Internet traffic. Reordering the network service order was covered previously in this chapter.

Configuring VPN

A VPN is an encrypted tunnel from your client to the network routing device providing the VPN service. Once established, your Mac will appear to have a direct connection to the LAN that the VPN device is sharing. So even if you're on a wireless Internet connection thousands of miles away from your LAN, a VPN connection provides a virtual network interface as if your computer were directly attached to that LAN. Mac OS X supports three common VPN protocols: the Layer 2 Tunneling Protocol over Internet Protocol Security (L2TP over IPSec), Point-to-Point Tunneling Protocol (PPTP), and—new in Mac OS X v10.6—Cisco's version of IPSec.

> **NOTE ▶** Some VPN services require a third-party VPN client. Third-party VPN clients usually include a custom interface for managing the connection. Although you may see the virtual network interface provided by the third-party VPN client appear in the Network preferences, it's usually not configurable from there.

To manage VPN connections:

1   Open and unlock the Network preferences.

Choose the network location you wish to edit from the Locations pop-up menu, or configure a new network location, as detailed previously in this chapter.

2   To add a VPN virtual network interface, click the small plus button at the bottom of the services list.

This reveals a dialog that allows you to add a new network interface and service.

3   Choose VPN from the Interface pop-up menu.

You must choose the appropriate VPN protocol from the VPN Type pop-up menu. Again, Mac OS X supports the L2TP over IPSec, PPTP, and Cisco IPSec VPN protocols. All three have similar configuration options, but for the purposes of this chapter L2TP will be used because it has a few more authentication and advanced options.

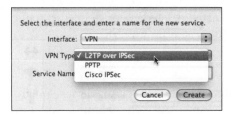

Finally, if you're going to have more than one type of VPN protocol, you may want to enter a descriptive name for the service. Otherwise, you can leave the service name as is because you can define multiple VPN configurations per VPN protocol. Click the Create button to make the new VPN virtual network interface and service.

4   To begin configuring VPN settings, select the VPN service from the network services list, and basic VPN configuration settings will appear to the right of the services list.

5   If you plan to have only one VPN configuration, leave the Configuration pop-up menu as is and continue to the next step. Multiple configurations are only needed if you will be switching between multiple VPN servers.

Conversely, if you want to set multiple VPN configurations, choose Add Configuration from the Configuration pop-up menu. This reveals a dialog where you can name and create a new VPN configuration. You can also delete and rename your configuration from this pop-up menu.

Continue editing VPN configurations, and when finished you will have to enter the settings for each VPN configuration, as outlined in the following steps.

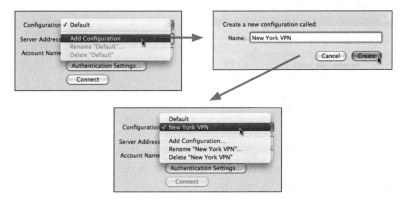

6   To configure VPN settings, first enter the VPN server address and then your VPN account name.

You must also define authentication methods by clicking the Authentication Settings button.

This will reveal a dialog allowing you to specify user and machine authentication settings. The VPN administrator should provide you with the appropriate authentication settings. Supplying a password here will add it to the system keychain. If left blank, the user will be prompted for the password when connecting. Once you have made your selections, click the OK button to save the authentication settings.

7   To configure advanced VPN settings, click the Advanced button in the bottom-right corner of the Network preferences. In the advanced settings dialog that opens, click the Options tab to view general VPN options.

The most important optional setting is to send all traffic over the VPN connection. By default, active VPN connections will not act as the primary network interface, so the system will route traffic to the VPN only if the destination IP address is part of the LAN that the VPN service is providing or the VPN server supplies special routing information. Selecting the "Send all traffic over VPN connection" checkbox will force the VPN connection to act as the primary network interface.

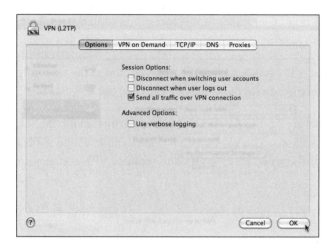

8   To enable automatic VPN connections, click the VPN on Demand tab. The options on this tab allow you to assign domains that, when accessed, will automatically activate specific VPN configurations.

Click the small plus button at the bottom of the list to add a domain and an associated VPN configuration. Double-click on a domain name to change it, and click once on the VPN configuration name to choose an alternate configuration from the pop-up menu. When you have finished, click the OK button to save the VPN on Demand settings.

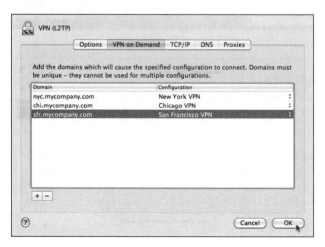

NOTE ▶ The built-in Cisco IPSec client does not feature any advanced options or VPN on demand settings.

9 Once you have completed all VPN settings, click the Apply button at the bottom-right corner of the Network preferences to save and activate the changes.

10 You can make accessing VPN connectivity options much easier by clicking the "Show VPN status in menu bar" checkbox. The VPN menu bar item allows you to easily select VPN configurations and connect, disconnect, and monitor VPN connections.

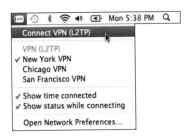

TIP VPN connections can be complicated and take a while to configure properly, so you can save time and prevent mistakes by using network configuration files. Click the gear icon at the bottom of the services list and use the Import and Export configuration menu options to use network configuration files.

TIP When troubleshooting VPN connections, it's useful to view the connection log info in /var/log/system.log. You can view the system log from the /Application/Utilities/Console application.

VPN connections are not typically always-on connections. As you saw in the instructions, Mac OS X supports automatic VPN connections with the VPN on Demand feature, but most users will manually enable VPN connections when necessary. You can manually connect and disconnect the VPN link from the VPN menu bar item or by clicking the Connect button in the Network preferences. VPNs are usually implemented in situations where security is required, so for many, initiating a VPN connection will prompt an authentication dialog.

Once the connection is authenticated and established, the VPN process will automatically configure TCP/IP and DNS settings using the PPP protocol. You can also manually configure these protocol settings, as outlined later in this chapter. VPN interfaces are, by default, set at the bottom of the network service order, so they will not automatically become the primary network interface when activated. This behavior is overridden when the optional "Send all traffic over VPN connection" checkbox is enabled, as covered in the instructions. You can also manually reorder the network service order, as explained previously in this chapter.

Configuring VLANs

VLANs are used to define separate independent logical LANs on a single network interface. In other words, your Mac could have a single Ethernet connection that allows it to simultaneously connect to multiple separate LANs. VLANs are configured in software, which gives network administrators much greater control over how network traffic is allocated and routed. VLAN services require special network infrastructure, but Mac OS X includes the appropriate network client software to support VLANs. Mac OS X supports the standard protocol used for VLAN configuration: the IEEE 802.1Q specification.

To manage VLANs:

1   Open and unlock the Network preferences.

Choose the network location you wish to edit from the Locations pop-up menu, or configure a new network location, as detailed previously in this chapter.

2 To add a VLAN interface, click the gear icon at the bottom of the services list and choose Manage Virtual Interfaces from the pop-up menu.

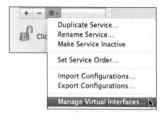

This will reveal a dialog allowing you add a new virtual network interface and services. Click the small plus button at the bottom of the virtual interface list and then choose New VLAN from the pop-up menu.

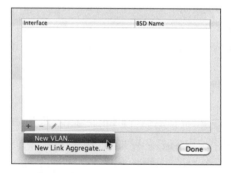

3 The dialog will transition to the VLAN creation dialog.

Enter a recognizable name for the new VLAN, and select a VLAN Tag as indicated by the network administrator. VLANs are tied to a specific wired Ethernet interface, so if you have multiple interfaces you must specify one from the Interface pop-up menu. When you have finished configuring the VLAN, click the Create button to continue.

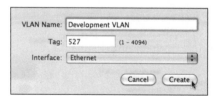

4 The dialog will transition back to the virtual interface dialog.

Here you can edit any virtual interface by double-clicking on its name. You can also delete a virtual interface by selecting it from the list and clicking the minus button at the bottom of the list.

When you have finished managing virtual interfaces, click the Done button.

5 Once you have completed all VLAN settings, click the Apply button at the bottom-right corner of the Network preferences to save and activate the changes.

If properly configured, the VLAN interface should activate a few moments after you click the Apply button. The VLAN interface will act like any other Ethernet interface and automatically attempt to configure using DHCP-supplied TCP/IP and DNS settings, but you can also manually configure these settings, as outlined later in this chapter. New virtual network interfaces are, by default, set at the bottom of the network service order, so they will not automatically become the primary network interface when activated. You can manually reorder the network service order as covered previously in this chapter.

Configuring Link Aggregation

Link aggregation, also known as interface bonding, allows you to define a single LAN interface using multiple separate hardware network interfaces. The advantage here is that you greatly increase network performance by using multiple physical connections. Link aggregation also increases network reliability by introducing connection redundancy, so if a network interface goes down there is at least one other interface to fall back on. Link aggregation services also require special network infrastructure, but again, Mac OS X includes the appropriate network client software to support link aggregation. Mac OS X supports the standard protocol used for link aggregation: the IEEE 802.3ad specification.

To manage link aggregation:

1 Open and unlock the Network preferences.

Choose the network location you wish to edit from the Locations pop-up menu, or configure a new network location, as detailed previously in this chapter.

2   To add a new aggregate virtual interface, click the gear icon at the bottom of the services list and choose Manage Virtual Interfaces from the pop-up menu.

This will reveal a dialog allowing you add a new virtual network interface and service. Click the small plus button at the bottom of the virtual interface list and then choose New Link Aggregate from the pop-up menu.

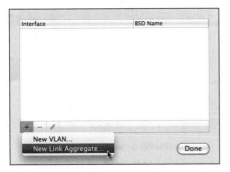

3   The dialog will transition to the link aggregate creation dialog.

Enter a recognizable name for the new aggregate interface, and select the checkboxes next to the Ethernet interfaces you want to bond together. Once bonded, these Ethernet interfaces cannot be used for another service. When you have finished configuring the aggregate interface, click the Create button to continue.

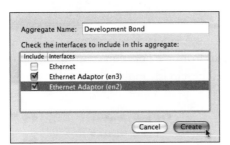

4 The dialog will transition back to the virtual interface dialog.

Here you can edit any virtual interface by double-clicking its name. You can also delete a virtual interface by selecting it from the list and clicking the minus button at the bottom of the list.

When you have finished managing virtual interfaces, click the Done button.

5 Once you have completed all link aggregation settings, click the Apply button at the bottom-right corner of the Network preferences to save and activate the changes.

If properly configured, the link aggregate interface should activate a few moments after you click the Apply button. You can check the status of the link aggregate interface by clicking the Advanced button in the bottom-right corner of the Network preferences, and then clicking the Bond Status tab. The Development Bond in the following example is obviously not properly configured.

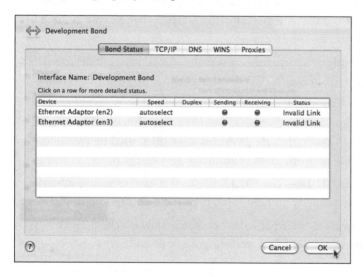

The link aggregate interface will act like any other Ethernet interface and automatically attempt to configure using DHCP-supplied TCP/IP and DNS settings, but you can also manually configure these settings, as outlined later in this chapter. New virtual network interfaces are, by default, set at the bottom of the network service order, so they will not automatically become the primary network interface when activated. You can manually reorder the network service order, as explained earlier in this chapter.

Using Network Protocols

Each hardware or virtual network interface provides connectivity for a number of standard networking protocols. The Network preferences shows primary protocol settings whenever you select a service from the services list, but many protocol configuration options are only available by clicking the Advanced button. The remainder of this section covers how to configure each built-in networking protocol supported by Mac OS X.

NOTE ▶ AppleTalk is no longer supported with Mac OS X v10.6.

Mac OS X includes built-in support for the following network protocols:

▶ TCP/IP configured via DHCP—As explained previously in this chapter, TCP/IP is the primary network protocol for LANs and WANs, and DHCP is a popular network service that will automatically configure TCP/IP clients.

▶ TCP/IP configured manually—If you do not have DHCP service on your local network or if you want to ensure that the TCP/IP settings never change, you can manually configure TCP/IP settings.

▶ DNS—As covered previously, DNS provides host names for IP network devices. DNS settings are often configured alongside TCP/IP settings either by DHCP or manual configuration. Mac OS X supports multiple DNS servers and search domains.

▶ Network Basic Input/Output System (NetBIOS) and Windows Internet Naming Service (WINS)—NetBIOS and WINS are protocols most often used by Windows-based computers to provide network identification and service discovery.

▶ Authenticated Ethernet via 802.1X—The 802.1X protocol is used to secure Ethernet networks by allowing only properly authenticated network clients to join the LAN.

▶ IP proxies—Proxy servers act as intermediaries between a network client and a requested service and are used to enhance performance or provide an additional layer of security.

▶ Wired Ethernet Protocol options—Mac OS X supports both automatic and manual Ethernet configuration.

▶ Wireless Ethernet (AirPort) Protocol options—The wireless nature of AirPort requires additional configuration to facilitate network selection and authentication.

▶ External (analog) Modem with PPP—Likewise, the very nature of analog modems requires manual configuration to activate a connection.

▶ Bluetooth DUN with PPP—Again, the wireless nature of Bluetooth requires additional configuration to facilitate peripheral selection and authentication.

▶ Point-to-Point Protocol (PPP)—As PPP is used for both analog modem and Bluetooth DUN connectivity, additional configuration is required.

Manually Configuring TCP/IP and DNS

Many network situations do not require any manual intervention to configure TCP/IP and DNS, as the DHCP or PPP service will automatically acquire these settings. The default configuration for all Ethernet and AirPort services is to automatically engage the DHCP process as soon as the interface port becomes active. To verify TCP/IP and DNS settings for hardware or virtual Ethernet services when using the DHCP service, simply select the service from the Network preferences.

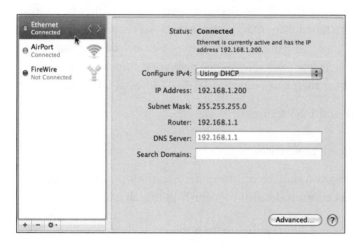

NOTE ▶ IPv6 addressing information is automatically detected as well if available. However, automatic IPv6 configuration is not provided by standard DHCP or PPP services.

NOTE ▶ Automatically configured DNS settings will show as gray text. This indicates that you can override these settings by manually entering DNS information.

Interfaces that may require a manual connection process, like AirPort, analog modems, VPN, and PPPoE interfaces, will automatically engage the DHCP or PPP process to acquire TCP/IP and DNS settings. To verify TCP/IP and DNS settings when using these interfaces, select the service from the services list, and then click the Advanced button in the bottom-right corner of the Network preferences. This will open the advanced settings dialog, where you can click the TCP/IP or DNS tabs to view their respective settings. You can also verify network settings of any other interface this way.

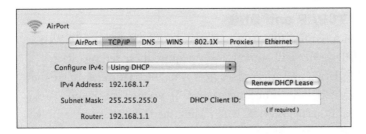

Despite the convenience of automatic TCP/IP and DNS configuration, there may be times where manual configuration is required. For example, the network server providing the DHCP service will require a manual configuration. In fact, most network devices that provide services, like servers or printers, use manually entered network configuration information so they don't run the risk of changing to a different TCP/IP address if DHCP resets.

To manually configure TCP/IP and DNS settings:

1   Open and unlock the Network preferences.

    Choose the network location you want to edit from the Locations pop-up menu, or configure a new network location, as detailed previously in this chapter.

2   Select the network service you wish to configure from the network services list.

    If you selected an Ethernet interface, at this point, you could configure TCP/IP settings from the general information area to the right of the services list, but for the purposes of this chapter you need to click the Advanced button in the bottom-right corner of the Network preferences to open the advanced settings dialog.

3   Click the TCP/IP tab at the top to view the TCP/IP settings.

4   If you want to keep using DHCP but only assign a manual IP address, choose "Using DHCP with manual address" from the Configure IPv4 pop-up menu.

You will have to manually enter an IPv4 address only for this Mac. When you have entered the appropriate IP address, click the OK button to dismiss the advanced network options dialog, and then click the Apply button in the bottom-right corner of the Network preferences to save and activate the changes.

You can disregard the rest of these steps because the DHCP service will continue to manage the rest of the TCP/IP and DNS settings.

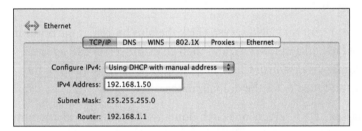

5   If you want to manually enter all TCP/IP settings, choose Manually from the Configure IPv4 pop-up menu.

At a minimum you will have to manually enter the IP address, the subnet mask (for this you can also use CIDR notation), and the router address. The user interface will cache the TCP/IP settings from the DHCP service so you may only have to enter a new IPv4 address.

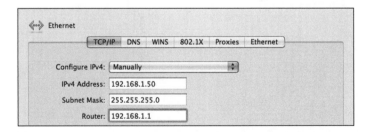

6   If you have to manually set up IPv6 settings as well, choose Manually from the Configure IPv6 pop-up menu.

At a minimum you will have to manually enter the IPv6 address, router address, and the prefix length. The user interface will cache any automatic IPv6 settings so you may only have to enter a new IPv6 address.

7 To configure DNS, click the DNS tab at the top to view the DNS settings.

Again, the user interface will cache the DNS settings from the DHCP service so you may not have to enter any DNS settings at all.

NOTE ▶ If the IP address of a DNS server is not specified, then the Mac will not be able to resolve DNS hostnames.

You should configure at least one DNS server. Click the plus button at the bottom of the DNS server list to add a new server, and then enter the server's IP address. Entering a search domain is optional. Click the plus button at the bottom of the Search Domains list, and then enter the domain name.

If you configure multiple DNS servers or search domains, the system will attempt to access those resources in the order they appear in the list. To edit an address, double-click on its entry in the list, or you can delete an entry by selecting it and clicking the minus button at the bottom of the list.

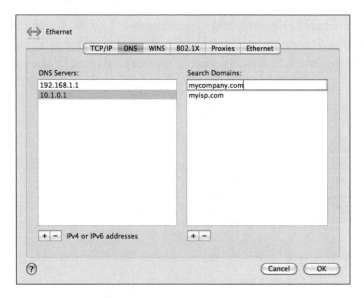

8   When you have entered all the appropriate IP and DNS settings, click the OK button
    to dismiss the advanced network options dialog, and then click the Apply button in
    the bottom-right corner of the Network preferences to save and activate the changes.

Whenever you manually configure TCP/IP or DNS settings, you should always test network connectivity to verify that you properly entered all information. Using standard
applications to access network and Internet resources is one basic test, but you could also
test more thoroughly using the included network diagnostic utilities. Using network diagnostic tools built into Mac OS X is covered later in this chapter.

Configuring NetBIOS and WINS

Network Basic Input/Output System (NetBIOS) and Windows Internet Naming Service
(WINS) run on top of TCP/IP to provide network identification and service discovery.
NetBIOS and WINS are used primarily by Windows-based systems to provide identification and service discovery on LANs, while WINS is used to identify and locate NetBIOS
network devices on WANs. You can think of WINS as a form of DNS for NetBIOS network clients.

> **NOTE ▶** Mac OS X supports NetBIOS and WINS on any active network interface
> except for VPN connections.

Mac OS X automatically configures your computer's NetBIOS name based on your Mac's
sharing name, and for many networks this should be sufficient. If your Mac is on a larger
network and you want to share resources from your Mac with other network clients, you
may want to manually select the NetBIOS workgroup. NetBIOS workgroups are used to
make navigation easier on large networks by grouping devices into smaller collections. You
may have to manually configure the WINS service to provide faster NetBIOS resolution.

> **NOTE ▶** It's not required to configure NetBIOS and WINS in order to connect to
> Windows resources. On certain networks, however, it may help when attempting to
> connect to those resources.

To manually configure NetBIOS and WINS settings:

1 Open and unlock the Network preferences.

Choose the network location you wish to edit from the Locations pop-up menu, or configure a new network location, as detailed previously in this chapter.

2 Select the network service you wish to configure from the network services list, and then click the Advanced button in the bottom-right corner of the Network preferences.

3 In the advanced settings dialog that opens, click the WINS tab at the top to view the NetBIOS and WINS settings.

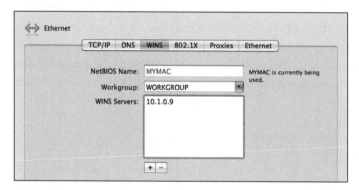

4 To manually configure NetBIOS, enter a unique name, and then choose a workgroup from the pop-up menu.

It may take a while for the NetBIOS workgroup list to refresh, thus preventing you from selecting it via the pop-up menu. If you already know the name of the work-group you want the Mac to be in, you can manually enter the workgroup name.

NOTE ▶ NetBIOS names and workgroup names are in all capital letters and cannot contain any special characters or spaces.

5 To enable WINS, enter at least one WINS server IP address. Click the plus button at the bottom of the WINS server list to add a new server, and then enter the server's IP address.

If you configure multiple WINS servers, the system will attempt to access those resources in the order they appear in the list. To edit a server address, double-click its entry in the list, or you can delete a server by selecting it and clicking the minus button at the bottom of the list.

6   When you have entered all the appropriate NetBIOS and WINS settings, click the OK button to dismiss the advanced network options dialog, and then click the Apply button in the bottom-right corner of the Network preferences to save and activate the changes.

If your network requires it, configuring specific NetBIOS and WINS settings will allow your Mac to interact with other Windows-compatible network clients as if you were running Windows natively. Accessing and sharing network services using these two protocols is covered in Chapter 8, "Network Services."

Configuring 802.1X

The 802.1X protocol is used to secure wired and wireless (AirPort) Ethernet networks by only allowing properly authenticated network clients to join the LAN. Networks using 802.1X will not allow any traffic until the network client properly authenticates to the network.

To facilitate 802.1X authentication, Mac OS X provides three types of authentication profiles:

▶   User Profile—With this configuration the user must manually choose to authenticate to the 802.1X network using account information you've configured. This method requires that users be logged in to the computer with a local account before they can join the 802.1X network. Also, this type of profile is automatically created if you join and authenticate to a wireless network that uses WAP or WAP2 Enterprise. Finally, it's important to note that user profiles are tied to a user's account but not to a network location or interface. Therefore, you can have multiple network locations that can take advantage of a single user 802.1X profile.

▶   Login Window Profile—Many larger networks use the same usernames and passwords for access to the computers and to their networks. Creating a login window profile allows the system to pass to the network the same credentials that are used to log in the user account to the Mac.

▶   System Profile—If you want the Mac to always have access to the 802.1X network, you can set a single 802.1X account for the computer as a whole. The account information is saved to the system keychain, and the system will automatically join the network on startup.

NOTE ▶ It's highly likely that you will have to acquire specific 802.1X configuration instructions from a network administrator. Many 802.1X implementations also require certificate files that must be copied to each Mac client. These can also be obtained from a network administrator.

To configure 802.1X on Ethernet or AirPort:

1 Open and unlock the Network preferences.

Choose the network location you wish to edit from the Locations pop-up menu, or configure a new network location, as detailed previously in this chapter.

2 Select the Ethernet or AirPort network service you wish to configure from the network services list, and then click the Advanced button in the bottom-right corner of the Network preferences.

This will reveal the advanced settings dialog.

Click the 802.1X tab at the top to view the 802.1X settings.

3 To add a new 802.1X configuration profile, click the small plus button at the bottom of the profiles list.

From the pop-up menu that appears select the appropriate 802.1X profile. You can add multiple login window and user profiles by reopening this pop-up menu.

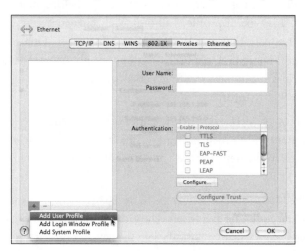

NOTE ▶ It's not recommended that you mix and match 802.1X profile types, as Login Window Profiles will override User Profiles and System Profiles will override both.

4   At this point you will perform one of three routines based on your 802.1X configuration profile choice:

▶ If you picked a User Profile, first enter a descriptive name for the profile to replace the default name "untitled." To the right in the configuration area, at a minimum you must enter the user's account name. Optionally you can choose to save the user's password or choose to always prompt for the password. Finally, configure authentication and trust settings as required by your 802.1X implementation.

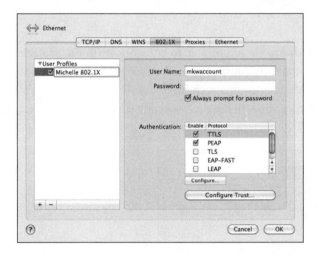

TIP ▶ To rename a User or Login Window Profile, simply double-click on its entry in the list, or you can delete a configuration by selecting it and clicking the minus button at the bottom of the list.

▶ If you picked a Login Window Profile, first you can enter a descriptive name for the profile to replace the default name "Login Window," though this is not necessary as most only need to configure a single profile for login window authentication. To the right in the configuration area, leave the username and password fields blank, as they are not saved. Finally, configure authentication and trust settings as required by your 802.1X implementation.

▶   If you picked a System Profile, to the right in the configuration area you must enter the 802.1X account information, including the password. Finally, configure authentication and trust settings as required by your 802.1X implementation.

5   When you have entered all the appropriate 802.1X settings, click the OK button to dismiss the advanced settings dialog, and then click the Apply button in the bottom-right corner of the Network preferences to save and activate the changes.

> **TIP** ▶ 802.1X settings can be complicated and take a while to configure properly, so you can save time and prevent mistakes by using network configuration files. Click the gear icon at the bottom of the services list and use the Import and Export configuration menu options to use network configuration files.

Once 802.1X is properly configured, you should be able to authenticate to the protected network. System Profiles will automatically connect as soon as you click the Apply button. Login Window Profiles will authenticate with the account information provided during login. Finally, to connect User Profiles you will have to manually click the Connect button in the Network preferences.

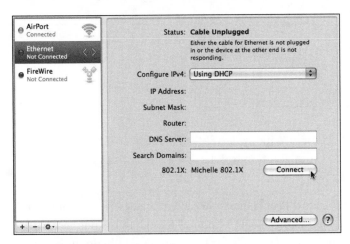

Configuring IP Proxies

Proxy servers act as intermediaries between a network client and a requested service. Proxy servers are often used to enhance the performance of slow WAN or Internet connections by caching recently requested data so future connections appear faster to local network clients. Primarily, though, proxy servers are implemented so network administrators can limit network connections to unauthorized servers or resources. Administrators can manage lists of approved resources, having the proxy servers allow access only to those resources.

Mac OS X supports proxy services for File Transfer Protocol (FTP), web protocols (HTTP and HTTPS), streaming (RTSP), SOCKS, and Gopher. For proxy configuration, Mac OS X supports manual configurations, automatic proxy configuration using local or network-hosted proxy auto-config (PAC) files, and full auto proxy discovery via the Web Proxy Autodiscovery Protocol (WPAD).

> **NOTE** ▶ It's highly likely that you will have to acquire specific proxy configuration instructions from a network administrator.

To configure proxy settings:

1 Open and unlock the Network preferences.

   Choose the network location you wish to edit from the Locations pop-up menu, or configure a new network location, as detailed previously in this chapter.

2 Select the network service you wish to configure from the network services list, and then click the Advanced button in the bottom-right corner of the Network preferences.

   This will reveal the advanced settings dialog.

3 Click the Proxies tab at the top to view the proxy settings.

4   At this point you will perform one of three routines based on your network's proxy implementation:

▶   If your proxy service supports the Web Proxy Autodiscovery Protocol (WPAD), then simply enable the Auto Proxy Discovery checkbox.

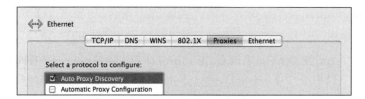

▶   If you have access to a proxy auto-config (PAC) file, enable the Automatic Proxy Configuration checkbox at the bottom of the proxy protocols list. You must then specify a PAX proxy configuration file. To specify a local file, click the Choose File button and then select the file using the file browser dialog. To specify a network-hosted file, enter the full network path to the file in the URL entry field.

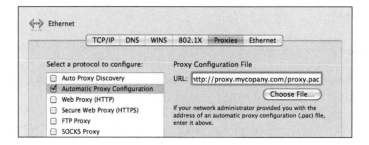

▶   To manually configure proxy settings, select the checkboxes next to each protocol you wish to send through the proxy servers. Select each protocol individually to enter the proxy connection information provided by the network administrator. At the bottom you can also elect to bypass the proxy for specific additional hosts and domains.

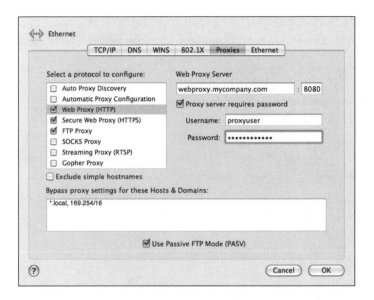

5   When you have entered all the appropriate proxy information, click the OK button to dismiss the advanced settings dialog, and then click the Apply button in the bottom-right corner of the Network preferences to save and activate the changes.

Manually Configuring Ethernet

Wired Ethernet connections are designed to establish connection settings automatically. Yet Mac OS X allows you to manually configure wired Ethernet options from the Network preferences should the automatic selections prove problematic.

To manually configure wired Ethernet settings:

1   Open and unlock the Network preferences.

Choose the network location you wish to edit from the Locations pop-up menu, or configure a new network location, as detailed previously in this chapter.

2   Select the wired Ethernet service you wish to configure from the network services list, and then click the Advanced button in the bottom-right corner of the Network preferences.

This will reveal the advanced settings dialog.

3   Click the Ethernet tab at the top to view the current automatically configured Ethernet settings.

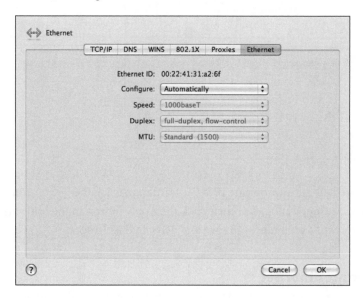

4   To manually configure Ethernet options, choose Manually from the Configure pop-up menu. The system will cache the current automatically configured Ethernet settings so you will not have to change all the settings.

The system will prepopulate the Speed, Duplex, and MTU Ethernet options based on your Mac's network hardwire. Make your custom selections from these pop-up menus.

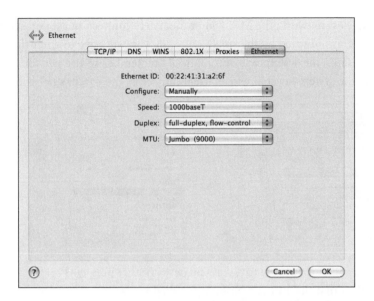

5   When you have selected all the appropriate Ethernet settings, click the OK button to dismiss the advanced settings dialog, and then click the Apply button in the bottom-right corner of the Network preferences to save and activate the changes.

Basic AirPort Configuration

As covered previously, Apple made basic wireless Ethernet (AirPort) network management a breeze with the AirPort menu item. The AirPort menu item will automatically appear in the menu bar if your Mac has an AirPort card installed. From this menu you can easily join established open and secure wireless networks. When you select this menu, the AirPort background process will automatically scan for any advertised networks that are within range for you to choose from. Mac OS X v10.6 introduced an improvement to this menu that shows the signal levels for wireless networks that are in range.

> **MORE INFO ▸** The AirPort menu in Mac OS X v10.6 is capable of several new tricks, including helping you quickly identify network issues, as outlined in Knowledge Base article HT3821, "Mac OS X 10.6 Snow Leopard: The AirPort status menu (AirPort Menu Extra) FAQ."

If you select an open wireless network, the Mac will immediately connect, but if you select a secure wireless network, as indicated by the small lock icon, you will have to enter the network password. By default, the system will automatically remember secure networks by saving the passwords to the system keychain so all users can access the wireless network.

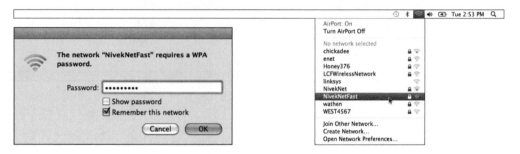

NOTE ▶ If you join and authenticate to a wireless network that uses WAP or WAP2 Enterprise, it's implied that the authentication is handled via 802.1X. Thus, joining this type of network will automatically create an 802.1X User Profile. Conversely, the system does not automatically recognize WEP networks with 802.1X authentication, so you will have to configure this manually as covered in the "Configuring 802.1X" section earlier in this chapter.

To increase security, some wireless networks do not advertise their availability. You can connect to these hidden wireless networks (also called closed networks) as long as you know their network name (or Service Set Identifier, aka SSID) by choosing Join Other Network from the AirPort menu item. This will reveal a dialog where you can enter all the appropriate information to join the hidden wireless network. Again, the system will save this information to the system keychain by default.

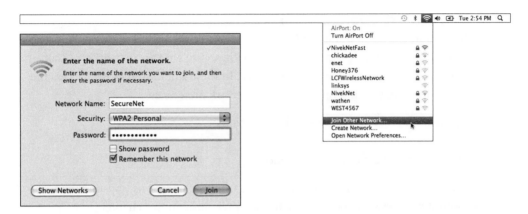

Lastly, if you are unable to connect to a standard wireless network, you can create an ad hoc wireless network using your Mac's AirPort card to share files wirelessly with other computers. Choose Create Network from the AirPort menu item and then enter the wireless network information that will be used to connect to your ad hoc network.

> **NOTE ▶** It is a security risk to leave an ad hoc network enabled on your Mac. To disable the ad hoc network, turn off AirPort or choose another wireless network from the AirPort menu.

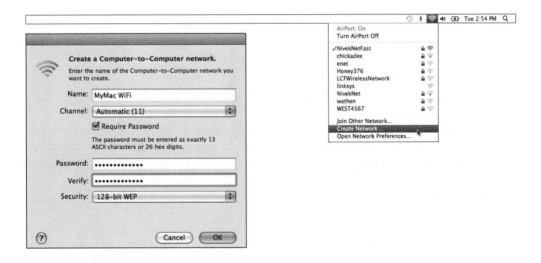

Advanced AirPort Configuration

Some administrators may find the need to restrict some of the wireless features. You may want to require that the Mac connect only to specific secure wireless networks, or that the Mac always connect to one particular network. In these situations you will access the advanced AirPort configuration options in the Network preferences.

To manage advanced AirPort options and connections:

1   Open and unlock the Network preferences.

Choose the network location you wish to edit from the Locations pop-up menu, or configure a new network location, as detailed previously in this chapter.

2   Select the AirPort service from the services list.

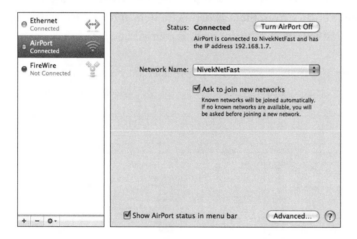

At this point you can configure basic AirPort settings in a manner similar to the AirPort menu item, including the ability to join or create another wireless network, from the Network Name pop-up menu.

3   You can also prevent non-administrative users from accessing AirPort settings by disabling the following:

▶   Deselecting the "Ask to join new networks" checkbox will prevent the user from being prompted when the Mac can't find a preconfigured wireless network but there are other networks in the area.

▶ Deselecting the "Show AirPort status in menu bar" checkbox will disable the AirPort menu item; however, this won't prevent a user from choosing a wireless network if the Mac presents a wireless discovery dialog.

4 Click the Advanced button in the bottom-right corner of the Network preferences to reveal the advanced settings dialog. Click the AirPort tab at the top to view the advanced AirPort settings.

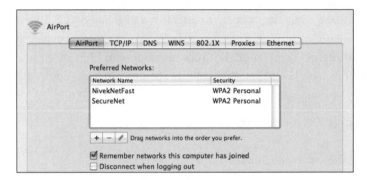

From the top half of the advanced AirPort settings pane, you can create a list of preferred wireless networks. By default, wireless networks that were added previously will appear here as well. If you disable the user access to AirPort settings as described in step three, the system will connect only to the preferred wireless networks in this list.

To add a new wireless network click the plus button at the bottom of the preferred network list, and then either join a wireless network in range or manually enter the information for a hidden or not-currently-in-range network. To edit a network, simply double-click on its entry in the list, or you can delete a network by selecting it and clicking the minus button at the bottom of the list.

5 At the bottom of the advanced AirPort settings pane you have several settings that allow for more specific AirPort administration options. Thus, if you choose to leave the AirPort menu item available to regular users, you can restrict certain settings to only administrative users.

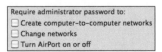

6   When you have entered the appropriate AirPort settings, click the OK button to dismiss the advanced settings dialog, and then click the Apply button in the bottom-right corner of the Network preferences to save and activate the changes.

Configuring Analog Modem Connections

The Point-to-Point Protocol (PPP) was developed to act as a control and transport mechanism for TCP/IP connections transferred via analog modems over phone lines. Though slow, the combination of using an analog modem to establish a PPP-based TCP/IP connection over the phone system, commonly known as a dial-up connection, provided the basis for many users' first Internet connection. With the abundance of high-speed Internet options, dial-up connections have been slowly dwindling. For some unlucky souls, however, this is still their only option.

To manage analog modem (PPP) connections:

1   Open and unlock the Network preferences.

Choose the network location you wish to edit from the Locations pop-up menu, or configure a new network location, as detailed previously in this chapter.

2   To begin configuring modem settings, select the analog modem service from the network services list, and basic modem configuration settings will appear to the right of the services list.

3   If you plan to have only one modem configuration, leave the Configuration pop-up menu as is and continue to the next step.

Conversely, if you want to set multiple modem configurations, choose Add Configuration from the Configuration pop-up menu. This will reveal a dialog where you can name and create a new modem configuration. You can also delete and rename configurations using this pop-up menu.

Continue adding modem configurations; then you will have to enter the settings for each modem configuration, as outlined in the following steps.

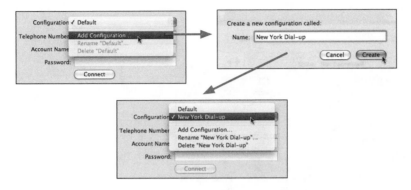

4   To configure basic modem settings, enter the dial-up phone number and account information as provided by your Internet service provider.

5   To configure advanced modem settings, click the Advanced button in the bottom-right corner of the Network preferences. This will reveal the advanced settings dialog. Click the Modem tab to view advanced modem options.

There are a lot of settings here, but for most situations the default settings are adequate. The most important configuration to double-check is the analog modem vendor and model selection.

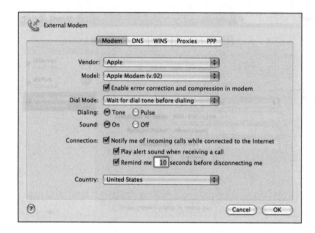

6   To configure advanced PPP settings, click the PPP tab.

Again, there are a lot of settings here, but the defaults are usually adequate. Probably the most significant settings are to optionally connect automatically when needed and to disconnect when logging out or switching to another user account. Click the OK button when you have made all your selections.

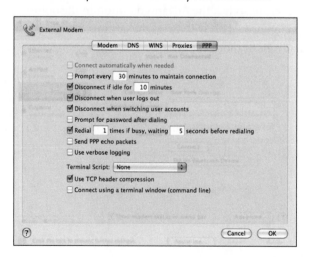

7   Once you have completed all modem settings, click the Apply button at the bottom-right corner of the Network preferences to save and activate the changes.

8   You can make accessing modem connectivity options much easier by clicking the "Show modem status in menu bar" checkbox. The modem menu bar item allows you to easily select modem configurations and connect, disconnect, and monitor modem connections.

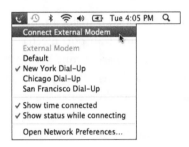

TIP ▶ Modem connections can be complicated and take a while to configure properly, so you can save time and prevent mistakes by using network configuration files. Click the gear icon at the bottom of the services list and use the Import and Export configuration menu options to use network configuration files.

TIP ▶ When troubleshooting PPP connections, it's useful to view the connection log info in /var/log/ppp.log. You can view the system log from the /Application/Utilities/Console application.

Modem connections are not typically always-on connections. Mac OS X supports automatically connecting the modem when needed, but you can also manually connect and disconnect the modem link from the modem menu bar item or by clicking the Connect button in the Network preferences. Once the connection is established, the PPP process will automatically configure TCP/IP and DNS settings. You can also manually configure these settings, as outlined earlier in this chapter. Modem interfaces are also automatically placed above all other interfaces in the network service order, so as soon as the modem interface is connected and completely configured it will be the primary network interface for all Internet traffic. Reordering the network service order was covered previously in this chapter.

Configuring Bluetooth DUN Connections

In Mac OS X, accessing the Internet via a Bluetooth DUN connection is similar to accessing it via an analog modem connection. The only difference is that instead of using an analog modem directly connected to your Mac, you're using a cell phone connected via a Bluetooth wireless connection, which requires a cell phone capable of resharing an Internet connection via Bluetooth and a Bluetooth-enabled Mac.

Configuring a Bluetooth DUN connection is similar to configuring an analog modem because Bluetooth DUN connections also use PPP as a control and transport mechanism for the TCP/IP connection. Only one extra step is required: pairing your Mac to the mobile phone providing the Internet access via Bluetooth. If you have already paired your Bluetooth-enabled mobile phone to your Mac, then all you have to do is enter the rest of the connection information as if you were configuring an analog modem. Again, your mobile phone service provider usually provides the configuration information. Otherwise, follow the instructions presented in Chapter 9, "Peripherals and Printing," to pair your Mac to a Bluetooth-enabled mobile phone.

Network Troubleshooting

The most important thing to remember about troubleshooting network issues is that it is often not the computer's fault. There are many other points of failure to consider when dealing with LAN and Internet connection issues. So the second most important thing to remember about troubleshooting network issues is to isolate the cause of the problem before attempting generic resolutions.

To help isolate network issues, you can categorize them into three general areas:

▶ Local issues—These issues are usually either related to improperly configured network settings or disconnected network connections.

▶ Network issues—Network issues are by far the hardest to nail down, as there could be literally hundreds of points of failure involved. In this case it always helps to be familiar with the physical topology of your network. Start by checking the devices that provide network access closest to your Mac. Something as simple as a bad Ethernet port on a network switch can cause problems. As you move on to investigating devices farther away from your Mac, you will find that it's often easiest to start your investigation using the network diagnostic utilities included with Mac OS X.

▶ Service issues—Service issues are related to the actual network device or service you are trying to access. For example, the devices providing DHCP or DNS services could be temporarily down or improperly configured. It's often easy to determine if the problem is with the service alone by testing other network services. If the other network services work, you're probably not dealing with network or local issues. Again, Mac OS X provides some useful diagnostic tools for testing service availability. Troubleshooting network services is also covered in Chapter 8, "Network Services."

You will be using three main tools for diagnosing network issues on Mac OS X: the Network preferences, the Network Diagnostics assistant, and the Network Utility.

Troubleshooting via Network Preferences

The first diagnostic tool you should always check is the Network preferences. Network preferences features a dynamically updating list that will show you the current status of any network interface. If a network connection is not working, you will find it here first.

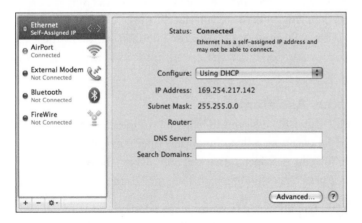

Network status indicators include:

▶ Green status—The connection is active and configured with TCP/IP settings. This, however, does not guarantee that the service is using the proper TCP/IP settings. For instance, in the previous screen shot of the Network preferences you'll note that the Ethernet service appears with a green status indicating proper TCP/IP settings. Nevertheless, if you look closer you'll see that the service is using a link-local TCP/IP configuration, indicating this interface is not receiving proper configuration from the DHCP service. If you are still experiencing problems with this service, double-check the network settings. If the settings appear sound, move on to the other diagnostic utilities.

▶ Yellow status—The connection is active but the TCP/IP settings are not properly configured. Double-check all the network settings until you get things right and the service goes green.

▶ Red status—These issues are usually either related to improperly configured network settings or disconnected network interfaces. If this is an always-on interface, check for proper physical connectivity. If this is a virtual or PPP connection, double-check the settings and attempt to reconnect.

TIP ▶ Remember that the interface order plays a huge part in how the Mac routes network traffic. Specifically, the primary network interface is the one that will be used to reach the Internet and primary DNS resolution. Become familiar with how the Mac uses multiple network connections, as covered earlier in this chapter.

Using Network Diagnostics Assistant

Mac OS X includes the Network Diagnostics assistant to help you troubleshoot common network issues. Some networking applications will automatically open this assistant when they encounter a network issue. You can also open it manually by clicking the Assist Me button at the bottom of the Network preferences, and then clicking the Diagnostics button.

The Network Diagnostics assistant will ask you a few simple questions about your network setup and then, based on your answers, run a battery of tests to determine where the problem might be occurring. Test results are displayed using colored indicators on the left side of the window. If there are problems, the assistant makes suggestions for resolution. In the following example, the modem connection has failed and the Network Diagnostics assistant is suggesting that you double-check your modem settings.

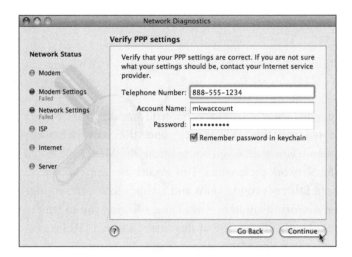

Using Network Utility

The Network preferences and Network Diagnostics assistant are good places to start troubleshooting network issues, but the most powerful application in Mac OS X for diagnosing network issues is /Applications/Utilities/Network Utility. The Network Utility provides an array of popular network identification and diagnostic tools. In fact, most of the tools in the Network Utility are based on UNIX command-line network utilities that have been used by network administrators for years.

The Network Utility is broken up into the following sections:

▶ Info—Allows you to inspect details regarding hardware network interfaces.

▶ Netstat—Shows routing information and network statistics.

▶ Ping—This fundamental network troubleshooting tool lets you test network connectivity and latency.

▶ Lookup—This very important tool lets you test DNS resolution.

▶ Traceroute—This powerful tool lets you analyze how your network connections are routed to their destination.

▶ Whois—Lets you query whois database servers and find the owner of a DNS domain name or IP address of registered hosts.

▶ Finger—Enables you to gather information based on a user account name from a network service.

▶ Port Scan—The most important tool for determining if a network device has services available.

The Network Utility can also be opened when your Mac is booted from the Mac OS X Install DVD. Any time you are booted from this DVD, you can open the Network Utility by choosing it from the Utilities menu. However, when booted from the Mac OS X Install DVD you do not have access to the Network preferences. This means that the Mac will automatically activate built-in wired Ethernet connections and attempt to acquire configuration via DHCP. Alternately, the AirPort menu item is available, allowing you to temporarily connect to wireless networks. Another limitation of this method is that DNS is not enabled; thus you will not be able to test for any DNS related issues.

Network Utility: Interface Information

When you open the Network Utility, you will first see the Info section. This section lets you view the detailed status of any hardware network interface. Even if you've opened the Network Utility to use another section, always take a few moments to verify that the network interface is properly activated.

Start by selecting the specific interface you're having issues with from the pop-up menu. You'll notice the selections here do not necessarily match the service names given in the Network preferences. Instead, this menu shows the interfaces using their interface type and UNIX-given names. When working properly, the en0 interface should be the first internal Ethernet port, and in most cases the en1 interface is the AirPort interface. If you have a Mac with two internal Ethernet ports, the second internal port will be en1 and the AirPort interface will be bumped to en2. The FireWire interface will be labeled as fw0.

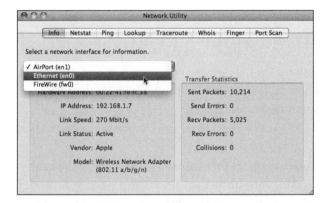

Once you have selected an interface, you can view general interface information to the left and transfer statistics to the right. The primary pieces of information you're looking for here are the Link Status, Link Speed, and IP Address(es). Only active hardware network interfaces will show as such, and the link speed will indicate if the interface is establishing a proper connection. Obviously, a proper IP address is required to establish a TCP/IP connection. You can also identify the selected interface's MAC address, which is used to identify this particular interface on the LAN.

As a final validation of the selected network interface, you can view recent transfer statistics. If you open other network applications to stir up some network traffic, you will be able to verify that packets are being sent and received from this interface. If you are seeing activity here but still experiencing problems, the issue is most likely due to a network or service problem and not the actual network interface. Or, if this interface is experiencing transfer errors, a local network hardware connectivity issue may be the root of your problem.

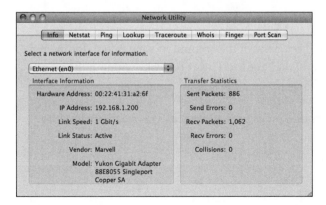

To resolve hardware network interface issues, always start by checking the physical connection. With wired networks, try different network ports or cabling to rule out physical connection issues. With wireless networks, double-check the AirPort settings and the configuration of any wireless base stations. On the rarest of occasions, you may find that the Mac's network hardware is somehow no longer working properly, in which case you should take your Mac to an Apple Authorized repair center.

Network Utility: Ping

If you have determined that your network settings are properly configured and that the hardware network interface appears to be working correctly but you are still experiencing network issues, your next step is to test network connectivity using the ping tool. The ping tool is the most fundamental network test to determine if your Mac can successfully send and receive data to another network device. Your Mac will send a ping data packet to the destination IP address, and the other device should return the ping packet to indicate connectivity.

To use ping:

1   Open /Applications/Utilities/Network Utility, and then click the Ping tab at the top.

2   Enter the IP address or host name of a network device to test connectivity to that device.

    Start by entering an IP address to a device on the LAN that should always be accessible, like the network router.

    Remember, using a domain name assumes that your Mac is properly communicating with a DNS server, which might not be the case if you're troubleshooting connectivity issues.

3   Click the Ping button to initiate the ping process.

    If the ping is successful, it should return with the amount of time it took for the ping to travel to the network device and then return. This is typically within milliseconds, so experiencing ping times any longer than a full second is unusual.

4   Once you have established successful pings to local devices, you can branch out to WAN or Internet addresses.

Using the ping tool, you may find that everything works except for the one service you were looking for that prompted you to start troubleshooting the network.

NOTE ▶ Some network administrators view excessive pinging as a threat, so many configure their firewalls to block pings or network devices to not respond to any network pings.

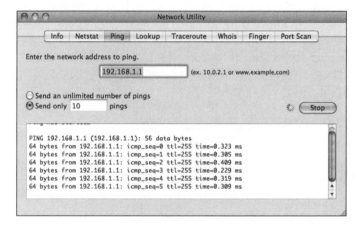

Network Utility: Lookup

If you are able to successfully ping other network devices by their IP address but attempting to connect to another device by its host name doesn't work, then you are experiencing issues related to DNS. The network lookup process will allow you to test name resolution against your DNS server.

To use lookup:

1   Open /Applications/Utilities/Network Utility, and then click the Lookup tab at the top.

2   Enter the IP address or host name of a network device to test DNS resolution.

Start by entering the host name of a device or service in your local domain. If you can resolve local host names but not Internet host names, this indicates that your local

DNS server is resolving local names but it's not properly connecting to the worldwide DNS network.

If you don't have a local domain, you can use any Internet host name as well.

3 Click the Lookup button to initiate the network lookup process.

A successful forward lookup will return the IP address of the host name you entered. A successful reverse lookup will return the host name of the IP address you entered.

4 If you are unable to successfully return any lookups, this means that your Mac is not connecting to the DNS server. You can verify this by pinging the DNS server IP address to test for basic connectivity.

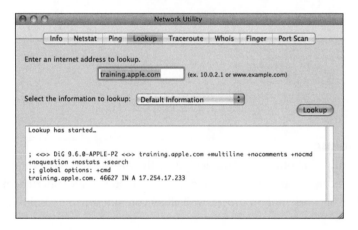

NOTE ▶ The Network Utility lookup feature is not designed to test Bonjour resolution; thus it cannot resolve ".local" names.

Network Utility: Traceroute

If you are able to connect to some network resources but not others, you should use the network traceroute utility to determine where the connection is breaking down. Remember that WAN and Internet connections require the data to travel through many network routers to find their destination. The traceroute tool will examine every network hop between routers using the ping tool to determine where connections fail or slow down.

To use traceroute:

1   Open /Applications/Utilities/Network Utility, and then click the Traceroute tab at the top.

2   Enter the IP address or host name of a network device to trace the connectivity to that device.

Start by entering an IP address to a device on the LAN that should always be accessible, like the network router.

Remember, using a domain name assumes that your Mac is properly communicating with a DNS server, which might not be the case if you're troubleshooting connectivity issues.

3   Click the Trace button to initiate the traceroute process.

If the traceroute is successful, it should return with the list of routers required to complete the connection and the amount of time it took for the ping to travel to each network router. Note that it sends three probes at each distance, so three times will be listed for each hop. Again, the delay is typically measured within milliseconds, so experiencing delay times any longer than a full second is unusual.

NOTE ▶ If traceroute doesn't get a reply from any router along the way, it will show an asterisk instead of listing the router address, as in the result for hop 15 in the example below.

4   Once you have established successful routes to local devices, you can branch out to WAN or Internet addresses.

Using the traceroute tool, you may find that a specific network router is the cause of the problem.

NOTE ▸ Some network administrators view excessive pinging as a threat, so many configure their firewalls to block pings or network devices to not respond to any network traceroute queries.

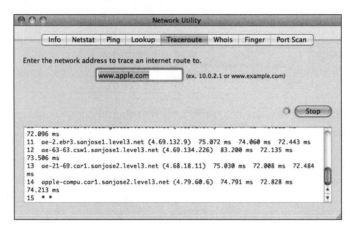

What You've Learned

▸   The Internet protocol suite, TCP/IP, provides the basis for nearly all local and wide area networks. DHCP provides automatic configuration for TCP/IP networks, and DNS provides local and worldwide TCP/IP host naming.

▸   Mac OS X supports a wide array of hardware network interfaces, virtual network interfaces, and network protocols, all managed via the Network preferences.

▸   Mac OS X includes a variety of network troubleshooting tools, among them the Network preferences, the Network Diagnostics assistant, and the Network Utility.

References

You can check for new and updated Knowledge Base documents at www.apple.com/support.

General Network

TS1629, " 'Well-known' TCP and UDP ports used by Apple software products"

HT3326, "Mac OS X 10.5: How to configure Network preferences for 802.1X"

HT3152, "Apple USB Modem: Frequently asked questions (FAQ)"

TA20531, "Mac OS X: Frequently Asked Questions (FAQ) for PPP Modem Connections"

TA20530, "Mac OS X: DSL/PPPoE Frequently Asked Questions (FAQ)"

HT3821, "Mac OS X 10.6 Snow Leopard: The AirPort status menu (AirPort Menu Extra) FAQ"

Network Troubleshooting

HT1714, "Mac OS X: Connect to the Internet, troubleshoot your Internet connection, and set up a small network"

HT1401, "AirPort troubleshooting guide"

TS2975, "Mac OS X v10.5 or later: Connecting to an 802.1X/WEP network with a saved 802.1X profile prompts for password"

TS2002, "Mac OS X: Slow startup, pauses at 'Initializing network' or 'Configuring network time' "

TS1843, "Mac OS: Troubleshooting 'A connection failure has occurred', 'The specified server could not be found' or Similar Messages

TS1853, "Mac OS X: Troubleshooting a dial-up (PPP) Internet connection"

TS1871, "Mac OS X: Troubleshooting a PPPoE Internet connection"

URLs

Wikipedia entry about the OSI reference model: http://en.wikipedia.org/wiki/OSI_model

IEEE's searchable database of OUIs used for MAC addresses: http://standards.ieee.org/regauth/oui/index.shtml

Wikipedia entry for CIDR notation: http://en.wikipedia.org/wiki/Classless_Inter-Domain_Routing

Wikipedia entry about the Internet protocol suite: http://en.wikipedia.org/wiki/Internet_protocol_suite

Wikipedia entry about DNS: http://en.wikipedia.org/wiki/Domain_Name_System

Wikipedia entry about DHCP: http://en.wikipedia.org/wiki/Dhcp

Review Quiz

1. What do the terms *interface*, *protocol*, and *service* mean in relation to computer networks?

2. What is the purpose of Internet Protocol (IP) addresses and subnet masks? What is their format?

3. How does the IP use the MAC address to send messages between computers on a local area network (LAN)?

4. How does the IP transfer messages between computers over a wide area network (WAN)?

5. How is the Domain Name Service (DNS) used to facilitate network naming?

6. How do Mac OS X computers acquire and use link-local TCP/IP addresses?

7. What interfaces and protocols are supported by default in Mac OS X?

8. How does network service order affect network connectivity?

9. In the Network preferences, how can you tell which interface is currently being used for network activities?

10. What functionality does Mac OS X 10.6 support with the AppleTalk protocol?

11. What are four common issues that can interrupt network services on a Mac OS X computer?

12. How can you identify the MAC addresses for all of the Mac's network interfaces?

Answers

1. An *interface* is any channel through which network data can flow. Hardware network interfaces are defined by physical network connections, while virtual network interfaces are logical network connections that ride on top of hardware network connections. A *protocol* is a set of rules used to describe a specific type of network communication. Protocols are necessary for separate network devices to communicate properly. Finally, a network *service* (as it pertains to the Network preferences) is the collection of settings that define a network connection.

2. The Internet Protocol (IP) address identifies the location of a specific network device. IP addresses are the primary identification used by the Internet protocol suite TCP/IP for both local and wide area networks. Subnet masks are used by network devices to identify their local network range and to determine if outgoing data is destined for a network device on the LAN. Most common IP addresses and subnet masks share the same IPv4 formatting. IPv4 addresses are a 32-bit number represented in four groups of four-digit numbers, known as octets, separated by periods. Each octet has a value between 0 and 255.

3. If a network device needs to send data to another network device on the same LAN, it will address the outgoing packets based on the destination device's MAC address.

4. A network client uses the subnet mask to determine if the destination IP address is on the LAN. If the destination IP address is not on the LAN, then it's assumed the destination address is on another network and it will send the data to the IP address of the local network router. The network router will then send the data, via a WAN connection, on to another router that it thinks is closer to the destination. This will continue across WAN connections from router to router until the data reaches its destination.

5. The DNS service is used to translate host names to IP addresses via forward lookups and translate IP addresses to host names via reverse lookups. DNS is architected as a hierarchy of worldwide domain servers. Local DNS servers provide name resolution and possibly host names for local clients. These local DNS servers connect to DNS servers higher in the DNS hierarchy to resolve both unknown host names and host local domain names.

6. If DHCP is specified as the configuration for a TCP/IP connection and no DHCP service is available, the computer will automatically select a random IP address in the 169.254.xxx.xxx range. It will check the local network to ensure that no other network device is using the randomly generated IP address before it applies the IP address.

7. Mac OS X supports the following network interfaces and protocols:

   Wired Ethernet IEEE 802.3 family of hardware network interface standards

   Wireless (AirPort) IEEE 802.11 family of hardware network interface standards

   FireWire IEEE 1394 hardware network interface

   Analog modem hardware network interface

   Bluetooth wireless hardware network interface

   Virtual private network (VPN) virtual network interface via the Point-to-Point Tunneling Protocol (PPTP)

   VPN virtual network interface via the Layer 2 Tunneling Protocol (L2TP) over Internet Protocol security (IPsec)

   Point-to-Point Protocol over Ethernet (PPPoE) virtual network interface

   6 to 4 virtual network interface

   Virtual local area network (VLAN) virtual network interface via the IEEE 802.1Q standard

   Link Aggregation virtual network interface via the IEEE 802.3ad standard

   Transmission Control Protocol/Internet Protocol (TCP/IP), also known as the Internet protocol suite

   Dynamic Host Configuration Protocol (DHCP)

   Domain Name Service (DNS) protocol

   Network Basic Input/Output System (NetBIOS) and Windows Internet Naming Service (WINS) protocols

   Authenticated Ethernet via the 802.1X protocol

   Point-to-Point Protocol (PPP)

8. The network service order list is used to determine the primary network interface if there is more than one active interface. All network traffic that isn't better handled via local connection to an active network interface is sent to the primary network interface. Thus, all Internet traffic is sent through the primary network interface.

9. In the Network preferences, all network interfaces with a green status indicator are being used for network activities. However, again all network traffic that isn't better handled via a local connection will be sent to the primary network interface. The primary network interface is the top-most active interface in the listing.

10. Mac OS X v10.6 does not support AppleTalk.

11. Four common issues that interrupt network services on Mac OS X are:

   A disconnected network cable will cause the hardware network interface to become inactive.

   A nonfunctioning network interface port will cause the hardware network interface to become inactive.

   A DHCP service issue will prevent proper TCP/IP configuration.

   A DNS service issue will prevent host name resolution.

12. You can identify all the MAC addresses for the Mac's network interfaces from the Info pane of the Network Utility.

8

Time   This chapter takes approximately 5 hours to complete.

Goals   Connect to common network services using built-in Mac OS X network applications

Browse and access network file services using the Finder

Configure Mac OS X client computers to provide network file-sharing and web-sharing services

Use remote control tools to access other network hosts

Provide and protect network sharing and host services

Access network directory service information

Troubleshoot network shared service issues

Chapter 8

Network Services

Modern operating systems provide a wide range of network and Internet service options, but all of them share the similar basic network architecture of client software, which accesses services, and server software, which provides services. Mac OS X includes support for many popular network protocols, allowing you to connect and access a wide variety of network services.

On the other hand, perhaps one of Apple's best-kept secrets is that Mac OS X and Mac OS X Server are nearly identical operating systems. Many of the core technologies that make Mac OS X a stable and secure client operating system also make a great server operating system. In fact, Mac OS X can provide many of the same network services as Mac OS X Server. With the exception of Mac OS X Server supporting several additional advanced network services and administration tools, the two systems even share the same software for providing many network services.

The majority of this network service functionality is a result of Mac OS X's UNIX foundation, which includes extensive use of open source software. Because of this diverse foundation, your Mac should integrate well with any other modern operating system for both accessing and providing network services.

In this chapter, you will focus on using Mac OS X as both a network client and shared resource for a variety of network and Internet services. First, you will be introduced to the key network service applications built in to Mac OS X. You will then learn how Mac OS X can both access and provide sharing via popular file and web-sharing services. Next, you will discover how to access and enable a variety of network and host sharing services. You will also learn techniques for securing and troubleshooting these services. Finally, you will be introduced to the client side of Mac OS X's directory services architecture, where you will learn how to manage and troubleshoot network identification and authorization technologies.

> **NOTE ▶** This chapter assumes you have fundamental knowledge of Mac OS X–related network topics such as the Internet Protocol (IP) and the Domain Name Service (DNS). These topics are covered in Chapter 7, "Network Configuration."

Understanding Network Services

From an architectural standpoint, network services are defined by client software (designed to access the service) and server software (designed to provide the service). The network service communication between the client and server software is facilitated by commonly known network protocols or standards. By adhering to such standards, software developers can create unique yet compatible network client and server software. This allows you to choose the software tool that best fits your needs. For instance, you can use the built-in Mac OS X Mail client created by Apple to access mail services provided by software created by Sun Microsystems or Microsoft.

Network Services Software

Some client software takes the form of dedicated applications, as is the case with many Internet services like email and web browsing. Other client software is integrated into the operating system—file and print services, for example. In either case, when you establish a network service connection, settings for that service are saved on the local computer to preference files. These client preferences often include resource locations and authentication information.

On the other side of this relationship is the server software. Properly setting up server software is usually a much more complicated affair. Server administrators may spend months designing, configuring, and administering the software that provides network services. Server-side settings include configuration options, protocol settings, and account information.

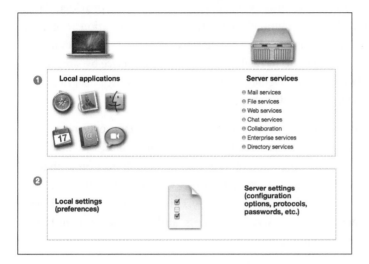

Network Services Communication

Network clients and servers, sometimes of different makes, communicate using commonly known network protocols or network standards. The distinction is that a protocol becomes a standard once it is widely adopted and ratified by a standards committee. Part of what defines a specific network protocol is which TCP or UDP ports are used for communications.

A primary feature of both the TCP and UCP transport mechanisms is the ability to handle multiple simultaneous connections and service protocols. This is accomplished by assigning each communication service to a specific port number or port range. Both TCP and UDP connection ports are defined between 0 to 65,535. For instance, the standard TCP port for web browser traffic is port 80. When troubleshooting a network service, you must know the port numbers or ranges for that service. Apple maintains a list of commonly used network services and their associated TCP or UDP ports at Knowledge Base document TS1629, "'Well Known' TCP and UDP ports used by Apple software products."

NOTE ▶ This book assumes the default port numbers and port ranges for each network service. Network administrators may choose to use a different port number than the default for testing, to "hide" a service, or to bypass router restrictions.

Network Services Identification

At a minimum, accessing a network service requires you to know the service's network location and often requires some way to prove your identity to the service provider. For some network services, you will have to manually identify the service's location with an Internet Protocol (IP) address or Domain Name Service (DNS) host name. Others feature dynamic service discovery that allows you to easily locate a network service by simply browsing from a list of available services. Details regarding dynamic network service discovery are covered in the next section of this chapter.

Once you have selected a network service to connect to, often you must prove your identity to that service provider. This process is called authentication. Successful authentication to a network service is usually the last step to establishing a connection to that service. Once a connection is established, security technologies are normally in place to ensure that you're allowed to access only certain resources. This process is called authorization. Both of these fundamental network service concepts, authentication and authorization, will be covered throughout this chapter.

Dynamic Network Service Discovery

Requiring users to manually enter network addresses to access a network service simply isn't very user-friendly. What if you were to join a new network where you don't know the exact names of all the available resources? Or what if the shared resource you need is hosted from another client computer that doesn't have a DNS host name or the same IP address every time? To address these issues, Mac OS X supports dynamic network service discovery protocols.

Dynamic network service discovery protocols allow you to browse local and wide area network resources without having to know specific service addresses. In a nutshell, network devices that are providing a service advertise their availability on the network, and clients that are looking for services request and receive this information to provide the user with a list of available network service choices. As available network resources change, or as you move your client to different networks, the service discovery protocols will dynamically update to reflect the current state of network resources.

Mac OS X makes ample use of dynamic network service discovery throughout. For example, dynamic network service discovery allows you to browse for available network file systems from the Finder and locate new network printers from the Print & Fax preferences.

Other network applications built into Mac OS X use it to locate a variety of shared resources, including iChat, Image Capture, iPhoto, iTunes, Safari, and the Mac OS X Server Admin Tools. Countless third-party network applications also take advantage of dynamic network service discovery.

It is important to remember the discovery protocol is only used to help you and the system locate the name and IP address of an available service. Once the discovery protocol provides your computer with a list of available services, their names, and their IP addresses, its job is done. When you connect to a discovered service, the Mac will establish a connection to the service using the service's native communications protocol. For example, the Bonjour protocol will provide the Mac with a list of available file services, but when you select a file server from this list the Mac will establish a connection to the server using the AFP protocol.

Mac OS X provides built-in support for the following dynamic network service discovery protocols:

▶ Bonjour on UDP port 5353—Bonjour is Apple's implementation of Zero Configuration Networking, or Zeroconf, an emerging standard that provides automatic local network configuration, naming, and service discovery. Bonjour is the primary dynamic network service discovery protocol used by Mac OS X native services and applications. Bonjour is preferred because it integrates well with other TCP/IP-based network services. Mac OS X v10.5 added support for Wide-Area Bonjour, allowing you to browse WAN resources as well as LAN resources. While local Bonjour requires no configuration, Wide-Area Bonjour requires that your Mac be configured to use a DNS server and search domain that supports the protocol. Configuring DNS is covered in Chapter 7, "Network Configuration."

   MORE INFO ▶ You can find out more about Zeroconf at www.zeroconf.org.

▶ Network Basic Input/Output System (NetBIOS) on UDP port 138 and Windows Internet Naming Service (WINS) on UDP port 137—NetBIOS and WINS are used primarily by Windows-based systems, but other operating systems have also adopted these protocols for discovering SMB-based file and print sharing services. Details regarding configuration of NetBIOS and WINS are also covered in Chapter 7, "Network Configuration."

NOTE ▶ Starting with Mac OS X v10.5 you can no longer disable Bonjour or NetBIOS/WINS from the graphical interface.

NOTE ▶ Mac OS X v10.6 no longer supports the AppleTalk network browsing protocol.

Host Network Identification

If you want to provide network services from your Mac or otherwise identify your Mac from another computer, you must configure it so that other network hosts can easily reach it. Even if you aren't providing file-sharing services from your Mac clients, if you plan to use any network administration tools, then you must have some way of identifying your Mac clients from across the network.

At a minimum your Mac can be reached by its IP address, but IP addresses are hard to remember and can change if your Mac is using DHCP. Thus, it is much more convenient for you and other network clients to locate your Mac using a network name and discovery service.

Mac OS X network identification methods include:

▶   IP address(es)—The primary network identifier for your Mac, it can always be used to establish a network connection.

▶   DNS host name—This name is hosted by a DNS server and set by administration at the DNS server. Many network clients don't have a DNS host name because of the administrative overhead required to create and update client DNS names.

▶   Computer name—This name is used by other Apple systems to identify your Mac. The computer name is part of Apple's Bonjour implementation and is set in the Sharing preferences.

▶   Bonjour name—As covered previously, Bonjour is Mac OS X's primary dynamic network discovery protocol; in addition, Bonjour provides a convenient naming system for use on a local network. The Bonjour name is usually similar to the computer name but differs in that it conforms to DNS naming standards and ends with ".local". This allows the Bonjour name to be supported by more network devices than the standard computer name, which is generally recognized only by Apple systems. This name is also set in the Sharing preferences.

▶ NetBIOS/WINS name—These are Windows' primary dynamic network discovery protocols. This name is set by either the Sharing or Network preferences.

Identifier	Example	Set by	Used by
IP address	10.1.17.2	Network preferences	Any network host
DNS hostname	client17.pretendco.com	Defined by DNS server	Any network host
Computer name	Client17	Sharing preferences	Mac systems (via Bonjour)
Bonjour name	client17.local	Sharing preferences	Any Bonjour host
NetBIOS name	CLIENT17	Network preferences	Any SMB host

Configuring Network Identification

You may be unable to control your Mac's IP address or DNS host name; the network administrator usually controls these. But as long as the Mac has properly configured TCP/IP settings as outlined in Chapter 7, "Network Configuration," your configuration is complete for these two identifiers. If your Mac has multiple IP addresses or DNS host names properly configured, it will also accept connections from those.

For dynamic network discovery protocols, though, your Mac will use network identification that can be set locally by an administrator. By default, your Mac will automatically choose a name based either on its DNS name or the name of the user created with the Setup Assistant. However, at any time an administrative user can change the Mac's network identifier from the Sharing preferences. Simply enter a name in the Computer Name field and the system will set the name for each available discovery protocol.

For example, if you enter a computer name of "My Mac", the Bonjour name will be set for "my-mac.local" and the NetBIOS/WINS name will be set for "MY_MAC". If the name you chose is already taken by another local device, the Mac will automatically append a number on the end of the name. NetBIOS/WINS may require additional configuration if your network uses multiple domains or workgroups, as covered in Chapter 7, "Network Configuration."

The local Bonjour service needs no additional configuration, but if you want to set a custom Bonjour name, click the Edit button below the Computer Name field to reveal the Local Hostname field. From this interface you can also register your Mac's identification for Wide-Area Bonjour. To do so, select the "Use dynamic global hostname" checkbox to reveal the Wide-Area Bonjour settings.

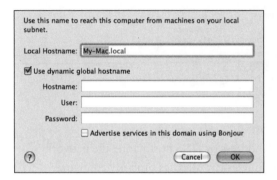

Using Network Applications

Because of the widespread adoption of the Internet protocol suite TCP/IP for nearly all LAN, WAN, and Internet communications, there really isn't any difference between how you access a "standard network service" and an "Internet service." With few exceptions, nearly all network services work the same way across a LAN as they do across the Internet. The primary difference between the two is scope of service. Services like email and instant messaging can certainly work on a local level, but these services are also designed to communicate across separate networks and between servers.

Mac OS X includes a range of client applications designed to access different network services. Although this book focuses on the network client software built into Mac OS X, many excellent third-party network clients are available for the Mac. In fact, when troubleshooting a network access problem, using an alternative network client is an excellent way to determine if the issue is specific to your primary client software.

> **MORE INFO** ▶ You can find third-party network client software at Apple's Macintosh Products Guide, http://guide.apple.com.

MORE INFO ▶ It's important to note that all of the network applications covered in this section, with the exception of iChat, can synchronize to Apple mobile devices via the iTunes application. Peripheral synchronization is covered later in Chapter 9, "Peripherals and Printing."

Safari 4 for Web Browsing

Mac OS X v10.6 includes Apple's Safari 4 web browser. Safari is an efficient and robust web browser that supports most websites. Apple has even made Safari available for the Windows operating system. However, you may find that some websites do not render properly or flat out don't work with Safari. If you are unable to access certain websites with Safari, try a third-party web browser. Several third-party web browsers are available for the Mac, including Firefox, OmniWeb, and Opera.

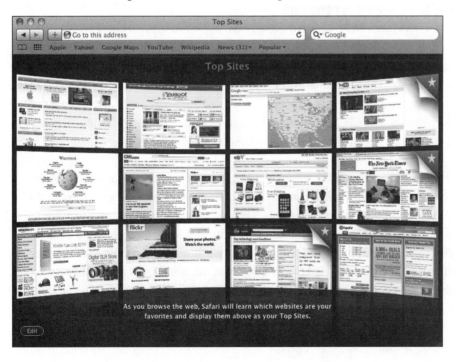

By far the most popular and ubiquitous network service, web communication is handled via the Hypertext Transfer Protocol (HTTP) using TCP port 80. Secure web communication, known by the acronym HTTPS, encrypts the HTTP protocol over a Secure Sockets Layer (SSL) connection and by default uses TCP port 443. Generally, little additional network configuration is required to use web services, as you only need to provide the web browser with the Uniform Resource Locator (URL) or web address of the resource you desire to connect to. The only exception is if you have to configure web proxies, as described in Chapter 7, "Network Configuration."

> **MORE INFO** ▶ You can find out more about Safari and download it for Windows from Apple's website, www.apple.com/safari.

Mail 4 for Email and Exchange

Mac OS X v10.6 includes Mail 4 for handling email communications along with mail-based notes and task lists. Mail supports all standard email protocols and their encrypted counterparts along with a variety of authentication standards. Also, new to Mail in Mac OS X v10.6 is support for Microsoft Exchange Server 2007.

> **NOTE** ▶ Mail in Mac OS X v10.6 requires Microsoft Exchange Server 2007 Service Pack 1 Update Rollup 4, with Outlook Web Access enabled.

With this many service options, properly configuring mail service settings can be quite daunting. Fortunately, Mail includes an account setup assistant to walk you through the process of configuring mail account settings. The assistant will even attempt to automatically determine the appropriate mail protocol security and authentication mail protocol settings. This includes support for the Autodiscovery feature of Microsoft Exchange Server 2007. Further, when you set up Mail to use Exchange, the system will automatically configure Address Book and iCal to use Exchange as well. Finally, email settings for users with MobileMe accounts will be configured automatically based on the MobileMe preferences.

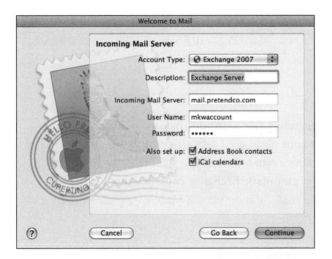

In summary, Mail 4 supports the following email services:

▶ Standard mailbox access protocols—The standard protocol used between mail clients and mail servers for receiving mail is either Post Office Protocol (POP) on TCP port 110 or Internet Message Access Protocol (IMAP) on TCP port 143. Both protocols can also be encrypted with an SSL connection. By default, encrypted POP uses TCP port 995 and encrypted IMAP uses TCP port 993. Finally, Apple's MobileMe service defaults to secure IMAP.

▶ Standard mail sending protocols—The standard protocol used for sending mail from clients to servers and from server to server is Simple Mail Transfer Protocol (SMTP) on TCP port 25. Again, SMTP can be encrypted with an SSL connection on ports 25, 465, or 587. The ports used for secure SMTP vary based on mail server function and administrator preference. Finally, Apple's MobileMe service defaults to secure SMTP.

▶ Microsoft Exchange Server 2007—Although popular, this does not use mail standards for client communication. Instead the Mail application relies on the Exchange Web Access (EWA) protocol for client communication. EWA, as its name implies, uses the standard ports for web traffic; TCP port 80 for standard transport and TCP port 443 for secure transport. Further, though the Exchange server itself uses SMTP for sending mail to other servers, the Mail client again uses the EWA protocol to send the outgoing mail message to the Exchange server.

> **MORE INFO** ▶ You can find out more about Exchange support in Mac OS X v10.6 from Knowledge Base article HT3748, "Mac OS X v10.6: Using Microsoft Exchange 2007 (EWS) accounts in Mail."

iCal 4 for Calendaring

Mac OS X v10.6 includes iCal 4 for handling calendar information. While iCal can certainly work on its own for managing your nonshared calendar information on your Mac, it also integrates with a variety of network synchronized and shared calendar services. iCal features an easy-to-use setup assistant, automatic Exchange configuration via the Mail application, and automatic MobileMe configuration via the MobileMe preferences.

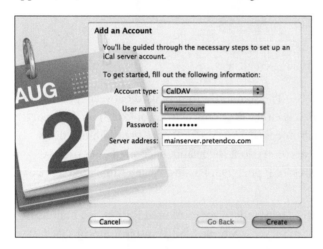

iCal 4 supports the following network calendar services:

▶ Local synchronized calendars—Calendars that are managed locally can be synchronized via the Internet to MobileMe, Yahoo, and Google calendar services. All three of these services use the encrypted HTTPS protocol over TCP port 443.

▶ Calendar web publishing and subscription— iCal allows you to share your calendar information by publishing iCalendar files to WebDAV-enabled web servers. Web-based Distributed Authoring and Versioning (WebDAV) is an extension to the HTTP protocol, so it runs over TCP port 80 or TCP port 443 if encrypted. You can also subscribe to iCalendar files hosted on WebDAV servers. Configuration is fairly easy, as accessing a shared calendar is identical to accessing a webpage. Simply provide iCal with the URL of the iCalendar file. Although calendar publishing allows you to easily share calendars one way over the web, it doesn't provide a true collaborative calendaring environment.

MORE INFO ▶ Apple hosts dozens of iCal compatible calendars at www.apple.com/ downloads/macosx/calendars.

▶ Calendar email invitation— iCal, again using iCalendar files, is integrated with Mail to automatically send and receive calendar invitations as email attachments. In this case the transport mechanism is whatever your primary mail account is configured to use. While this method isn't a widespread standard, most popular mail and calendar clients can use this method. Ultimately, this method should be used only if no dedicated collaborative calendaring system is in place.

▶ CalDAV collaborative calendaring—iCal supports an emerging calendar collaboration standard known as CalDAV. As the name implies, this standard uses WebDAV as a transport mechanism on TCP port 8008 or 8443 for encrypted, but CalDAV adds the administrative processes required to facilitate calendar and scheduling collaboration. Mac OS X Server's iCal service is based on CalDAV. Furthermore, CalDAV is being developed as an open standard so any vendor can create software that provides or connects to CalDAV services.

▶ Exchange 2007 collaborative calendaring—With the latest version of iCal, Apple included support for this popular calendar service. Again, Mac OS X's Exchange integration relies on EWA, which uses TCP port 80 for standard transport and TCP port 443 for secure transport.

Address Book 5 for Contacts

Mac OS X v10.6 includes Address Book 5 for handling contact information. Similar to iCal, while Address Book can certainly work on its own for managing nonshared contact information on your Mac, it also integrates with a variety of network synchronized and shared contact services. Again, also similar to iCal, Address Book features an easy-to-use setup assistant, automatic Exchange configuration via the Mail application, and automatic MobileMe configuration via the MobileMe preferences.

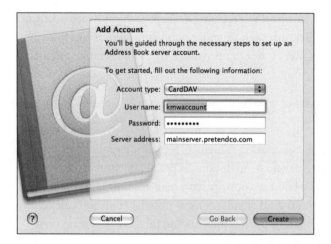

Address Book 5 supports the following network contact services:

▶ Local synchronized contacts—Contacts that are managed locally can be synchronized via the Internet to MobileMe, Yahoo, and Google contact services. All three of these services use the encrypted HTTPS protocol over TCP port 443.

▶ Directory service contacts—Address Book can search against contact databases via the standard for network directory services, the Lightweight Directory Access Protocol (LDAP). Address Book can be configured for LDAP services either directly from the setup assistant or via integration with Mac OS X's system-wide directory service, as covered later in this chapter.

▶ CardDAV contact sharing—Address Book supports an emerging calendar collaboration standard known as CardDAV. Again, as the name implies, this standard uses WebDAV as a transport mechanism on TCP port 8800 or 8843 for encrypted, but CardDAV adds the administrative processes required to facilitate contact sharing. Mac OS X Server's Address Book service is based on CardDAV. Furthermore, CardDAV is being developed as an open standard so any vendor can create software that provides or connects to CardDAV services.

▶ Exchange 2007 contact sharing—With the latest version of Address Book, Apple included support for this popular contact sharing service. Again, Mac OS X's Exchange integration relies on EWA, which uses TCP port 80 for standard transport and TCP port 443 for secure transport.

iChat 5 for Instant Messaging

Instant messaging has grown well beyond text chatting with iChat 5, included with Mac OS X v10.6. The latest iChat supports ten-way audio conferencing, four-way video conferencing, peer-to-peer file sharing, remote screen sharing, and high-resolution iChat Theater for sharing video from supported applications. iChat also features an account setup assistant that walks you through the configuration process.

NOTE ▶ iChat's advanced features, such as videoconferencing, screen sharing, and iChat Theater are not supported by many third-party chat clients. When you select a chat participant, iChat will automatically determine the client software's messaging capabilities and allow you to use only supported features.

iChat 5 supports three categories of chat services:

▶ Messaging services that are open to the public—iChat supports MobileMe, AOL Instant Messenger, and Google Talk accounts. Assuming you have already registered for an account through one of these service providers, configuring iChat simply involves entering your account name and password. Once again, MobileMe accounts will be configured automatically based on the MobileMe preferences.

▶ Privately hosted messaging services—iChat supports open source Jabber servers, including Mac OS X Server's iChat service. If your Mac is connected to a directory server that is hosting Jabber account information, iChat will be automatically configured based on those settings. Otherwise, you will have to manually enter Jabber server and account information. Jabber servers are based on the eXtensible Messaging and Presence Protocol (XMPP) that uses TCP port 5222 or 8223 for encrypted.

▶ Ad hoc messaging—iChat will use the Bonjour network discovery protocol to automatically find other iChat users. No configuration is necessary to access Bonjour messaging. Bonjour details are covered previously in the "Dynamic Network Service Discovery" section of this chapter.

iChat supports a wide variety of messaging features and instant messaging protocols—which means it uses far too many TCP and UDP ports to list here. However, Knowledge Base document HT1507, "Using iChat with a firewall or NAT router," lists all the possible ports iChat may attempt to use.

Using File-Sharing Services

There are many protocols for transferring files across networks and the Internet, but the most efficient are those designed specifically to share file systems. Network file servers can make entire file systems available to your client computer across the network. The key distinction is that client software built into Mac OS X's Finder can mount a network file service similar to mounting a locally connected storage volume. Once a network file service is mounted to the Mac, you will be able to read, write, and manipulate files and folders as if you were accessing a local file system. Additionally, access privileges to network file services are defined by the same ownership and permissions architecture used by local file systems. Details regarding file systems, ownership, and permissions are covered in Chapter 4, "File Systems."

Mac OS X provides built-in support for these network file service protocols:

▶ Apple Filing Protocol (AFP) version 3 on TCP port 548 or encrypted on TCP port 22—This is Apple's native network file service. The current version of AFP supports all the features of Apple's native file system, Mac OS X Extended.

▶ Server Message Block (SMB) on TCP ports 139 and 445—This network file service is mainly used by Windows systems, but many other platforms have adopted support for this protocol. SMB also supports many of the advanced file system features used by Mac OS X.

▶ Network File System (NFS) version 4, which may use a variety of TCP or UDP ports—Used primarily by UNIX systems and supports many advanced file system features used by Mac OS X.

▶ Web-based Distributed Authoring and Versioning (WebDAV) on TCP port 80 (HTTP) or encrypted on TCP port 443 (HTTPS)—This protocol is an extension to the common HTTP service and provides basic read/write file services.

> **TIP** Apple uses the WebDAV protocol to facilitate MobileMe iDisk services.

▶ File Transfer Protocol (FTP) on TCP ports 20 and 21 or encrypted on TCP port 989 and 990 (FTPS)—This protocol is in many ways the lowest common denominator of file systems. FTP is supported by nearly every computing platform, but it provides only the most basic of file system functionality. Further, the Finder supports only read capability for FTP or FTPS volumes.

> **NOTE** ▶ Don't confuse FTPS with another similar protocol SFTP. The distinction is that FTPS uses SSL encryption on TCP port 990 and SFTP uses SSH encryption on TCP port 22. The Finder does not support FTPS. However, both are supported at the command line.

> **NOTE** ▶ The command line includes a full FTP/FTPS client with the ftp command. Additionally, you will find several third-party FTP/FTPS clients on Apple's Macintosh Products Guide.

The Finder provides two methods for connecting to a network file system: automatically discovering shared resources by browsing to them in the Finder's Network folder or manually connecting by entering the address of the server providing the file service.

Browsing File Services

You can browse for dynamically discovered file services from two locations in the Finder. The first location is the Shared list located in the Finder's Sidebar. If enabled in the Finder preferences, the Shared list is ideal for quickly discovering computers providing file services on a small network. The Shared list will show only the first eight discovered computers providing services. If additional servers are discovered, the last item in the Shared list, All Items, is a link to the Finder's Network folder.

TIP ▶ The Finder's Shared list will also show servers that you are currently connected to even if they didn't originally appear in the Shared list.

TIP ▶ The Finder will also let you browse to screen-sharing (VNC) hosts via Bonjour, as covered later in this chapter.

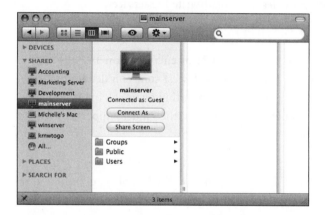

The Finder's Network folder is a special place on Mac OS X. The Network folder is not a standard folder at all; it's an amalgamation of all dynamically discovered network file services and all currently mounted file systems, including manually mounted file systems. Obviously, the Network folder is constantly changing based on information gathered from the two dynamic network service discovery protocols supported by Mac OS X—Bonjour and NetBIOS/WINS—so you can only browse AFP or SMB file services from the Network folder.

On smaller networks there may only be one level of network services. Conversely, if you have a larger network that features service discovery domains, they will appear as subfolders inside the Network folder. Each subfolder will be named by the domain it represents. Items inside the domain subfolders represent shared resources configured for that specific network area.

NOTE ▶ From the command line, the Network folder will show only file systems that were mounted by Mac OS X's automatic network file mounting system. Automatic mounts are covered in Chapter 4, "Using File Services," of *Apple Training Series: Mac OS X Server Essentials v10.6*.

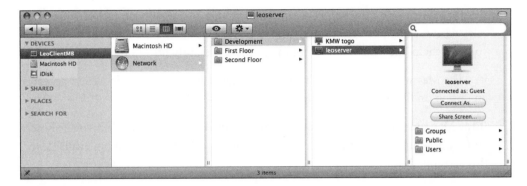

To browse and connect to an AFP or SMB file service:

1   From the Finder's Sidebar, select the computer you wish to connect to from the
    Shared list, or select a computer from the Finder's Network folder. The quickest routes
    to the Network folder are to either choose Go > Network from the menu bar or use
    the Shift-Command-K keyboard shortcut.

    Selecting a computer from either the Shared list or the Network folder will yield simi-
    lar results.

2   The moment you select a computer providing services, the Mac will attempt to auto-
    matically authenticate using one of three methods:

    ▶   If you are using Kerberos authentication, the Mac will attempt to authenticate to
    the selected computer using your Kerberos credentials. Kerberos is covered later in
    this chapter.

▶   If you are using non-Kerberos authentication but you have connected to the selected computer previously and chose to save the authentication information to your keychain, the Mac will attempt to use the saved authentication information.

▶   The Mac will attempt to authenticate as a guest user. Keep in mind guest access is an option on file servers that many administrators disable.

If the Mac succeeds in authenticating to the selected computer, the Finder will show you the account name it connected with and also list the shared volumes available to this account.

3   If the Mac was unable to automatically connect to the selected computer, or you need to authenticate with a different account, click the Connect As button to open an authentication dialog.

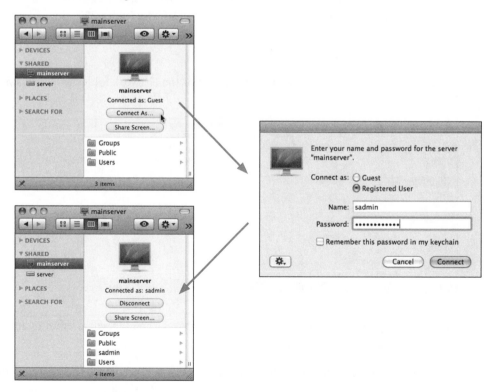

Choosing the Connect as Guest radio button will indicate that you wish to connect anonymously to the file service. Otherwise, if you have proper authentication information, enter it here. Optionally, you can select the checkbox that will save this authentication information to your login keychain.

Click the Connect button and the Mac will re-authenticate with the new account and show you a new list of shared volumes available to the account.

4   Each available shared volume will appear as a folder. Click once on a shared volume to connect and mount its file system.

5   Once the Mac has mounted the network file volume it can appear in several locations from the Finder, including the Computer location, the desktop, and the Sidebar's Shared list depending on configuration.

By default, connected network volumes will not show up on the desktop. You can change this behavior from the General tab of the Finder Preferences dialog.

TIP From the command line, mounted network volumes will appear where all other non-system volumes appear, in the /Volumes folder.

Manually Connecting File Services

To manually connect to a file service, you must specify a network identifier (URL) for the file server providing the service. You may also have to enter authentication information and choose or enter the name of a specific shared resource path. When connecting to an AFP or SMB service, you can authenticate first and then choose a shared volume. Conversely, when connecting to an NFS, WebDAV (HTTP), or FTP service you specify the shared volume or full path as part of the server address and then you authenticate if needed.

Manually Connect to AFP or SMB

To manually connect an AFP or SMB file service:

1   From the Finder, choose Go > Connect to Server from the menu bar or use the Command-K keyboard shortcut.

     This will open the Finder's Connect to Server dialog.

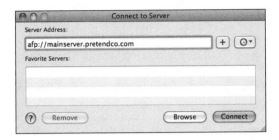

2   In the Server Address field, enter afp:// or smb:// followed by the server's IP address, DNS host name, computer name, or Bonjour name.

Click the Connect button to continue.

TIP ▶ If you don't specify a protocol, the Connect to Server dialog will default to the AFP protocol.

TIP ▶ Optionally, after the server address you can enter another slash and then the name of a specific shared volume. This will allow you to skip step 4.

3   A dialog will appear requiring you to enter authentication information.

Selecting the Connect as Guest radio button indicates that you wish to connect anonymously to the file service. Remember that guest access is an option on file servers that many administrators will disable.

If you do have proper authentication information, enter it here. Optionally, you can select the checkbox that saves this information to your login keychain.

Click the Connect button to continue.

NOTE ▶ If you are using Kerberos or you have previously saved your authentication information to a keychain, the computer will automatically authenticate for you and will not present the authentication dialog. Kerberos is covered later in this chapter.

4 You will be presented with the list of shared volumes that your account is allowed to access.

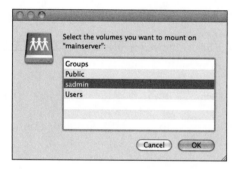

Select the volume or volumes you wish to mount. Hold down the Command key to select multiple volumes from the list.

Click the OK button to mount the selected shared volumes.

Manually Connect to NFS, WebDAV, or FTP

To manually connect an NFS, WebDAV, or FTP file service:

1 From the Finder choose Go > Connect to Server from the menu bar or use the Command-K keyboard shortcut.

The Finder's Connect to Server dialog opens.

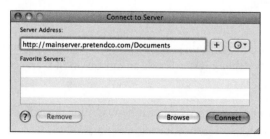

2   In the Server Address field, enter one of the following:

▶   `nfs://` followed by the server address, another slash, and then the absolute file path of the shared volume.

▶   `http://` for WebDAV (or `https://` for WebDAV encrypted via SSL), followed by the server address. Each WebDAV site only has one mountable volume, but you can optionally enter another slash and then specify a folder inside the WebDAV volume.

▶   `ftp://` (or `ftps://` for FTP encrypted via SSL) followed by the server address. FTP servers also have only one mountable root volume, but you can optionally enter another slash and then specify a folder inside the FTP volume.

Click the Connect button to continue.

TIP ▶   Clicking the Browse button in the Connect to Server dialog will bring you to the Finder's Network folder, allowing you to browse for a server, as covered in the previous section of this chapter.

3   Depending on the protocol settings, you may be presented with an authentication dialog.

NFS connections will never display an authentication dialog. The NFS protocol uses the local user that you're already logged in as for authorization purposes or Kerberos.

If you are presented with an authentication dialog, enter the appropriate authentication information here. Optionally you can select the checkbox that will save this authentication information to your login keychain.

Click the OK button to mount the shared volume.

NOTE ▶ If you are using Kerberos or you have previously saved your authentication information to a keychain, the computer will automatically authenticate for you and will not display the authentication dialog. Kerberos is covered later in this chapter.

Again, once the Mac has mounted the network file volume it can appear in several locations from the Finder, including the Computer location, the desktop, and the Sidebar's Shared list, depending on configuration. However, mounted network volumes will *always* appear at the Computer location in the Finder, accessible by choosing Go > Computer from the menu bar or by pressing Shift-Command-C. Again, you can also set Finder preferences to show mounted network volumes on the desktop and in the Sidebar's Shared list, as covered in the previous section. Finally, from the command line, mounted network volumes will appear where all other non-system volumes appear: in the /Volumes folder.

Manually entering server information every time you connect to a server is a hassle. Two features in the Connect to Server dialog make this process efficient for your users. The Connect to Server dialog maintains a history of your past server connections. You can access this history by clicking the small clock icon to the right of the Server Address field. Also, you can create a list of favorite servers in the Connect to Server dialog by clicking the plus button to the right of the Server Address field.

Managing Connected Volumes

It is important to recognize that the Mac treats mounted network volumes similarly to locally attached volumes, so you must remember to always properly unmount and eject network volumes when you are done with them. Mounted network volumes are unmounted and ejected from the Finder using the exact same techniques you would use on a locally connected volume. Unmounting and ejecting mounted volumes is covered in Chapter 4, "File Systems."

In practice, though, it's difficult for users to remember they have network volumes mounted, as there is no locally attached hardware device to remind them. Further, laptop users will often roam out of wireless network range without even thinking about what network volumes they may have mounted. If a network change or problem disconnects the Mac from a mounted network volume, the Mac will spend several minutes attempting to reconnect to the server hosting the volume. If after several minutes the Mac cannot reconnect to the server, you will see an error dialog allowing you to fully disconnect from the server.

Automatically Connecting Network Volumes

On a positive note, because the Finder treats mounted network volumes similar to other
file system items, you can save time and make life easier for you and your users by creating automatic connections to network volumes. One method is to have a network volume
mount automatically when a user logs in by adding the network volume to the user's login
items. Managing login items is covered in Chapter 2, "User Accounts."

Alternately, you can create easy-to-use shortcuts to often-used network volumes. One
method involves creating Dock shortcuts by dragging network volumes or their enclosed
items to the right side of the Dock. You can also create aliases on the user's desktop that
link to often-used network volumes or even specific items inside a network volume.
Creating aliases is covered in Chapter 5, "Data Management and Backup." Either method
you use will automatically connect to the network volume when the user selects the item.

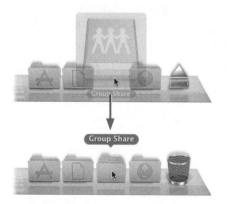

TIP ▶ Remember that by using Kerberos authentication or by saving authentication
information to the keychain you can bypass authentication dialogs as well.

Providing Network File Services

Mac OS X has built-in support for providing access via three popular file-sharing services—AFP, FTP, and SMB—along with web-sharing services via HTTP. When you enable any network service, always confirm proper configuration by testing access to the service from another computer, as covered previously in this chapter.

> **MORE INFO** ▶ Mac OS X includes support for providing NFS services, though not via the graphical interface. You can find out more about providing NFS services by reading the nfsd manual page from the command line.

Mac OS X's network file-sharing services are, for the most part, enabled and managed entirely from the Sharing preferences (choose Apple menu > System Preferences and click the Sharing preferences icon). Three primary steps are required to properly configure your Mac so other computers can access its shared file resources: setting your Mac's network identification as covered previously in this chapter, enabling the network file service, and defining access to file system resources.

> **NOTE** ▶ Users will not be able to access services on a Mac in sleep mode. You can disable your Mac's automatic sleep activation or enable automatic waking for network access from the Energy Saver preferences. Mac OS X v10.6 supports automatic wake on both wired and wireless networks if your network hardware supports it. You can find out more from Knowledge Base article HT3774, "Mac OS X v10.6: About Wake on Demand."

Enabling File Sharing

If your Mac's network identification is set up correctly, it's easy to enable AFP, FTP, and SMB file-sharing services with the default access settings.

To enable network file sharing:

1   Choose Apple menu > System Preferences, then click the Sharing icon.

2   Click the lock icon in the bottom-left corner and authenticate as an administrative user to unlock Sharing preferences.

3 Select the File Sharing checkbox to enable the AFP network file service.

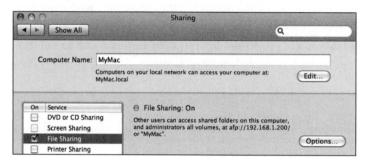

This is the only service that will be enabled by default when you select the File Sharing checkbox. The launchd control process will now listen for AFP service requests on TCP port 548, and automatically start the AppleFileServer process as necessary to handle any requests.

MORE INFO ▶ Details regarding the launchd control process are covered in Chapter 10, "System Startup."

4 To enable the FTP network file service, make sure File Sharing is selected in the Service list, and then click the Options button in the bottom-right corner of the Sharing preferences.

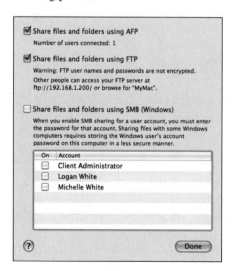

Select the "Share files and folders using FTP" checkbox in the dialog. The launchd control process will now listen for FTP service requests on TCP ports 20 and 21 and automatically start the ftpd process as necessary to handle any requests.

TIP ▶ From this dialog you can also choose to disable the AFP service if you intend to provide only FTP or SMB services. You can also view the number of connected AFP clients.

5   To enable the SMB network file service, make sure File Sharing is selected in the Service list, and then click Options.

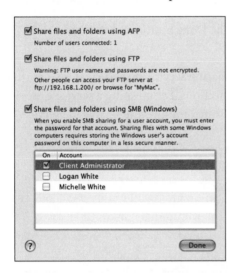

Select the "Share files and folders using SMB" checkbox. The launchd control process will now listen for SMB service requests on TCP ports 139 and 445 and automatically start the smbd process as necessary to handle any requests.

MORE INFO ▶ Mac OS X uses the open source Samba software suite to provide SMB file services. To learn how to configure custom Samba service settings, visit www.samba.org.

6 The SMB service stores passwords in a different format than the standard Mac OS X account password. Therefore, you will have to select the checkbox next to each account for which you wish to grant SMB access and reenter the password for that account.

7 Once you have made your selections, click the Done button and then close the Sharing preferences.

Now that you have enabled a network file-sharing service, if the Mac is up and running the service is actively listening for connections. Deactivating a service closes any current connections, and they remain deactivated until you re-enable the service.

NOTE ▶ Deselecting the File Sharing checkbox deactivates all network file services.

NOTE ▶ Deactivating a File Sharing service disconnects any currently active AFP and SMB connections. Only the AFP service will remind you of this and allow you to warn currently connected users that the service will soon be unavailable. Also, FTP connections will remain until you disconnect from the network or restart the Mac.

The AFP service is limited to ten simultaneous connections. All other services remain limited only by your Mac's resources. For more simultaneous connections, look at Mac OS X Server. The unlimited-client edition of Mac OS X Server does not have this restriction.

While modern Macs are able to handle many simultaneous connections and multiple services, it's not a good idea to leave these services running all the time because they can be a security risk. This is especially true for portable Macs that often connect to public wireless networks, or any time you enable Guest access.

Be especially wary of the FTP service since all transactions are in clear text. Always be aware of exactly which files and folders you are allowing others to access. Next you will cover the default access configuration and how to change access settings to better fit your needs.

Understanding File-Sharing Authorization

Enabling a network file-sharing service enables other users on the network to connect to your computer; however, they will still need to supply a username and password to make any changes to your files or to access files beyond your Public folder.

By default, both the AFP and SMB services allow others to authenticate to your Mac anonymously or as a guest user. For security reasons, anonymous FTP access is disabled by default on Mac OS X. Still, all three protocols also allow sharing, standard, and administrative users to authenticate to your Mac with their user account information. If you only want to grant known user accounts with the ability to access network file-sharing resources on your Mac, you can easily disable guest access from the Accounts preferences. Configuring user accounts was covered in Chapter 2, "User Accounts."

Once a user has been authenticated, the authorization services take over to control which files, folders, or volumes the user account is allowed to access on your Mac. File-sharing access is controlled by these three authorization settings:

▶ Default Shared Items—AFP and SMB network file services will automatically grant default access to connect and mount specific folders or volumes based on the account type. The default shared items are covered in the next section.

▶ Custom Shared Items—For AFP and SMB, you can define custom folders or volumes as shared items, sometimes called share points, on your Mac. Making a folder or volume a shared item defines it as a location that other users can connect to and mount on their network client.

▶ File System Permissions—Once users have mounted a shared item from your Mac, they will have access to files and folders inside the mounted file system based on your Mac's file system permissions settings.

Understanding Default File-Sharing Access

To keep things simple, Mac OS X uses a predefined set of file-sharing access rules for AFP and SMB services. You don't have to define a single shared item or configure any file system permissions settings to provide file-sharing services on Mac OS X. You can simply enable file sharing and users will be able to access their items based on the default file-sharing access settings. These default settings are based on user account types as defined in the Accounts preferences:

▶ Guest User—The guest user, if enabled, is normally only allowed access to other standard and administrative users' Public folders.

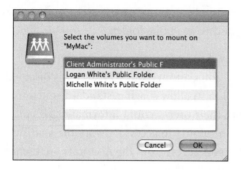

▶ Sharing User—By default, sharing users have the same access as the guest user. This allows you to disable anonymous access but still restrict certain users to Public folder access only.

▶ Standard User—Because standard users have local home folders, they will be allowed full access to their home folder contents as if they were using the Mac locally. Standard users also have access to all users' Public folders.

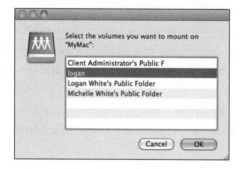

▶ Administrative User—Having full control over the Mac, administrative users can access every locally mounted volume on the shared Mac, including attached external drives and inserted optical media. Administrative users can also mount their home folder and all users' Public folders.

NOTE ▶ The exception to all these file-sharing rules applies to any FileVault user. Nothing in these user's home folders can be shared because of the FileVault encryption. However, these users will be able to connect to their home folder via file sharing, but they will have to take the additional step of authenticating and mounting their FileVault home folder disk image.

These default access settings will fulfill many users' file-sharing needs, but for those Macs that are used as full-time network file-sharing resources, these defaults are often not good enough. In the next section you will learn how to override these defaults and configure custom file-sharing access.

Customize File-Sharing Access

Earlier versions of Mac OS X provided flexibility for configuring custom file-sharing access by allowing you to edit file system permissions settings from the Finder's Get Info window. However, you could not enable additional shared folders or volumes using the built-in interface tools. Mac OS X v10.5 introduced a revamped Sharing preferences that allows you to configure custom shared folders and volumes and easily edit permissions for shared items. You can use the Finder's Get Info window to set ownership and permissions, but you can also use the Get Info window to configure custom shared folders and volumes.

Before you begin configuring custom file-sharing access, you should be aware of a few file-sharing access rules. First, administrative users will always be allowed to remotely mount any volume, and both standard and administrative users will always be allowed to remotely mount their home folders. Second, as you create new standard and administrative users, their Public folders will be automatically set as a shared item. But you can easily disable the shared setting for each Public folder separately from the Sharing preferences or the Finder's Get Info window.

Ultimately, all file-sharing access is controlled by Mac OS X's file system permissions settings. When you enable a folder or volume as a shared item, the file permissions settings dictate which users can access the shared item. For example, the Public folders' Everyone permission setting is what grants all users, including guest and sharing-only users, local and file-sharing access to the Public folders contents. So, if you want to properly configure custom file-sharing access, you must be familiar with the file system permissions architecture, as detailed in Chapter 4, "File Systems."

Custom File Sharing via Finder

To configure custom file-sharing settings from the Finder:

1 If you're setting up a new shared item, prepare the folder or volume to be shared. If you're sharing a new folder, create and name the folder with the Finder. If you're sharing a volume, be sure the volume is properly mounted and formatted as Mac OS Extended (Journeyed), as outlined in Chapter 4, "File Systems."

2 In the Finder, select the folder or volume for which you wish to configure the sharing settings, and then open the Get Info window (choose File > Get Info or press Command-I). You may have to click the General disclosure triangle to reveal the general information section.

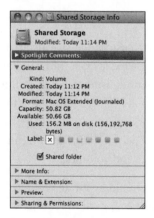

3 Select the "Shared folder" checkbox to share the selected folder or volume.

Deselecting this checkbox will stop sharing the item.

NOTE ▶ If you are not an administrative user, you'll have to authenticate with an administrative user account to enable or disable a shared item.

4   Click the Sharing & Permissions disclosure triangle.

You'll see the item's ownership and permissions settings. Click the small lock icon in the bottom-right corner of the Get Info window and authenticate as an administrative user to unlock the Sharing & Permissions section.

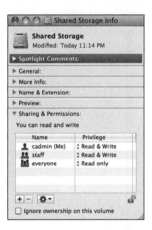

5   From the Sharing & Permissions area, you can configure custom file-sharing access settings for any number of users or groups.

Only users or groups with read access will be able to mount the shared item. Always test newly shared items using multiple account types to ensure you have configured appropriate access settings.

Custom File Sharing via the Sharing Preferences

To configure custom file-sharing settings from the Sharing preferences:

1   If you're setting up a new shared item, prepare the folder or volume to be shared.

2   Open the Sharing preferences and authenticate as an administrative user to unlock their settings.

3   Select File Sharing from the Service list to access the network file-sharing settings. The Shared Folder list will show currently shared items, including the Public folders that are shared by default.

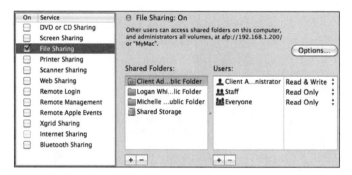

4   To share a new folder or volume, click the small plus icon at the bottom of the Shared Folders list.

A file browser dialog appears. Select the folder or volume you wish to share, then click the Add button to start sharing that item.

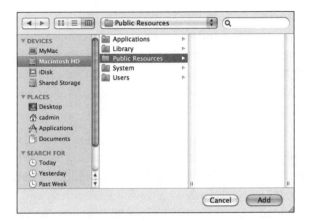

To stop sharing an item, select it from the Shared Folders list and click the small minus button at the bottom of the list.

5   Select a shared item to reveal its access settings in the Users list. The Users list is identical to the Sharing & Permissions area in the Finder's Get Info window.

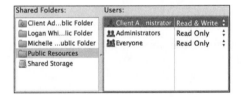

Again, only users or groups with read access will be able to mount the shared item, and you should always thoroughly test newly shared items to ensure you have configured appropriate access settings.

Understanding FTP Limitations

Mac OS X's default FTP file-sharing service configuration does not allow connections from guest or sharing-only users. The FTP service also relies on file system permissions to dictate user access. With Mac OS X, when users connect to the FTP service, they start in their home folder but can access and navigate to any other items on the Mac for which they have the appropriate file system permissions.

Apple also disabled anonymous FTP access, because it is by far the least secure file-sharing protocol available and is often exploited by malicious attackers. It's fair to say that authenticated FTP access poses an even greater security risk, since users' passwords travel across the network in an unprotected form. If security is paramount, avoid FTP entirely and instead use AFP or SMB services. Another secure alternative is the SFTP service, which is part of the SSH service covered later in the "Understanding Remote Login" section.

> **MORE INFO** ▶ Find out how to enable custom FTP service settings by reading the ftpd manual page from the command line.

Configure Web Sharing

Mac OS X also includes the Apache 2.2 web server to allow users to share web pages and files from their own systems. Apple has preconfigured the web-sharing service so that it can be enabled with literally a single click.

To enable basic web sharing:

1   Open Sharing preferences by choosing Apple menu > System Preferences and clicking the Sharing icon.

2   Click the lock icon in the bottom-left corner and authenticate as an administrative user.

3   Select the Web Sharing checkbox to enable the Apache 2.2 web service.

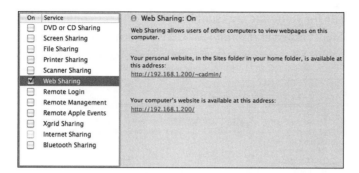

The `launchd` control process now starts the `httpd` background process, which listens for web service requests on TCP port 80.

With the web-sharing service enabled, other users can browse websites hosted from your Mac. This service is preconfigured with a main computer website and individual websites for each user who has a local home folder.

Configuring Computer Website

With web sharing enabled, you can browse to your Mac's primary computer website by entering `http://<yourmac>/`, where `<yourmac>` is your Mac's IP address, DNS host name, or Bonjour name. For example, if your Mac's IP address was 192.168.1.200 and its sharing name was My Mac, then you could enter http://192.168.1.200/ or http://my-mac.local/. If you navigate to this website with the default configuration, you will see the Apache 2.2 test page, which simply proclaims, "It Works!"

Configuring a custom website for your Mac is as simple as replacing the contents of your Mac's computer website folder (located at /Library/WebServer/Documents/). To use your own custom website, replace this folder's contents with the website resources you created.

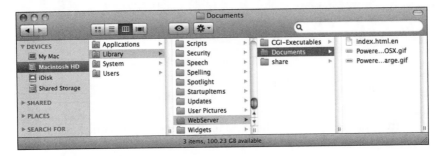

You can use any website creation tool that you like, such as iWeb or Pages, but you must keep in mind a few rules. First, the main page of your website must be named index.html. Second, you must ensure that file system permissions settings for your website files allow read access to the web server, which accesses them as a system user named "_www". The easiest way to accomplish this is to grant Everyone read access to the website items. Finally, if you want to use advanced website features such as server-side scripts or secure transfers, you have to manually enable these services from the Apache 2.2 configuration files.

> **MORE INFO** ► The Apache 2.2 web server has capabilities that go well beyond basic web sharing. To find out more, access the built-in locally hosted documentation at http://localhost/manual/, or visit the Apache web server project page at http://httpd. apache.org.

Configuring User Websites

Mac OS X's web-sharing service is also preconfigured to allow individual websites for each user with a local home folder on your Mac. You can browse to user websites by entering http://<yourmac>/~<username>/, where <yourmac> is your Mac's IP address, DNS host name, or Bonjour name, and <username> is the short name of the user account. For example, if your computer, with the sharing name of My Mac, has two user accounts with the short names of mike and debbie, then you could enter http://My-Mac.local/~mike/ or http:// My-Mac. local/~debbie/. If you navigate to this website with the default configuration, you will see the Mac OS X user test page.

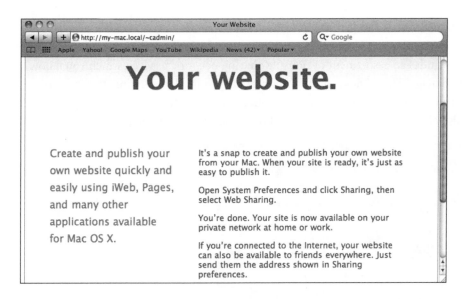

Each user's website is located inside the Sites folder within her home folder. To configure a custom website for the user, replace this folder's contents with the website resources you created. Again, you can use any website creation tools you like, and you must also follow the same website rules listed in the previous section.

Using Host-Sharing Services

In addition to the file- and web-sharing services covered in the previous section, Mac OS X includes an assortment of non-file-sharing network services, which you'll now see how to manage. These "host-sharing" services vary in implementation and purpose, but they all allow users to remotely access resources on the Mac providing the service. They are also all easily enabled and managed from the Sharing preferences.

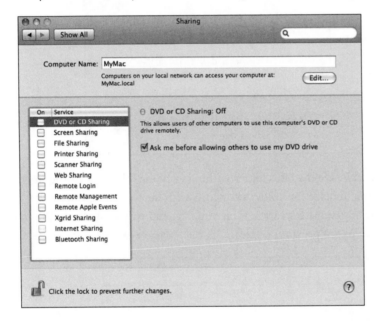

NOTE ▶ Users will not be able to access services on a Mac in sleep mode. You can disable your Mac's automatic sleep activation or enable automatic waking for network access from the Energy Saver preferences. Mac OS X v10.6 supports automatic wake on both wired and wireless networks if your network hardware supports it. You can find out more from Knowledge Base article HT3774, "Mac OS X v10.6: About Wake on Demand."

It's important to recognize the security risk involved in providing a service that allows other users to control processes on your Mac. Obviously, if you're providing a service that allows remote control and execution of software, it's certainly possible for an attacker to cause trouble. Thus, it's paramount that when you enable these types of services you choose strong security settings. Using strong passwords is a good start, but you can also configure limited access to these services from the Sharing preferences.

Mac OS X network host-sharing services include:

▶ DVD or CD Sharing (Remote Disk)—This service, also known as Remote Disk, allows you to share your Mac's optical drive via the network. It's primarily designed to let you install software for MacBook Air, which lacks a built-in optical drive. Do not confuse Remote Disk with the standard file-sharing services covered previously in this chapter. This service differs in several key respects; it shares only what is in the optical drive, you cannot configure user-specific access, and it can only be accessed via Bonjour. By enabling this service, the launchd control process starts the ODSAgent background process, which listens for Remote Disk requests on a very high randomly selected TCP port. This service can be accessed only by other Macs from the Finder's sidebar, the Migration Assistant application, or the Remote Install Mac OS X application.

MORE INFO ▶ Several Apple Knowledge Base articles contain more information about Remote Disk, including HT1131, HT1777, and HT2129.

▶ Screen Sharing—Allows remote control of your Mac's graphical interface. Using this service is covered later in this chapter.

▶ Printer Sharing— Allows network access to printers that are directly attached to your Mac. Using this service is covered in Chapter 9, "Peripherals and Printing."

▶ Scanner Sharing—Allows network access to document scanners that are directly attached to your Mac. This service only works with other Macs on a local network (Bonjour) via the Image Capture application. This service is also enabled only on a per-user basis, and available only when the user is logged in. By enabling this service, the launchd control process listens for scanner sharing requests on a very high randomly selected TCP port and starts the Image Capture Extension background process as needed to handle any requests. The only additional configuration is that you can, from the Sharing preferences, enable specific scanners if you have more than one attached.

▶ Remote Login—Allows remote control of your Mac's command line via Secure Shell (SSH). Using this service is covered later in this chapter.

▶ Remote Management—Augments the screen-sharing service to allow remote administration of your Mac via the Apple Remote Desktop 3.3 (ARD) application. Using this service is covered later in this chapter.

▶ Remote Apple Events—Allows applications and Apple Scripts on another Mac to communicate with applications and services on your Mac. This service is most often used to facilitate automated Apple Script workflows between applications running on separate Macs. By enabling this service, the `launchd` control process listens for remote Apple Events requests on TCP and UDP port 3130 and starts the `AEServer` background process as needed to handle any requests. By default, all nonguest user accounts will be allowed to access the service, but this can be limited to specific users from the Sharing preferences.

MORE INFO ▶ AppleScript is covered in Chapter 3, "Command Line and Automation."

▶ Xgrid Sharing—Allows you to join an Xgrid system, which is Apple's distributed computing solution that allows you to turn a collection of networked Macs into a supercomputer. The Xgrid software built into Mac OS X only allows your Mac to become an agent of the Xgrid system. An Xgrid agent performs tasks at the behest of an Xgrid controller, which can only be a Mac OS X Server. Further, though Xgrid is the easiest distributed computing solution to date, it is not designed for the casual user. You cannot just send any application process through the Xgrid system. At the very least, issuing jobs to Xgrid requires familiarity with the command line or that you use software designed to take advantage of the Xgrid service. By enabling this service, the `launchd` control process starts the `xgridagentd` background process, which contacts the Xgrid controller on TCP port 4111 and waits for any available jobs. Finally, to join an Xgrid system, you must configure a password on your Mac to authenticate it to the Xgrid controller.

MORE INFO ▶ You can find out more about Xgrid at www.apple.com/server/macosx/ technology/xgrid.html.

▶ Bluetooth Sharing—Allows access to your Mac via Bluetooth short-range wireless. Using this service is covered in Chapter 9, "Peripherals and Printing."

Understanding Screen Sharing

Providing remote phone support can be arduous. Inexperienced users don't know how to properly communicate the issues they are experiencing or even what they are seeing on the screen. Further, attempting to describe the steps involved in performing troubleshooting or administrative tasks to an inexperienced user over the phone is at best time consuming and at worst a painful experience for both parties.

When it comes to troubleshooting or administration, nothing beats actually seeing the computer's screen and controlling its mouse and keyboard. Mac OS X includes built-in software that allows you to view and control the graphical interface via three methods; Mac OS X screen sharing, iChat screen sharing, and Apple Remote Desktop 3.3 (ARD) remote management.

Both Mac OS X screen sharing and iChat screen sharing are included with the standard system software and their use is covered in the following sections of this chapter. However, the standard installation of Mac OS X includes only the client-side software for ARD v3.3, as the administrative side of ARD used to control other Macs is a separate purchase. Yet, screen sharing is a subset of ARD, so when you enable ARD remote management you can also enable screen sharing at the same time. In other words, you can save yourself a step by initially configuring remote management, which allows for both ARD and screen-sharing access. Thus, configuring ARD remote management is also covered later in this chapter, as it can still be used to provide basic screen sharing.

All Apple screen sharing is based on a slightly modified version of the Virtual Network Computing (VNC) protocol. The primary modification is the use of optional encryption for both viewing and controlling traffic. VNC is a cross-platform standard for remote control, so if configured properly, Mac OS X's screen-sharing technology integrates well with other third-party VNC-based systems. Thus, your Mac can control (or be controlled by) any other VNC-based software regardless of operating system.

> **NOTE ▶** Mac OS X v10.6 screen sharing is fully backward compatible with Mac OS X v10.5 screen sharing. Further, Mac OS X v10.6 computers can control older Mac OS X systems that have ARD 3.3 remote management or other VNC software enabled.

Using Mac OS X Screen Sharing

This service, as its name implies, allows users to remotely view and control a Mac's graphical interface via a network connection. Obviously, in order to access a Mac remotely via screen sharing, the remote Mac must first have the screen-sharing service enabled.

Enabling the Screen-Sharing Service

To enable the screen-sharing service:

1   Open the Sharing preferences by choosing Apple menu > System Preferences, then clicking the Sharing icon.

2 Click the lock icon in the bottom-left corner and authenticate as an administrative user to unlock the Sharing preferences.

> **NOTE ►** The screen-sharing service is part of the ARD remote management service. Thus, if Remote Management is enabled, the Screen Sharing checkbox will be inaccessible.

3 Select the Screen Sharing checkbox in the Service list to enable the screen-sharing service.

The launchd control process starts the AppleVNCServer background process, which listens for screen-sharing service requests on TCP and UDP port 5900. By default, all nonguest user accounts will be allowed to access the service.

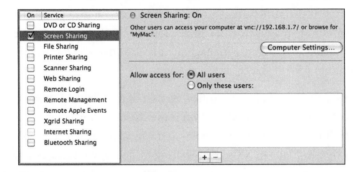

4 Optionally, to limit screen-sharing access, select the "Only these users" radio button, and then click the plus icon at the bottom of the users list.

In the dialog that appears, select the specific users or groups for whom you wish to grant screen-sharing access. You can select existing users or groups, or create a new Sharing user account by clicking the New Person button or selecting a contact from your Address Book.

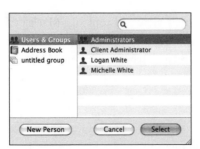

5   Optionally, to allow a wider range of users to access your Mac's screen-sharing service, click the Computer Settings button. Enable guest and VNC screen-sharing access
in the resulting dialog.

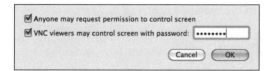

Select the top checkbox to allow anyone (from another Mac) to ask permission to
share the screen. When attempting to access your Mac's screen sharing, the currently
logged-in user must authorize the session.

Standard third-party VNC viewers cannot authenticate using the secure methods
employed by screen sharing, so you must set a specific password for VNC access.
Remember that all standard VNC traffic is unencrypted.

Control Another Computer via Screen Sharing

The process to connect to and control another computer for screen sharing is similar to
how you connect to a shared file system. From the Finder you can connect to another
computer for screen sharing by either browsing to the computer from the Shared list or
Network folder, or you can manually enter its network address in the Connect to Server
dialog. The latter method will also allow you to connect and control any host providing
standard VNC services.

NOTE ▶ Browsing for screen-sharing computers works only for Bonjour-
compatible clients.

To control the graphical interface of another computer with screen sharing, ARD 3 remote
management, or VNC enabled:

1   From the Finder initiate a connection to the computer you wish to control using one
of two methods:

▶   Browse to and select the computer from the Finder Sidebar's Shared list, or select
the computer from the Finder's Network folder. Then click the Share Screen button
to continue.

▶ In the Finder's Connect to Server dialog, enter vnc:// followed by the computer's IP address, DNS host name, or Bonjour name. Then click the Connect button to continue.

The Mac will automatically open the /System/Library/CoreServices/Screen Sharing application and initiate a connection to the specified host.

2 You are presented with a dialog where you must enter the authentication information. Optionally, you can select the checkbox that will save this information to your login keychain.

NOTE ▶ If you are using Kerberos or you have previously saved your authentication information to a keychain, the computer will automatically authenticate for you and will not present the authentication dialog.

3   Click the Connect button to continue. The Screen Sharing application will establish a connection to the other computer.

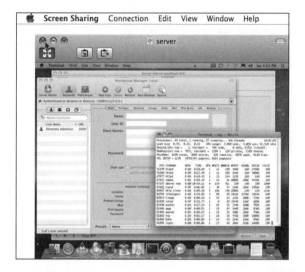

A new window opens, titled with the controlled computer's name, showing a live view of the controlled computer's screen(s). Any time this window is active, all keyboard entries and mouse movements will be sent to the controlled computer.

For example, using the Command-Q keyboard shortcut will quit the active application on the computer being controlled. Thus, in order to quit the Screen Sharing application you have to click the close (X) button at the top-left corner of the window.

TIP ▶ Click the toolbar button in the top right hand corner of the window to reveal additional screen-sharing features, including the ability to copy and paste between your Mac and the remote Mac.

While using the Screen Sharing application, be sure to check out the preference options by choosing Screen Sharing > Preferences from the menu bar. Use these preferences to adjust screen size, encryption, and quality settings. If you are experiencing slow performance, adjust these settings for fastest performance. Keep in mind that some network connections, such as crowded wireless or dial-up connections, are so slow that these preferences won't matter much and you will simply have to wait for the screen to redraw.

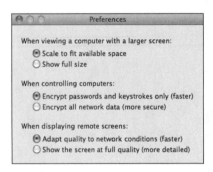

Using iChat 5 Screen Sharing

The included iChat 5 instant messaging application can be used to initiate screen sharing, and as an added bonus will simultaneously provide voice chat services between the administrator Mac and the controlled Mac. iChat screen sharing also makes it much easier to locate other Macs to control, as iChat will automatically resolve the location of remote computers based on your active chats or available buddies. Further, iChat also supports reverse screen sharing—the administrator Mac can push its screen to display on another Mac for demonstration purposes.

> **NOTE** ▶ iChat does not require either Mac to have screen sharing enabled in the Sharing preferences because iChat includes a quick and easy authorization process to initiate each screen-sharing session.

> **NOTE** ▶ iChat 5's screen-sharing feature is only compatible with other Macs running iChat 4 or iChat 5. When you select chat participants, iChat will automatically determine if their computer is using a compatible version of iChat.

To initiate an iChat screen-sharing session:

1   From iChat, select an available chat user from a buddy list and then click the screen-sharing button at the bottom of the buddy list.

   This opens the screen-sharing pop-up menu, where you can choose "Share My Screen with <chatuser>" or "Ask to Share <chatuser>'s Screen," where <chatuser> is the name of the user whose machine you are asking to control.

2   The user on the other computer will see an authorization dialog where he can choose to accept or decline your request to share screens.

3   If the other user clicks the Allow button, the screen-sharing session will begin. The following screen capture shows the screen-sharing "controller's" point of view. The other user will see the same screen without the small My Computer window in the bottom-left corner.

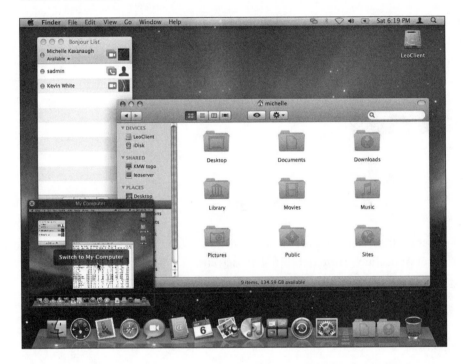

Further, if both computers support voice chat, iChat will automatically start a voice chat session between the two computers. You may need to configure Audio/Video settings in the iChat preferences for this feature to work properly.

4   Both users will have simultaneous control of the Mac being shared, including the ability to end the screen-sharing session at any time from the screen-sharing menu item on the right side of the menu bar.

NOTE ▶ Even as an administrative user, you cannot force other users to share screens using iChat; they have the sole power to allow or deny your request. However, with Finder-initiated screen sharing, any user or group in the allowed access list can force a screen-sharing connection.

Understanding Remote Login

Mac OS X includes support for command line remote login via the Secure Shell (SSH) protocol, which by default runs on TCP port 22. Apple's implementation of remote login is based on the popular OpenSSH project, and defaults to the more secure SSH version 2 standard. OpenSSH provides a robust and secure environment for remotely accessing the command line of another network host.

With graphical interface screen sharing so readily accessible in Mac OS X, you may wonder why the ability to remotely log in to the command line is still relevant. After all, if you need to remotely access another Mac's command line you can always use screen sharing to open and control the Terminal application on the remote Mac. Well, aside from screen sharing being a bandwidth hog, there are many uses for remote login and SSH that remote screen sharing does not provide.

For starters, using remote login is much more efficient than screen sharing because only text is transmitted. Often, remote login is so fast that it's indistinguishable from using the command line on a local computer. From an administration standpoint, remote login is a much more subtle approach for remote management, as users logged in to the graphical interface can't tell that someone has remotely logged in to their Mac's command line. So as an administrative user, you can remotely log in to a Mac and resolve an issue from the command line without the user even knowing you were there. Even if the Mac is sitting idle at the login window, you can still remotely log in to the command line and take care of business.

Aside from providing a secure network connection for remote login, the SSH protocol can also provide secure connections for any other network protocol. You can use SSH to create an encrypted tunnel between two SSH-enabled network devices and then pipe any other TCP- or UDP-based network protocol through the SSH connection. Further, SSH remote login allows you to securely transfer files using Secure File Transfer Protocol (SFTP) or the secure copy command scp.

Finally, because SSH is a network standard, it's compatible across many platforms. In other words, your Mac can securely log in remotely via the command line to any compatible network host with SHH enabled. Conversely, any systems with a command line prompt and SSH client software can securely log in remotely to your Mac.

> **MORE INFO** ▶ As with any command-line tool, you can learn more about SSH by reading the ssh manual page.

Using Remote Login (SSH)

This service, as its name implies, allows users to remotely log in to your Mac's command line via an SSH network connection. Obviously, in order to access a Mac via remote login, the remote Mac must first have the remote login service enabled.

NOTE ▶ If you aren't already comfortable with navigation in the UNIX command line, then it's strongly recommended that you study the command-line concepts in Chapter 3, "Command Line and Automation," before reading the remainder of this section.

Enabling the Remote Login (SSH) Service

To enable the Remote Login service:

1 Open the Sharing preferences and authenticate as an administrative user to unlock the preferences.

2 Select the Remote Login checkbox in the Service list to enable the SSH Remote Login service.

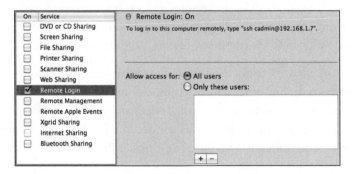

The launchd control process listens for remote login service requests on TCP 22 and starts the sshd background process as needed to handle any requests. By default, all standard and administrative user accounts will be allowed to access the service.

3 Optionally, to limit remote login access, select "Only these users" and click the plus icon. In the resulting dialog, select the standard users, administrative users, or groups for whom you wish to grant access.

TIP Enabling the Remote Login service also enables the SFTP service, a secure version of the FTP protocol, and allows for use of the remote secure copy command, scp.

Control Another Host via SSH

The primary interface for SSH is the ssh command. The syntax for initiating a remote login connection is ssh followed by the name of the user you will be logging in as, then the @ symbol, and then the address or host name of the computer you wish to log in to. If you're logging in to a computer for the first time using SSH with standard password authentication, you'll be prompted to trust the authenticity of the remote host. If a network administrator has given you a public key file for authentication, you won't have to enter a user password.

TIP From the Terminal you can also browse for ssh hosts by choosing Shell > New Remote Connection from the menu.

In the following example, Michelle starts off at the command line on a Mac named "client." She issues the ssh command to connect to the "server.pretendco.com" Mac using the user name "sadmin." She has never established an SSH connection between these two computers, so she is asked if she wants to trust the authenticity of the "server" computer. In most cases, the answer to this question is "yes." Michelle then enters the sadmin user's password, but note that it is never shown onscreen.

Notice how the command prompt changes to show that Michelle is using the "server" computer. Using the command line remotely via SSH is nearly indistinguishable from using it locally. Michelle issues the who command on "server" to see who is currently using that computer. You can see that a user has logged in to the graphical interface, "console," also using the sadmin account, and you can see Michelle's SSH connection, "ttys000." Finally, in this example, Michelle logs out and closes the SSH connection by issuing the exit command.

```
client:~ michelle$ ssh sadmin@server.pretendco.com
The authenticity of host 'server.pretendco.com (10.0.1.200)' can't be established.
RSA key fingerprint is bd:34:8c:1e:c6:bf:9a:46:e9:2a:b1:cc:81:7c:a3:02.
Are you sure you want to continue connecting (yes/no)? yes
Warning: Permanently added 'server.pretendco.com,10.0.1.200' (RSA) to the list of
known hosts.
Password:
Last login: Sat Oct 6 18:19:09 2009
server:~ sadmin$ who
sadmin console Oct 2 11:57
sadmin ttys000 Oct 6 22:13 (client.pretendco.com)
server:~ sadmin$ exit
logout
Connection to server.pretendco.com closed.
client:~ michelle$
```

TIP ▶ The OpenSSH software includes a secure copy command, scp, and a secure FPT client, sftp. These commands can be used to securely transfer files to and from a Mac with remote login enabled.

Enable ARD Remote Management

The Remote Management service is client-side software that allows the Apple Remote Desktop 3.3 (ARD) administration tool to access your Mac. ARD is the ultimate remote management tool for Mac OS X computers. In addition to screen sharing, ARD allows administrators to remotely gather system information and usage statistics, change settings, add or remove files and software, send UNIX commands, and perform nearly any other management task you can think of. The real power of ARD is that you can execute all these tasks simultaneously on dozens of Macs with just a few clicks. Again, if you plan to use ARD in the future, but you want to enable screen sharing for now, you can enable Remote Management in one step and take advantage of both remote control features.

MORE INFO ▶ The Apple Remote Desktop 3.3 (ARD) administration software provides advanced functionality that goes well beyond simple screen sharing. You can find out more about ARD at www.apple.com/remotedesktop.

To enable the ARD Remote Management service:

1 Open the Sharing preferences and authenticate as an administrative user to unlock the preferences.

2 Select the Remote Management checkbox in the Service list to enable both screen sharing and the ARD client-side services.

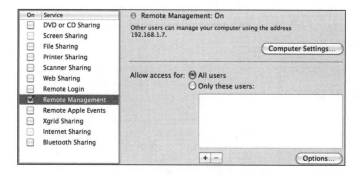

The launchd control process starts the ARDAgent background process which listens for incoming administration requests on UDP port 3283, and also starts AppleVNCServer which listens for screen-sharing requests on TCP port 5900.

NOTE ▶ The screen-sharing service is part of the ARD remote management service. Thus, if Remote Management is enabled, the Screen Sharing checkbox will be inaccessible.

3   If this is the first time you have enabled remote management, you'll see a dialog that allows you to select the ARD options you wish to allow for all nonguest local users. You can individually select options, or you can hold down the Option key and then select any checkbox to enable all options. Click OK once you have made your selections.

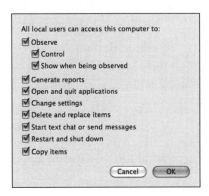

4   Optionally, to further limit ARD access, select "Only these users" and click the plus icon.

Then select a standard or administrative local user for whom you wish to grant ARD access. When you're done, another dialog appears, from which you select the ARD options this user can access.

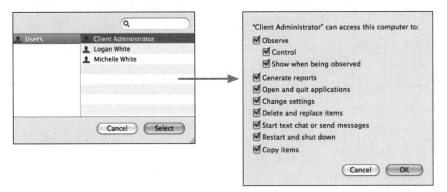

You can edit a user's ARD options at any time by double-clicking that user's name in the user access list.

5   Additional optional ARD computer options are available by clicking the Computer Settings button.

This opens a dialog that allows you to enable guest and VNC screen-sharing access (covered earlier in this chapter) and the Remote Management menu bar item that allows users to request help from administrators, and add any additional information to help identify this particular Mac.

```
☑ Show Remote Management status in menu bar
☐ Anyone may request permission to control screen
☐ VNC viewers may control screen with password: [          ]

Computer Information
These fields are displayed in the System Overview Report.

Info 1: [Room 245        ]      Info 3: [              ]
Info 2: [                ]      Info 4: [              ]

                            ( Cancel )  ( OK )
```

Sharing an Internet Connection

Mac OS X includes the Internet Sharing service, which can "reshare" a single network or Internet connection to any other network interface. Suppose you're traveling with a portable Mac that can obtain an Internet connection using a wireless broadband service, but your travel companions' computers have no such service. You can share your Mac's wireless broadband service via your Mac's AirPort and turn your Mac into a wireless access point for the other computers.

When you enable the Internet Sharing service, the launchd process starts several background processes to facilitate these additional network services:

▶   InternetSharing—Manages the Internet Sharing service as a whole.

▶   natd—Performs the Network Address Translation (NAT) service that allows multiple network clients to share a single network or Internet connection.

▶   bootpd—Provides the DHCP automatic network configuration service for the network devices connected via your Mac. When a network device connects to your Mac's shared network connection, it will automatically obtain an IP address, usually in the 10.0.2.X range.

▶ named—Provides DNS services for network devices connected via your Mac. It's responsible for forwarding requests between these network devices and your Mac's primary DNS server.

Configure and Enable Internet Sharing

To enable the Internet Sharing service:

1 Configure your Mac's primary network connection to the Internet as outlined in Chapter 7, "Network Configuration."

You need not configure the network settings for the interface that the other network devices will connect to, but you should connect any wired network interfaces at this point.

NOTE ▶ You can only reshare a network or Internet connection to devices connected via your Mac's wired Ethernet, wireless Ethernet (AirPort), or FireWire interfaces.

2 Select the Internet Sharing item in the Service list, but do not select the Internet Sharing checkbox until you configure the service settings.

3 Select the interface you wish to share from the pop-up menu. In most cases this will be your Mac's primary connection to the Internet. It can be any active network connection.

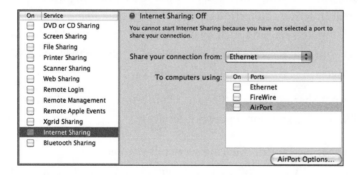

4 Select the checkboxes next to the network interfaces that other network devices will use to access your Mac's shared network.

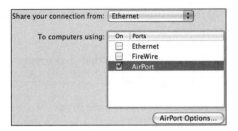

NOTE ▶ It's a bad idea to select the checkbox next to the same interface that you are sharing from—this means that your Mac will be resharing an interface back onto itself. Fortunately, the system will present you with a warning dialog if you attempt to choose this potentially bad configuration. Further, Internet Sharing will automatically shut off if it detects DHCP services on any of the networks you are attempting to share to.

5 If you are sharing to an AirPort wireless Ethernet network, click the AirPort Options button to reveal these settings.

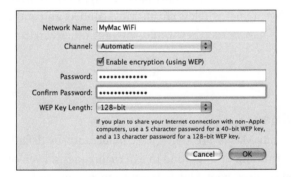

At a minimum you'll need to choose a network name so others know how to connect to your wireless service, but you should leave the wireless channel setting on Automatic for the best performance. It's also strongly recommended that you enable Wired Equivalent Privacy (WEP) encryption and set a password to protect your wireless Ethernet network. Further, choose 128-bit from the WEP Key Length pop-up menu—it's slightly more secure, and nearly all wireless Ethernet cards support this higher standard.

Click OK after you have configured your wireless Ethernet network.

6 Once you have configured all the Internet Sharing settings, select the checkbox next to Internet Sharing in the Service list to enable the service.

You'll see a warning dialog reminding you of the potential issues that may arise should you improperly configure the Internet Sharing service.

Click the Start button only if you're absolutely certain that you have properly configured the Internet Sharing settings.

7 If you're resharing to your Mac's AirPort wireless interface, the AirPort menu item changes appearance to indicate that you're sharing the interface.

8 Other wired Ethernet and FireWire network clients only have to physically connect to your Mac's shared network interface. Other wireless clients must connect and authenticate to your Mac's shared wireless network as they would with any other wireless access point.

Securing Network Services

From a network services standpoint, your Mac is already very secure because, by default, there are only a few essential services running that respond to external requests. Even once you start providing individual shared services, your Mac is designed to respond only to those services that are enabled. Further, services that could cause trouble if compromised, like file or screen sharing, can be configured to have limited access authorization, as covered previously in this chapter. Still, users can open third-party applications or background services that could leave a Mac vulnerable to a network attack.

TIP To maintain a high level of network security, you should leave sharing services disabled unless absolutely necessary. If you do enable sharing services, be sure to limit authorization access as best you can.

Understanding the Mac OS X Personal Application Firewall

The most common method to secure network services is to configure a firewall, which will block unauthorized network service access. Most networks use a firewall to limit inbound traffic from an Internet connection. In fact, most personal routers, like AirPort base stations, are by design also network firewalls. While network-level firewalls will block unauthorized Internet traffic into your network, they will not block traffic that originated from inside your network to your Mac. Also, if your Mac is mobile and is often joining new networks, odds are that every new network you join will have different firewall rules.

Thus, to prevent unauthorized network services from allowing incoming connections to your specific Mac, you can enable the built-in personal application firewall. A personal firewall will block unauthorized connections to your Mac no matter where they originated. The Mac OS X firewall also features a single click configuration that provides a high level of network service security, which will work for most users.

A standard firewall uses rules based on service port numbers. As you've learned previously in this lesson each service defaults to a standard port or set of ports. However, some network services, like iChatAgent (a background process that receives incoming connections for iChat), use a wide range of dynamic ports. If we were to manually configure a traditional firewall, we would have to make dozens of rules for every potential port that the user may need.

To resolve this issue, Mac OS X's firewall uses an adaptive technology that allows connections based on applications and service needs, without you having to know the specific ports they use. For example, you can authorize iChatAgent to accept any incoming connection without configuring all of the individual TCP and UDP ports used by the iChatAgent application.

> **TIP** A more traditional port-based firewall, `ipfw`, is still in place on Mac OS X and can be configured from the command line or the `ipfw` configuration files if that's your preferred method.

The Mac OS X firewall also leverages another built-in feature, code signing, to ensure that allowed applications and services aren't changed without you knowing. Further, code signing allows Apple and third-party developers to provide a guarantee that their software hasn't been tampered with. This level of verifiable trust allows you to configure the Mac OS X firewall in default mode with a single click, which will automatically allow signed applications and services to receive incoming connections.

Finally, because the Mac OS X firewall is fully dynamic it will open only the necessary ports when the application or service is running. Again, using iChatAgent as an example, the Mac OS X firewall will allow only incoming connections to the required ports if the iChatAgent application is running. If the application quits because the user logs out, the firewall will close the associated ports. Having the required ports open only when an application or service needs them provides an extra layer of security not found with traditional firewalls.

Configure the Mac OS X Firewall

To enable and configure the Mac OS X personal application firewall:

1   Open Security preferences by choosing Apple menu > System Preferences, then clicking the Security icon.

2   Click the lock icon in the bottom-left corner and authenticate as an administrative user to unlock Sharing preferences.

3   Select the Firewall tab at the top, and then click the start button to turn on the Mac OS X personal application firewall using the default rules.

     Once enabled, the Start button changes to a Stop button, allowing you to disable the firewall.

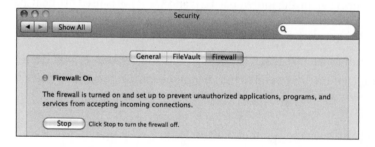

The default configuration is to allow incoming traffic for established connections (connections that were initiated from your Mac and are expecting a return) and for any signed software or enabled service. This level of security is adequate for most users.

> **TIP** ▶ Firewall logging is always enabled and can be viewed from the Console application. The firewall log is located at /private/var/log/appfirewall.log.

4   If you want to customize the firewall, any additional firewall configuration is revealed by clicking the Advanced button.

From the Advanced dialog you can see which services are currently being allowed. Without any additional configuration, sharing services enabled from the Sharing preferences will automatically appear in the list of allowed services.

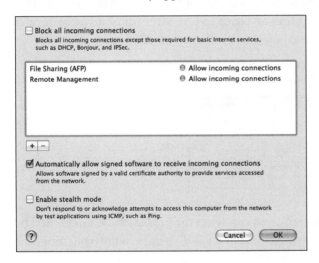

5   Optionally, for a bit more control you can manually set which applications and services the firewall allows by deselecting the checkbox to automatically allow signed software.

With this firewall choice, as you open new network applications for the first time or update existing network applications, you will see a dialog where you can allow or deny the new network application. This dialog will appear outside the Security preferences any time a new network application requests incoming access.

6   If you are manually setting network application and service firewall access, you can always return to the Advanced firewall dialog to review the list of items, and either delete items from the list or even specifically disallow certain items.

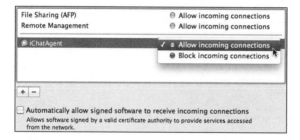

7   Optionally, for a bit more security, you can select the Enable stealth mode checkbox to prevent response or acknowledgement of a failed attempt to the requesting host.

With this enabled, your Mac will not respond to any unauthorized network connections, including network diagnostic protocols like ping, traceroute, and port scan. In other words, your computer will simply ignore the request instead of returning a response of failure to the requesting host.

However, your Mac will still respond to other services that are allowed. This includes by default, Bonjour, which will dutifully announce your Mac presence, thus preventing your Mac from being truly hidden on the network.

8 Optionally, when the utmost security is needed, you can select the "Block all incoming connections" checkbox. Notice that selecting this option also automatically selects stealth mode as well.

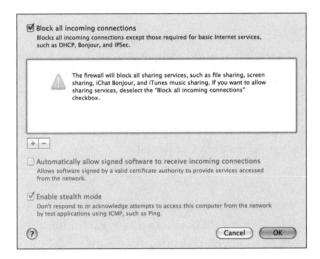

With this enabled, your Mac will not respond to any incoming network connections except for those required for basic network services or established connections, such as those needed to browse the web or check email. Obviously, this will prevent any shared service or application hosted on your Mac from working remotely.

Troubleshooting Network Services

To effectively troubleshoot a network issue you must isolate the issue into one of three categories: local, network, or service. Most issues involving failure to access network services will probably fall under the service category. This means that you should probably focus most of your efforts toward troubleshooting the specific service that you're having issues with.

However, before digging too deep into troubleshooting the specific network service, quickly check for general network issues. First, check to see if other network services are working. Opening a web browser and navigating to a few different local and Internet websites is always a good general network connectivity test. To be thorough, also test other network services, or test from other computers on the same network. If you're experiencing problems connecting to a file server but you can connect to web servers, chances are your TCP/IP configuration is fine, and you should concentrate on the specifics of the file server. If you're only experiencing problems with one particular service, you probably don't have local or network issues and you should focus your efforts on troubleshooting just that service.

Conversely, if other network clients or services aren't working either, your issue is likely related to local or network issues. Double-check local network settings to ensure proper configuration from both the Network preferences and Network Utility. If you find that other computers aren't working, you might have a widespread network issue that goes beyond troubleshooting the client computers. For more information, general network troubleshooting was detailed in Chapter 7, "Network Configuration."

Using Network Port Scan

Once you decide to focus on troubleshooting a problematic network service, one of your most important diagnostic tools will be the network port scan utility. Part of the Network Utility application, port scan will scan for any open network service ports on the specified network address. As covered earlier in this chapter, network service protocols are tied to specific TCP and UDP network ports. Network devices providing a service must leave the appropriate network ports open in order to accept incoming connections from other network clients. A port scan will reveal if the required ports are indeed open. If the ports aren't open, that device is either not providing the expected service or is configured to provide the service in a nonstandard method. Either way, this indicates that the issue lies with the device providing the service, not your Mac.

> **NOTE** ▶ Network administrators view repeated network pings and broad port scans as a threat. Thus, some network devices are configured to not respond even when working properly. In general you should avoid excessive network pinging and scanning an unnecessarily broad range of ports when testing others' servers.

To use network port scan:

1 Open /Applications/Utilities/Network Utility and click the Ping tab at the top.

Before performing a port scan, check for basic network connectivity by attempting to ping the device that is supposed to be providing the service. Enter the device's network address or host name and click the Ping button.

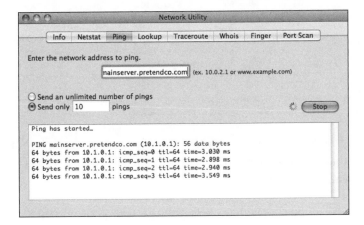

If the ping is successful, it should return with the amount of time it took for the ping to travel to the network device and then return. Assuming you have network connectivity to the other device, continue to the next step.

2 Click the Port Scan tab at the top of the Network Utility window.

Again, enter the network address or host name of the device that is supposed to be providing the service.

3 If you're only troubleshooting a specific service, limit the port scan to just that service's default ports, by selecting the appropriate checkbox and entering a beginning and ending port range.

There are 65,535 available TCP and UDP network ports, so a full port scan is unnecessary and can take some time. Even if you don't know the specific port, most common ports are between 0 and 1024.

4   Click the Scan button to initiate the port scan process.

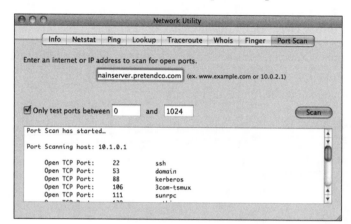

Depending on the scan range you chose, it may take several minutes to complete the scan. Any open ports that were discovered will be listed along with the associated network protocol if known.

NOTE ▶ There are some inaccuracies with the protocol reporting of the port scan feature. For example port 106 (listed as 3com-tsmux) is actually the Mac OS X Password Server and port 625 (listed as dec_dlm) is actually the directory service proxy.

Troubleshooting Network Applications

Aside from general network service troubleshooting, there are a few application-specific troubleshooting techniques you can try. First, double-check any application-specific configuration and preference settings. It takes only a few moments, and you may find that users have inadvertently caused the problem by changing a setting they shouldn't have.

Be aware of these specifics when troubleshooting network applications:

▶   Safari—Safari is a good web browser, but it's not perfect. There are certain webpages that Safari just can't get right. The only resolution is to try a different web browser. Several third-party web browsers are available for the Mac, including popular alternatives like Firefox, OmniWeb, and Opera.

▶ Mail—Improper mail account configuration settings are the most common cause of Mail application issues. Fortunately, the Mail application includes a built-in account diagnostic tool called the Mail Connection Doctor that will attempt to establish a connection with all configured incoming and outgoing mail servers. To open the Mail Connection Doctor, choose Window > Connection Doctor within the Mail application. If a problem is found a suggested resolution will be offered, but for a more detailed diagnostic view click the Show Detail button to reveal the progress log and then click the Check Again button to rerun the tests.

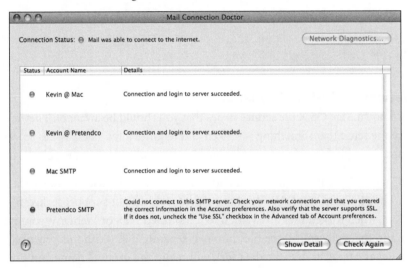

TIP Apple also provides an online mail setup assistant database that may help you identify mail client configuration issues, www.apple.com/support/macosx/mailassistant.

▶ iChat—iChat also suffers from occasional improper account configuration, but it's a less frequent occurrence than with the Mail application. More often iChat suffers from connectivity issues when attempting advanced messaging features like voice and videoconferencing. As such, iChat also features a Connection Doctor that will let you view conference statistics, chat capabilities, and the iChat error log. To open the iChat Connection Doctor, within the iChat application choose Video > Connection Doctor.

If you have experienced recent errors the Connection Doctor will open to the error log, but you can view other information from the Show pop-up menu.

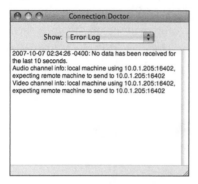

Specific Network File-Sharing Issues

There are a few known Mac OS X file service issues that you should be aware of. They aren't software bugs in the sense that something is broken and requires a fix. These issues represent compatibility and design choices that are intentional but may still cause you problems.

As covered in Chapter 5, "Data Management and Backup," Mac files use separate data and resource forks. The NFS and WebDAV file-sharing protocols do not support forked files of this type. Thus, when forked files are written to a mounted NFS or WebDAV volume, Mac OS X will automatically split these files into two separate files. With this practice, commonly known as AppleDouble, the data fork will retain the original name, but the resource fork will be saved with a period and underscore before the original name. The Finder will recognize these split files and show only a single file to the user. However, users on other operating systems will see two separate files and may have trouble accessing the appropriate file.

You may encounter another issue when trying to access an AFP network volume from a Windows file server. Windows servers include Services for Macintosh (SFM), which provides only the legacy AFP 2 file service. Mac OS X is still compatible with AFP 2 but is optimized for AFP 3.1. There are many known performance issues with AFP 2, so you should avoid it at all costs. Ideally, you should use a Mac OS X Server to provide AFP services for your network. However, if you must keep the Windows file server, you can add AFP 3.1 support by installing Group Logic's ExtremeZ-IP (www.grouplogic.com).

Also remember that Mac OS X v10.6 clients include a robust SMB client that will natively connect to your Windows server with a high degree of reliability and performance.

Troubleshooting Shared Services

If you're providing a shared service from your Mac, and others are having trouble reaching it, you must first consider how established the service is to determine where to focus your efforts. So, if your Mac has been reliably providing a shared service for a while but now a single client computer has trouble accessing the service, troubleshoot the client computer before troubleshooting your shared Mac.

Otherwise, if multiple clients cannot access your shared Mac, you may indeed have an issue with the sharing service. After ruling out other potential local client and network issues, you can safely assume that the problem lies with the Mac providing shared services. If so, shared network service issues fall into two general categories: service communication or service access.

Service communication issues are manifested by an inability to establish a connection to the shared service. Keep in mind that if you are presented with an authentication dialog, the client and server are establishing a proper connection and you should troubleshoot the issue as a service access issue. However, if you are unable to authenticate, or you can authenticate but you're not authorized to access the service, then you are experiencing a service access issue.

Network Service Communication Issues

If you are unable to establish a connection to the shared service, this may signal a network service communication issue.

To troubleshoot service communication issues:

▶ Double-check the shared Mac's network configuration—From the Network preferences, make sure the Mac's network interfaces are active and configured with the appropriate TCP/IP settings. You can also use Network Utility to verify the network configuration. If a DNS server is providing a host name for your shared Mac, use the Lookup tool in Network Utility to verify the host name.

▶ Double-check the Mac's sharing service configuration—From the Sharing preferences, verify the Mac's sharing name and ensure that the appropriate services are enabled and configured.

▶ Double-check the Mac's firewall configuration—From the Security preferences, first temporarily stop the firewall to see if disabling it makes a difference. If you are able to establish a connection, adjust the list of allowed services and applications before you restart the firewall.

▶ Check for basic network connectivity to the shared Mac—First, turn off the firewall's stealth mode, and then from another Mac use Network Utility's Ping tool to check for basic connectivity to the shared Mac. If you can't ping the shared Mac, you're probably having a network-level issue that goes beyond service troubleshooting.

▶ Check for network service port connectivity to the shared Mac—First, turn off the firewall's stealth mode, and then from another Mac use Network Utility's Port Scan tool to verify whether the expected network service ports are accessible. If the shared Mac is configured properly, the appropriate network service ports should register as open. If network routers exist between the network clients and the shared Mac, consider the possibility that a network administrator has decided to block access to those ports.

Network Service Access Issues

Failure to authenticate or be granted authorization to a shared service is considered a network service access issue. The following list provides methods for troubleshooting these access issues. However, if your services also rely upon a network directory service, you should also consider the directory service troubleshooting methodology covered later in the "Troubleshooting Directory Service" section of this chapter.

▶ Verify the local user account settings—When using local user accounts, make sure the correct authentication information is being used. You may find that the user is not using the correct information, and you may have to reset the account password. Troubleshooting user account issues was covered in Chapter 2, "User Accounts." Also, keep in mind that some services do not allow the use of guest and sharing-only user accounts. Further, the VNC-compatible and Xgrid services use password information that is not directly linked to a user account.

▶ Double-check directory service settings—If you use a network directory service in your environment, verify that the Mac is properly communicating with the directory service by checking its status in the Directory Utility application. Even if you're only trying to use local accounts, any directory service issues can cause authentication problems. Also, keep in mind that some services, like ARD remote management, do not by default allow you to authenticate with accounts hosted from network directories.

▶ Double-check shared service access settings—Several authenticated sharing services allow you to configure access lists. Use the Sharing preferences to verify that the appropriate user accounts are allowed to access the shared service.

▶ Verify file system ownership and permissions—If you're able to authenticate or connect to file- and web-sharing services, but you're unable to access files and folders, then file system permissions are probably getting in the way. In this case the Finder may display a message indicating that you cannot complete your action because of insufficient permissions to access the item. Use the Finder's Get Info window to inspect the file and folder permissions of the inaccessible items. Sometimes the easiest resolution is to simply create a new permission setting just for the user who is experiencing access issues. Mac OS X's adoption of file system ACLs allows you to make as many permission rules as you want. Also, remember that any files accessed by the web-sharing service should be readable by Everyone. Detailed information about file system permissions, including troubleshooting access issues, is covered in Chapter 4, "File Systems."

Understanding Directory Services

Directory service is a generic term used to describe the technologies that are used to locate network and resource information. Apple's implementation of directory services is branded as Open Directory (OD). It's responsible for providing Mac OS X with fundamental network and resource information. The OD background process daemon, appropriately named DirectoryService, is started during system startup and is always running as a background system process.

The primary directory service function is to act as the authority for resource information. Directory services can provide information about a variety of resources, but the most common resource type is account information. OD resolves all account identification requests and through secondary processes coordinates account authentication and authorization services. The primary focus of the remainder of this chapter is managing and troubleshooting directory services on Mac OS X, aka OD, as it relates to account identification, authentication, and authorization.

Directory Resources

The "directory" in directory services and Open Directory (OD) refers to the fact that it provides a directory of information similar in many ways to an online phone book. The most commonly accessed directory resource is account information. With Mac OS X, all account information, including user and group information, is stored in a directory. OD, or more specifically, the DirectoryService daemon, handles all directory interaction for Mac OS X, making it the single source for providing account information to every Mac OS X application, command, or background service.

Common directory resources used by Mac OS X include:

▶ User Accounts—The primary resource used to identify a human user to the computer. Detailed information regarding user accounts is covered in Chapter 2, "User Accounts."

▶ User Groups—A collection of user accounts used to provide greater control over management and security settings. Detailed information regarding group accounts is also covered in Chapter 2.

▶ Computer Accounts—This is information used to identify a specific computer for purposes of authentication and client management settings.

▶ Computer Groups—A collection of computer accounts used to facilitate efficient client management settings for many computers.

▶ Network File Mounts—Information used by Mac OS X's automatic network file mounting system. Automatic mounts are covered in Chapter 4, "Using File Services," of *Apple Training Series: Mac OS X Server Essentials v10.6.*

▶ Client Management Settings—Information used to automatically apply specific user and computer preferences based on administrator-controlled settings. Directory-based client management settings are covered in Chapter 9, "Managing Accounts," of *Apple Training Series: Mac OS X Server Essentials v10.6.*

▶ Collaboration Information—This includes any information used to facilitate collaboration services, including iCal, iChat, and Wiki Services. Collaboration services are covered in Chapter 7, "Using Collaborative Services," of *Apple Training Series: Mac OS X Server Essentials v10.6.*

Directory Types

Through OD, Mac OS X is able to easily access multiple directory services simultaneously. This allows Mac OS X to integrate into a mixed directory environment with little difficulty and few compromises. As a result, Mac OS X has become very popular among administrators who manage large networks with complicated directory service infrastructures.

Directory types supported by Mac OS X include:

► Local—OD maintains a local directory database with a series of XML-encoded files located in the /var/db/dslocal/nodes/Default/ folder. Any locally stored resource information, including local user account information, is saved to this directory. The local directory is consulted first for any requested resource information.

► Berkeley Software Distribution (BSD) Flat File and Network Information Systems (NIS)—Stand-alone UNIX systems typically use BSD flat files to store local directory information, or use the NIS protocol to access network directory information. Both are still supported by Mac OS X but disabled by default. If support is enabled, these systems will always be consulted second for any requested resource information.

► Lightweight Directory Access Protocol version 3 (LDAPv3)—LDAPv3 has emerged as one of the most popular network directory standards. In fact, Mac OS X Server's built-in directory service, appropriately dubbed Open Directory Server, uses the LDAPv3 protocol. Configuring Mac OS X to connect, or bind, to an LDAPv3 service is covered in the "Configuring Network Directory Services" section later in this chapter.

► Active Directory (AD)—This is Microsoft's implementation of the LDAPv3 protocol. Though it's based on LDAPv3, Microsoft made so many changes to meet its design goals that AD is considered a unique network directory protocol unto itself. Configuring Mac OS X to connect, or bind, to an AD service is also covered in the "Configuring Network Directory Services" section.

TIP ▶ Third-party developers can create their own Open Directory plug-ins to provide additional access to network directory services.

Advantages of Network Directory Services

Implementing network directory services is certainly more complicated than simply using the default local directory service. However, the administrative benefits of using resource and account information hosted on a network directory far outweigh the extra time spent setting it up.

Advantages of using network directory services are:

▶ User accounts are no longer tied to individual Macs—Users with a network or mobile account can log in to any Mac connected to the network directory service. Because the directory service maintains the account information, their entire user environment can be accessed from any Mac they can log in to.

▶ The same user account information can be used for multiple network services— Devices providing network services can connect to the network directory service. You can use the same user name and password for any network service even if those services are hosted on multiple separate servers.

▶ You can use Kerberos to provide secure single-sign-on authentication—Kerberos also happens to be the most secure popular authentication service to date. Details regarding Kerberos are covered in the "Managing Network Authentication" section later in this chapter.

▶ You can define user and computer settings from a centralized location—In addition to providing a single location for all account attributes, you can manage application and system settings from a single location. In other words, you can save client configuration information to a centralized network directory service, and any Mac connected, or bound, to the directory service will be automatically configured with those settings. Again, directory-based management settings are covered in Chapter 9, "Managing Accounts," of *Apple Training Series: Mac OS X Server Essentials v10.6*.

User Account Types

Until now, this text has covered only locally hosted directories, which contain resources and account information available to only a single Mac system. Even so, OD gives Mac OS X the ability to access resource and account information hosted by network-based directory services. Thus, Mac OS X can simultaneously access accounts located in both local and network directories.

Mac OS X account location types include:

▶ Local account—Account information is stored on the local Mac and is available only to that Mac. Obviously, this account type can be created only on a local Mac.

▶ Network account—Account information is stored on a network server that is providing a shared directory to any connected, or bound, network client. The Mac must be connected to the network directory in order for you to access a network account.

▶ Local account tied to a Mac OS X Server account—Account information is still stored on the local Mac and is available only to that Mac. However, this local account is also directly associated with another account stored on a Mac OS X Server that is providing a shared directory. The server account must be hosted from a Mac OS X Server that is being managed via Server Preferences. The primary mechanisms through which the two accounts are associated is Kerberos authentication and client management. The system will initially synchronize the password between the two accounts and automatically configure the local account for server access. Thus, when the user logs into a Mac with her local account she is able to access resources on the server without additional configuration.

▶ Mobile account—Account information is stored on a network server providing a shared directory, but the account information can also be cached to the Mac's local directory. Every time you log in using a mobile account, the account information will be cached to the Mac's local directory. As long as the cached information remains on the Mac, you'll still be able to access the mobile account if the Mac isn't connected to the network directory.

Configuring Network Directory Services

The process of connecting Mac OS X to a network directory service is called *directory binding*. The term *bind* is used to describe this connection because, unlike other types of network connections that come and go, the connection between a client and a network directory service is designed to be persistent.

Once you bind Mac OS X to a network directory service, it will allow all services to request information from those network directories. Whenever directory service information is requested, the Mac will attempt to communicate with the network directories to which it's bound. Most important, you will be able to log in and authenticate to the Mac with user accounts hosted on the network directory.

Mac OS X Directory Binding Methods

There are several methods for binding your Mac to a network directory service:

▶ During Setup Assistant—If your network directory service is being hosted from a local Mac OS X Server that is being managed via Server Preferences, then you can bind it during the Setup Assistant. As covered in Chapter 1, "Installation and Initial Setup," the first time a Mac starts up with a new copy of Mac OS X, Setup Assistant handles the initial setup. If Setup Assistant discovers a Mac OS X Server on the local network you can use a server account to bind your Mac client to the network directory service. This process will also automatically create a local administrator account tied to the server account. Further, any services hosted by the Mac OS X Server and managed via Server Preferences will be automatically configured for the user; this can include Address Book, iCal, iChat, and Mail client configuration.

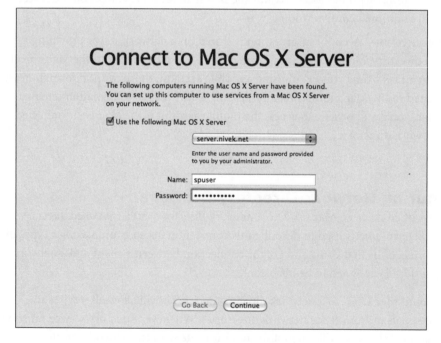

NOTE ▶ Any directory binding method attempted after initial setup with Setup Assistant requires administrator authentication.

NOTE ▶ On a single Mac you can configure multiple local accounts tied to server accounts. You must log in to each local account separately and then, via the Accounts preferences, manually delete and rebind to the server in order to set up each account. Manually managing directory service binding is covered later in this chapter.

▶ From a Mac OS X Server Invitation dialog— If your network directory service is being hosted from a local Mac OS X Server that is being managed via Server Preferences, and your local account name matches the name of a server account, then you may be presented with a Mac OS X Server Invitation dialog. Clicking the Set Up button will open the Accounts preferences and bind your Mac to the Mac OS X Server and tie your local account to the server account. Again, this process will synchronize the account passwords and can automatically configure client services.

▶ From a Mac OS X Server email invitation—If your network directory service is being hosted from a local Mac OS X Server that is being managed via Server Preferences, then you can bind it automatically from an email invitation sent by the server's administrator. Clicking the "Automatically Configure My Mac" button in this email will open the Accounts preferences and bind your Mac to the Mac OS X Server and tie your local account to the server account. Again, this process will synchronize the account passwords and can automatically configure client services. Further, the invitation email can have clickable links to other services hosted from the server like file and web services.

MORE INFO ▶ You can find out more about Mac OS X Server accounts managed via Server Preferences from Apple's Mac OS X Server Getting Started v10.6 guide available at http://images.apple.com/server/macosx/docs/Getting_Started_v10.6.pdf.

▶ Manually via the Accounts preferences—This manual method allows you a bit more control over the directory binding process. Primarily, this method allows you to avoid linking local accounts to Mac OS X Server accounts. Also, this method allows you to bind your Mac to both Mac OS X Server providing OD services and Microsoft Active Directory services. This method is covered in the following sections of this chapter.

▶ Manually via the Directory Access application—This manual method allows for completely customizable configuration of the directory binding process. Using this method you can bind your Mac to any LDAPv3 directory service (including OD services), Microsoft Active Directory services, or any additional network directory via third-party directory service plug-ins. This method is also briefly covered in the following sections of this chapter.

Manually Configure Network Open Directory Binding

To configure binding for Mac OS X Open Directory (OD) services:

1   Open Accounts preferences by choosing Apple menu > System Preferences, then clicking the Accounts icon.

2   Click the lock icon in the bottom-left corner and authenticate as an administrative user to unlock Accounts preferences.

3   Click the Login Options button at the bottom of the user list and then click the Join button to the right.

This will open a dialog allowing you to configure a directory service bind.

4   To bind your Mac to an OD server, enter the IP address or DNS host name of a server providing OD services in the server field, or you can click the pop-up menu button to select a local Mac OS X Server via Bonjour.

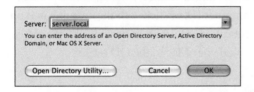

Depending on the server configuration this may be the only dialog you see. If the dialog doesn't automatically change, simply click the OK button to bind your Mac to the OD server. Skip to step 7.

5   If the server is a Mac OS X Server providing services managed via Server Preferences, you will be prompted to choose if you want to automatically set up services. Choosing the Only Join service button will simply bind your Mac to the OD service, whereas choosing the Set Up Services button will tie the currently logged in local account to a server account. Click the button of your choice.

If you chose to set up services, you will be prompted to authenticate with the server account. Enter the authentication information provided by the server administrator and click Continue to bind your Mac to the OD server and tie your local account to the server account. Skip to step 7.

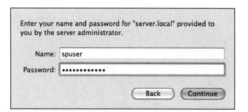

6   If the OD server requires authentication to bind but you are not automatically setting up other services, the dialog will change to require authentication information. Optionally, you can pick a different name for your Computer ID, or stick with the default based on your Mac's sharing name. Enter the authentication information provided by the server administrator and click the OK button to bind your Mac to the OD server.

7 Once the directory service bind is complete, if your Mac is successfully communicating with the OD service, you will see a green status indicator next to the server name.

Configure Active Directory Binding

To configure binding for Microsoft Active Directory (AD) services:

1 Open Accounts preferences by choosing Apple menu > System Preferences, then clicking the Accounts icon.

2 Click the lock icon in the bottom-left corner and authenticate as an administrative user to unlock Accounts preferences.

3 Click the Login Options button at the bottom of the user list and then click the Join button to the right.

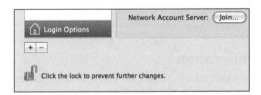

This will open a dialog allowing you to configure a directory service bind.

4 To bind your Mac to AD, enter the AD domain name in the server field.

The dialog will automatically change once it recognizes the AD domain.

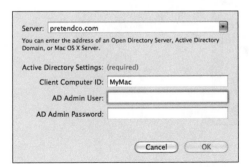

5   Optionally, you can pick a different name for your Computer ID, or simply stick with the default based on your Mac's sharing name.

6   Enter the authentication information provided by the server administrator and click the OK button to bind your Mac to the AD domain.

Depending on your AD implementation it may take several minutes to bind your Mac to the AD domain.

7   Once the AD bind is complete, if your Mac is successfully communicating with the AD service, you will see a green status indicator next to the domain name.

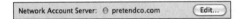

MORE INFO ▶ Attempting to fully integrate Mac OS X into an AD system may require additional configuration. Find out more from Apple's Active Directory integration technical white paper: http://images.apple.com/business/solutions/it/docs/ Best_Practices_Active_Directory.pdf.

Advanced Directory Service Configuration

As mentioned previously, Mac OS X's OD infrastructure allows for more complex directory service configurations, including the ability to simultaneously bind to multiple network directory services. The Accounts preferences allows for initial setup of multiple network directory services as long as they are either OD- or AD-based. After you have set up your initial network directory service in the Accounts preferences, click the Edit button to reveal the list of currently bound network directory servers.

This dialog shows the current state of all bound network directory services. The dialog will also allow you to bind your Mac to additional network directory servers or delete existing bindings. Simply click the small plus button at the bottom of the list to initiate another network directory service bind. Again, follow the steps outlined previously to bind your Mac to an additional OD or AD service.

However, for more advanced configuration you will need to use the Directory Utility application. You can open the Directory Utility from either the previously mentioned network directory service list dialog, or from the Finder by opening /System/Library/CoreServices/Directory Utility.app. This application requires administrative access but once authenticated will allow you to change many more directory service settings. The initial view allows you to configure various directory service settings by double-clicking on the service.

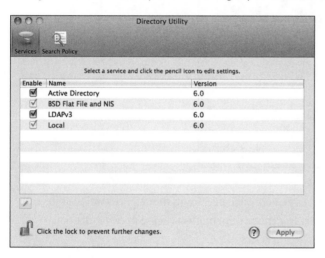

From Directory Utility you can also manage the directory service search policy by clicking the Search Policy button in the toolbar. If your Mac has access to multiple directory services, the system will search for account information in local directories first, followed by network directories. If multiple network directory services are available, the system will search for account information based on this service order. If a similarly named account exists in multiple directories, the first account located is the one that's used. To change the search order simply click and drag the server entries in this list.

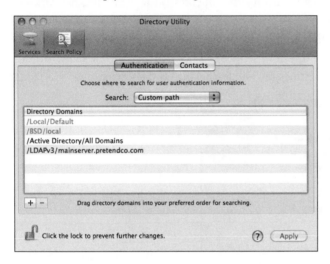

MORE INFO ▶ Directory services is a complicated topic that can extend well beyond the scope of this reference guide. For more information please check out *Apple Training Series: Mac OS X Directory Services v10.6.*

Managing Network Authentication

The concept of authentication has been covered previously, but to reiterate, authentication is the process of proving your identity to the computer. More specifically, you are proving to the computer that you should be allowed to access an account because you know a secret about the account that only the account's holder should know. Mac OS X supports elaborate authentication systems that require special hardware to validate your identity, but alphanumeric passwords are still the most commonly used authentication secret.

Understanding Authentication and Authorization

Authorization is closely tied to authentication, but they are not the same thing. Authentication is only used to prove your account identity to the system, but authorization defines which items or services the account is allowed to access. In other words, authentication is who you are, and authorization is what you can do.

Authentication and authorization are used throughout Mac OS X to ensure a safe computing environment. Open Directory (OD) coordinates authentication for Mac OS X, but authorization is handled by each service differently. For example, Chapter 2, "User Accounts," showed how each user account type has different levels of access to the system. The login window uses the OD service to identify and authenticate the user, but Mac OS X's system authorization services dictate which applications and services the user is authorized to access. A large part of Chapter 4, "File Systems," covered how access to files and folders is granted. Again, OD provides identification and authorization services, but the file system permissions determine which files and folders the user is authorized to access.

Understanding Network Authentication

Authentication systems vary as widely as the services they help secure. Often legacy technologies use authentication techniques that are considered rudimentary and unsecured in today's world of Internet thieves and spyware. Local account authentication tends to be more relaxed, but as you come to rely more on network and Internet services the need to provide strong authentication becomes paramount. In general you can categorize an authentication service into one of four groups:

▶ Basic or clear-text password—In this simplest form of authentication, passwords are passed between client and service in standard text. Obviously, this provides no network security, as passwords could be easily recovered using common network diagnostic tools. The few services that still rely on basic password authentication do so to support the widest possible audience. Mac OS X avoids using this type of encryption whenever possible, and so should you.

▶ Encrypted password—Many variations of this type of authentication exist, but they all involve sending password information between client and service in an encrypted format. This is a more secure technique than clear text, but it still involves passing secrets across the network, so a determined individual could possibly uncover your password. The likelihood of a nefarious person decrypting your password depends on the strength of encryption being used. Mac OS X uses encrypted passwords for local accounts, as do some generic LDAP directory services. In fact, most network services now rely on encrypted passwords if they don't already rely on the next two types of authentication.

▶ Kerberos—This advanced authentication system provides highly secure, single-sign-on authentication. Both Apple's OD and Microsoft's Active Directory (AD) rely on Kerberos to provide authentication for a variety of network and Internet services. Details on Kerberos follow.

Understanding Kerberos Authentication

Kerberos is a secure authentication service that's popular with many universities and corporations. Both Apple and Microsoft have implemented Kerberos as their primary authentication mechanism for network directory services. Originally developed by the Massachusetts Institute of Technology (MIT), Kerberos provides ticket-based single-sign-on authentication services.

Single sign-on means that you have to enter your account password only once per session, often at the login window. As long as you remain logged in to the Mac or connected to the Kerberos system, it will use your previous credentials to satisfy the authentication for any other network service that supports Kerberos. A network service that supports Kerberos authentication is often called a *kerberized* service. Many primary network applications and services included with Mac OS X are kerberized, including Mail, iChat, iCal, Screen Sharing, SSH, AFP, SMB, and NFS.

Kerberos was designed with the idea that you can't trust network traffic to be secure. So, Kerberos ensures that account passwords are never transmitted across the network. This system also provides mutual authentication, where both the client and server can verify each other's identity. Kerberos provides these features by generating tickets that are used to validate the authenticity of each Kerberos participant.

The only downside to ticket-based authentication is its relative complexity when compared with other techniques. Kerberos authentication requires a special trusted service known as the Key Distribution Center (KDC). In the case of OD and AD, the server providing directory services is often also the primary KDC. Starting with the introduction of Mac OS X v10.5, every Macintosh can also provide local KDC services. However, to keep things simple this chapter will focus on the authentication relationship between a Mac OS X client and a centralized KDC tied to a network directory service.

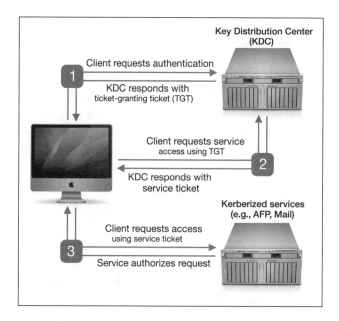

An example of the basic Kerberos authentication process:

1   Enter your user name and password at the login window.

The login window, via OD, negotiates a connection to the KDC. The KDC issues you an encrypted ticket-granting ticket (TGT). The TGT is encrypted in such a way that it can be unlocked and used only if you entered the correct password.

Think of the TGT as a "day pass" that can be used to access other services. TGTs are usually good for several hours, but if they expire before you log out, the Kerberos system will automatically generate a new one for you.

2   Upon attempting to connect to a kerberized network service, such as an AFP network volume or an email service, OD will use the TGT to request a service ticket from the KDC.

If the KDC trusts your TGT and trusts the service you're attempting to connect to, it issues you a ticket for that service.

3 OD uses the service ticket to authenticate your account to the requested network service. Assuming your service ticket is good, the kerberized service will trust your identity and allow the connection.

Notice that you only had to enter your user name and password once at the login window; after that, steps 2 and 3 are repeated for each different kerberized service you connect to. Further, at no point did your password ever travel across the network, nor did the requested network service have to communicate with the KDC to verify your authenticity.

> **MORE INFO** ▶ The information presented here is merely an introduction to the Kerberos authentication system. For more, please visit MIT's Kerberos website at http://web.mit.edu/Kerberos.

Finally, it is important to not confuse Kerberos's single-sign-on ability with the keychain systems' ability to save authentication information locally. Even though both services are used to automatically authenticate network services, they are quite different in architecture and scope. Kerberos can be used only to authenticate kerberized services and is often managed on a network-wide scale. The keychain system can be used to save a wide variety of authentication information, but saved keychain information is accessible only to the local Mac. The keychain system is covered in detail in Chapter 2, "User Accounts."

Verifying Kerberos Authentication

Kerberos is so well integrated in Mac OS X that it is possible to extensively use Kerberos without once having to manage its configuration. Assuming you have bound your Mac to an OD or AD service, Kerberos is already configured for you. The system configures the Kerberos settings automatically during the binding process. Users probably won't even know that they are using Kerberos because the login window and OD will automatically handle all future authentications.

Despite this level of integration, you should be aware of methods for testing and verifying Kerberos authentication. As covered previously, initial Kerberos authentication typically takes place during login. However, it's important to understand that you can test Kerberos authentication at any point, even if the user account you're testing isn't logged into the Mac. In other words, you can log into a Mac using a known working account, like a local administrator, and then use the Kerberos tools to verify authentication to a different user's account.

Using the Kerberos Ticket Viewer Application

Basic Kerberos functionality can be tested from the Kerberos Ticket Viewer application:

1   Log in to the Mac using any working account you have access to.

If the account you're trying to verify doesn't work, log in using another working account, possibly a local account that doesn't rely on Kerberos.

2   Open the Kerberos Ticket Viewer application using one of the following methods:

▶   Open /Applications/Utilities/Keychain Access.app and then select Keychain Access > Ticket Viewer from the menu.

▶   Open /System/Library/CoreServices/Ticket Viewer.app.

3   If you were able to log in with the user account you wish to test, it may already appear in the Ticket Viewer Kerberos user identities list.

▶   If no user identities appear, skip to step 4.

▶   If a user identity is present, and the date and time for when the TGT expires is listed, then Kerberos authentication should be working. You can click the Get Ticket button to verify a renew of the TGT.

▶ If a user identity is present but there is no ticket, select the user in the list, and click the Get Ticket button in the toolbar to test Kerberos authentication. In the dialog that appears, enter the user's password and then click the Continue button. Skip to step 5.

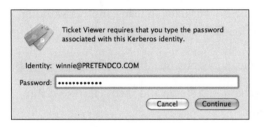

4   If the Ticket Viewer application opens with no Kerberos user identities listed, click the Add Identities button.

From the dialog that appears enter the user's fully qualified Kerberos identity. This usually includes the user's name, followed by the @ symbol, followed by the Kerberos realm in all capital letters.

Also enter the user's password, and then click the Continue button.

5   If authentication was successful, then the user's identity in the list will show the date and time when the TGT expires.

If authentication failed then you will receive an error message that should help you identify the problem. In the following example, the client's time is not correct, therefore Kerberos authentication fails.

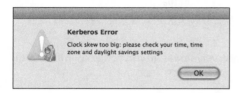

6   If you are done testing Kerberos, for the sake of security, you should click the Destroy Ticket button in the toolbar to de-authenticate the user.

NOTE ▶ From the Ticket Viewer you can also change a user's Kerberos password, but if Kerberos authentication is working properly, the user can also accomplish this if he changes his own password at the login window or the Accounts preferences. Password changes are covered in Chapter 2, "User Accounts."

Using the Kerberos Commands

The Ticket Viewer application is convenient for verifying Kerberos TGTs, but as covered previously, the TGT is only the first part of Kerberos authentication. Again, if you want to connect to a kerberized service, you must also acquire service tickets. Unfortunately, the Ticket Viewer application doesn't show service tickets. To view service tickets you must use the Kerberos command-line utilities. These Kerberos commands, however, are very easy to use. They also allow you to test Kerberos regardless of the user you're currently logged in with.

The command to acquire a Kerberos TGT is simply kinit followed by the user's Kerberos identity. You will, of course, be prompted to enter the user's password to acquire the TGT. To list any Kerberos tickets for the current user, simply enter klist. Finally, to deauthenticate from Kerberos, enter kdestroy to destroy all the currently held tickets.

In the following example, Michelle has already authenticated via Kerberos with the "spuser" account and in the Finder she has connected to an AFP share point. She enters klist to verify the TGT and service tickets. As you can see, the second ticket is an AFP service ticket, indicating that Kerberos authentication for that service is working as well.

```
MyMac:~ michelle$ klist
Kerberos 5 ticket cache: 'API:Initial default ccache'
Default principal: spuser@SERVER.NIVEK.NET

Valid Starting     Expires               Service Principal
08/30/09 21:43:07  08/31/09 07:43:04  krbtgt/SERVER.NIVEK.NET@SERVER.NIVEK.NET
renew until 09/06/09 21:43:04
08/30/09 21:43:12  08/31/09 07:43:04  afpserver/server.nivek.net@SERVER.NIVEK.NET
     renew until 09/06/09 21:43:04
```

Troubleshooting Directory Services

Directory services and authentication services are tightly linked to each other. Also, Open Directory (OD) is responsible for both of these services in Mac OS X, so they share similar troubleshooting techniques. Almost all common OD issues are initially discovered because of a single symptom: A user is unable to access or authenticate to his or her account. Other symptoms might indicate an issue with OD, but an inability to authenticate is often the first and most significant issue a user will experience. After all, if the Mac has OD issues, then the user probably won't even make it past the login window.

> **NOTE** ▸ Again, before digging too deep into troubleshooting a specific network service, take a few moments to check for general network service issues as outlined earlier in this chapter.

Common troubleshooting techniques specific to directory services and authentication services include:

▸   Attempt to authenticate with another user account—Remember, Mac OS X supports multiple directory services, so first test another user account hosted from the same directory. Also, keep in mind that if a similarly named account exists in multiple directories, the first account OD locates is the one that's used. Otherwise, if the other account works properly, the problem lies only with the account record. Yet if you are unable to authenticate from multiple accounts, you are experiencing a problem with the directory service as a whole.

▶ Reset the account password—This approach often requires that you have administrative access to the directory server hosting the account. Not only will this technique resolve any potential human errors, it will also reset the account's authentication information, which may have become compromised.

▶ Verify network directory service connectivity and configuration—As covered previously, the network directory listing in the Accounts preferences shows you the current status of bound network directory services. If a service isn't responding properly, you can reset the network directory service configuration by unbinding and then rebinding to the service using the plus and minus buttons at the bottom of the network directory list.

▶ Verify Kerberos authentication and configuration—As explained earlier, the Kerberos application will show you currently connected Kerberos accounts and tickets. First attempt a quick fix by destroying all current tickets and then re-authenticating. If multiple Kerberos KDCs or accounts are available, make sure the appropriate account is being used. Finally, Kerberos is a time-sensitive protocol, so verify that your Mac and the server(s) all have the correct date and time set. Ideally, all Kerberos participants will be configured to use the Network Time Protocol (NTP) to ensure clock synchronization.

▶ Check directory service log files—If none of these techniques work, fall back on information collected by the OD log files. OD generates very thorough log information that can help pinpoint directory service and authentication service issues. From the /Application/Utilities/Console application, inspect the system.log, as it contains relevant network and authentication information, and the three directory service specific log files located in /Library/Logs: DirectoryService.server.log has OD general usage and configuration information; DirectoryService.error.log has all OD error messages; and SingleSignOnTools.log has all Kerberos configuration and error messages.

What You've Learned

▶ Mac OS X includes built-in support for accessing and sharing a wide variety of network services, including Internet, network file, and remote control services.

▶ Your Mac is accessible to other network clients via static network identifiers like its IP address(es) and DNS host name, or dynamic network service identifiers like Bonjour, and NetBIOS/WINS.

▶ The Finder allows you to connect to and mount network file systems by either manually entering a server address or browsing the network for servers via dynamic network discovery services.

▶ Mac OS X can provide AFP, SMB, and FTP file-sharing services.

▶ Mac OS X also includes the Apache 2.2 web server, which is preconfigured to share a single computer website and individual websites for each user.

▶ Mac OS X can provide several types of client-sharing services that allow others to remotely control or execute software on your Mac.

▶ Mac OS X's core network software lets you protect other network services by enabling adaptive firewall filtering, or share a network or Internet connection with others by acting as a network router.

▶ Mac OS X includes Open Directory for resolving network and directory resource information. Open Directory supports several network directory services, including LDAP services and Microsoft's Active Directory service.

▶ Open Directory also coordinates account authentication via a variety of authentication protocols, including the popular Kerberos authentication system.

References

Check for new and updated Knowledge Base documents at www.apple.com/support.

General Network Services

TS1629, "'Well known' TCP and UDP ports used by Apple software products"

HT2250, "Bonjour: Frequently asked questions (FAQ)"

Network Applications

TS1594, "Mac OS X 10.5: What you can do if Safari quits unexpectedly"

TA25586, "Mac OS X Mail: About secure email communications (SSL)"

HT2008, "iChat: Frequently asked questions (FAQ)"

HT2579, "Frequently asked questions about iCal"

HT1507, "Using iChat with a firewall or NAT router"

HT3748, "Mac OS X v10.6: Using Microsoft Exchange 2007 (EWS) accounts in Mail"

HT3778, "MobileMe: Microsoft Exchange data in iCal and Address Book will not sync with MobileMe"

HT3861, "iCal, Mac OS X v10.6: About adding an iCal account stored on a Mac OS X Server v10.5 iCal Server via Kerberos authentication"

TS2998, "Mac OS X v10.6: Can receive email, but not send email"

Providing Network Services

HT1810, "Mac OS X 10.5 Leopard: About the application firewall"

HT1344, "Choosing a Password for networks that use Wired Equivalent Privacy (WEP)"

HT2370, "Apple Remote Desktop: Configuring remotely via command line (kickstart)"

HT1131, "MacBook Air: Sharing DVDs or CDs with Remote Disc"

HT1777, "MacBook Air: How to use Remote Disc to share DVDs or CDs on a Mac- or Windows-based computer"

HT2129, "MacBook Air: Reinstalling software using Remote Install Mac OS X"

HT3774, "Mac OS X v10.6: About Wake on Demand"

URLs

Official Zeroconf dynamic network discovery service website: www.zeroconf.org

Apple's product guide: http://guide.apple.com

Apple's Safari 4 web browser: www.apple.com/safari

Apple's iCal shared calendars website: www.apple.com/downloads/macosx/calendars

Official Samba SMB software suite resource website: www.samba.org

Your Mac's locally hosted Apache 2.2 documentation: http://localhost/manual

Official Apache web server software resource website: http://httpd.apache.org

Apple's Xgrid distributed computing solution resource website: www.apple.com/server/macosx/technology/xgrid.html

Apple Remote Desktop network client management software: www.apple.com/remotedesktop

Apple's Online Mail Setup Assistant: www.apple.com/support/macosx/mailassistant

Group Logic's ExtremeZ-IP AFP server for Windows: www.grouplogic.com

Apple's Mac OS X Server Getting Started v10.6 guide: http://images.apple.com/server/macosx/docs/Getting_Started_v10.6.pdf

Apple's Active Directory integration technical white paper: http://images.apple.com/business/solutions/it/docs/Best_Practices_Active_Directory.pdf

Official Kerberos authentication resource website: http://web.mit.edu/Kerberos

Review Quiz

1. What is the relationship between clients and servers as it relates to network service access?

2. What is the relationship between a network service and a network port?

3. What two dynamic network service discovery protocols are supported by Mac OS X?

4. How does Mac OS X use dynamic network service discovery protocols to access network services?

5. What five network file services can you connect to from the Finder's Connect to Server dialog?

6. How are items inside the Finder's Network folder populated?

7. How do you provide Mac OS X file-sharing services so other computers can access them?

8. What password issues may arise related to the SMB service?

9. What shared items are accessible to an administrative user who connects via AFP or SMB? What about a standard user?

10. What items are shared by default to all users?

11. What shared items are accessible to any user who connects via FTP?

12. How do you provide Mac OS X web-sharing services?

13. What files are associated with the computer's website? What about an individual user's website?

14. What client-sharing services can Mac OS X provide?

15. What is the security risk of enabling client-sharing services?

16. How is Xgrid implemented in Mac OS X?

17. What network services are provided by your Mac to facilitate Internet sharing? What options are available for Internet sharing via your Mac's AirPort wireless Ethernet interface?

18. How does Mac OS X's built-in firewall work? What advanced firewall settings are available?

19. What are some known issues that arise when connecting to network file services?

20. What are three common troubleshooting techniques for issues involving failure to connect to network services?

21. What is a directory as it relates to directory services?

22. What are seven common types of resources Mac OS X can access from a directory service?

23. What are the primary differences between local, network, and mobile accounts?

24. What are four advantages of using network directory services to store account information?

25. What four directory service types can be used in Mac OS X?

26. What is authentication? What is authorization?

27. What are three common authentication methods?

28. What is a Kerberos ticket? What is a Key Distribution Center (KDC)?

29. How do Kerberos and the keychain system differ for managing authentication services?

30. What are five common directory services and authentication services troubleshooting techniques?

Answers

1. Client software is used to access network services provided by server software. The connection is established using a common network protocol known by both the client and server software. Thus, the client and server software can be from different sources.

2. Network services are established using a common network protocol. The protocol specifies which TCP or UDP port number is used for communications.

3. Mac OS X supports Bonjour, and Network Basic Input/Output and Windows Internet Naming Service (NetBIOS and WINS) dynamic network service discovery protocols.

4. Devices providing a network service advertise their availability via a dynamic network service discovery protocol. Clients that are looking for services request and receive this information to provide the user with a list of available network service choices.

5. From the Finder's Connect to Server dialog, you can connect to Apple File Protocol (AFP), Server Message Blocks/Common Internet File System (SMB), Network File System (NFS), Web-Based Distributed Authoring and Versioning (WebDAV), and File Transfer Protocol (FTP) network file services.

6. The Finder populates the Network folder using information provided by the dynamic network services discovery protocols. Computers providing services appear as resources inside the Network folder, while service discovery zones or workgroups appear as folders. Any currently connected servers will also appear in the Network folder.

7. To provide services to other network clients you first set your Mac's network identification, then enable the desired network file service, and finally define access to file system resources.

8. To support SMB authentication, users' passwords must be stored in a special format, which must be enabled in Sharing preferences.

9. Administrators who connect to your Mac via AFP or SMB have access to any locally mounted volume. By default, standard users can only access their home folder and other users' Public folders.

10. The items shared to all users by default are the local users' Public folders inside their home folders.

11. Users who connect to your Mac via FTP have access based on the local file system ownership and permissions; by default they'll start in their home folders but can navigate anywhere file permissions allow them to.

12. To enable the web-sharing service select the checkbox next to Web Sharing in the Sharing preferences.

13. The computer's website files are located in the /Library/WebServer/Documents folder. Each user's website files are located in the Sites folder inside their home folder.

14. Mac OS X's client-sharing services are: Screen Sharing, Remote Login, Remote Management, Remote Apple Events, and Xgrid Sharing.

15. If a client-sharing service is compromised, an unauthorized user can control your Mac and execute unwanted applications or processes.

16. Mac OS X includes the ability to share its computing resources as an Xgrid agent. A computer running Mac OS X Server is required to act as an Xgrid controller.

17. When Internet sharing is enabled, your Mac provides network routing NAT, DHCP, and DNS forwarding services for any network device connected to your Mac's shared network interfaces. When sharing a network or Internet connection to your Mac's AirPort wireless Ethernet interface, you can specify a wireless network name, channel, and (optionally) WEP security settings.

18. Mac OS X's built-in firewall inspects each incoming network connection to determine if it's allowed. Connections are allowed or denied on a per-application basis. The advanced firewall settings allow you to control whether signed applications are automatically allowed through the firewall, to control the list of allowed (or denied) applications, and to enable stealth mode (which means your Mac will not respond to any unsolicited connections).

19. Forked files may cause problems for NFS or WebDAV network file systems. Also, avoid AFP 2 services as provided by Windows file servers.

20. Review the Network preferences, review the Network Utility statistics, and attempt to connect to different network services.

21. A directory is a database of information that in some cases can be shared to the network. The most commonly accessed directory resource is account information.

22. Common directory resources that Mac OS X can access include user accounts, user groups, computer accounts, computer groups, network file mounts, management settings, and collaboration information.

23. Local accounts are available only to a single Mac, network accounts are available to Macs connected to a network directory service, and mobile accounts are network accounts that are cached to the local Mac for offline use.

24. Four advantages of using network directory services to store account information are: 1) user accounts are no longer tied to individual Macs; 2) the same user account information can be used for multiple network services; 3) you can use Kerberos to provide secure single-sign-on authentication; and 4) you can define user and computer settings from a centralized location.

25. The directory service types that can be used in Mac OS X are Local, Berkeley Software Distribution (BSD) Flat File and Network Information Systems (NIS), Lightweight Directory Access Protocol version 3 (LDAPv3), and Active Directory (AD).

26. Authentication is the process of proving your identity to the computer; authorization defines which items or services you are allowed to access.

27. Three common authentication methods are basic or clear-text passwords, encrypted passwords, and Kerberos ticket–based authentication.

28. Kerberos tickets are used to validate an account's identity. Kerberos uses ticket-granting tickets (TGTs) and service tickets. Kerberos requires a special trusted service known as the KDC. In most cases the KDC service is running alongside the network directory service.

29. Kerberos can only be used to authenticate kerberized services and is often managed on a networkwide scale. The keychain system can be used to save a wide variety of authentication information, but saved keychain information is accessible only to the local Mac.

30. Common directory services and authentication services troubleshooting techniques are: 1) attempting to authenticate with another user account; 2) resetting the account password; 3) verifying network directory service connectivity and configuration; 4) verifying Kerberos authentication and configuration; and 5) checking the directory service log files.

9

Time   This chapter takes approximately 2 hours to complete.

Goals   Understand, manage, and troubleshoot peripheral connectivity from both a hardware and a software perspective

Pair Bluetooth devices to your Mac

Manage peripherals that use synchronizing technologies

Understand, manage, and troubleshoot printing and faxing systems

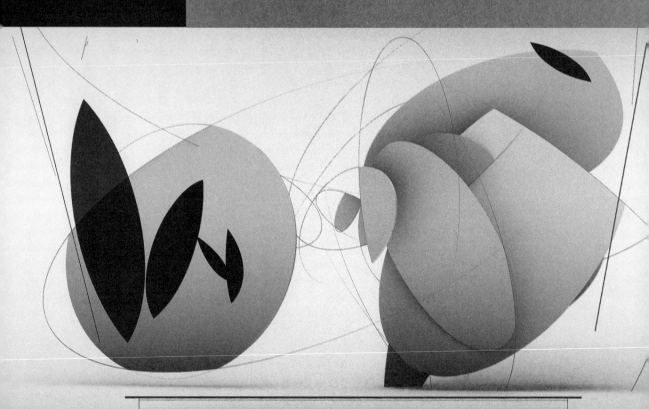

## Chapter 9

Peripherals and Printing

Apple pioneered the concept of automatic peripheral support with the original Macintosh. This feature, commonly known as plug-and-play, is now supported with varying success in all modern operating systems. Peripheral hardware has also improved, as now the most common connectivity standards support hot-pluggable or even wireless connections. Mac OS X supports all popular modern peripheral standards, demonstrating Apple's continued commitment to making peripheral use as easy as possible. Nowhere is this commitment made clearer than by Apple's foray into the consumer electronics market with products like iPod, Apple TV, and iPhone.

Similarly, Apple and Adobe pioneered the desktop publishing revolution by introducing the first high-quality printing solution for personal computers. Although Adobe created the PostScript printing system, Apple was the first to include it in both the Macintosh operating system and the very first PostScript printer, the Apple LaserWriter. Apple has continued to pioneer advancements in printing software with Mac OS X by adopting a printing workflow based on Adobe's Portable Document Format (PDF) and the Common UNIX Printing System (CUPS).

At the start of this chapter, you'll learn how Mac OS X supports different peripheral technologies, and then you'll manage and troubleshoot peripherals connected to your Mac. You'll also learn how Mac OS X supports different print and fax technologies and how to manage and troubleshoot printers and fax modems connected to your Mac.

Understanding Peripherals

For the purposes of this chapter, a peripheral is any non-networked device to which your computer system can be directly connected. A peripheral is directly connected to and controlled by the Mac, whereas network devices are shared.

Given the wide range of devices included in this definition, this chapter shows you how to categorize devices based on their connectivity type and device class. Understanding the available connection methods and device types is necessary to manage and troubleshoot peripherals, which is your ultimate goal in the first half of this chapter.

Understanding Peripheral Connectivity

Most peripherals communicate with the Mac system via a connection mechanism commonly known as a bus. Bus connections are the most common peripheral connection type because they allow multiple peripherals to connect to your Mac simultaneously. In fact, the only connection types that are not buses are those used for audio and video connectivity. Even then, your Mac is connected via a peripheral bus to intermediary hardware responsible for encoding or decoding the audio and video signals.

You can categorize peripheral connectivity into four types:

▶ Peripheral buses—General-purpose buses primarily used to connect an external device to your Mac.

▶ Expansion buses—Designed to expand your Mac's hardware capabilities, often by adding extra connectivity options.

▶ Storage buses—Used only for accessing storage devices.

▶ Audio and video connectivity—Standard interfaces used to send audio or video signals from one device to another.

Each connection is specialized for a particular type of communication, so a combination of technologies is often required to use a peripheral. For example, your Mac's graphics hardware is obviously designed to output a standard video signal, but it communicates with the processor via an expansion bus. You'll see many examples of combined connection types as you explore various peripheral devices.

Given this, it's a good thing Mac OS X includes the System Profiler application to help you identify connected peripherals, including their connection types. Access the System Profiler by choosing Apple menu > About This Mac and clicking the More Info button in the resulting dialog. Once System Profiler is open, select a hardware interface from the Contents list to view its information. Using System Profiler for further troubleshooting peripherals is covered in this chapter's "Troubleshooting Peripherals" section.

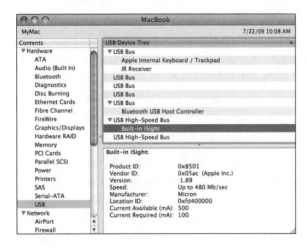

NOTE ▶ This chapter will only cover connection technologies included with Mac systems that support Mac OS X v10.6.

Peripheral Buses

Peripheral buses are the connection type most commonly associated with computer peripherals. Because they are designed to provide a general-purpose communications link between the computer and the peripheral, a variety of devices can use these connections. There have been dozens of peripheral connectivity standards developed over the years, but in the last decade three peripheral standards have dominated the market: Universal Serial Bus (USB), FireWire, and Bluetooth.

Universal Serial Bus (USB) 1.1/2.0

Standard on every Mac that supports Mac OS X v10.6, USB is by far the most popular peripheral connection. In fact, it has become so popular that every single type of peripheral can be found in USB versions. You're probably already aware of the external USB ports on your Mac, but you may not know that Intel-based Macs also use USB for internal connectivity. For example, the MacBook's keyboard, trackpad, infrared receiver, iSight camera, and Bluetooth controller are all connected via internal USB connections.

USB was originally designed by Intel and is a hot-pluggable interface that allows the user to connect and disconnect devices while they are on, or "hot." USB is also a highly expandable connection platform that allows for daisy-chained connections. So, you can connect one USB device to your Mac, then connect another USB device to the first, and so on. With USB hubs, this allows for up to 127 simultaneous devices per host controller. Most Macs have at least two externally accessible USB host controllers.

A USB port may supply up to 2.5 watts of power (500 mA of current at 5 volts) to the connected devices, which is all that some types of devices need to operate. Unpowered hubs, including those built into many USB keyboards, split the available power between their ports, usually supplying only 0.5 watts (100 mA) to each, enough for only very low-power devices. When Mac OS X detects that there is not enough power for a connected device, it displays a low-power warning and disables the device.

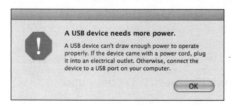

If you see this dialog, you can verify the power issue by opening /Applications/Utilities/ System Profiler and selecting USB from the report list. Selecting any USB device will display the electric current available to, and required by, the device.

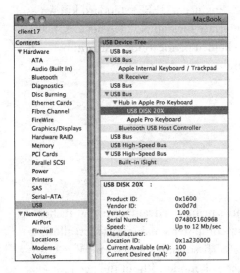

You can try resolving USB power issues by connecting the peripheral directly to the Mac or through a powered hub, which uses an external power connection to supply full power to the attached device. Peripherals that require even more power to operate, such as printers or large disk drives, generally also include a separate power source.

At the time of this writing there are two primary USB versions: USB 1.1 and USB 2.0. USB 2.0 ports are backward-compatible with USB 1.1 cabling and devices. USB 1.1 supports low-speed connections at 1.5 megabits per second (Mbit/s) and full-speed connections at up to 12 Mbit/s. USB 2.0 supports high-speed connections up to a theoretical maximum of 480 Mbit/s. In practice, though, high-speed USB 2.0 connections fall short of the theoretical maximum. Then again, if you require a higher-performance peripheral connection bus, consider the next technology: FireWire.

MORE INFO ▶ You can find out more about USB at the official USB Implementer's Forum website: www.usb.org.

FireWire

Also standard on many Macs that support Mac OS X v10.6, FireWire is a high-speed, general-purpose peripheral connection originally developed by Apple. FireWire has been ratified as an Institute of Electrical and Electronics Engineers (IEEE) standard known as IEEE-1394, and has been adopted as a standard interface for digital video devices. Like USB, FireWire supports hot-pluggable and daisy-chained connections. Using hubs, each FireWire host controller can support up to 63 simultaneous devices.

FireWire has several advantages over USB. FireWire's primary advantage is that its host controllers work without placing a burden on your computer's main processor, allowing for higher overall performance compared with USB. These sophisticated FireWire host controllers also allow your Mac to be used in target disk mode without the need for a functional operating system, as covered in Chapter 4, "File Systems."

All Macs support FireWire 400 with a maximum transfer rate of up to 400 Mbit/s, and higher-end Macs also support FireWire 800 with a maximum transfer rate of up to 800 Mbit/s. These two FireWire standards use different port connections, but Macs with FireWire 800 ports can connect to FireWire 400 devices with the appropriate adapter. Because FireWire is designed to move large quantities of data efficiently, FireWire 400 outperforms high-speed USB 2.0 even though it has a higher theoretical maximum throughput. This is mainly why FireWire has become a standard for digital video recording devices that require high-bandwidth connectivity.

Also, Apple's FireWire ports generally supply about 7 watts per port, compared with USB's 2.5 watts. This increased power capacity makes FireWire ideal for use with external portable hard drives, as no additional power source is required to run the drive. But the additional cost and complexity of FireWire host controllers makes the technology overkill for many simple peripherals, such as mice, keyboards, and flash drives, which are well served by USB.

MORE INFO ► You can find out more about FireWire at Apple's developer website: http://developer.apple.com/hardwaredrivers/firewire/index.html.

Bluetooth

Bluetooth is a short-range wireless peripheral connection standard originally developed by Ericsson for cell phone headsets. Most Bluetooth devices have a range of only 1 to 10 meters, ideal for peripherals but inadequate for wireless networking. Further, it's not nearly as fast as wireless Ethernet; Bluetooth 1.2 has a maximum transfer speed of up to 721 kbit/s and Bluetooth 2.0 + Extended Data Rate (EDR) a maximum transfer speed of up to 3.0 Mbit/s. However, Bluetooth's primary advantage is that it works with low-power devices.

As Bluetooth increased in popularity, computer manufacturers adopted it for wireless peripherals as well. In addition to providing a wireless connection between your Mac and cell phone, Bluetooth allows your Mac to use wireless headsets, mice, keyboards, and printers. Most Macs that support Mac OS X v10.6 include Bluetooth wireless, and for those that don't, you can easily add it with a USB-to-Bluetooth adapter. You can find out if your Mac has Bluetooth support by opening the System Preferences application and looking for the Bluetooth icon in the Internet & Wireless section. You may also see a small Bluetooth icon in the menu bar near the clock. Configuring Bluetooth is covered in the "Using Bluetooth Peripherals" section later in this chapter.

MORE INFO ▶ You can find out more about Bluetooth at the official Bluetooth Technology Information website: www.bluetooth.com.

Expansion Buses

With expansion buses you can add additional hardware functionality to your Mac, usually in the form of a small computer board often referred to as a *card*. Expansion buses are only found built into the main computer board inside your Mac. Though designed to allow for the addition of any type of technology, expansion buses are most often used to add support for another type of bus or connection. For example, most graphics cards are connected to your Mac via an expansion bus. Other common expansion cards add additional network ports, peripheral bus ports, storage bus connections, or audio and video input/output connections.

Even if you never add an expansion card to your Mac, several internal components are still connected via an expansion bus. Many Mac computers feature a space-saving design that accommodates most users' needs without additional expansion connections. Yet, for those who require hardware expansion, certain Mac OS X v10.6-compatible computers have additional expansion bus connections: Mac Pros, older model 15-inch MacBook Pros, and 17-inch MacBook Pros. The specific type of expansion ports varies by Mac model. As always, you can use the System Profiler application to identify your Mac's expansion bus capabilities.

As of this writing, the three main expansion buses supported by Mac OS X v10.6 compatible hardware are:

▶ PCI Express 1.0 (PCIe or PCI-E)—This more recent version of the PCI standard supports a maximum connection bandwidth of up to 4 GB/s, depending on configuration. All Intel-based Macs use PCIe internally, and Mac Pro features PCIe expansion ports.

▶ PCI Express 2.0 (PCIe or PCI-E)—This latest version of the PCI standard supports a maximum connection bandwidth of up to 8 GB/s, depending on configuration, and is backward compatible with PCIe 1.0 cards. The latest Mac Pros feature PCIe 2.0 expansion ports.

▶ ExpressCard 34—Based on PCIe and USB technology, this expansion format is primarily designed for portable computers and features a maximum connection bandwidth of up to 2.5 Gbit/s. The slot supports both PCIe and USB signaling, so it will use whichever is most appropriate for the inserted card. Some MacBook Pro models feature a single ExpressCard 34 slot.

NOTE ► Some MacBook Pro models feature an SD card slot. While convenient for those needing regular access to SD cards, this is not an expansion-bus technology, as it only allows for connections to SD cards.

Storage Buses

Storage buses are designed to connect your computer to disk or optical storage drives. The age and model of your Mac determines which storage bus technologies are used. But if your Mac features free expansion bus connections, you can generally add any storage bus connections you require via an expansion card.

Some storage buses are designed for internal use, and others can be used externally as well. It's important to know that external storage disk and optical drives connected via USB or FireWire are still using a dedicated storage bus inside the external drive case. So, every disk or optical drive is designed to use a specific storage bus, but those signals can also be retransmitted via a USB or FireWire connection. Therefore, you can purchase empty external drive enclosures that include hardware that bridges the storage bus connection to USB or FireWire, and then install your own internal drive in the case. This is extremely useful for recovering data from a Mac with a functional internal hard drive but otherwise inoperable hardware.

Storage buses supported in various Mac hardware include:

▶ Advanced Technology Attachment (ATA)—Sometimes called Parallel ATA, this storage bus was the most common standard for internal storage for many years and supports a maximum connection bandwidth of up to 133 megabytes per second (MB/s). ATA host controllers are inexpensive because they support only two drives per controller. Many Macs still use ATA-based internal optical drives to reduce product costs.

▶ Serial ATA (SATA)—This improvement on ATA is now the most common storage bus for internal storage. Most current Macs support SATA 3Gbit/s, which sports a maximum connection bandwidth of up to 384 MB/s. SATA host controllers are also inexpensive, but they support only a single drive per controller. All Intel-based Macs use SATA-based internal disk drives. External SATA connectivity can be added to your Mac via an expansion card.

▶ Small Computer System Interface (SCSI)—Sometimes also called Parallel SCSI, this was the original drive interface designed for personal computers. Over the years SCSI has evolved to become the most common storage bus for use in high-end or server computers, and though it supports internal storage, it's more often used for external storage. The latest SCSI supports a maximum connection bandwidth of up to 320 MB/s and up to 16 drives per controller. SCSI connectivity can be added to MacPro via an expansion card.

▶ Serial Attached SCSI (SAS)—This improvement on SCSI is becoming a popular storage bus for use in high-end or server computers. SAS also allows internal and external connections and currently supports a maximum connection bandwidth of up to 3Gbit/s or 384 MB/s and up to 16,384 devices through the use of expanders. The Intel-based Xserve supports internal SAS drives, but again, you can add additional SAS connectivity to your Mac via an expansion card.

▶ Fibre Channel—This is the most advanced SCSI variant and adds network-like features such as long-distance cabling and packet-based communication switching. Fibre Channel can offer speeds up to gigabytes per second. Fibre Channel host controllers are more complicated than other storage controllers, so they are also quite expensive and only available via an expansion card. Apple's Xsan network storage technology is built around Fibre Channel hardware.

Audio and Video Connectivity

Most audio and video connections are point-to-point and don't support multiple devices (like the previously covered bus connections). An audio or video signal is typically output from one device and directly connected to another single device designed to receive the signal.

All Macs, with the exception of some Xserve computers, have a variety of audio and video output connections. Most Macs also include audio input connections that allow you to record audio to digital files. Conversely, no Mac includes built-in support for direct video input. Nevertheless, there are a wide variety of video input options that allow you to capture video files to your Mac via USB, FireWire, or an expansion card.

Audio connections supported by various Macs include:

▶ Analog stereo audio—The standard stereo signal used by most consumer-grade audio equipment, which takes the form of either the 3.5 mm minijack or twin RCA connectors. Nearly every device made by Apple features built-in analog stereo output via minijack, and most Macs also feature analog stereo input.

▶ TOSLINK digital audio—This optical connection has become the most common digital audio connection for consumer-grade audio equipment. While both analog and digital audio connections support varying audio resolutions, digital audio connections do not suffer from electromagnetic interference. Thus, digital audio connections typically provide a much clearer audio signal. Most Intel-based Macs feature digital audio input and output. The Mac Pro uses standard TOSLINK ports, while all other Macs use special audio ports that support both analog stereo minijack and mini-TOSLINK connections.

Video connections supported by various Macs include:

▶ Composite video—This RCA connection is the most common connection for analog standard-definition consumer-grade video. Many older Intel-based Macs can output a composite video signal using an Apple video adapter. However, composite video has an effective resolution of only 640 x 480 pixels, so it's not ideal for computer use.

▶ S-Video—This mini-DIN connection is also a common connection for analog standard-definition consumer-grade video, but it provides a slightly better picture than composite video. Many older Intel-based Macs can output an S-Video signal using an Apple video adapter. S-Video is also hindered by an effective resolution of 640 x 480 pixels.

▶ Video Graphics Array (VGA)—This is the most common connection used for analog computer video displays. Most Macs can output a VGA signal up to a resolution of 1600 x 1200 pixels, with some going as high as 2048 x 1536 pixels. Although older Macs feature built-in VGA ports, Intel-based Macs all require an Apple VGA adapter.

▶ Digital Video Interface (DVI)—This is the most common connection used for digital computer video displays and also high-definition televisions. DVI supports resolutions of up to 1920 x 1200 pixels. For a while Apple used smaller connections for DVI on some Macs to save space. These connections, known as Mini-DVI and Micro-DVI, are electronically identical to DVI; they simply use smaller connections. Many older Macs feature built-in DVI ports, but more recent Macs require an Apple DVI adapter.

▶ Dual-Link DVI (DVI-DL)—This is an extension to the DVI standard that supports resolutions of up to 2560 by 1600 pixels. Older high-end Macs directly support DVI-DL connections, while some newer Macs support this through an Apple DVI-DL adapter.

▶ Mini DisplayPort—This is the most recent display standard used by Apple that's based on a smaller connector version of the DisplayPort standard. DisplayPort is quickly becoming the standard connection for computer-based digital displays because of its support of new technologies and less complicated, ultimately less expensive, display hardware. Apple has stated that going forward all Macs will use Mini DisplayPort for external displays. Both Apple and third parties have created adapters for Mini DisplayPort to other video standards.

▶ High-Definition Multimedia Interface (HDMI)—This is fast becoming the standard connection for consumer-grade digital audio and high-definition video equipment. HDMI combines a DVI-based digital video signal with multichannel digital audio signals in a single, inexpensive copper connection. Although no Mac features built-in HDMI ports, you can convert any DVI connection to HDMI by using an inexpensive cable adapter. However, no current Mac supports audio over HDMI even when using an adapter.

MORE INFO ▶ To identify the various Apple video adapters available, please refer to Apple Knowledge Base article HT3235, "Monitor and Display Adapter Table."

Using Bluetooth Peripherals

Because Bluetooth is a wireless technology, some configuration is required to connect your Mac to a Bluetooth peripheral. The process of connecting Bluetooth devices is known as *pairing*. Once two devices are paired, they will act as if they were directly connected to each other. Mac OS X v10.6 includes a revamped Bluetooth interface that makes the process of configuring peripherals even easier.

NOTE ▶ Desktop Macs can be purchased with only Bluetooth wireless keyboards and mice. If this is the case you will have already paired these devices during first startup with the Mac OS X Setup Assistant.

To set up and manage Bluetooth peripherals:

1   Select the Bluetooth menu extra near the clock on the right side of the menu bar.

Make sure your Mac's Bluetooth is turned on. It's also advisable to disable Discoverable mode, as leaving it enabled is a potential security risk.

NOTE ► Discoverable mode advertises your Mac as a Bluetooth resource to any device within range, which could invite unwanted attention to your Mac. The only time you should enable Discoverable mode is when you are having difficulty pairing your Mac to a Bluetooth peripheral; then you can try it the other way around and attempt to pair the peripheral to your Mac.

2   Enable Discoverable mode on the Bluetooth peripheral you're going to pair with your Mac.

Each device is different, so you may need to consult the device's user guide to enable Discoverable mode. In this example we will be using an Apple Bluetooth keyboard, which is automatically discoverable any time it's not pared to a Mac.

3   From the Bluetooth menu extra select Set Up Bluetooth Device to open the Bluetooth Setup Assistant, which walks you through the setup process.

4 Once open the Bluetooth Setup Assistant scans for any Bluetooth peripherals in range that are in Discoverable mode. It may take several moments for the device's name to appear; once it does, select it and click Continue.

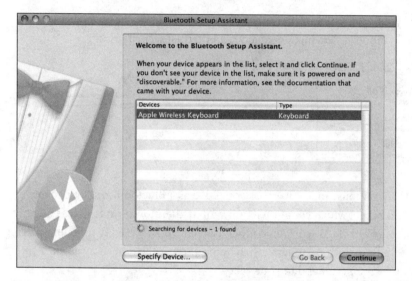

5 For many Bluetooth peripherals, you'll have to enter a passkey to authorize the pairing. Depending on the device, you will perform either of the following:

▶ On your Mac, enter a predefined passkey as given in the device's user guide and click Continue to authorize the pairing.

▶ Allow the Bluetooth Setup Assistant to create a random passkey that you then enter into the Bluetooth device to authorize the pairing. In this example of pairing to an Apple Bluetooth keyboard, this is the case.

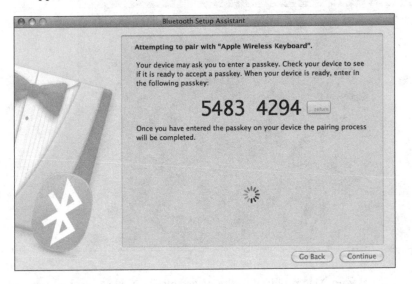

6   The Bluetooth Setup Assistant will automatically detect the capabilities of your Bluetooth peripheral and may present you with additional configuration screens. Continue through these screens until you complete the setup process.

TIP ▶ If you choose to set up iSync using the Bluetooth Setup Assistant, it automatically opens and configures the iSync application. For more, see "Peripherals That Synchronize" later in this chapter.

7 When the pairing is complete you can choose to Quit the Bluetooth Setup Assistant or Set Up Another Device.

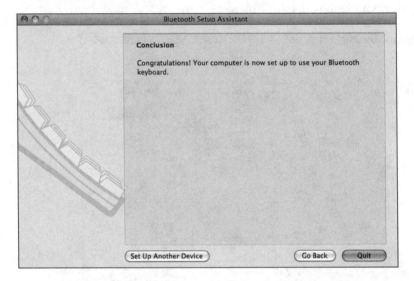

8 You can verify that your Mac is paired to the device by again selecting the Bluetooth menu extra.

Notice that the Bluetooth menu extra indicates that the setup has changed the name of the keyboard to match the user account. You can adjust settings like the peripheral's name from the Bluetooth preferences.

9 To access all the Bluetooth management settings open Bluetooth preferences from either the Apple menu > System Preferences or the Bluetooth menu extra > Open Bluetooth Preferences.

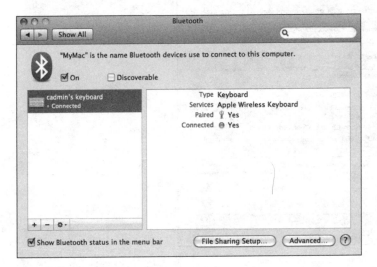

10 To manage a Bluetooth peripheral, select it from the list and then click the Action (gear) button to reveal a pop-up menu with management choices.

You can also use the plus and minus keys at the bottom of the Bluetooth devices list to add or delete peripheral pairings.

11 Optionally, click the Advanced button to reveal a dialog allowing you to adjust additional Bluetooth settings.

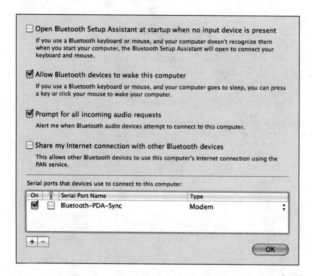

12 Optionally, click the File Sharing Setup button to open the Bluetooth pane of the Sharing preferences, which allows you to adjust Bluetooth sharing settings.

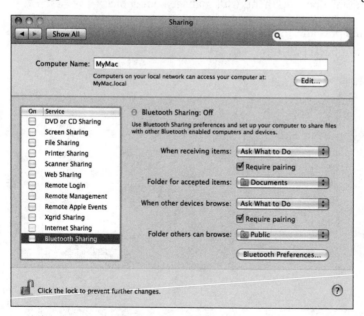

Peripherals that Synchronize

Some peripherals are sophisticated enough that they are computers themselves, managing personal information such as contacts and calendar events. Examples include Bluetooth-enabled cell phones, iPods, iPhones, and Apple TVs. As you use your Mac and the peripheral separately to make changes to this information, the two devices will invariably have conflicting information. Thus, synchronization software is required to consolidate any differences between your Mac and the peripheral.

Mac OS X features three synchronization methods, each supporting a specific type of peripheral or service: the iTunes application, the iSync application, and the MobileMe service. Fortunately, these three separate methods all draw from the same personal information applications. For instance, no matter which methods are used, your Mac's Address Book application will always take part in the synchronization process to ensure that your contacts are properly updated.

NOTE ▶ Third-party personal information applications, like Entourage, tie into these synchronization systems with varying degrees of compatibility. Always read the application's documentation to be aware of any compatibility issues.

NOTE ▶ As of this writing no built-in Mac OS X sync technology supports mobile devices that run BlackBerry, Palm, or Windows Mobile systems. However, third-party syncing solutions are available from www.markspace.com.

Synchronization methods in Mac OS X include:

▶ iTunes application—This application, located at /Applications/iTunes, is responsible for managing and synchronizing iPods, iPhones, and Apple TVs. Though iTunes was originally used to synchronize audio files to iPods, as Apple's mobile devices advanced so did iTunes, which now synchronizes audio, pictures, video, podcasts, contacts, calendars, email settings, notes, and bookmarks. By default, iTunes automatically opens when you attach an iPod or iPhone to your Mac.

MORE INFO ▸ iTunes has grown so powerful, it's practically another platform. You can find out more about iTunes at Apple's website: www.apple.com/itunes.

▸ iSync application—Located at /Applications/iSync, this application allows you to sync Bluetooth-enabled cell phones. To enable Bluetooth cell phone syncing, pair your Mac to your cell phone as outlined previously in the "Using Bluetooth Peripherals" section of this chapter.

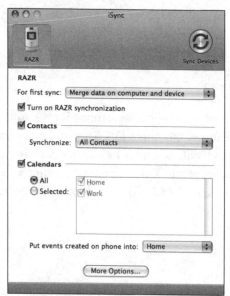

MORE INFO ▶ A full list of supported iSync mobile phones can be found in Apple Knowledge Base article HT2824, "iSync: Supported mobile phones in Mac OS X 10.4, 10.5."

▶ MobileMe service—Subscribers to the MobileMe service can synchronize their personal information to Apple's servers for safekeeping and online access. This also allows MobileMe subscribers to easily maintain the consistency of their personal information between separate computers via the Internet. MobileMe automatically synchronizes your information between Macs, PCs, iPhones, and the MobileMe web portal. You can manage MobileMe settings including synchronization from the MobileMe preferences.

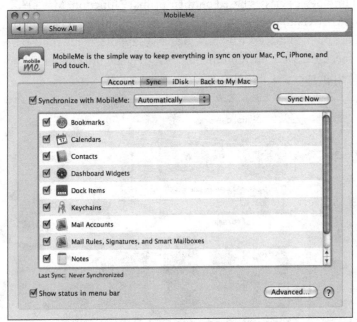

MORE INFO ▶ The MobileMe service provides many more features than synchronization; you can find out more about the MobileMe service at Apple's website: www.apple.com/mobileme.

MORE INFO ▶ If you're having trouble with MobileMe sync you can use the Sync Diagnostics assistant to send diagnostic information to Apple regarding your issue. For more information please refer to Apple Knowledge Base article HT3783, "Mac OS X v10.6: About Sync Diagnostics Assistant."

Troubleshooting Peripherals

Troubleshooting peripheral issues can be difficult because of the wide variety of devices out there. However, peripheral issues can usually be categorized as either software related or hardware related. The first part of this section looks at how the system software interacts with peripherals and how to identify peripheral issues related to software. As for peripheral hardware issues, ultimately replacing or repairing the peripheral or its connections usually resolves the issue. Yet there are a few general troubleshooting techniques you can use to help identify and possibly resolve the problem.

Peripheral Device Classes

Peripherals are divided into device classes based on their primary function. Mac OS X includes built-in software drivers that allow your Mac to interact with peripherals from all device classes. While these built-in drivers may provide basic support, many third-party devices require device-specific drivers for full functionality. Detailed information about software drivers is covered in the next section.

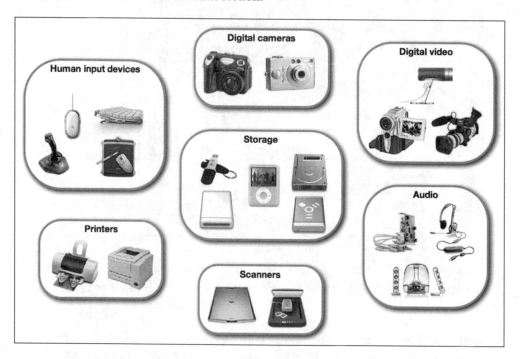

Device classes as defined in Mac OS X include:

▶ Human input devices (HID)—Peripherals that allow you to directly input information or control the Mac's interface. Examples are keyboards, mice, trackpads, game controllers, tablets, and even Braille interfaces.

▶ Storage devices—Disk drives, flash drives, optical drives, and iPods. Storage peripherals are covered in Chapter 4, "File Systems."

▶ Printers—Printers of all types, plotters, and fax machines. Printing is covered later in this chapter.

▶ Scanners—Flatbed, negative, slide, and drum scanners. Mac OS X supports scanners via the Image Capture framework, which allows you to control scanners from /Applications/Image Capture or any other compatible third-party capture application, such as Photoshop.

> **TIP** The Image Capture application supports both locally attached scanners and scanners being shared via the network. Further, the Sharing preferences also allow you to share a locally attached scanner to the network. Network scanner discovery is accomplished using Bonjour, so usually no additional setup is required to locate shared scanning resources.

▶ Digital cameras—These peripherals include both directly connected cameras and camera storage cards mounted to the Mac's file system. Recall that many digital cameras, when connected to a computer, simply extend their internal storage to the computer. In this case, Mac OS X accesses the camera's internal storage, or any directly attached camera storage cards, as it does any other storage device. Applications like iPhoto or Aperture then take over to essentially copy the picture files from the camera storage to the Mac's storage. Some cameras support a tethered capture mode in which they are directly controlled by the Mac and send the captured picture data directly to the Mac. Mac OS X supports this type of camera connection via the Image Capture framework, which also allows you to use /Applications/Image Capture or another compatible third-party capture application.

▶ Video devices—These peripherals include video cameras and video converters connected via USB, FireWire, or an expansion bus. Mac OS X supports these video devices via the QuickTime framework, which allows you to use /Applications/QuickTime Player or any other compatible video application, such as iMovie or Final Cut Pro.

▶   Audio devices—These peripherals include external audio interfaces connected via USB, FireWire, or an expansion bus. Mac OS X supports these audio devices via the Core Audio framework, so you can use any compatible audio application, such as GarageBand or Logic Pro.

Peripheral Device Drivers

One of the primary responsibilities of the system software is to act as an intermediary between peripherals and applications. If an application supports a general device class, the operating system handles all the technical details of communicating with each model of peripheral in that class. Here's an example: For an application to receive user input, it needs to receive information from Mac OS X's human input system, but it doesn't need to know any details about how to interpret the electrical signals from the keyboard or mouse because that's handled by the operating system. This separation of peripherals and applications by the operating system allows you to use nearly any combination of the two with few incompatibilities.

Mac OS X supports peripherals using device drivers, specialized pieces of software that allow peripherals to interoperate with Mac OS X. Some peripherals are supported via a generic driver, but many require a device driver created specifically for the peripheral. Although Mac OS X includes a decent selection of common device drivers, you may have to install third-party device drivers to support your peripherals. Nearly all device drivers are installed using an installer utility that places the driver software in the correct resource folder on your Mac. Device drivers are implemented in one of three ways: kernel extensions, framework plug-ins, or applications.

NOTE ▶ Mac OS X will only use a driver if it's already installed. In other words, if you're adding support for a new third-party peripheral that requires custom drivers, install those drivers first before you connect the peripheral to the Mac.

NOTE ▶ It's always best to check the peripheral manufacturer's website to obtain the latest version of the driver software.

Device driver implementations in Mac OS X include:

▶   Kernel extensions (KEXTs)—This is a special type of software created to add peripheral support at the lowest level of Mac OS X: the system kernel. KEXTs load and unload from the system automatically, so there's no need to manage them aside from making sure they are installed in the correct locations. While some KEXTs are hidden inside application bundles, most are located in the /System/Library/Extensions or /Library/Extensions folders. Remember, in general, nearly all the items in the /System folder are part of the standard Mac OS X install. Examples of peripherals that use KEXTs are human input devices, storage devices, audio and video devices, and other expansion cards.

▶ Framework plug-ins—This type of device driver adds support for a specific peripheral to an existing system framework. For example, support for additional scanners and digital cameras is facilitated via plug-ins to the Image Capture framework.

▶ Applications—In some cases a peripheral is best supported by an application written just for that peripheral. Examples are the iPod and iPhone, which are managed by the iTunes application.

Inspecting Loaded Extensions

Even though the Mac OS X kernel is designed to manage KEXTs without user interaction, you may still need to verify that a specific KEXT is loaded. You can view currently loaded KEXTs from the System Profiler application (choose Apple menu > About This Mac, and click the More Info button in the resulting dialog). Once System Profiler is open, select the Extensions item in the Contents list; it may take a few moments for the system to scan all currently loaded KEXTs. Once the list appears, you can further inspect individual KEXTs by selecting them from this list.

A key feature introduced with Mac OS X v10.6 is support for a 64-bit kernel, thus necessitating 64-bit KEXTs. From System Profiler you can easily identify which loaded extensions support 64-bit mode. Though Mac OS X boots the kernel in 32-bit mode by default, you can force it to boot the kernel in 64-bit mode as outlined in Chapter 10, "System Startup." Using the kernel in 64-bit mode may help performance with certain applications, but before you enable this mode you should make sure all your KEXTs support it. Any KEXTs that don't support 64-bit mode will simply be ignored when booting the kernel in 64-bit mode.

General Peripheral Troubleshooting

General peripheral troubleshooting techniques include:

▶ **Always check System Profiler first.** If you remember only one peripheral troubleshooting technique, it should be this: Connected peripherals appear in System Profiler regardless of functioning software drivers. In other words, if a connected peripheral does not show up in System Profiler, then you are almost certainly experiencing a hardware failure. If a connected peripheral appears as normal in System Profiler, you are probably experiencing a software driver issue. In that case, use System Profiler to validate whether the expected extensions are loaded.

▶ **Unplug and then reconnect the peripheral.** Doing this will reinitialize the peripheral connection and force Mac OS X to reload any peripheral-specific drivers.

▶ **Plug the peripheral into a different port or use a different cable.** This will help you rule out any bad hardware, including host ports, cables, and inoperable hubs.

▶ **Unplug other devices on the same bus.** There may be another device on the shared bus that is causing an issue.

▶ **Resolve potential USB power issues.** As covered previously in this chapter, the USB interface can prove problematic if devices are trying to draw too much power. Try plugging the USB device directly into the Mac instead of any USB hubs.

▶ **Shut down and then restart the Mac.** This tried-and-true troubleshooting technique reinitializes all the peripheral connections and reloads all the software drivers.

▶ **Try the peripheral with another Mac.** This helps you determine whether the issue is with your Mac or the peripheral. If the device doesn't work with other computers, your Mac is not the source of the issue.

▶ **Check for system software and driver software updates.** Software bugs are constantly being fixed, so it's always a good time to check for software updates. You can use Mac OS X's built-in Software Update application, but you should also check the peripheral manufacturer's website for the latest driver updates.

▶ **Check for computer and peripheral firmware updates.** Like software updates, firmware updates may also be necessary to resolve your peripheral issue. This is especially true for more sophisticated devices like iPods and iPhones, which have their own internal firmware.

Configuring Printing and Faxing

Though printing may seem like a trivial task, the software that facilitates it is complex enough to merit devoting a significant portion of this chapter to it. Mac OS X's printing system also handles faxing—after all, a fax is essentially a printer connected via modems communicating across the phone system.

Robust printing has always been an important part of the Mac operating system because of its popularity with graphic design users. Mac OS X v10.5 continued this tradition with an updated printing system featuring redesigned and simplified printing interfaces. In this part of the chapter, you will configure printers and faxes, as well as manage print jobs. You will also learn how to troubleshoot printing issues.

Print and Fax Technology Architecture

Mac OS X v10.6 uses the open source Common UNIX Printing System 1.4 (CUPS) to manage local printing and faxing. Originally an independent product, CUPS was recently purchased by Apple and remains an open source project. Architecturally, CUPS uses the Internet Printing Protocol (IPP) standard as the basis for managing printing and faxing tasks and uses PostScript Printer Description (PPD) files as the basis for printer drivers. Though still used by CUPS, the PPD name is a bit of a misnomer, as non-PostScript printers can also be described by these files.

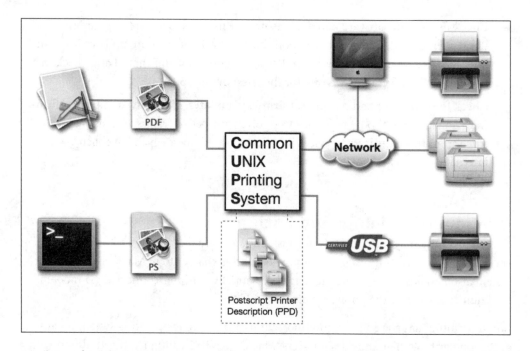

A print or fax job starts when a user prints from either an application in the graphical user interface or the print commands in the command-line interface. When you print from an application, Mac OS X's Quartz graphics system generates a Portable Document Format (PDF) file. When you print from the command line, a PostScript (PS) file is generated. In either case, the file created is called a spool file and is placed inside the /var/spool/cups folder. The CUPS background process, cupsd, takes this spool file and passes it through a series of filter processes known as the print chain. These processes convert the spool file to a format that is understood by the destination printer or fax, and then ultimately communicate this information to the printer (or in the case of a local fax, your Mac's modem).

MORE INFO ▶ CUPS provides capabilities beyond the scope of this text. To find out more visit the official CUPS website at www.cups.org.

Printing and Faxing Drivers

Before you can print or fax, you must configure printer or fax modem settings, which includes associating an appropriate printer driver with the printing device. This association happens automatically as you configure a new printing device; however, the system must have the printer driver installed before it can use the printer. Apple supplies printer drivers for most popular models, among them Brother, Canon, Epson, EFI, Hewlett-Packard, Lexmark, Ricoh, Samsung, and Xerox.

> **MORE INFO** ▶ For a complete list of printer and scanner drivers available from Apple for Mac OS X, please refer to Knowledge Base article HT3669, "Mac OS X v10.6: Printer and scanner software."

Depending on the install options that were selected during system installation, you may or may not have to install additional printer drivers. The default selection, designed to save space on the system volume, is to install only drivers for printers in use by the Mac, or nearby and popular printers. During installation you can choose to install all available printer drivers at the time of the disc's creation. This installer is also available after system installation from the Optional Installs on the Mac OS X Install DVD. Installing all the available printer drivers occupies well over 1 GB of storage space, so you can choose to install no third-party printer drivers during system installation.

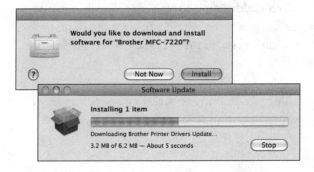

If you attempt to add a printer that the Mac does not have the driver for and you are connected to the Internet, the system will prompt you to automatically download and install the driver using Apple's Software Update service. Obviously if you aren't connected to the Internet, then you will have to acquire the printer driver manually, though some standard PostScript and PCL printers can use the built-in generic printer drivers. Also, if Apple doesn't provide the printer driver via its Software Update mechanism you will have to manually acquire the appropriate driver, often directly from the printer's manufacturer.

> NOTE ▶ You must log in or authenticate as an administrative user to install printer drivers either manually or via Software Update.

> NOTE ▶ The automatic printer driver installer from Software Update will often install multiple printer drivers from the same manufacturer simultaneously.

A few of the built-in Apple printer drivers are installed in /System/Library/Printers, but all of the third-party printer drivers will be installed to the /Library/Printers folder. The primary folder for drivers is the PPD folder, but you may notice other vendor folders that contain ancillary printer driver resources.

Once you've added a printer or fax configuration, a copy of the PPD with the name of the device is placed in the /etc/cups/ppd folder and two configuration files are modified: /etc/cups/printers.conf and /Library/Preferences/org.cups.printers.plist. Finally, the first time a user prints or accesses a printer or fax queue, the system will create a printer or fax queue application, again with the name of the device, in the ~/Library/Printers folder in the user's home folder.

> TIP ▶ When adding supported multifunction printers, scanning and faxing services will also be configured along with general printing services.

Configuring a Directly Attached Printer

If your Mac already has the correct printer driver for a directly attached USB or FireWire printer, the system automatically detects the appropriate settings and configures the new printer for you as soon as you plug it in. It's important to note, however, that this automatic configuration only occurs if an administrative user is currently logged into the Mac. You can verify the printer has been added by simply opening the Print dialog from any application (File > Print in the menu bar) or the Print & Fax preferences. In the Print & Fax preferences you can tell which printers are locally connected if their location is shown as the same name as the local Mac's sharing name.

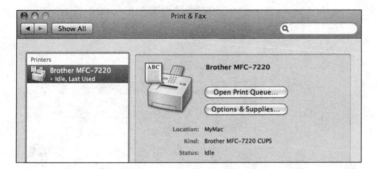

If the driver isn't installed but is available from Apple, you will be prompted with the automatic Software Update install mechanism when you plug the printer in. If an administrative user chooses to install the printer driver, after installation the printer will be automatically configured as well. Finally, if a printer driver for a directly attached printer is unavailable from Apple, then nothing will happen automatically when you plug it in. You will have to manually acquire and install the printer driver to get it working.

Configuring a Local Network Printer

Conversely, network printer and all fax configurations have to be manually added, but Apple has made this process incredibly easy for locally networked printers. If the printer you wish to add is on the local network, either as a standalone printer advertising via Bonjour (also known as mDNS) or being shared via another Mac or AirPort base station, then all you need to do is select it from the Print dialog (File > Print in the menu bar) from any application. Once in the Print dialog, select the Printer pop-up menu and the system will scan the local network for available printers to select from. As covered previously, the Mac will either configure the printer with a preinstalled driver or prompt to download the driver from Apple's Software Update service. Again, note that only adminis-trative users can add printers.

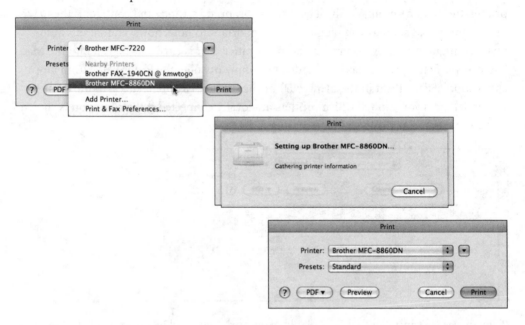

NOTE ► If a network printer requires authentication you may be presented with an authentication dialog in order to print to the shared printer.

NOTE ► Your Mac will automatically acquire the appropriate printer drivers from any Mac that is sharing a printer via the network. In other words, the Mac hosting a shared printer will automatically send your Mac the drivers if they aren't preinstalled.

Manually Configuring a Printer

If the network printer doesn't support automatic network discovery via Bonjour, then you will have to configure it manually via the Add Printer window. Also, if a directly attached printer does not automatically configure, then you can manually add it. You can open the Add Printer window at any time to manually add new printers or faxes. Again, non-administrative users will have to provide administrator authentication to access the Add Printer window.

NOTE ▶ Mac OS X v10.6 no longer supports the AppleTalk network protocol and thus no longer supports printing via AppleTalk network printers.

NOTE ▶ Bluetooth printers are configured via the Bluetooth Setup Assistant as covered in the "Using Bluetooth Peripherals" section earlier in this chapter.

To manually add a new printer or fax:

1 Open the Add Printer window via one of the following methods:

▶ From any application open a Print dialog by choosing File > Print from the menu bar. Next, from the Printer pop-up menu select Add Printer.

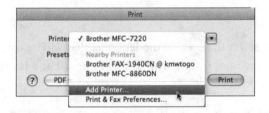

▶ Open the Print & Fax preferences by choosing Apple menu > System Preferences, then clicking the Print & Fax icon. Click the lock icon in the bottom-left corner and authenticate as an administrative user to unlock the Print & Fax preferences. Finally, click the small plus button at the bottom of the Printers list.

▶ From the Finder open the /System/Library/CoreServices/AddPrinter application. This application's icon can also be placed in your Dock.

2 The Add Printer window features several panes for selecting a printer or fax. These panes are accessed by clicking the following buttons in the toolbar:

▶ Default—This browser lets you select directly attached USB and FireWire printers and network printers discovered using Bonjour or network directory services.

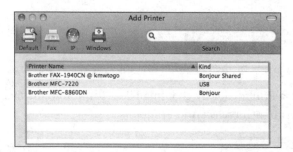

▶ Fax—This browser allows you to select the specific modem port that will be used for incoming and outgoing fax transmissions. Configuring your Mac to act as a fax is covered in the next section of this chapter.

▶ IP—This dialog allows you to manually enter the IP address or DNS hostname of a Line Printer Daemon (LPD), IPP, or HP JetDirect printer. You must select the appropriate protocol from the pop-up menu and enter the printer's address. Entering a printer queue is optional.

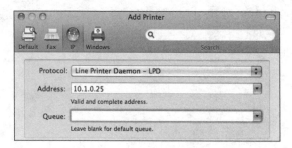

▶ Windows—This browser lets you select printers shared via the SMB printer sharing protocol. Double-click on a SMB server and authenticate to access the server's shared printers.

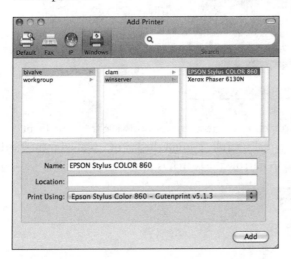

3   Once you have selected a printer or fax modem from the top half of the new printer configuration dialog, the system will complete the bottom half for you using information it has discovered. This includes automatically selecting the appropriate printer driver if possible.

Often this information isn't ideal, and you can easily change it. The Name and Location fields are only there to help you identify the device, so you can set those to anything you like.

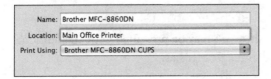

4 If you're configuring an LPD, HP JetDirect, or SMB printer the odds are very high that you will have to manually specify the appropriate printer driver.

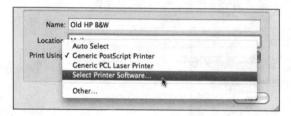

To specify a specific printer driver, choose Select Printer Software from the Print Using pop-up menu. You can manually scroll through the list of installed printer drivers, but using the Spotlight field to narrow the search is much quicker.

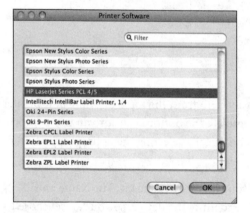

5 Once you have selected and configured the new printer or fax, click the Add button to finish the printer's configuration.

If you are configuring an IP printer, then you may be presented with an additional dialog to select any special options that the printer has.

6 You can verify the printer has been added by simply opening the Print dialog from any application or the Print & Fax preferences.

In the Print & Fax preferences you can tell which printers are connected via network if their location is shown as something different than your local Mac's sharing name.

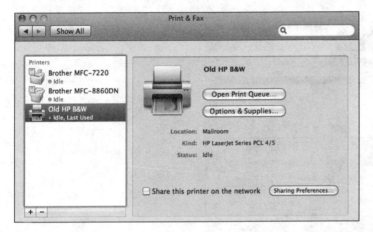

Configuring Fax Services

Creating a fax printer configuration, similar to adding a printer, is all that's required to prepare your Mac to send faxes. However, a few more steps are required to configure your Mac to *receive* faxes.

TIP You can also share your Mac's faxing capabilities via the network as detailed in the "Sharing Printers and Faxes" section later in this chapter.

To configure your Mac to send faxes:

1   Open and unlock the Print & Fax preferences, and then click the small plus button at the bottom of the Printers list to open the Add Printer dialog.

2   From the Add Printer dialog click the Fax button in the toolbar and then select a fax connection.

You will be able to choose either using Bluetooth DUN for faxing via a paired Bluetooth enabled mobile phone or External Modem for faxing via the Apple USB

Modem. The system will automatically complete the lower half of the Add Printer dialog, but you can change both Name and Location to whatever is most convenient.

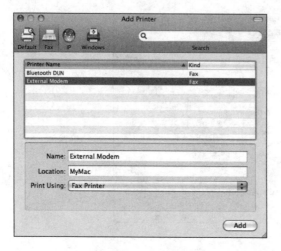

3   After you have selected a fax configuration, click the Add button to add the fax printer to your printer list.

4   Back at the Print & Fax preferences you should at least enter the fax number for the line configured as your Mac's fax.

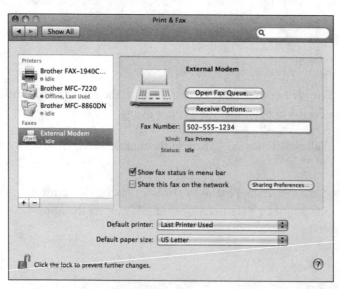

TIP ▶ Quickly view the status of your Mac's fax configuration by selecting "Show fax status in menu bar," which enables the fax status menu item on the far-right side of the menu bar near the time.

At this point you can now send faxes from any application that can print. From any Print dialog simply start a print job that specifies the fax printer you just created. At that point the Print dialog will automatically expand and allow you to enter a phone number for the destination fax and optionally create a fax cover page. To enable your Mac to receive faxes you must perform a few more configuration steps.

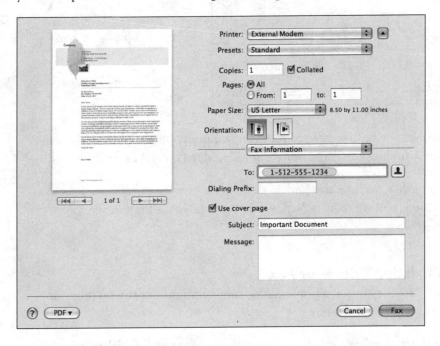

MORE INFO ▶ Detailed print job settings are covered in "Managing Print Jobs" later in this chapter.

To configure your Mac to receive faxes:

1   Open and unlock the Print & Fax preferences, and then select a fax printer from the printers list.

2 Click the Receive Options button to reveal a dialog where you'll enable and configure your Mac to receive incoming faxes. At the very least, you must select the "Receive faxes on this computer" checkbox.

You can also define the number of rings before the fax will answer and the destination folder for the received fax documents, which are saved as PDF files. Optionally, you can have the Mac automatically print or email received fax documents.

3 Click OK when you have completed your configuration options, and the Mac will wait patiently for incoming faxes as long as it's powered on and awake.

NOTE ▶ Your Mac can't receive faxes in sleep mode. You can disable your Mac's automatic sleep activation or enable wake for network access from the Energy Saver preferences.

Modify an Existing Printer or Fax

You may find it necessary to edit a printer or fax configuration after you set it up. From the Print & Fax preferences, you can:

▶ Delete a printer or fax configuration—Select the item you wish to delete from the printer and fax list, and then click the small minus button at the bottom of the list.

▶ Set printing defaults—From the two pop-up menus at the bottom of the Print & Fax preferences, select the default printer and paper size. Use caution when setting the default printer for Last Printer Used; because you will effectively have no permanent default printer, the default destination for print jobs may constantly change.

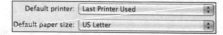

▶ Edit an existing configuration and check supply levels—Simply select the configuration from the printer and fax list and click the Options & Supplies button. In the resulting dialog you can easily edit the printer's configuration including changing the selected printer driver and, if available, check the printer supply levels and open the printer's hardware configuration utility.

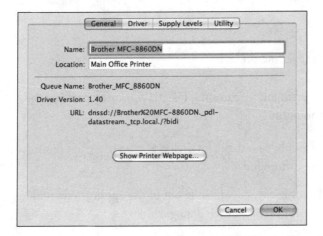

NOTE ▶ The only way to edit a fax configuration is by accessing its print queue application, as covered in "Managing Print Jobs" later in this chapter.

Managing Print Jobs

Mac OS X features a unified Print dialog that combines previously separate Page Setup and Print dialogs. The Page Setup dialog typically contains document size, orientation, and scale settings, and the Print dialog has all other printer settings. For backward compatibility, Mac OS X 10.6 allows older applications to continue to use separate Page Setup and Print dialogs, but older apps will still be able to use the new unified printing interface when you open a Print dialog. In other words, some older applications will have document settings in both the Page Setup and the Print dialogs.

This unified Print dialog also features two modes: Basic mode allows you to quickly start a print job based on print setting presets, and advanced mode allows you to specify any page or print option and save print setting presets.

NOTE ▶ Some applications, especially graphic design and desktop publishing applications, use custom print dialogs that may look different from the standard Print dialog covered in this chapter.

NOTE ▶ If a network printer requires authentication you may be presented with an authentication dialog in order to print to the shared printer.

Basic Printing

To start a print job based on print setting presets:

1   From an application, start a print job by choosing File > Print or by pressing the Command-P keyboard combination.

NOTE ▶ Some applications will bypass the Print dialog and issue a print job to your default printer when you use Command-P.

The Print dialog appears. In some cases it will slide out of the application's window title bar; in other cases it will appear as its own dialog window.

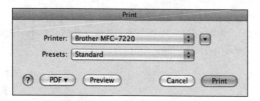

2   The default printer and print preset will be selected, but you can choose any other configured printer or preset from the associated pop-up menu.

Creating your own printer presets is covered in the next section of this chapter.

3   Click the Print button to start the print job.

The system will automatically open the print queue application associated with the destination printer. Though no window will open if the print job is successful, you will be able to click on the print queue in the Dock.

Advanced Printing and Print Presets

To start a print job based on custom print settings:

1   From an application open the Print dialog by choosing File > Print or by pressing Command-P.

2   The default printer and print preset will be selected, but you can choose any other configured printer or preset from the associated pop-up menu.

3   Click the small arrow button to the right of the selected printer, and the Print dialog will expand to its advanced mode.

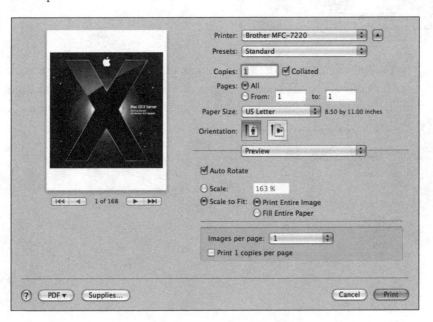

The arrow button will toggle the Print dialog between basic and advanced modes. The Print dialog also remembers which mode you were in last for each application. In other words, every application will start with a simple Print dialog the first time you print, but for subsequent print jobs, the Print dialog will open to the mode last used for each individual application.

4   On the left side of the advanced Print dialog, you can page through a preview of the print job. Any changes you make to the page layout settings are instantly reflected in the preview.

5   On the right side of the dialog, you can configure all possible print settings for most applications. The top half features basic page setup and print settings.

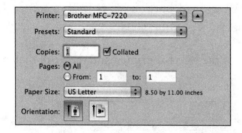

Settings on the bottom half vary based on the application you're printing from and your selected printer's driver. You can select a category of print settings to modify by choosing it from the pop-up menu that separates the print settings from top to bottom.

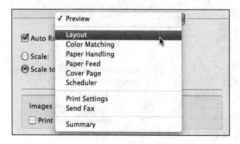

Explore each settings category and don't forget to review your settings from the print Summary category, again accessed via the pop-up menu.

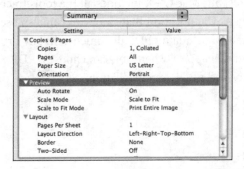

6 To save the current print settings as a preset, choose Save As from the Presets pop-up menu. Select if you want this preset to apply to all printers or just the currently selected printer. Give the preset a name in the resulting dialog and click OK to save it.

NOTE ▶ Print presets do not save application-specific settings.

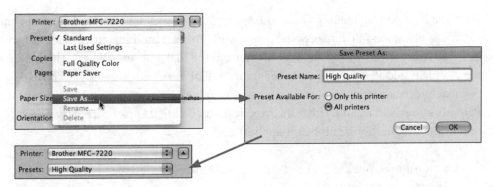

The preset will now be accessible from the Preset pop-up menu from both basic and advanced Print dialogs. The print presets are saved to the ~/Library/Preferences/com. apple.print.custompresets.plist file, so each user has her own custom print presets.

7 Click the Print button to start the job based on your print settings.

Using PDF Tools

Mac OS X includes a built-in PDF workflow architecture and editing tools. The full Adobe Acrobat suite has more advanced PDF features, but Mac OS X includes all the tools to create PDF documents or perform basic editing. Any application that can print can also use Mac OS X's Quartz imaging system to generate high-quality PDF documents. In any Print dialog, click the PDF button. A pop-up menu will appear where you can choose a PDF workflow destination, including the ability to save a PDF to any location.

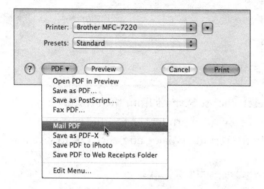

From the PDF pop-up menu you can also specify a PDF workflow designed to accept and automatically process PDF files. Some preset workflows are built in, but you can add your own PDF workflows by choosing Edit Menu from the PDF pop-up menu. Alternately, you can manually add PDF workflows to the /Library/PDF Services, or the ~/Library/PDF Services folders, depending on who needs access to the PDF workflows. To create custom PDF workflows you can use either the /Applications/Utilities/AppleScript Editor application or the /Applications/Automator application.

> **MORE INFO** ▶ You can find out more about AppleScript, Apple's English-like automation technology, and Automator in Chapter 3, "Command Line and Automation."

Mac OS X's /Applications/Preview application also offers comprehensive PDF editing functionality—you can edit and adjust individual elements, reorder pages, crop the document, add annotations, and fill out form data. From Preview you can also convert PDF files to other formats or resave the PDF file using more appropriate settings.

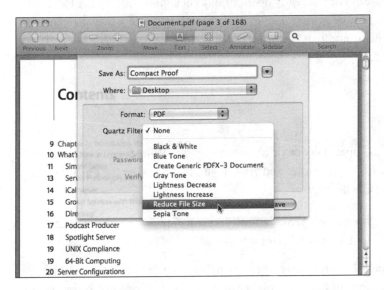

Managing Printer Queues

As stated previously, when a print or fax job is started the spool file is placed inside the /var/spool/cups folder, and then CUPS takes over to process the file and send it to the printer or fax modem. When you print from the graphical interface, Mac OS X opens a print queue application to manage the print job. If a job completes quickly, the file will only be in the print or fax queue for a few moments and the print queue application will quit when done. However, printers always seem to be the most problematic of peripherals, so often your Mac will not be able to complete the print job. The printer or fax queue application will remain open until the print job finishes or you resolve the print issue.

> **NOTE ▶** If Mac OS X detects an error with the printer or fax modem, it will stop all print jobs to that device. You will still be able to issue print jobs, but they will simply fill up in the device's queue.

To manage print and fax job queues:

1 You can access the print or fax queue application using one of the following methods:

▶ If a printer or fax queue is already open, simply click on its icon in the Dock. In the example screen shot the printer queue's Dock icon is indicating that there are currently two jobs in queue and that the printer is disconnected.

▶ You can manually open a fax or print queue from the Print & Fax preferences by selecting the device from the printer and fax list, and then clicking the Open Print Queue or Open Fax Queue button.

2 When the printer or fax queue opens, you will immediately see the current status of the printer and any current queued print jobs.

Here is a typical example print queue when the printer is offline and the user has printed multiple versions of the same job because he incorrectly assumed this would fix the issue. Mac OS X will automatically detect when the printer becomes available again, assuming the queue isn't paused.

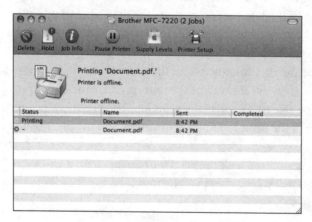

3   To pause or resume the printer queue, click the Pause Printer or Resume Printer button in the queue application toolbar.

4   To hold or resume a specific print job, select it from the job list and then click the Hold or Resume button in the queue application toolbar.

You can also delete a job by selecting it from the job list and then clicking the Delete button in the queue application toolbar.

TIP Selecting a job and pressing the Space bar will open a Quick Look preview window of the print job.

Once you are done managing a printer or fax queue, it's acceptable to leave the application running. You may find it useful to leave often-used print and fax queues in the Dock for direct access. Simply right-click or Control-click on the queue application's Dock icon and from the shortcut menu choose Keep in Dock. You can also provide quick access to all your print and fax queues by dragging the ~/Library/Printers folder to your Dock. Clicking on this folder in your Dock reveals all configured devices.

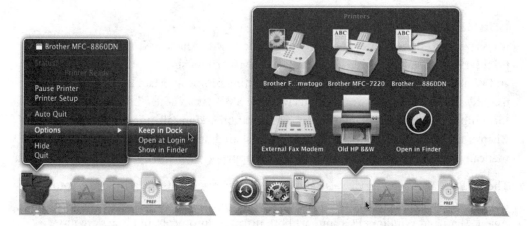

There are also some other features available in the printer queue application's toolbar. For instance, to check the printer's supplies click the Supply Levels button. You can also reconfigure nearly all of the printer's settings by clicking the Printer Setup button in the toolbar. Finally, if the queue is for a supported multifunction printer, you can click the Scanner button in the toolbar to change the printer queue window into an image capture window. Mac OS X supports scanning to multifunction devices both locally and via the network.

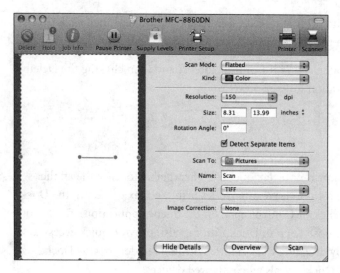

Sharing Printers and Faxes

It's very easy to share printer and fax configurations with Mac OS X. Your Mac's shared print service is made available via the IPP and SMB printer sharing protocols. While Macs and Windows PCs technically support both printing protocols, Macs are more likely to use IPP, and Windows PCs are more likely to use SMB. As an added bonus, the IPP protocol supports automatic printer driver configuration and installation for Mac systems, so when another Mac user connects to your Mac's shared print service, her system will automatically select, and download if necessary, the appropriate printer drivers.

The CUPS shared print service also allows other network clients to easily locate your shared printer and fax configurations with Bonjour for IPP or NetBIOS/WINS for SMB. Again, Macs and Windows PCs support both discovery protocols, but Macs are more likely to use Bonjour, and Windows PCs are more likely to use NetBIOS/WINS. Or, network clients can manually enter your Mac's IP address or DNS hostname to access your Mac's shared print service. Configuring your Mac's identification for providing network services is covered in Chapter 8, "Network Services."

NOTE ▶ Users will not be able to access shared print services on a Mac in sleep mode. You can disable your Mac's automatic sleep activation or enable wake for network access from the Energy Saver preferences.

To share printers and faxes from your Mac:

1 Open and unlock the Sharing preferences.

2 Select the Printer Sharing checkbox to enable printer and fax sharing.

Selecting this checkbox tells the cupsd process (which is always running in the background) to listen for IPP print service requests on TCP port 631. By default, only locally connected printers will be shared.

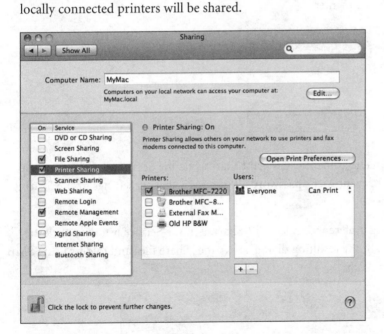

3 To enable sharing for additional printer or fax configurations, simply select the checkboxes next to the printers or faxes you wish to share.

You can also enable specific printing devices for sharing from the Print & Fax preferences.

NOTE ▶ It may be a bad idea to reshare network printers using your Mac's shared print services if network printers are already available on your network.

4 Optionally, you can limit who is allowed to print to your shared printers or faxes. By default all users are allowed access to your shared printing devices. To limit access select a shared device from the Printers list and then click the small plus button at the bottom of the Users list.

A dialog will appear allowing you to select user or group accounts that you wish to grant access to the printing device. By adding additional accounts you can also choose to deny access to guest users by selecting No Access to Everyone in the Users list. Also, with limited printing access enabled, all users will have to authenticate in order to print to your shared printer.

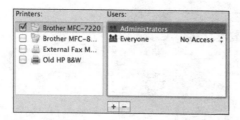

5 If you need to enable authenticated print sharing via the SMB protocol, you must also enable the relevant user's passwords in the SMB sharing settings of the Sharing preferences.

From the Sharing preferences, select File Sharing in the Service list, then click the Options button. In the resulting dialog, select the "Share files and folders using SMB (Windows)" checkbox.

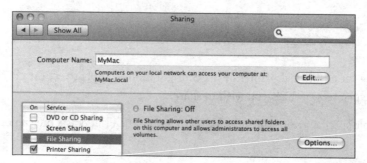

NOTE ▶ SMB file sharing does not need to be enabled for SMB print sharing.

Finally, you'll select and enter passwords for the user accounts you wish to allow to connect to your SMB shared resources. Click the Done button once you have made your selections.

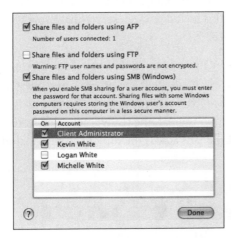

The launchd control process will now listen for SMB service requests on TCP port 139, and automatically start the smbd background process as necessary to handle any requests.

MORE INFO ▶ You can find out more about file sharing services in Chapter 8, "Network Services."

Advanced Printing Management

The CUPS software in your Mac OS X system was first built as a print server, though most of the time it only serves printing for one system. CUPS was also originally designed for UNIX systems, so it provides comprehensive print management tools for the command-line interface. To foster adoption of the CUPS architecture, it's licensed as free and open source software, so any system can take advantage of its printing capabilities.

CUPS Web-Based Administration

All these CUPS attributes—being server-based, UNIX-based, and open source—led to the need for a common interface to manage the CUPS system that doesn't require specific system software. While it's true that all CUPS-compatible systems have a command line, most users simply aren't comfortable navigating the command line, especially for something as fundamental as printing. Thus, CUPS also includes a web server that provides a full web-based graphical administration interface.

You can access your Mac's CUPS web interface by opening a web browser and entering the following URL: http://localhost:631/. This URL essentially tells the browser to request a website on your local Mac via TCP port 631. The CUPS web interface home page lists the available documentation. While the documentation is great, the really interesting features from a management perspective are the rest of the tabs across the top of the page including Administration, Jobs, and Printers.

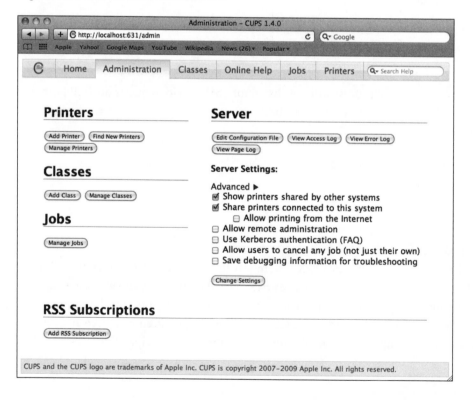

Exploring the details of the CUPS web interface is beyond the scope of this guide, but the page is well documented and is the best place to start digging deeper into CUPS. A few of the web interface highlights include the ability to enable remote CUPS administration, essentially allowing you to access the Mac's CUPS web interface from another computer. Also new in CUPS with Mac OS X v10.6 is the ability to create web RSS feeds with print accounting information. This allows you to use an RSS aggregator application to keep tabs on printing statistics.

> **NOTE** ► If you aren't already comfortable with navigation in the UNIX command line, it's strongly recommended that you study the command line concepts in Chapter 3, "Command Line and Automation," before reading the remainder of section.

Modifying Printer Administration Rights

As stated previously, by default, you must be an administrative user to make changes to printer and fax settings. However, you can change this default and give any number of specific users and groups the ability to administrate printer and fax settings. With CUPS, only those belonging to the system group "_lpadmin" can do this. You can't edit this group using the Accounts preferences, so if you want to grant additional administration rights for printing and faxing you will have to use the command line group editor dseditgroup.

In the following example, Michelle, as an administrative user, adds the Logan user account to the _lpadmin group using the dseditgroup command. Thus, Michelle is giving Logan the ability to manage printing and fax settings. Note that Michelle has to put her account name in the dsedigroup command arguments and then provider her password.

```
MyMac:~ michelle$ dseditgroup -o edit -u michelle -a logan _lpadmin
```

Here is a different example in which Michelle uses the same command, but this time adds the staff group to the _lpadmin group. As covered in Chapter 2, "User Accounts," all local users are in the staff group. Thus, Michelle is effectively giving local users the ability to manage printing and fax settings.

```
MyMac:~ michelle$ dseditgroup -o edit -u michelle -t group -a staff _lpadmin
```

TIP ▶ To delete a user or group using `dseditgroup`, instead of using
`-o edit`, use `-o delete`.

Command Line Print Management

The first generally useful printing command is `lpq`. This command will let you view current jobs in print and fax queues. The syntax is `lpq` followed by any command options. In the following example, Michelle uses the `lpq` command with the `-a` option to view all jobs on all print devices:

```
MyMac:~ michelle$ lpq -a
Rank Owner Job File(s) Total Size
1st michelle 10 Boot Camp.pdf 444416 bytes
2nd michelle 13 APSG Jan06.pdf 869376 bytes
```

The `lprm` command lets you delete current print jobs in print and fax queues. The syntax is simply `lprm`, and if no more information is provided it deletes the first job in the default printer queue. Here, Michelle uses the `lprm` command to delete the first print job from the previous example, then checks the queue with the `lpq -a` command. She enters the `lprm` command again to delete the final job, and then checks the queue one last time:

```
MyMac:~ michelle$ lprm
MyMac:~ michelle$ lpq -a
Rank Owner Job File(s) Total Size
1st michelle 13 APSG Jan06.pdf 869376 bytes
MyMac:~ michelle$ lprm
MyMac:~ michelle$ lpq -a
no entries
```

The `lpr` command lets you print a file from the command line. The syntax is simply `lpr` and then the path to a print-ready file. A print-ready file is any PDF- or PS-formatted document. In the following example, Michelle uses the `lpr` command to print the MyDoc.pdf file in her Desktop folder, and then she checks the print queue with the `lpq -a` command:

```
MyMac:~ michelle$ lpr Desktop/MyDoc.pdf
MyMac:~ michelle$ lpq -a
Rank Owner Job File(s) Total Size
1st michelle 13 MyDoc.pdf 235123 bytes
```

Troubleshooting the Printing System

You will probably experience more printing issues caused by hardware than by software. However, this being a reference about Mac OS X, the following is a series of mostly software-based general print system troubleshooting techniques. These techniques are based on information from Apple Knowledge Base document HT1465, "Troubleshooting printing issues in Mac OS X":

▶ **Always check the printer queue application first.** The print and fax queue application will always show the first symptoms of an issue, and odds are you were made aware of the issue by the queue. The print queue will let you know if there is a printer connection issue, but you should also check to make sure the queue is not paused and that none of the jobs are on hold. Sometimes deleting old print jobs from the queue will help clear the problem.

▶ **Double-check page and print settings.** If the job is printing but doesn't print correctly, double-check page and print settings using the Print dialog's advanced mode.

▶ **Review the PDF output of the application.** Remember that the CUPS workflow is application > PDF > CUPS > printer. Thus, verifying if the PDF looks correct will let you know if the source of the problem is with the application or the printing system.

▶ **Print from another application.** If you suspect the application is at the root of the problem, try printing from another application. You can also print a test page while in the printer queue application by choosing Printer > Print Test Page.

▶ **Check the printer hardware.** Many modern printers have diagnostic screens or printed reports that can help you identify a hardware issue. Many also have a software utility or a built-in webpage that may report errors. Clicking the Printer Setup button in the printer queue application's toolbar will access these management interfaces. Also, don't forget to double-check cables and connections. Finally, you may be well served by contacting the printer manufacturer to diagnose printer hardware issues.

▶ **For fax issues, check phone line and phone settings.** As with any fax system issue, you need to check for modem and phone line problems. When sending faxes via the print system, you may encounter issues that are outside of your control because you are relying on the phone system and another user's fax hardware.

▶ **For directly connected printers, use peripheral troubleshooting techniques.** For printers connected via USB or FireWire, use the peripheral troubleshooting techniques outlined earlier in this chapter.

▶ **For network printers, use network troubleshooting techniques.** For printers connected via a network connection, use the network troubleshooting techniques described in Chapter 7, "Network Configuration."

▶ **Delete and then reconfigure printers or faxes.** From the Print & Fax preferences, delete and then reconfigure a troublesome printer or fax using the techniques outlined earlier in this chapter. This will reset the device's drivers and queue.

▶ **Reset the entire print system.** Sometimes it's necessary to reset the entire printing system. From the Print & Fax preferences, right-click or Control-click anywhere in the printers and fax list and choose "Reset printing system" from the shortcut menu. Click OK in the verification dialog. Next you'll have to authenticate as an administrative user. This clears all configured devices, shared settings, custom presets, and queued print jobs. While this may seem drastic, it's likely to clear up any software-related printing issues.

▶ **Review CUPS log files.** Like other system services, CUPS writes all important activity to log files. You can access these logs while in any printer queue application by choosing Printer > Log & History. This opens the Console utility to the CUPS error_log file. While in the Console you can also check the CUPS access_log and page_log files located in /private/var/log/cups.

NOTE ▶ The CUPS error_log file may not exist if the CUPS service hasn't yet logged any serious print errors.

▶ **Reinstall or update printer drivers.** Again, software bugs are always being fixed, so it's always a good time to check for printer driver updates. You can use Mac OS X's built-in Software Update application to check for system updates and many printer updates. However, be sure to also check the printer manufacturer's website for the latest printer driver updates.

▶ **Repair installed software disk permissions.** Third-party installers tend to sometimes mess up system software permissions. Use Disk Utility's Repair Permissions feature to resolve permissions issues with printer drivers and other print system files (see Chapter 4, "File Systems").

What You've Learned

▶ Mac OS X supports a wide variety of peripherals, expansion cards, storage devices, and audio/video connections.

▶ Bluetooth peripherals require paring for the Mac to securely access their services.

▶ These devices are supported in groups of device classes, and Mac OS X includes a selection of generic software drivers.

▶ Built-in and third-party drivers are supported via kernel extensions, framework plug-ins, and stand-alone applications.

▶ Mac OS X uses CUPS to provide print and fax services for both local and shared users.

▶ A rich PDF workflow capability is also built into Mac OS X.

▶ You learned a variety of peripheral and printing troubleshooting techniques.

References

Check for current Knowledge Base documents at www.apple.com/support.

Peripherals

HT1720, "USB Device Troubleshooting"

TA26476, "FireWire: Frequently Asked Questions"

HT3039, "What you can do with Bluetooth wireless technology"

HT3235, "Monitor and Display Adapter Table"

HT2824, "iSync: Supported mobile phones in Mac OS X 10.4, 10.5"

HT3783, "Mac OS X v10.6: About Sync Diagnostics assistant"

HT3825, "Mac OS X v10.6: Digital camera RAW formats supported"

Printing

HT3771, "Mac OS X v10.6: Mac 101 – Printing"

HT1465, "Troubleshooting printing issues in Mac OS X"

HT3669, "Mac OS X v10.6: Printer and scanner software"

URLs

Official USB Implementer's Forum resource website: www.usb.org

Apple's official FireWire developer website: http://developer.apple.com/hardwaredrivers/firewire/index.html

Official Bluetooth Technology Information website: www.bluetooth.com

Mark/Space provides sync software drivers for third-party mobile devices: www.markspace.com

Apple's official iTunes website: www.apple.com/itunes

Apple's official MobileMe service website: www.apple.com/mobileme

Official CUPS print server resource website: www.cups.org

Your Mac's local CUPS management website: http://localhost:631

Review Quiz

1. Which peripheral, expansion, and storage buses are supported by Mac OS X?

2. What does iSync do?

3. What are the device classes used in Mac OS X to categorize peripherals? What are some example peripherals of each class?

4. What is a device driver? What three primary types of device drivers are there?

5. What does CUPS do?

6. What are PPD files responsible for?

7. How do you share printers with other Mac and Windows users?

Answers

1. Mac OS X supports Universal Serial Bus (USB), FireWire, and Bluetooth peripheral buses; PCI Express (PCIe), PC Card, and ExpressCard 34 expansion buses; and Advanced Technology Attachment (ATA), Serial ATA (SATA), Small Computer System Interface (SCSI), Serial Attached SCSI (SAS), and Fibre Channel storage buses.

2. iSync allows you to synchronize personal information between Mac OS X applications and peripherals like Palm PDAs and Bluetooth-enabled cell phones.

3. Device classes as defined by Mac OS X are: human input devices (HID) like keyboards and mice; storage devices like hard drives and optical drives; printers; scanners; digital cameras; video devices, including both input and output devices; and audio devices, including both input and output devices.

4. A device driver is software specially designed to facilitate the communication between Mac OS X and a peripheral. They can be kernel extensions, framework plug-ins, or stand-alone applications.

5. Common UNIX Printing System (CUPS) manages all printing and faxing for Mac OS X, including both local and shared printing.

6. PostScript Printer Description (PPD) files are printer driver files that instruct the CUPS system on how to communicate with specific printer models.

7. You can enable printer sharing for Mac clients from the Print & Fax or Sharing preferences, but to enable authenticated print sharing to Windows clients you must also enable user's passwords in the SMB file sharing settings from the Sharing preferences.

10

Time

This chapter takes approximately 1 hour to complete.

Goals

Understand the Mac OS X startup process

Identify the essential files and processes required to successfully start up Mac OS X

Troubleshoot the startup and login processes

Chapter 10

System Startup

System startup certainly isn't the most glamorous part of Mac OS X, but it's clearly important and technically quite impressive. Apple has improved startup and runtime processes with every revision of Mac OS X. When things work correctly, the startup process on Intel-based Macs is often under 30 seconds. Obviously, users appreciate a quick startup, but most don't and shouldn't have to care what goes on during system startup because they expect their Macs to work properly.

However, when things do go wrong during system startup, users often fear the worst. Novice users may assume that if their Macs won't start up, they will lose important documents. But the system startup process can fail due to many issues that probably won't result in any user data loss. So, it's important to properly diagnose startup issues so you can get the Mac up and running, or at least try to recover data.

This chapter focuses on the process that your Mac goes through from the moment you press the power button until you ultimately reach the Finder. First you will identify the essential files and processes required to success-fully start up Mac OS X. This allows you to effectively troubleshoot startup and login issues covered in the remaining portion of this chapter.

Understanding the Startup Sequence

This section examines the main stages of the Mac OS X system startup procedure. The stages of system startup can be categorized into either *system initiation*, the processes required to start the operating system, or *user session*, the processes required to initialize the user environment. At each stage the Mac will present an audible or visual cue to help you validate startup progress. The startup cues discussed here are what you'll experience during a typical startup. Any deviation will be covered throughout this section as you learn more about the startup process.

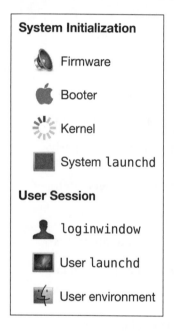

The four main Mac OS X system initialization stages are, in order:

▶   Firmware—At this stage the Mac's hardware initializes and the booter is located and started. Successfully completing this stage results in an audible startup chime and a bright flash from the power-on light, and all displays show a light gray background.

▶   Booter—The booter's main job is to load the system kernel and essential hardware drivers, known as kernel extensions (KEXTs), into main memory and then allow the kernel to take over the system. The booter stage is indicated by a dark gray Apple logo on the main display.

▶ Kernel—The kernel provides the system's foundation and loads additional drivers and the core BSD UNIX system. It is indicated by a dark gray spinning gear below the Apple logo on the main display.

▶ System `launchd`—Once the core operating system is loaded, it starts the first process, the system `launchd`, which is responsible for loading the remainder of the system. This stage is indicated by a bright blue background on all displays. Successful completion of this stage results in either the login screen or the Finder, if the user is set to automatically log in.

The three main Mac OS X user environment stages are, in order:

▶ `loginwindow`—This is the process responsible for presenting the login screen and eventually logging the user into the system. Successful completion of this stage results in initialization of the user environment, thus allowing user applications to run.

▶ User `launchd`—This process works in conjunction with the `loginwindow` process to initialize the user environment and start any user processes or applications.

▶ User environment—This is the "space" the user's processes and applications exist in when she is logged into the system. Obviously, the user environment is maintained by the `loginwindow` and user `launchd` processes.

System Initialization: Firmware

Your Mac's firmware, also called BootROM, resides on flash memory chips built into the Mac's main computer board. This way, when you power on your Mac, even before it starts a "real" operating system, the firmware acts as a mini-operating system with just enough software to get things going. Specifically, the firmware tests and initializes the hardware, and then locates and starts the system software booter.

Intel-based Macs feature firmware based on Intel's Extensible Firmware Interface (EFI) technology. Aside from supporting Intel's processor hardware, EFI is what allows your Mac to start up from Mac OS X, Windows, or any other Intel-compatible operating system.

> **MORE INFO** ▶ EFI is an extremely flexible boot architecture and is now managed by the Unified EFI Forum. In fact, EFI will soon be known as Unified Extensible Firmware Interface (UEFI). You can find out more at www.uefi.org.

Power-On Self-Test

The first thing your Mac's firmware does at power on is the Power-On Self-Test (POST). The POST tests built-in hardware components such as processors, system memory, network interfaces, and peripheral interfaces. When your Mac passes the POST, you hear the startup chime and see a light gray background on all displays. After a successful POST, the firmware will go on to locate the booter file.

If your Mac fails the POST, the displays will remain blank or off, and you may get hardware error codes. Depending on the age and model of your Mac, these error codes may manifest as audible tones or a series of flashes from the external power-on light, or internal diagnostic lights may illuminate. You may even see a combination of these things. Regardless of which error code you experience, it indicates a hardware problem exists outside of Mac OS X's control. You can visit Apple's support website at www.apple.com/support to identify your specific Mac's error code, or you can take your Mac to an Apple Authorized Service Provider.

Booter Selection

By default, the firmware will pick the system booter file that was last specified from the Startup Disk preferences in Mac OS X or the Boot Camp control panel in Windows. The booter file's location is saved in your Mac's nonvolatile RAM (NVRAM) so that it remains persistent across system restarts. If the booter file is found, EFI will start the booter process and Mac OS X will begin to start up. This is indicated by the dark gray Apple logo in the center of the main display.

If the firmware cannot locate a booter file, you will see a flashing folder icon with a question mark. Troubleshooting this issue will be covered in the second portion of this chapter.

Startup Modifiers

Your Mac's firmware also supports many keyboard combinations, which, when pressed and held during initial power-on, allow you to modify the startup process. Some of these combinations modify the booter selection, while others modify how Mac OS X starts up. Alternate Mac OS X startup modes are covered later in the "Troubleshooting Startup" section.

> **NOTE** ▶ If the Mac has a firmware password set then all the startup modifiers will be disabled save for the Option key (Startup Manager), which will prompt for the firmware password. For more information see Knowledge Base article HT1352, "Setting up firmware password protection in Mac OS X."

> **NOTE** ▶ Some hardware does not support startup modifier keyboard combinations, including some third-party keyboards and keyboards connected via some USB hubs or keyboard-video-mouse (KVM) switch. Also, Bluetooth wireless keyboards may not work either.

Mac startup modifiers include:

▶ C—Starts up from a bootable CD or DVD in the optical drive.

▶ D—Starts up from the Apple Hardware Test partition on the first restore DVD included with your Intel-based Mac. Later models also include this diagnostic built-in to the hardware ROM and thus don't require the DVD.

▶ N—Starts up from a compatible NetBoot server. The Mac will show a flashing globe icon in the center of the main display until it locates the NetBoot server, at which point it will show the dark gray Apple logo.

▶ T—For Macs with built-in FireWire ports, holding this key powers on the Mac in FireWire target disk mode, allowing other computers to access your Mac's internal drives. Target disk mode details are covered in Chapter 4, "File Systems."

▶ Shift—Starts up Mac OS X in Safe Mode.

▶ Option—Starts up into the Startup Manager, which allows you to select any volume containing Mac OS X to start up from. This includes internal volumes, optical drive volumes, some external volumes, and on later Intel-based Macs, NetBoot images.

> **NOTE** ▶ Startup volumes selected with the Startup Manager are not saved to NVRAM, so this setting will not persist between system restarts.

▶   Option-N—Starts up from the NetBoot server using the default system image.

▶   Command-V—Starts up Mac OS X in verbose mode.

▶   Command-S—Starts up Mac OS X in single-user mode.

▶   6 and 4—Starts up Mac OS X with a 64-bit kernel on supported Mac hardware. The 64-bit kernel mode is covered in the "Startup Stage Three: Kernel" section later in this chapter.

▶   3 and 2—If your Mac has been set to always start in 64-bit kernel mode, this will force it back to the standard 32-bit kernel mode.

▶   Command-Option-P-R—Resets NVRAM settings and restarts the Mac.

▶   Eject key, F12 key, mouse or trackpad button—Ejects any removable media, including optical discs.

Firmware Updates

Boot read-only memory, or boot ROM, refers to older versions of firmware technology that are not upgradable. Your Mac's firmware, however, is upgradable, and on Intel-based Macs it's even replaceable if it has become damaged. Mac OS X's Software Update service may automatically update some Macs' firmware, but you can also check Apple's Knowledge Base for the latest list of Mac firmware updates. Document HT1237, "EFI and SMC firmware updates for Intel-based Macs," maintains a list of Mac firmware updates. You can replace your Intel-based Mac's firmware using a firmware restoration CD as outlined in document HT2213, "About the Firmware Restoration CD (Intel-based Macs)."

> **MORE INFO** ▶ You can easily extend your Intel-based Mac's EFI capabilities using the open source rEFIt toolkit available at http://refit.sourceforge.net.

System Initialization: Booter

The booter process is launched by your Mac's firmware and is responsible for loading the Mac OS X kernel and enough essential kernel extensions, or KEXTs, so the kernel can take over the system and continue the startup process. Your Mac's firmware also passes on any special startup mode instructions for the booter to handle, such as when the user is holding down the Shift key, indicating that Mac OS X should start up in Safe Mode. The booter process itself resides at /System/Library/CoreServices/boot.efi.

To expedite the startup process, the booter will load cached files whenever possible. These cached files contain an optimized kernel and KEXTs that load much quicker than if the system had to load them from scratch. These caches are located in the /System/Library/ Caches/com.apple.kernel.caches folder. If the system detects a problem or you start Mac OS X in Safe Mode, these caches will be discarded and the kernel-loading process will take much longer.

As covered previously, the booter process is indicated at startup by the dark gray Apple icon in the center of the main display. If the booter successfully loads the kernel, this will be indicated by a small, dark gray spinning gear icon below the Apple icon.

If your Mac is set to NetBoot and the firmware successfully locates the booter file on the NetBoot server, you will again see the dark gray Apple icon. However, in this case the booter and the cached kernel information must be downloaded from the NetBoot server. This process is indicated by a small, dark gray spinning earth icon below the Apple icon. The earth icon will be replaced by the standard spinning gear icon once the kernel has been successfully loaded from the NetBoot server.

Finally, if the booter is unable to load the kernel, a dark gray prohibitory icon will take the place of the Apple icon. Again, troubleshooting this issue will be covered later in this chapter.

System Initialization: Kernel

Once the booter has successfully loaded the kernel and essential KEXTs, the kernel itself takes over the startup process. The kernel has now loaded enough KEXTs to read the entire file system, allowing it to load any additional KEXTs and start the core BSD UNIX system. A spinning gray gear icon below the Apple icon indicates the kernel's startup progress. Finally, the kernel starts the first normal (nonkernel) process, the system launchd, which is ultimately the parent process for every other process. The appearance of anything besides the white startup screen with the Apple logo is an indication that the kernel has fully loaded and the launchd process is starting other items.

Again, in most cases the kernel is loaded by the booter from cached files. However, the kernel is also located on the system volume at /mach_kernel. This file is normally hidden from users in the graphical user interface, because they don't need access to it. Many other hidden files and folders at the root of the system volume are necessary for the BSD UNIX system, and again the average user doesn't need access to these items. As covered in Chapter 9, "Peripherals and Printing," KEXTs reside in the /System/Library/Extensions and /Library/Extensions folders.

64-bit Kernel Mode

Mac OS X v10.6 features an optional 64-bit kernel mode on supported Mac hardware. Although the default for Mac OS X is to start the kernel in 32-bit mode, you can have it start in 64-bit kernel mode if you have a specific application or service that can benefit from it. At the time of this writing the 64-bit kernel is only supported on late model iMac, Mac Pro, MacBook Pro, and Xserve computers.

> **MORE INFO** ▶ Mac OS X Server v10.6 defaults to 64-bit kernel mode on Xserve and Mac Pro computers with 4 GB or more system memory.

In general, 64-bit kernel mode is only beneficial if your Mac has a very large amount of system memory (8+ GB), and even then it benefits only specific types of processes. It's important to recognize that most users will see almost no benefit from a 64-bit kernel, as 64-bit applications and services can already run on the Mac OS X kernel in its default 32-bit mode. Further, running Mac OS X with a 64-bit kernel will prevent you from using any 32-bit KEXT. Many third-party KEXTs only support 32-bit mode. As covered in

Chapter 9, "Peripherals and Printing," you can use /Applications/Utilities/System Profiler to identify which installed KEXTs support 64-bit mode.

To force a supported Mac OS X computer to start up in 64-bit kernel mode, hold down the 6 and 4 keys during system startup. As with all startup modifiers this is not a permanent solution. To permanently configure 64-bit kernel mode you will need to use the `systemsetup` command. Specifically, from the command line enter `sudo systemsetup -setkernelbootarchitecture x86_64` to set the default startup for 64-bit kernel mode. Conversely, you can set the default back to 32-bit kernel with `sudo systemsetup -setkernelbootarchitecture i386`. Finally, you can verify that your Mac is running with a 64-bit kernel by opening System Profiler and selecting the Software overview.

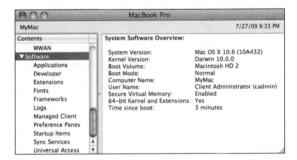

System Initialization: System launchd

Once the kernel is up and running, the Mac is ready to start running processes at the behest of the system and eventually human users. The first normal (non-kernel) process started is the system `launchd`, located at /sbin/launchd, which runs as root and is given the process identification number of 1. In UNIX terms, the system `launchd` is the first parent process that spawns all other child processes, and those processes go on to spawn other child processes.

The first task for the system `launchd` process is to complete the system initialization by starting all other system processes. Previous versions of Mac OS X show the "Welcome to Mac OS X" dialog with a progress bar to indicate system initialization status as the various system processes start up. However, beginning with Mac OS X v10.5 the `launchd` process was highly optimized, so the system initialization process takes only a few moments and is indicated by a bright blue background on all displays. This bright blue background is actually a result of `launchd` starting the `WindowServer` process, which is responsible for drawing the Mac OS X user interface, but it's still a good indication that things are progressing through the system startup process.

The launchd process is designed to expedite system initialization by starting multiple system processes simultaneously whenever possible and starting only essential system processes at startup. After startup, the system launchd process automatically starts and stops additional system processes as needed. By dynamically managing system processes, launchd keeps your Mac responsive and running as efficiently as possible.

> **MORE INFO ▶** launchd is an extremely powerful open source system for managing services. Learn more about launchd at Apple's developer website, http://developer. apple.com/macosx/launchd.html.

System launchd Items

As covered in Chapter 5, "Data Management and Backup," launchd manages system processes as described by launchd preference files in the /System/Library/LaunchDaemons folder. Third-party processes can also be managed when described by launchd preference files in the /Library/LaunchDaemons folder.

Apple strongly encourages all developers to adopt the launchd system for all automatically started processes. But the system launchd process also supports legacy startup routines. This includes support for running the traditional UNIX /etc/rc.local script during system initialization if present, though this script is not included on Mac OS X v10.6 by default. The system launchd process also starts the /sbin/SystemStarter process, which manages system processes as described by legacy Mac OS X startup items. Mac OS X v10.6 does not include any built-in startup items, but SystemStarter will still look in the /System/Library/ StartupItems and /Library/StartupItems folders for third-party startup items.

Viewing the launchd Hierarchy

The /Applications/Utilities/System Profiler application lists all processes along with their identification numbers and parent/child relationships. In the System Profiler, you can sort the process list by clicking on the title of the Process ID column, and you can view a process's parent process by double-clicking on its name in the list. You will find it beneficial to open the System Profiler and examine the process listing as you learn about how Mac OS X starts up the user environment. Detailed information about using the System Profiler application is covered in Chapter 5, "Applications and Boot Camp."

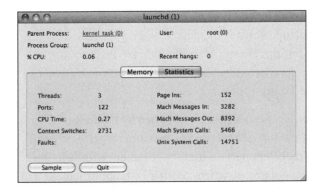

User Session

Eventually, after enough system processes have started, the system launchd process will start /System/Library/CoreServices/loginwindow.app. The loginwindow process is unique in its ability to run as both a background process and a graphical interface application. The loginwindow coordinates the login screen and, in coordination with the DirectoryService process, authenticates the user. After authentication the loginwindow, in coordination with the user's launchd, also initializes the graphical interface user environment and continues to run as a background process to maintain the user session.

A user can authenticate manually using the login screen, or the loginwindow can be set to automatically authenticate a user at startup, which is the default when your Mac has only a single user account. The loginwindow settings are stored in the /Library/Preferences/com. apple.loginwindow.plist preference file. As covered in Chapter 2, "User Accounts," you can configure loginwindow settings from the Accounts preferences.

If no users are logged into the Mac, the loginwindow process is owned by the root user. Once a user successfully authenticates, the loginwindow process switches ownership to this user and then proceeds to set up the graphical interface user environment with help from the user's launchd. In fact, the system launchd process starts another instance of launchd that is also owned by the authenticated user. All user processes and applications, even those that the user manually opens, will be started by the user-specific launchd process. If fast user switching is enabled, the system launchd process will start additional loginwindow and launchd processes to initialize and maintain each user's environment.

Initialize the User Environment

The user's loginwindow and launchd processes set up the graphical interface user environment by:

▶ Retrieving the user account information from DirectoryServices and applying any account settings

▶ Configuring the mouse, keyboard, and system sound using the user's preferences

▶ Loading the user's computing environment: preferences, environment variables, devices and file permissions, and keychain access

▶ Opening the Dock, Finder, and SystemUIServer, which is responsible for user interface elements like menu extras on the right side of the menu bar

▶ Automatically opening the user's login items

It's important to understand the differences between the various autostarting mechanisms in Mac OS X; LaunchDaemons, Startup Items, launch agents, and login items. Again, LaunchDaemons and Startup Items are started during system initialization by the system launchd process on behalf of the root user. On the other hand, launch agents and login items are only started on behalf of a specific user. In other words, launch daemons and startup items affect the system as a whole, while launch agents and login items affect only a single user.

Specifically, launch agents are started by the user's launchd process on behalf of the user. Launch agents can be started at any time as long as the user's launchd process is running. Most launch agents are started during the initialization of the user environment, but they could also be started afterward or on a regular repeating basis depending on need. Launch agents provided by the system can be found in /Library/LaunchAgents, whereas third-party launch agents should be located in either /Library/LaunchAgents or ~/Library/LaunchAgents.

Finally, login items are started only at the very end of the initialization of the user environment. The loginwindow process, again with help from the user's launchd process, is responsible for starting a user's login items. The user's login item list is stored in the ~/Library/Preferences/loginwindow.plist preference file. As covered previously in Chapter 2, "User Accounts," you can configure a user's login item list from the Accounts preferences.

Maintaining the User Environment

The user-owned launchd and loginwindow processes will continue to run as long as the user is logged in to the session. The user's launchd process will start all user processes and applications, while the user's loginwindow process will monitor and maintain the user session.

The user's loginwindow process monitors the user session by:

▶ Managing logout, restart, and shutdown procedures

▶ Managing the Force Quit Applications window, which includes monitoring the currently active applications and responding to user requests to forcibly quit applications

▶ Writing any standard-error output to the user's console.log file

While the user is logged in to the session, the user's launchd process automatically restarts any user application that should remain open, such as the Finder or the Dock. If the user's loginwindow process is ended, whether intentionally or unexpectedly, all the user's applications and processes will also immediately quit without saving changes. If this happens, the system launchd process will then automatically restart the loginwindow process as if the Mac had just started up. In other words, the loginwindow will, depending on configuration, either display the login screen or automatically log in the specified user.

Sleep Modes, Logout, and Shutdown

At the other end of the spectrum, but still related, are the processes required to pause or end the user session. The main distinction is that your Mac's sleep function does not quit any open processes, whereas the user logout and system shutdown functions will quit open processes. In most cases, the user manually issues a sleep, logout, or shutdown command from the Apple menu or by pressing the Mac's power button.

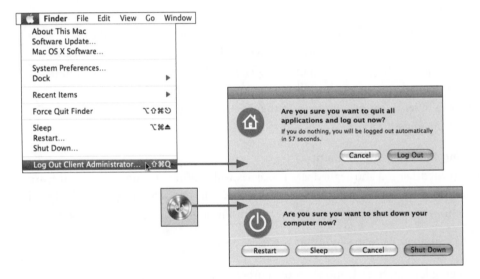

However, other processes and applications can also initiate sleep, logout, or shutdown commands. For instance, the Installer and Software Update applications can request a restart when the installation of new software requires it. Further, you can configure the Mac to automatically perform certain commands such as: put the system to sleep after inactivity with settings in the Energy Saver preferences; set a schedule to sleep, shut down, or start up the Mac with settings in the Schedule dialog of the Energy Saver preferences; automatically log out users after inactivity with settings in the Security preferences; and automatically log out managed users with settings in the Parental Controls preferences. Many of these settings can be managed remotely from Apple Remote Desktop or from managed client settings hosted on a network directory server.

Sleep Modes

Your Mac's sleep function is convenient because it does not quit any active processes or applications. Instead, the system kernel pauses all processes and then essentially shuts down all the hardware except for system memory and power to the USB and FireWire ports. This greatly reduces the amount of power used; as an example, portable Macs can remain in sleep mode for several days on a single battery charge. Waking your Mac from sleep mode restarts all hardware, and the kernel will resume all processes and applications from the point you left them.

All Intel-based portable Macs support a safe sleep mode. When these Macs go to sleep, they also copy the entire contents of system memory to an image file on the system volume. This way, if these Macs stay in sleep mode long enough to completely drain the battery, no data is lost when the system has to fully shut down. When you restart a Mac from safe sleep mode, the booter process will reload the saved memory image from the system volume instead of proceeding with the normal startup process. The booter process indicates the Mac is restarting from safe sleep mode by showing a light gray version of your Mac's screen when it was put to sleep and a small progress bar at the bottom of the main display. It should take only a few moments to reload system memory, and the kernel will resume all processes and applications.

Logout

Users can log out any time they want to end their user session, but they also have to log out to shut down or restart the Mac. When the currently logged-in user chooses to log out, the user's loginwindow process manages all logout functions with help from the user's launchd process. Once the user authorizes the logout, the user's loginwindow process issues a Quit Application Apple event to all applications. This gives applications a chance to save any changes or ask the user if changes should be saved. If the application fails to reply or quit itself after 60 seconds, the logout process will be stopped and loginwindow will display an error message.

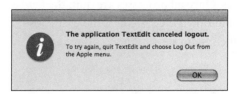

If all the user's applications successfully quit, the user's loginwindow process will then forcibly quit any background user processes. Finally, the user's loginwindow process will close the user's graphical interface session, run any logout scripts, record the logout to the main system.log file, and reset device permissions and preferences to their defaults. If the user chose only to log out, as opposed to shutting down or restarting, the user's loginwindow and launchd processes will quit, the system launchd process will restart a new loginwindow process owned by the root user, and the login screen will appear.

Shutdown and Restart

When a logged-in user chooses to shut down or restart the Mac, again the user's loginwindow process manages all logout functions with help from the system launchd process. First the user's loginwindow process logs out the current user. If other users are logged in via fast user switching, the loginwindow process will ask for administrative user authentication and, if granted, will forcibly quit all other users' processes and applications, possibly losing user data.

After all user sessions are logged out, the user's loginwindow process tells the kernel to issue the quit command to all remaining system processes. Processes like loginwindow should quit promptly, but the kernel must wait for processes that remain responsive while they are going through the motions of quitting. If system processes don't respond after a few seconds, the kernel will forcibly quit those processes. Once all processes are quit, the kernel will stop the system launchd process and then shut down the system. If the user chose to restart the Mac, the Mac's firmware will begin the system startup process once again.

Troubleshooting Startup

The most important part of troubleshooting system startup is fully understanding the startup process. Once you can identify the various stages—and know which processes and files are responsible for each—you are well on your way to diagnosing any startup issue. In the second portion of the chapter, you'll troubleshoot each of these stages as well as investigate logout and shutdown problems.

Here you will learn about the three primary Mac OS X diagnostic startup modes: verbose mode, Safe Mode, and single-user mode. These three modes are initiated at the firmware stage but can affect the remaining startup process at each stage. The ramifications of each diagnostic startup mode are covered with each stage throughout this section.

The Mac OS X diagnostic startup modes are:

▶ Verbose mode—This mode is initiated by holding down Command-V during system startup. In verbose mode, the system will not hide the startup progress from you with the light gray or blue screens. Instead, you will see a black background with white text showing all details of the startup process.

▶ Safe Boot/Safe Mode/Safe Login—This mode is initiated by holding down the Shift key during system startup and user login. Safe Boot occurs when the system is starting up; Safe Mode is when the system is actually running; and Safe Login is when the system starts up the user session. During Safe Boot, the system will more carefully test startup procedures and limit automatically launched processes during each stage.

▶ Single-user mode—This mode is initiated by holding down Command-S during system startup. When starting up in single-user mode, the system will only start core kernel and BSD UNIX functionality. You must be familiar with the command-line interface to use single-user mode. Using the command line is detailed in Chapter 3, "Command Line and Automation."

Troubleshooting the Firmware

Issues at the firmware stage are indicated by an inability of your Mac to reach the light gray screen with the dark gray Apple icon. The key to troubleshooting at this point is to determine whether this issue is related to the Mac's hardware or system volume.

Hardware Issues

If you don't hear the startup chime or see the power-on light flash, the Mac's hardware did not pass the POST. You may also hear a series of diagnostic tones or see a series of power-on flashes. If this is the case, your Mac has a fundamental hardware issue.

To troubleshoot hardware issues:

▶ Always check for simple things first. Is the Mac plugged into an electrical outlet? Are the keyboard and mouse working properly?

▶ Run the Apple Hardware Test (AHT) included on the first restore disc packaged with your Mac. Insert the disc in the optical drive, and start up holding down the D key to automatically select the AHT volume.

▶ You can also attempt to reset your Mac's firmware by using a firmware restoration CD as outlined in Apple Knowledge Base document HT2213, "About the firmware restoration CD (Intel-based Macs)."

▶ Ultimately, if this is a serious hardware issue, you will have to take your Mac to an Apple Authorized Service Provider.

System Volume Issues

If your Mac passes the POST but you are left with a flashing dark-gray question mark folder icon, it means the firmware cannot locate a valid system volume or booter file. The Mac's main processor and components are probably working correctly, and you may only have a software issue. Hold down the Option key during startup and use the Startup Manager to locate system volumes.

To troubleshoot system volume issues:

▶ If the original system volume appears, select it to start up from. If your Mac starts up from the system on the volume, open the Startup Disk preferences to reset the volume as the startup disk. You can attempt to define the startup disk when booted from another system volume like the Mac OS X Install DVD.

▶ If the original system volume appears but your Mac still cannot find a valid system or booter, you may need to reinstall Mac OS X on that volume. As always, back up any important data from that volume before you make significant changes.

▶ If your original system volume does not appear, the issue lies with that storage device. Start up from another system, like the Mac OS X Install DVD, and use the storage troubleshooting techniques outlined in Chapter 4, "File Systems."

Troubleshooting the Booter

Issues at the booter stage are indicated by a flashing dark gray prohibitory icon—evidence of a failure to load the kernel.

To troubleshoot the booter:

▶ If you're starting up the Mac from a volume containing a system this Mac has never booted from, the prohibitory icon usually indicates that the version of Mac OS X on the volume is not compatible with your Mac's hardware.

▶ Start up the Mac while holding down the Shift key to initiate a Safe Boot. The booter will first attempt to verify and repair the startup volume, indicated by a dark gray progress bar across the bottom of the main display. If repairs were necessary, the Mac will automatically restart before continuing. If this happens, continue to hold down the Shift key. The booter will verify the startup volume again, and if the volume appears to be working properly, the booter will attempt to load the kernel and essential KEXTs again. The booter uses the most judicial, and slowest, process to load these items. If successful, the booter will pass off the system to the kernel, which will continue to safe-boot.

▶ If the booter cannot find or load a valid kernel, you may need to reinstall Mac OS X on that volume.

Troubleshooting the Kernel

Issues at the kernel stage are indicated by an inability to reach the bright blue screen, as evidence of a failure to load all KEXTs, the core BSD UNIX system, and ultimately the system launchd process. If this is the case, your Mac is stuck at the light gray screen with the dark gray spinning gear icon.

To troubleshoot the kernel:

▶ Start up the Mac while holding down the Shift key to initiate a Safe Boot. In addition to the Safe Boot procedures covered in the "Troubleshooting the Booter" section earlier, this will force the kernel to ignore all third-party KEXTs. If successful, the kernel will start the system launchd process, which will continue to safe-boot. Completing the kernel startup stage via a Safe Boot indicates the issue may be a third-party KEXT, and you should start up in verbose mode to try to identify the problem KEXT.

▶ Start up the Mac while holding down Command-V to initiate verbose mode. The Mac will show you the startup process details as a continuous string of text. If the text stops, the startup process has probably also stopped, and you should examine the end of the text for troubleshooting clues. When you find a suspicious item, move it to a quarantine folder and then restart the Mac without Safe Boot, to see if the problem was resolved. This may be easier said than done, as accessing the Mac's drive to locate and remove the item may not be possible if the Mac is crashing during startup. This is an example of where FireWire target disk mode really shines. As covered in Chapter 4, "File Systems," you can easily modify the contents of a problematic Mac's system volume using target disk mode and a second Mac.

NOTE ▶ If your troublesome Mac successfully starts up in Safe Boot mode and you're trying to find the issue, do not use Safe Boot and verbose mode at the same time. If the startup process succeeds, verbose mode will eventually be replaced by the standard startup interface and you will not have time to identify problematic items.

▶ If the kernel cannot completely load while safe-booting or you are unable to locate and repair the problematic items, you may need to reinstall Mac OS X on that volume.

Troubleshooting the System launchd

Issues at this stage are indicated by an inability to reach the login screen or log in a user (evidence of a failure by the system launchd process). If the system launchd process is not able to complete the system initialization, the loginwindow process will not start. Your Mac will be either stuck with a black screen or a bright blue screen, depending on how far the system launchd got.

To troubleshoot system launchd issues:

▶ Start up the Mac while holding down the Shift key to initiate a Safe Boot. In addition to the Safe Boot procedures covered earlier in the "Troubleshooting the Booter" and "Troubleshooting the Kernel" sections of this chapter, this will force the system launchd process to ignore all third-party fonts, LaunchDaemons, and Startup Items. If successful, the system launchd process will start the loginwindow. At this point the Mac system has fully started up and is now running in Safe Mode. Completing the system initialization process via Safe Boot indicates the issue may be a third-party system initialization item, and you should start up in verbose mode to try to identify the problematic item.

▶ Start up the Mac while holding down Command-V to initiate verbose mode. Again, if the text stops, examine the end of the text for troubleshooting clues; if you find a suspicious item, move it to a quarantine folder and then restart the Mac normally.

▶ At this point you might be able to successfully safe-boot into the Finder. If so, use the Finder's interface to quarantine suspicious items.

▶ While working in Safe Mode, you may also consider removing or renaming system cache and preference files, as they can be corrupted and cause startup issues. Begin by removing /Library/Caches because those files contain easily replaced information. As far as system preferences go, you can remove any setting stored in the /Library/Preferences or /Library/Preferences/SystemConfiguration folders you're comfortable with having to reconfigure. A much safer solution would be to simply rename individual system preference files in these folders. Once you have moved or replaced these items, restart the Mac, and the system will automatically replace these items with clean versions.

▶ If Safe Boot continues to fail or you have located a suspicious system item that you need to remove, start up the Mac while holding Command-S to initiate single-user mode. You'll see a minimal command line interface that will allow you to move suspicious files to a quarantine folder. If you want to modify files and folders in single-user mode, you will have to prepare the system volume. Start by entering /sbin/fsck -fy to verify and repair the startup volume. Repeat this command until you see a message stating that the drive appears to be OK. Only then should you enter /sbin/mount -uw / to mount the startup volume as a read and write file system. Use the techniques covered in Chapter 3, "Command Line and Automation," to deal with potentially troublesome files. Once you have made your changes, you can exit single-user mode and continue to start up the system by entering the exit command, or you can shut down the Mac by entering the shutdown -h now command.

TIP ▶ If you find single-user mode daunting, then you may want to install AppleJack, which is a third-party command line interface that makes running common troubleshooting commands easy. Find it at http://applejack.sourceforge.net.

▶ If the system initialization process cannot complete while safe-booting or you are unable to locate and repair the problematic items, you may need to reinstall Mac OS X on that volume.

Troubleshooting User Initialization

If the loginwindow process is not able to initialize the user environment, the user will never be given control of the graphical interface. You may see the user's desktop background picture, but no applications will load, including the Dock or the Finder. Or it may appear that the user session starts, but then the login screen will reappear. At this point you should first attempt a Safe Login, which is initiated by holding down the Shift key while you click the Log In button at the login screen. Safe Login is also part of the Safe Boot startup mode. In addition to the Safe Boot procedures covered previously in this chapter, the loginwindow displays the login screen with the words "Safe Boot" in bright red text under the Mac OS X logo.

With Safe Login enabled, the loginwindow process will not automatically open any user-defined login items, and the user's launchd process will not start any user-specific LaunchAgents. Obviously, if a Safe Login resolves your user session issue, you need to adjust this user's Login Items list from the Accounts preferences or any items in the /Library/LaunchAgents or ~/Library/LaunchAgents folders.

If a Safe Login doesn't resolve your user session issue, there are other troubleshooting sections in this book you should refer to. Primarily, you should follow the troubleshooting steps outlined in Chapter 2, "User Accounts." Additionally, the loginwindow process relies heavily on directory services, so you may also be well served by the troubleshooting steps outlined in Chapter 8, "Network Services."

Troubleshoot Logout and Shutdown

An inability to log out or shut down is almost always the result of an application or process that refuses to quit. If you're unable to log out, as long as you still maintain control of the graphical interface, you can attempt to forcibly quit stubborn processes using the techniques outlined in Chapter 6, "Applications and Boot Camp." You may find the loginwindow process has closed your user session, but the Mac refuses to shut down. This is indicated by a small spinning gear icon on top of your desktop background or the bright blue screen after all your applications have quit. You should let the system attempt to shut down naturally, but if it takes any longer than a few minutes, it means a system process is refusing to quit. You can force your Mac to shut down by holding down the power-on key until the Mac powers off, as indicated by a blank display.

> **NOTE ▶** When you restart the Mac, the firmware does not perform a full POST during the subsequent startup process. Thus, if you're troubleshooting hardware issues you should always shut down and then start up, never restart.

What You've Learned

▶ The Mac OS X system initialization happens in four stages: firmware, booter, kernel, and system launchd. The Mac OS X user environment happens in three stages: loginwindow, user launchd, and the user environment.

▶ At each stage there are audible or visual cues that help you recognize startup progress.

▶ Your Mac's firmware features a variety of startup modes that help you administer and troubleshoot the system.

▶ The launchd and loginwindow processes are primarily responsible for managing the user environment, including processes such as system initialization, graphical interface user session setup, and login, logout, and shutdown.

▶ Safe Mode, verbose mode, and single-user mode are the three primary Mac OS X startup diagnostic modes.

References

Check for current Knowledge Base documents at www.apple.com/support.

Firmware

HT1547, "Power On Self-Test Beep Definition - Part 2"

HT2341, "Intel-based Mac Power-On Self-Test RAM error codes"

HT1533, "Startup key combinations for Intel-based Macs"

HT1343, "Mac OS X keyboard shortcuts"

HT1310, "Startup Manager: How to select a startup volume"

HT1352, "Setting up firmware password protection in Mac OS X"

HT1237, "EFI and SMC firmware updates for Intel-based Macs"

HT2213, "About the firmware restoration CD (Intel-based Macs)"

General Startup

TS1892, "Mac OS X: 'Broken folder' icon, prohibitory sign, or kernel panic when computer starts"

HT2674, "Intel-based Mac: Startup sequence and error codes, symbols"

HT1564, "What is Safe Boot, Safe Mode?"

HT1757, "Progress bar appears after waking from sleep"

TS1388, "Isolating issues in Mac OS X"

URLs

Official Unified Extensible Firmware Interface (UEFI) resource website: www.uefi.org

rEFIt alternative EFI booter with advanced features website: http://refit.sourceforge.net

Apple's official `launchd` developer documentation: http://developer.apple.com/macosx/launchd.html

Easy to use single-user mode software: http://applejack.sourceforge.net

Review Quiz

1.   What are the primary system initialization stages and user environment stages in Mac OS X, and in what order do they start?

2.   What are the visual and/or audible cues of the stages of system initialization?

3.   What does the firmware do? What is the POST?

4.   What role does the system `launchd` process serve during system startup?

5.   What items are automatically started by the system `launchd` during the system initialization process?

6.   What role does the `loginwindow` process serve in system startup?

7.   What is the difference between launch daemons, startup items, launch agents, and login items?

8.   What happens during user logout?

9. What happens during system shutdown?

10. What is the difference between Safe Boot, Safe Mode, and Safe Login?

11. Which items are not loaded when Mac OS X safe-boots?

12. What keyboard combination is used to safe-boot Mac OS X?

13. How do you further resolve an issue that disappears when the Mac successfully safe-boots?

Answers

1. The primary system initialization stages are: firmware, booter, kernel, and system launchd (in that order). The primary user environment stages are loginwindow, user launchd, and user environment.

2. Each stage is indicated by the following: firmware, startup chime or bright flash of the power-on light followed by a light gray screen on the primary display; booter, a dark gray Apple logo on the primary display; kernel, a small dark gray spinning gear or spinning earth icon below the Apple logo; and system launchd, a bright blue screen on all displays followed by the login screen.

3. The firmware initializes the Mac's hardware and locates the booter file on a system volume. The Power-On Self-Test (POST) checks for basic hardware functionality when your Mac powers on.

4. The system launchd process is ultimately responsible for starting every system process. It also manages system initialization and starts the loginwindow process.

5. During system initialization the system launchd process automatically starts /System/Library/LaunchDaemons, /Library/LaunchDaemons, /Library/StartupItems (via SystemStarter), and the /etc/rc.local UNIX script if it exists.

6. The loginwindow process displays the login screen that allows the user to authenticate, and then sets up and manages the graphical interface user environment.

7. Launch daemons and startup items are opened during system initialization by the system launchd process on behalf of the root user. Launch agents and login items are opened during the initialization of the user environment by the user's specific launchd process.

8. During user logout the user's `loginwindow` process does the following: requests that all user applications quit; automatically quits any user background processes; runs any logout scripts; records the logout to the main system.log file; resets device permissions and preferences to their defaults; and finally quits the user's `loginwindow` and `launchd` processes.

9. At system shutdown the `loginwindow` process logs all users out and then tells the kernel to quit all remaining system processes. Once the kernel quits all system processes, the Mac will shut down.

10. Safe Boot refers to when the system is starting up; Safe Mode is when the system is actually running; and Safe Login is when the system starts up the user session.

11. When Mac OS X safe-boots, it will not load third-party KEXTs, third-party LaunchAgents, third-party LaunchDaemons, third-party StartupItems, third-party fonts, any user login items, or any user-specific LaunchAgents.

12. A Safe Boot is initiated by holding down the Shift key during system startup.

13. If an issue disappears when the Mac successfully safe-boots, then you must find and remove or quarantine the third-party startup resource that caused the issue. The best way to isolate the problematic item is to start up the Mac in verbose mode and then observe where the startup process fails. Verbose mode is initiated by holding down Command-V during system startup.

Index